Lecture Notes in Computer Science 5292

Commenced Publication in 1973
Founding and Former Series Editors:
Gerhard Goos, Juris Hartmanis, and Jan van Leeuwen

Ron Morrison   Dharini Balasubramaniam
Katrina Falkner (Eds.)

Software Architecture

Second European Conference, ECSA 2008
Paphos, Cyprus, September 29–October 1, 2008
Proceedings

 Springer

Volume Editors

Ron Morrison
Dharini Balasubramaniam
University of St Andrews
School of Computer Science
North Haugh, St Andrews, Fife KY16 9SX, UK
E-mail: {ron, dharini}@cs.st-andrews.ac.uk

Katrina Falkner
University of Adelaide
School of Computer Science
Adelaide, SA 5005, Australia
E-mail: katrina@cs.adelaide.edu.au

Library of Congress Control Number: 2008935446

CR Subject Classification (1998): D.2.11, D.3, H.2.3

LNCS Sublibrary: SL 2 – Programming and Software Engineering

ISSN   0302-9743
ISBN-10   3-540-88029-1 Springer Berlin Heidelberg New York
ISBN-13   978-3-540-88029-5 Springer Berlin Heidelberg New York

Springer is a part of Springer Science+Business Media

springer.com

© Springer-Verlag Berlin Heidelberg 2008
Printed in Germany

Typesetting: Camera-ready by author, data conversion by Scientific Publishing Services, Chennai, India
Printed on acid-free paper   SPIN: 12525850   06/3180   5 4 3 2 1 0

Preface

The European Conference on Software Architecture (ECSA) is the premier European conference dedicated to the field of software architecture, covering all architectural features of software engineering. It is the follow-up of a successful series of European workshops on software architecture held in the UK in 2004 (Springer LNCS 3047), Italy in 2005 (Springer LNCS 3527), and France in 2006 (Springer LNCS 4344). It evolved into a series of European conferences whose first edition was ECSA 2007, held in Madrid, Spain during September 24–26, 2007 (Springer LNCS 4758). This year's conference was held at the beautiful Coral Beach Hotel and Resort near Paphos in Cyprus.

As with the previous versions of the conference, ECSA 2008 (Springer LNCS 5292) provided an international forum for researchers and practitioners from academia and industry to present innovative research and to discuss a wide range of topics in the area of software architecture. It focused on formalisms, technologies, and processes for describing, verifying, validating, transforming, building, and evolving software systems. Covered topics included architecture modelling, architecture description languages, architectural aspects, architecture analysis, transformation and synthesis, architecture evolution, quality attributes, model-driven engineering, built-in testing and architecture-based support for component-based and service-oriented systems.

The conference attracted paper submissions from 29 countries (Australia, Belgium, Brazil, Canada, China, Chile, Denmark, Finland, France, Germany, Greece, Ireland, Italy, Lithuania, Luxembourg, Malta, The Netherlands, Norway, Pakistan, Peru, Poland, Portugal, Romania, South Africa, Spain, Turkey, the UK, USA, and Venezuela). In all, 110 abstracts were submitted of which 83 papers were submitted via the conference website.

Each submission was reviewed by three members of the Program Committee. Papers were selected based on originality, quality, soundness, and relevance to the conference.

The Program Committee selected papers according to four types for presentation in paper sessions:

- Full research papers describe novel contributions to software architecture research and cover work that has a sound scientific/technological basis and has been fully validated. These are allocated 16 pages in the proceedings.
- Experience papers describe significant experiences related to software architecture practice and present case studies or real-life experiences of benefit to practitioners and researchers. These are allocated 16 pages in the proceedings.
- Research challenge papers present significant research challenges in theory or practice of software architecture or the state of the art on different topics related to software architecture. These are allocated eight pages in the proceedings.
- Emerging research papers present promising results from work-in-progress in a topic of software architecture research and cover work that has a sound basis, but has not yet been validated in full. These are allocated four pages in the proceedings.

The Program Committee selected 12 full research papers, 4 experience papers and 7 emerging research papers out of 83 submissions. This gives an acceptance rate of 14% for full papers, 4% for experience (long) papers, 9% for emerging research papers. In addition, 12 papers were selected to be presented as posters in Research Challenge paper sessions.

The conference included two keynote talks. The opening day keynote was presented by one of the founders of Software Architecture, Dewayne E. Perry of the University of Texas at Austin, USA, on "Issues in Architecture Evolution: Using Design Intent in Maintenance and Controlling Dynamic Evolution" and the second keynote was delivered by Colin Atkinson, from the University of Mannheim, Germany, on "Component-Oriented Verification of Software Architectures Through Built-in Tests."

We would like to thank the members of the Program Committee for providing thoughtful and knowledgeable reviews and for their substantial effort in making ECSA 2008 a successful conference.

The ECSA 2008 submission and review process was extensively supported by the EasyChair Conference Management System.

On the organizational front, we deeply acknowledge all the members of the Organizing Committee for their excellent service. Finally, we acknowledge the prompt and professional support from Springer, who published these proceedings in printed and electronic volumes as part of the *Lecture Notes in Computer Science* series.

September 2008   Ron Morrison
George A. Papadopoulos

Organization

Conference Chair

George A. Papadopoulos   University of Cyprus, Cyprus
george@cs.ucy.ac.cy

Program Committee

Program Committee Chair

Ron Morrison   University of St. Andrews, UK
ron@cs.st-andrews.ac.uk

Program Committee Members

Yamine Ait Ameur   ENSMA, France
Dharini Balasubram   University of St. Andrews, UK
Thais Batista   University of Rio Grande do Norte UFRN, Brazil
Marco Bernardo   University of Urbino, Italy
Antoine Beugnard   ENST Bretagne, France
Jan Bosch   Intu, USA
Alan W. Brown   IBM Rational, USA
Carlos E. Cuesta   Rey Juan Carlos University, Spain
Paulo Roberto Freire Cunha   Federal University of Pernambuco, Brazil
Rogerio de Lemos   University of Kent, UK
Khalil Drira   LAAS-CNRS, University of Toulouse, France
Laurence Duchien   INRIA and University of Lille, France
Katrina Falkner   University of Adelaide, Australia
Régis Fleurquin   University of South Brittany VALORIA, France
David Garlan   Carnegie Mellon University, USA
Carlo Ghezzi   Polytechnic of Milan, Italy
Ian Gorton   Pacific Northwest National Lab, USA
Paul Grefen   Eindhoven University of Technology,
                                      The Netherlands
Volker Gruhn   University of Leipzig, Germany
Wilhelm Hasselbring   University of Oldenburg, Germany
Juan Hernández   University of Extremadura, Spain
Paola Inverardi   University of L'Aquila, Italy

René Krikhaar	ICT NoviQ and Vrije Universiteit Amsterdam, The Netherlands
Frédéric Lang	INRIA Rhône-Alpes, France
Nicole Levy	University of Versailles St.-Quentin en Yvelines RiSM, France
Antonia Lopes	University of Lisbon, Portugal
Jeff Magee	Imperial College London, UK
Esperanza Marcos	Rey Juan Carlos University, Spain
Carlo Montangero	University of Pisa, Italy
Ron Morrison	University of St. Andrews, UK
Robert L. Nord	Software Engineering Institute, USA
Henk Obbink	Philips Research Europe, The Netherlands
Flavio Oquendo	University of South Brittany VALORIA, France
Mourad Oussalah	University of Nantes LINA, France
Claus Pahl	Dublin City University, Ireland
Mike P. Papazoglou	Tilburg University, The Netherlands
Jennifer Pérez	Technical University of Madrid (UPM), Spain
Dewayne E. Perry	University of Texas at Austin, USA
Frantisek Plasil	Charles University, Czech Republic
Eltjo Poort	Logica, The Netherlands
Amar Ramdame-Cherif	University of Versailles St.-Quentin en Yvelines PRiSM, France
Isidro Ramos	Polytechnic University of Valencia, Spain
Ralf Reussner	University of Karlsruhe, Germany
Clemens Schäfer	University of Leipzig, Germany
Bradley Schmerl	Carnegie Mellon University, USA
Judith Stafford	Tufts University, USA
Clemens Szyperski	Microsoft Research, USA
Richard N. Taylor	University of California at Irvine, USA
Miguel Toro	University of Seville, Spain
J.C. (Hans) van Vliet	VU University Amsterdam, The Netherlands
Brian Warboys	University of Manchester, UK
Eoin Woods	UBS Investment Bank, UK

Poster Sessions

Dharini Balasubramaniam	University of St. Andrews, UK
Katrina Falkner	University of Adelaide, Australia

Organizing Committee Members

Pyrros Bratskas	University of Cyprus, Cyprus
Pericles Cheng	University of Cyprus, Cyprus
Constantinos Kakousis	University of Cyprus, Cyprus
Nearchos Paspallis	University of Cyprus, Cyprus

Steering Committee

Flavio Oquendo	University of South Brittany VALORIA, France
Carlos E. Cuesta	Rey Juan Carlos University, Spain
Esperanza Marcos	Rey Juan Carlos University, Spain
John Favaro	Consorzio Pisa Ricerche, Italy
Volker Gruhn	University of Leipzig, Germany
Ron Morrison	University of St. Andrews, UK
Mourad Oussalah	University of Nantes LINA, France
George A. Papadopoulos	University of Cyprus, Cyprus
Brian Warboys	University of Manchester, UK

Table of Contents

Keynotes

Full Research Papers

Experience Papers

Emerging Research Papers

Research Challenge Papers

Issues in Architecture Evolution: Using Design Intent in Maintenance and Controlling Dynamic Evolution

Dewayne E. Perry

The University of Texas at Austin, USA
`perry@ece.utexas.edu`

Abstract. Issues in Architecture Evolution: 1) Using design intent in maintenance & 2) Controlling dynamic evolution   In this keynote talk I will address two issues in software architecture evolution. In Alex Wolf's and my original architecture model, we proposed rationale as one of the major components. Over the years very little has been explored about this issue. The primary purpose of rationale was to record architecture design intent: why are things the way they are? It is only recently that architecture researchers have become interested in capturing design intent. Unfortunately the focus has been (as it was in the 80's on capturing design decisions) on what can we capture and how. I will focus instead on the problem of what design intent do we need when we evolve the architecture design and discuss the work I am doing with my student Paul Grisham. There are a number of interesting contexts where the dynamic evolution of software architectures are of critical importance - for example, self-managing, self-adapting systems, etc. Another interesting context is that of simulating very large, very complex systems. In all these cases, the control of dynamic architecture evolution is a critical issue. In the case of complex simulations we have foreknowledge (indeed, control) of the desired architecture evolution. I will focus on our approach in handling this issue in this context. While this is a fairly narrow context, I believe our approach has applicability in a wider context.

Keywords: Design intent, dynamic evolution, architectural maintenance.

R. Morrison, D. Balasubramaniam, and K. Falkner (Eds.): ECSA 2008, LNCS 5292, p. 1, 2008.
© Springer-Verlag Berlin Heidelberg 2008

Component-Oriented Verification of Software Architectures through Built-in Tests

Colin Atkinson

University of Mannheim, Germany
`atkinson@informatik.uni-mannheim.de`

Abstract. Although the technologies used to implement and assemble components have improved significantly in recent years, techniques for verifying systems created from them have changed very little. In fact, the correctness and reliability of component-based systems are still usually checked using the traditional testing techniques employed before components and services became widespread. These techniques are not only expensive because they treat a system as a monolithic black box, they are not very helpful because they fail to use architectural knowledge to pin-point the source of failures. As a result, many of the potential benefits of component-based development are outweighed by the costs involved in verifying the resulting systems. In this talk, Colin Atkinson will present an approach that addresses this problem by making the system verification process component-oriented as well. Based on the notion of built-in tests - tests that are packaged with components and are executed at run-time - the approach reduces the level of manual effort needed to verify a system by partially automating the testing process. It involves a method to define how services/components should be written to support and exploit built-in tests, and a resource-aware infrastructure that arranges for tests to be executed when they have a minimal impact on the delivery of system services.

Keywords: Verification, built-in tests, system services.

R. Morrison, D. Balasubramaniam, and K. Falkner (Eds.): ECSA 2008, LNCS 5292, p. 2, 2008.

Non-synchronous Communications in Process Algebraic Architectural Description Languages

Marco Bernardo and Edoardo Bontà

Università di Urbino "Carlo Bo" – Italy
Istituto di Scienze e Tecnologie dell'Informazione

Abstract. Architectural description languages are a useful tool for modeling complex software systems at a high level of abstraction and, if based on formal methods, for enabling the early verification of various properties among which correct component coordination. This is the case with process algebraic architectural description languages, as they have been equipped with several techniques for verifying the absence of coordination mismatches in the case of synchronous communications. The objective of this paper is twofold. On the modeling side, we show how to enhance the expressiveness of a typical process algebraic architectural description language by including the capability of representing non-synchronous communications, in such a way that the usability of the original language is preserved. On the analysis side, we show how to modify the compatibility check for acyclic topologies and the interoperability check for cyclic topologies, in such a way that both checks can still be applied in the presence of non-synchronous communications.

1 Introduction

Several architectural description languages have been proposed in the literature. Many of them – like, e.g., Wright [2], Darwin/FSP [8], PADL [1], and π-ADL [10] – are based on process algebra [9] due to its support to compositional modeling. On the analysis side, process algebraic ADLs inherit all the techniques applicable to process algebra, like model checking and equivalence checking. In addition, such languages are equipped with ad-hoc analysis techniques (see, e.g., [2,7,4,1]) mostly based on behavioral equivalences. These techniques are useful for (i) detecting coordination mismatches – deriving from components that are correct if taken separately but that do not satisfy certain requirements when assembled together – and (ii) generating diagnostic information – in order to pinpoint those components from which mismatches arise.

The ad-hoc analysis techniques proposed in the literature deal only with synchronous communications. In that setting, all ports of software components are blocking. A component waiting on a synchronous input port cannot proceed until an output is sent by another component. Similarly, a component issuing an output via a synchronous output port cannot proceed until another component is willing to receive. This is an important case, especially when verifying coordination properties like the deadlock freedom of software systems resulting

R. Morrison, D. Balasubramaniam, and K. Falkner (Eds.): ECSA 2008, LNCS 5292, pp. 3–18, 2008.

from the assembly of individually deadlock-free components. However, in general software components can be involved not only in synchronous communications, but also in non-synchronous communications.

The first contribution of this paper is to show how to enhance the expressiveness of a typical process algebraic architectural description language by including the capability of representing non-synchronous communications, in such a way that the usability of the original language is preserved. More specifically, we focus on PADL [1] and we extend it by means of additional qualifiers useful to distinguish among synchronous, semi-synchronous, and asynchronous ports.

Semi-synchronous ports are not blocking. A semi-synchronous port of a component succeeds if there is another component ready to communicate with it, otherwise it raises an exception so as not to block the component to which it belongs. For example, a semi-synchronous input port can be used to model accesses to a tuple space via (non-blocking) input or read probes [6]. A semi-synchronous output port can instead be used to model the (non-blocking) interplay between a graphical user interface and an underlying application whenever the latter cannot do certain tasks requested by the user.

Analogously, asynchronous ports are not blocking. Here the reason is that the beginning and the end of the communications in which these ports are involved are completely decoupled. For instance, an asynchronous output port can be used to model output operations on a tuple space. An asynchronous input port can instead be used to model the periodical check for the presence of information received from an event notification service [5].

The semantic treatment of non-synchronous communications is completely transparent to PADL users. They only have to specify appropriate synchronicity-related qualifiers in their descriptions, hence the degree of usability of PADL is unaffected. We will see that semi-synchronous ports can easily be handled with suitable semantic rules generating exceptions whenever necessary, whereas asynchronous ports require the addition of implicit repository-like components.

The second contribution of this paper is to show how to modify the compatibility check for acyclic topologies and the interoperability check for cyclic topologies introduced in [1], in such a way that both checks can still be applied in the presence of non-synchronous communications.

This paper is organized as follows. In Sect. 2 we recall PADL. In Sect. 3 we extend its syntax with semi-synchronous and asynchronous ports and we consequently revise its semantics. In Sect. 4 we modify the architectural compatibility and interoperability checks in order to deal with non-synchronous communications as well. The modified checks are illustrated via an applet-based simulator for a cruise control system. In Sect. 5 we provide some concluding remarks.

2   The Architectural Description Language PADL

PADL [1] is a process algebraic architectural description language. In this section we present the syntax and the semantics for PADL after recalling some basic notions of process algebra.

2.1 Process Algebra

Process algebra [9] provides a set of operators by means of which the behavior of a system can be described in an action-based, compositional way. Given a set *Name* of action names including τ for invisible actions, we will consider a process algebra PA with the following process term syntax:

$$
\begin{array}{lll}
P ::= \underline{0} & \text{inactive process} & \\
\quad | \quad B & \text{process constant} & (B \stackrel{\Delta}{=} P) \\
\quad | \quad a.P & \text{action prefix} & (a \in Name) \\
\quad | \quad P + P & \text{alternative composition} & \\
\quad | \quad P \parallel_S P & \text{parallel composition} & (S \subseteq Name - \{\tau\}) \\
\quad | \quad P/H & \text{hiding} & (H \subseteq Name - \{\tau\}) \\
\quad | \quad P[\varphi] & \text{relabeling} & (\varphi : Name \to Name, \varphi^{-1}(\tau) = \{\tau\})
\end{array}
$$

Operational semantic rules map every closed and guarded process term P of PA to a state-transition graph $[\![P]\!]$ called labeled transition system, where each state corresponds to a process term derivable from P, the initial state corresponds to P, and each transition is labeled with the corresponding action.

Process terms are compared and manipulated by means of behavioral equivalences. Among the various approaches, for PA we consider weak bisimilarity, according to which two process terms are equivalent if they are able to mimic each other's visible behavior stepwise.

A symmetric relation $\mathcal{R}$ is a weak bisimulation if for all $(P_1, P_2) \in \mathcal{R}$ and $a \in Name - \{\tau\}$: *(i)* whenever $P_1 \stackrel{a}{\longrightarrow} P_1'$, then $P_2 \stackrel{\tau^* a \tau^*}{\Longrightarrow} P_2'$ and $(P_1', P_2') \in \mathcal{R}$; *(ii)* whenever $P_1 \stackrel{\tau}{\longrightarrow} P_1'$, then $P_2 \stackrel{\tau^*}{\Longrightarrow} P_2'$ and $(P_1', P_2') \in \mathcal{R}$. Weak bisimilarity $\approx_B$ is the union of all the weak bisimulations.

2.2 PADL Textual and Graphical Notations

A PADL description represents an architectural type, which is a family of software systems sharing certain constraints on the observable behavior of their components as well as on their topology.

The textual description of an architectural type starts with the name and the formal parameters (initialized with default values) of the architectural type. The available data types are boolean, integer, real, list, array, record, and generic object. The textual description then comprises two sections.

The first section defines the behavior of the system family by means of types of software components and connectors, which are collectively called architectural element types. The definition of an AET starts with its name and its formal parameters and consists of the specification of its behavior and its interactions.

The behavior of an AET has to be provided in the form of a sequence of defining equations written in a verbose variant of PA allowing only for the inactive process (rendered as `stop`), the value-passing action prefix operator with a possible boolean guard condition, the alternative composition operator (rendered as `choice`), and recursion.

The interactions are those actions occurring in the process algebraic specification of the behavior that act as interfaces for the AET, while all the other actions are assumed to represent internal activities. Each interaction has to be equipped with two qualifiers. The first qualifier establishes whether the interaction is an input or output interaction.

The second qualifier describes the multiplicity of the communications in which the interaction can be involved. We distinguish among uni-interactions mainly involved in one-to-one communications (qualifier `UNI`), and-interactions guiding inclusive one-to-many communications (qualifier `AND`), or-interactions guiding selective one-to-many communications (qualifier `OR`). It can also be established that an output or-interaction depends on an input or-interaction, in order to guarantee that a selective one-to-many output is sent to the same element from which a selective many-to-one input was received (keyword `DEP`).

The second section of the PADL description defines the topology of the system family. This is accomplished in three steps. First we have the declaration of the instances of the AETs – called AEIs – which represent the actual system components and connectors, together with their actual parameters. Then we have the declaration of the architectural (as opposed to local) interactions, which are some of the interactions of the AEIs that act as interfaces for the whole systems of the family. Finally, we have the declaration of the architectural attachments among the local interactions of the AEIs, which make the AEIs communicate with each other. An attachment is admissible only if it goes from an output interaction of an AEI to an input interaction of another AEI. Moreover, a uni-interaction can be attached to only one interaction, whereas an and-/or-interaction can be attached to (several) uni-interactions only.

```
ARCHI_TYPE                        ◁name and initialized formal parameters▷

   ARCHI_BEHAVIOR
         ⋮                                  ⋮
      ARCHI_ELEM_TYPE             ◁AET name and formal parameters▷
         BEHAVIOR                 ◁sequence of PA defining equations built from
                                     stop, action prefix, choice, and recursion▷
         INPUT_INTERACTIONS       ◁input uni/and/or-interactions▷
         OUTPUT_INTERACTIONS      ◁output uni/and/or-interactions▷
         ⋮                                  ⋮

   ARCHI_TOPOLOGY
      ARCHI_ELEM_INSTANCES        ◁AEI names and actual parameters▷
      ARCHI_INTERACTIONS          ◁architecture-level AEI interactions▷
      ARCHI_ATTACHMENTS           ◁attachments between AEI local interactions▷

END
```

Besides the textual notation, PADL comes equipped with a graphical notation that is an extension of the flow graph notation [9]. In an enriched flow graph, AEIs are depicted as boxes, local (resp. architectural) interactions are depicted as small black circles (resp. white squares) on the box border, and attachments are depicted as directed edges between pairs each composed of a local output interaction and a local input interaction. The small circle/square of an interaction is extended with a triangle (resp. bisected triangle) outside the AEI box if the interaction is an and-interaction (resp. or-interaction).

Example 1. Suppose we need to model a scenario in which there is a server that can be contacted at any time by two identically behaving clients. Assume that the server has no buffer for holding incoming requests and that, after sending a request, a client cannot proceed until it receives a response from the server. Since the behavior of the two clients is identical, a single client AET suffices:

```
ARCHI_ELEM_TYPE Client_Type(void)
  BEHAVIOR
    Client(void; void) =
      process . send_request . receive_response . Client()
  INPUT_INTERACTIONS  UNI receive_response
  OUTPUT_INTERACTIONS UNI send_request
```

where `process` is an internal action. The server AET can be defined as follows:

```
ARCHI_ELEM_TYPE Server_Type(void)
  BEHAVIOR
    Server(void; void) =
      receive_request . compute_response . send_response . Server()
  INPUT_INTERACTIONS  OR receive_request
  OUTPUT_INTERACTIONS OR send_response   DEP receive_request
```

where `compute_response` is an internal action, while `send_response` is declared to depend on `receive_request` in order to make sure that each response is sent back to the client that issued the corresponding request. Finally, we declare the topology of the system as follows:

```
ARCHI_TOPOLOGY
  ARCHI_ELEM_INSTANCES
    C_1 : Client_Type();
    C_2 : Client_Type();
    S   : Server_Type()
  ARCHI_INTERACTIONS
    void
  ARCHI_ATTACHMENTS
    FROM C_1.send_request TO S.receive_request;
    FROM C_2.send_request TO S.receive_request;
    FROM S.send_response  TO C_1.receive_response;
    FROM S.send_response  TO C_2.receive_response
```

where the dot notation has to be used so as to avoid ambiguities in cases in which the same action name denotes interactions belonging to different AEIs. ∎

2.3   The Semantics for PADL

The semantics for PADL is given by translation into PA. The meaning of a PADL description is a process term stemming from the parallel composition of the process algebraic specifications of the behavior of the AEIs declared in the description, with synchronization sets being determined by attachments.

Let $\mathcal{C}$ be an AET with formal parameters $fp_1, \ldots, fp_m$ and behavior given by the sequence $\mathcal{E}$ of defining equations. Let C be an AEI of type $\mathcal{C}$ with actual parameters $ap_1, \ldots, ap_m$. Then the semantics of C is defined as follows:

$$\llbracket C \rrbracket \;=\; \textit{or-rewrite}(\mathcal{E}\{ap_1/fp_1, \ldots, ap_m/fp_m\})$$

where $\{\_/\_, \ldots, \_/\_\}$ denotes a syntactical substitution, while function $\textit{or-rewrite}$ inductively rewrites the body of any defining equation of $\mathcal{E}$ by replacing each occurrence of any or-interaction with fresh uni-interactions. More precisely, if or-interaction a of C is involved in $\textit{attach-no}(C.a) = l \geq 2$ attachments, then:

$$\textit{or-rewrite}(a.P) \;=\; \texttt{choice}\{a_1.\textit{or-rewrite}(P),$$
$$\vdots$$
$$a_l.\textit{or-rewrite}(P)\}$$

Consider now a set $\{C_1, \ldots, C_n\}$ of AEIs and let us denote by $\mathcal{LI}_{C_j}$ the set of local interactions of C_j and by $\mathcal{LI}_{C_j;C_1,\ldots,C_n} \subseteq \mathcal{LI}_{C_j}$ the set of local interactions of C_j attached to $\{C_1, \ldots, C_n\}$. In order to make such AEIs interact in the framework of PA – where only actions with the same name can synchronize – we need a set $\mathcal{S}(C_1, \ldots, C_n)$ of fresh action names, one for each pair of attached local uni-interactions in $\{C_1, \ldots, C_n\}$ and for each set of local uni-interactions attached to the same local and-interaction in $\{C_1, \ldots, C_n\}$.

Then we need suitable injective relabeling functions $\varphi_{C_j;C_1,\ldots,C_n}$ mapping each $\mathcal{LI}_{C_j;C_1,\ldots,C_n}$ to $\mathcal{S}(C_1, \ldots, C_n)$ in such a way that:

$$\varphi_{C_j;C_1,\ldots,C_n}(a_1) \;=\; \varphi_{C_g;C_1,\ldots,C_n}(a_2)$$

if and only if $C_j.a_1$ and $C_g.a_2$ are attached to each other or to the same and-interaction. To ensure renaming uniqueness, $\mathcal{S}(C_1, \ldots, C_n)$ can be built by concatenating the original names of attached interactions – e.g., $C_j.a_1 \# C_g.a_2$.

The interacting semantics of C_j with respect to $\{C_1, \ldots, C_n\}$ is defined as follows:

$$\llbracket C_j \rrbracket_{C_1,\ldots,C_n} \;=\; \llbracket C_j \rrbracket[\varphi_{C_j;C_1,\ldots,C_n}]$$

In general, the interacting semantics of $\{C'_1, \ldots, C'_{n'}\} \subseteq \{C_1, \ldots, C_n\}$ with respect to $\{C_1, \ldots, C_n\}$ is defined as follows:

$$\llbracket C'_1, \ldots, C'_{n'} \rrbracket_{C_1,\ldots,C_n} \;=\; \llbracket C'_1 \rrbracket_{C_1,\ldots,C_n} \parallel_{\mathcal{S}(C'_1,C'_2;C_1,\ldots,C_n)}$$
$$\llbracket C'_2 \rrbracket_{C_1,\ldots,C_n} \parallel_{\mathcal{S}(C'_1,C'_3;C_1,\ldots,C_n)\cup\mathcal{S}(C'_2,C'_3;C_1,\ldots,C_n)} \cdots$$
$$\cdots \parallel_{\bigcup_{i=1}^{n'-1} \mathcal{S}(C'_i,C'_{n'};C_1,\ldots,C_n)} \llbracket C'_{n'} \rrbracket_{C_1,\ldots,C_n}$$

where $\mathcal{S}(C'_j, C'_g; C_1, \ldots, C_n) = \mathcal{S}(C'_j; C_1, \ldots, C_n) \cap \mathcal{S}(C'_g; C_1, \ldots, C_n)$ is the pairwise synchronization set of C'_j and C'_g with respect to $\{C_1, \ldots, C_n\}$, with $\mathcal{S}(C'_j; C_1, \ldots, C_n) = \varphi_{C'_j; C_1, \ldots, C_n}(\mathcal{LI}_{C'_j; C_1, \ldots, C_n})$ being the synchronization set of C'_j with respect to $\{C_1, \ldots, C_n\}$. Finally, the semantics of an architectural type $\mathcal{A}$ formed by the set of AEIs $\{C_1, \ldots, C_n\}$ is defined as follows:

$$\boxed{[\![\mathcal{A}]\!] = [\![C_1, \ldots, C_n]\!]_{C_1, \ldots, C_n}}$$

Example 2. Consider the client-server system described in Ex. 1. Then $[\![\texttt{C\_1}]\!]$ and $[\![\texttt{C\_2}]\!]$ coincide with the defining equation for `Client`, whereas $[\![\texttt{S}]\!]$ is given by the following defining equation obtained from the one for `Server` after manipulating the occurring or-interactions:

```
Server'(void; void) =
  choice
  {
     receive_request_1 . compute_response . send_response_1 . Server'(),
     receive_request_2 . compute_response . send_response_2 . Server'()
  }
```

The semantics of the whole description is given by the following process term:

$[\![\texttt{C\_1}]\!][\texttt{send\_request} \mapsto \texttt{C\_1.send\_request\#S.receive\_request\_1},$
$\qquad \texttt{receive\_response} \mapsto \texttt{S.send\_response\_1\#C\_1.receive\_response}]$
$\qquad \|_\emptyset$
$[\![\texttt{C\_2}]\!][\texttt{send\_request} \mapsto \texttt{C\_2.send\_request\#S.receive\_request\_2},$
$\qquad \texttt{receive\_response} \mapsto \texttt{S.send\_response\_2\#C\_2.receive\_response}]$
$\qquad \|_{\{\texttt{C\_1.send\_request\#S.receive\_request\_1},}$
$\qquad\quad {\texttt{S.send\_response\_1\#C\_1.receive\_response},}$
$\qquad\quad {\texttt{C\_2.send\_request\#S.receive\_request\_2},}$
$\qquad\quad {\texttt{S.send\_response\_2\#C\_2.receive\_response}\}}$
$[\![\texttt{S}]\!][\texttt{receive\_request\_1} \mapsto \texttt{C\_1.send\_request\#S.receive\_request\_1},$
$\qquad \texttt{send\_response\_1} \mapsto \texttt{S.send\_response\_1\#C\_1.receive\_response},$
$\qquad \texttt{receive\_request\_2} \mapsto \texttt{C\_2.send\_request\#S.receive\_request\_2},$
$\qquad \texttt{send\_response\_2} \mapsto \texttt{S.send\_response\_2\#C\_2.receive\_response}]$ ∎

3   Semi-synchronous and Asynchronous Interactions

All the interactions occurring in a PADL description can be involved only in synchronous communications, thus causing input interactions and output interactions to be blocking operations. In order to increase the expressiveness of PADL, within the interface of each AET we will provide support for distinguishing among synchronous, semi-synchronous and asynchronous interactions. The usability of the language will be preserved by means of suitable synchronicity-related qualifiers that are made available to PADL users.

In this section we enrich the textual and graphical notations in order to express non-synchronous interactions, then we revise the semantics accordingly. The nine

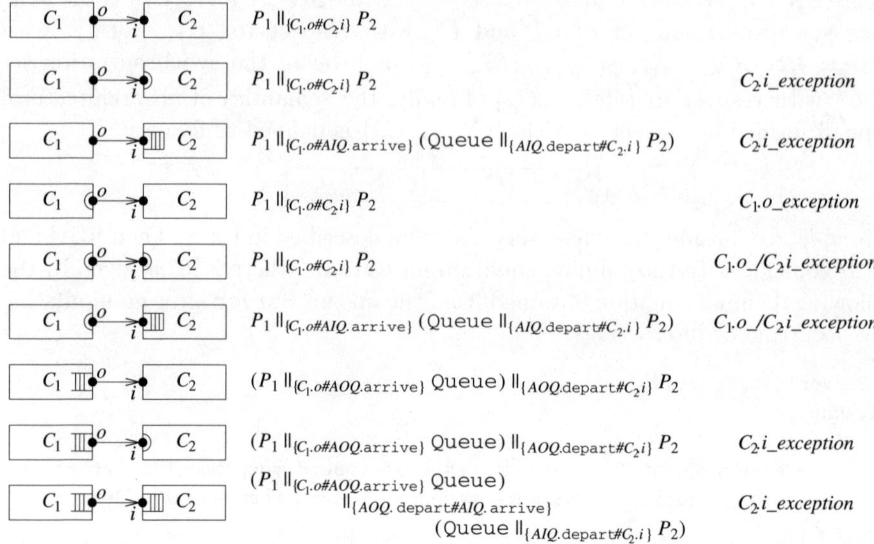

Fig. 1. Synchronous, semi-synchronous and asynchronous communications

resulting forms of communication are summarized by Fig. 1, with the first one being the only one originally available in PADL.

3.1   Enriching PADL Textual and Graphical Notations

In the textual notation of PADL we introduce a third qualifier for interactions, to be used in the definition of the AETs. Such a qualifier establishes whether an interaction is synchronous, semi-synchronous, or asynchronous. The related keywords are SYNC (default value), SSYNC, and ASYNC, respectively.

While a synchronous interaction blocks the AEI executing it as long as the interactions attached to it are not ready, this is not the case with non-synchronous interactions. More precisely, a semi-synchronous interaction raises an exception if it cannot take place immediately due to the (temporary or permanent) unavailability of the interactions attached to it, so that the AEI executing it can proceed anyway. Likewise, in the case of an asynchronous interaction the beginning and the end of the communication are decoupled, hence the AEI executing the interaction will never block.

A boolean variable $s.\texttt{success}$ is associated with each semi-synchronous interaction s. This implicitly declared variable is made available to PADL users in order to catch exceptions. In this way situations in which different behaviors have to be undertaken depending on the outcome of s can easily be managed.

In the graphical notation a semi-synchronous interaction is depicted by extending the small circle/square of the interaction with an arc inside the AEI box. An asynchronous interaction, instead, is depicted by extending the small circle/square with a buffer inside the AEI box.

Example 3. Consider again the client-server system described in Ex. 1. Since the server has no buffer for incoming requests, each client may want to send a request only if the server is not busy, so that the client can keep working instead of passively waiting for the server to become available. This can be described by transforming `send_request` into a semi-synchronous interaction:

```
ARCHI_ELEM_TYPE Client_Type(void)
  BEHAVIOR
    Client(void; void) =
      process . send_request .
        choice
        {
          cond(send_request.success = true) ->
                                  receive_response . Client(),
          cond(send_request.success = false) ->
                                  keep_processing . Client()
        }
  INPUT_INTERACTIONS  SYNC  UNI receive_response
  OUTPUT_INTERACTIONS SSYNC UNI send_request
```

On the other hand, the server should not make any assumption about the status of its clients, as these may be much more complicated than the description above. In particular, when sending out a response to a client, the server should not be blocked by the temporary or permanent unavailability of that client, as this would decrease the quality of service. This can be achieved by using keyword `ASYNC` in the declaration of interaction send response within `Server_Type`. ∎

3.2   Semantics of Semi-synchronous Interactions: Additional Rules

A semi-synchronous interaction s executed by an AEI C gives rise to a transition labeled with s within $[\![C]\!]$. However, in an interacting context this transition has to be relabeled with $s\_exception$ if s cannot immediately participate in a communication. This is accomplished by means of additional semantic rules.

Suppose that the output interaction o of an AEI C_1 is attached to the input interaction i of an AEI C_2. Let $C_1.o\#C_2.i$ be the fresh action name associated with their synchronization, P_1 (resp. P_2) be the process term representing the current state of $[\![C_1]\!]_{C_1,C_2}$ (resp. $[\![C_2]\!]_{C_1,C_2}$), and $S = \mathcal{S}(C_1, C_2; C_1, C_2)$.

If o is synchronous and i is semi-synchronous – which is the second form of communication depicted in Fig. 1 – then the following additional semantic rule is necessary for handling exceptions:

$$\frac{P_1 \xrightarrow{\;\;C_1.o\#C_2.i\;\;}\!\!\!\!\!\!\!/ \qquad P_2 \xrightarrow{\;\;C_1.o\#C_2.i\;\;} P_2'}{P_1 \parallel_S P_2 \xrightarrow{\;\;C_2.i\_exception\;\;} P_1 \parallel_S P_2' \qquad C_2.i.\texttt{success} = \texttt{false}}$$

In the symmetric case in which o is semi-synchronous and i is synchronous – which corresponds to the fourth form of communication depicted in Fig. 1 – the following additional semantic rule is necessary for handling exceptions:

$$\frac{P_1 \xrightarrow{\;C_1.o\#C_2.i\;} P_1' \qquad P_2 \xrightarrow{\;C_1.o\#C_2.i\;}\!\!\!/}{P_1 \,\|_S\, P_2 \xrightarrow{\;C_1.o\_exception\;} P_1' \,\|_S\, P_2 \qquad C_1.o.\texttt{success} = \texttt{false}}$$

Finally, in the case in which both o and i are semi-synchronous – which corresponds to the fifth form of communication depicted in Fig. 1 – we have the previous two semantic rules together.

3.3 Semantics of Asynchronous Interactions: Implicit AEIs

While semi-synchronous interactions are dealt with by means of suitable semantic rules accounting for possible exceptions, asynchronous interactions need a different treatment because of the decoupling between the beginning and the end of the communications in which those interactions are involved.

After the or-rewriting process, for each asynchronous uni-/and-interaction we have to introduce an additional implicit AEI that behaves as an unbounded buffer, as shown in the third, sixth, seventh, eighth and ninth form of communication depicted in Fig. 1. This AEI is of the following type, where `arrive` is an always-available synchronous interaction, whereas `depart` is a synchronous interaction enabled only if the buffer is not empty.

```
ARCHI_ELEM_TYPE Async_Queue(void)
  BEHAVIOR
    Queue(int i := 0; void) =
    choice
    {
      cond(true)  -> arrive . Queue(i + 1),
      cond(i > 0) -> depart . Queue(i - 1)
    }
  INPUT_INTERACTIONS  SYNC --- arrive
  OUTPUT_INTERACTIONS SYNC --- depart
```

In the case of an asynchronous output interaction o, this is implicitly converted into a synchronous uni-interaction and attached to `arrive`, which is declared as a uni-interaction. By contrast, `depart`, which is declared as a uni-/and-interaction depending on whether o was a uni-/and-interaction, is attached to the input interactions originally attached to o.

In the case of an asynchronous input interaction i, `depart` is declared as a uni-interaction and implicitly attached to i, which is implicitly converted into a semi-synchronous uni-interaction. By contrast, the output interactions originally attached to i are attached to `arrive`, which is declared as a uni-/and-interaction depending on whether i was a uni-/and-interaction.

Note that i becomes semi-synchronous because the communications between `depart` and i must not block the AEI executing i whenever the buffer is empty. Thus i is subject to the first additional semantic rule defined in Sect. 3.2.

3.4 Revising PADL Semantics

Due to the way non-synchronous interactions have been handled, we only need to revise the definition of the semantics of an AEI in isolation, while all the subsequent definitions given in Sect. 2.3 are unchanged. More precisely, we only have to take into account the possible presence of additional implicit AEIs acting as unbounded buffers for asynchronous interactions.

Suppose that AEI C has $h \in \mathbf{N}_{>0}$ asynchronous input interactions $i_1, \ldots, i_h$ – handled through the related additional implicit AEIs $AIQ_1, \ldots, AIQ_h$ – and $k \in \mathbf{N}_{>0}$ asynchronous output interactions $o_1, \ldots, o_k$ – handled through the related additional implicit AEIs $AOQ_1, \ldots, AOQ_k$. Then $[\![C]\!]$ is defined as follows:

$$\begin{aligned}
&((\overbrace{\mathbf{Queue} \parallel_\emptyset \ldots \parallel_\emptyset \mathbf{Queue}}^{h}) [\varphi_{C,\mathrm{async}}]) \parallel_{\{AIQ_1.depart\#C.i_1,\ldots,AIQ_h.depart\#C.i_h\}} \\
&\quad or\text{-}rewrite(\mathcal{E}\{ap_1/fp_1, \ldots, ap_m/fp_m\}) [\varphi_{C,\mathrm{async}}] \\
&\qquad \parallel_{\{C.o_1\#AOQ_1.arrive,\ldots,C.o_k\#AOQ_k.arrive\}} ((\underbrace{\mathbf{Queue} \parallel_\emptyset \ldots \parallel_\emptyset \mathbf{Queue}}_{k}) [\varphi_{C,\mathrm{async}}])
\end{aligned}$$

where $\varphi_{C,\mathrm{async}}$ transforms $C.i_1, \ldots, C.i_h, C.o_1, \ldots, C.o_k$ and the related attached interactions of $AIQ_1, \ldots, AIQ_h, AOQ_1, \ldots, AOQ_k$ into the corresponding fresh names occurring in the two synchronization sets.

4 Modifying Architectural Checks

The objective of the architectural checks developed in [1] is to infer certain architectural properties – which thus involve only interactions – from the properties of the individual AEIs through a topological reduction process based on equivalence checking. In case of failure, such checks provide diagnostic information useful to single out components responsible for possible property violations.

The starting point in [1] is given by abstract variants of enriched flow graphs, where vertices correspond to AEIs and two vertices are linked by an edge if and only if attachments have been declared among their interactions. These graphs are arbitrary combinations of stars and cycles, which are thus viewed as basic topological formats.

The strategy proposed in [1] is to reduce the whole topology of an architectural type to a single equivalent AEI that satisfies the properties of interest. This is accomplished by applying specific checks locally to stars and cycles occurring in the abstract enriched flow graph of the architectural type. If passed, each check allows the star/cycle in which it has been employed to be replaced by an equivalent AEI in the star/cycle itself that satisfies the properties of interest.

In this section we show how to modify the compatibility check for stars and the interoperability check for cycles, in such a way that both checks can still be applied in the presence of non-synchronous interactions. Although these checks are conceived for an entire class of properties [1], for the sake of simplicity here the considered property is deadlock freedom and the behavioral equivalence chosen among those preserving deadlock freedom is weak bisimilarity $\approx_{\mathrm{B}}$ (Sect. 2.1).

4.1 Revising Closed Interacting Semantics

The considered architectural checks must be applied to closed variants of the interacting semantics of AEIs, where all the internal actions are hidden. In the framework of PADL enriched with non-synchronous interactions, also the asynchronous interactions have to be hidden together with the interactions of the related additional implicit AEIs to which they are re-attached. The reason is that all of those interactions cannot communicate with the rest of the system, hence they cannot affect architectural properties.

Let $\{C_1, \ldots, C_n\}$ be a set of AEIs and let C_j be one of its AEIs having $h \in \mathbf{N}_{>0}$ asynchronous input interactions $i_1, \ldots, i_h$ and $k \in \mathbf{N}_{>0}$ asynchronous output interactions $o_1, \ldots, o_k$. The closed interacting semantics of C_j with respect to $\{C_1, \ldots, C_n\}$ is defined as follows:

$$
\begin{aligned}
\llbracket C_j \rrbracket^{\mathrm{c}}_{C_1,\ldots,C_n} = {} & \llbracket C_j \rrbracket_{C_1,\ldots,C_n} / (\mathit{Name} - \mathcal{LI}_{C_j;C_1,\ldots,C_n}) \\
& / \{ AIQ_1.\mathit{depart}\#C_j.i_1, \ldots, AIQ_h.\mathit{depart}\#C_j.i_h, \\
& \quad\; C_j.o_1\#AOQ_1.\mathit{arrive}, \ldots, C_j.o_k\#AOQ_k.\mathit{arrive}, \\
& \quad\; C_j.i_1\_\mathit{exception}, \ldots, C_j.i_h\_\mathit{exception} \}
\end{aligned}
$$

The closed interacting semantics $\llbracket C'_1, \ldots, C'_{n'} \rrbracket^{\mathrm{c}}_{C_1,\ldots,C_n}$ and the closed semantics $\llbracket \mathcal{A} \rrbracket^{\mathrm{c}}$ are defined accordingly.

4.2 Adapting Architectural Compatibility

A star is an acyclic portion of the abstract enriched flow graph of an architectural type, which is formed by a central AEI K and a border $\mathcal{B}_K = \{C_1, \ldots, C_n\}$ including all the AEIs attached to K. In order to achieve a correct coordination between K and each $C_j \in \mathcal{B}_K$, the actual observable behavior of each C_j should coincide with the one expected by K. In other words, the observable behavior of K should not be altered by the addition of C_j to the border of the star.

Definition 1. *We say that K is compatible with $C_j \in \mathcal{B}_K$ iff:*

$$
\left(\llbracket K \rrbracket^{\mathrm{c}}_{K,\mathcal{B}_K} \, \|_{\mathcal{S}(K,C_j;K,\mathcal{B}_K)} \, \llbracket C_j \rrbracket^{\mathrm{c}}_{K,\mathcal{B}_K} \right) / H_j \; \approx_{\mathrm{B}} \; \llbracket K \rrbracket^{\mathrm{c}}_{K,\mathcal{B}_K} / H_j
$$

where the hiding set H_j includes all the semi-synchronous interactions involved in attachments between K and C_j together with the related exceptions, as well as all the interactions of implicit AEIs associated with K (resp. C_j) that are attached to interactions of C_j (resp. K). ∎

Note that $H_j = \emptyset$ whenever neither K nor C_j has semi-synchronous or asynchronous interactions. In fact, the presence of H_j is the novelty with respect to the definition of compatibility given in [1].

The reason why it makes sense to hide those semi-synchronous and asynchronous interactions is that they are not blocking, hence similarly to internal actions they cannot negatively affect component coordination.

The reason why it is necessary to hide each of them is that, within an AEI executing one of them the interaction takes place at a specific point with a specific outcome, while in the parallel composition of that AEI with other AEIs the same interaction can have a different outcome (semi-synchronous case) or can be delayed (asynchronous case). This may lead to detect inequivalence between the behavior of the individual AEI and the behavior of a set of AEIs including it – a compatibility violation – even in the absence of a real coordination mismatch.

We now extend the compatibility theorem of [1] to non-synchronous interactions. The additional constraint to satisfy is that no and-interaction occurring in the star can be non-synchronous or attached to a non-synchronous interaction.

Theorem 1. *Let $H = H_1 \cup \ldots \cup H_n$. Whenever $[\![K]\!]^c_{K,\mathcal{B}_K} \, / \, H$ is deadlock free and K is compatible with any $C_j \in \mathcal{B}_K$, then the whole star $[\![K, \mathcal{B}_K]\!]^c_{K,\mathcal{B}_K} \, / \, H$ is deadlock free provided that $H_j \cap H_g = \emptyset$ for all $j \neq g$.* ∎

4.3 Adapting Architectural Interoperability

Consider a cycle $\{C_1, \ldots, C_n\}$ in the abstract enriched flow graph of an architectural type $\mathcal{A}$. As shown in [1], compatibility is not enough to deal with it. The reason is that the AEIs in the cycle can no longer be considered two-by-two, because each of them may interfere with any of the others. In order to achieve a correct coordination between any C_j and the rest of the cycle, the actual observable behavior of C_j should coincide with the one expected by the rest of the cycle. In other words, the observable behavior of the rest of the cycle should not be altered by the addition of C_j to the cycle.

Definition 2. *We say that C_j interoperates with the rest of the cycle iff:*

$$\boxed{[\![C_1, \ldots, C_n]\!]^c_{\mathcal{A}} \, / \, (Name - \mathcal{S}(C_j; \mathcal{A})) \, / \, H_j \, \approx_{\mathrm{B}} \, [\![C_j]\!]^c_{\mathcal{A}} \, / \, H_j}$$

where H_j includes all the semi-synchronous interactions involved in attachments between C_j and the rest of the cycle together with the related exceptions, as well as all the interactions of implicit AEIs associated with C_j (resp. the rest of the cycle) that are attached to interactions of the rest of the cycle (resp. C_j). ∎

As in Sect. 4.2, the presence of H_j is the novelty with respect to the definition of interoperability given in [1]. We now extend the interoperability theorem of [1] to non-synchronous interactions.

Theorem 2. *Whenever there exists C_j in the cycle such that $[\![C_j]\!]^c_{\mathcal{A}} \, / \, H_j$ is deadlock free and C_j interoperates with the rest of the cycle, then the whole cycle $[\![C_1, \ldots, C_n]\!]^c_{\mathcal{A}} \, / \, (Name - \mathcal{S}(C_j; \mathcal{A})) \, / \, H_j$ is deadlock free.* ∎

4.4 Example: An Applet-Based Simulator

In this section we discuss the application of the modified architectural checks by revisiting the cruise control system considered in [8,3].

This system is governed by two pedals – accelerator and brake – and three buttons – on, off, and resume. When on is pressed, the cruise control system records the current speed and maintains the automobile at that speed. When the accelerator, the brake, or off is pressed, the cruise control system disengages but retains the speed setting. If resume is pressed later on, then the system is able to accelerate or decelerate the automobile to the previously recorded speed.

The cruise control system is formed by four software components: a sensor, a speed controller, a speed detector, and a speed actuator. The sensor detects the driver commands and forwards them to the speed controller, which in turn triggers the speed actuator. The speed detector periodically measures the number of wheel revolutions per time unit. The speed actuator adjusts the throttle on the basis of the triggers received from the controller and of the speed measured by the detector.

As an example, we report the definition of the sensor AET:

```
ARCHI_ELEM_TYPE Sensor_Type(void)
  BEHAVIOR
    Sensor_Off(void; void) =
      detected_engine_on . turn_engine_on . Sensor_On();
    Sensor_On(void; void) =
      choice
      {
        detected_accelerator . press_accelerator . Sensor_On(),
        detected_brake . press_brake . Sensor_On(),
        detected_on . press_on . Sensor_On(),
        detected_off . press_off . Sensor_On(),
        detected_resume . press_resume . Sensor_On(),
        detected_engine_off . turn_engine_off . Sensor_Off()
      }
    INPUT_INTERACTIONS  UNI detected_engine_on; detected_engine_off;
                            detected_accelerator; detected_brake;
                            detected_on; detected_off; detected_resume
    OUTPUT_INTERACTIONS UNI press_accelerator; press_brake;
                            press_on; press_off; press_resume
                        AND turn_engine_on; turn_engine_off
```

Suppose we want to design an applet-based simulator for such a system. The applet will have seven software buttons – corresponding to turning the engine on/off, the two pedals, and the three hardware buttons – together with a text area showing the sequence of buttons that have been pressed. When pressing one of the seven software buttons, the corresponding operation either succeeds or fails. In the first case, the applet can interact with the sensor and the text area is updated accordingly. In the second case – think, e.g., of pressing the accelerator button when the engine is off – the applet cannot interact with the sensor, rather it emits a beep.

In order not to block the simulator in case of failure, we need to model several operations of the applet through semi-synchronous interactions, as shown below:

```
ARCHI_ELEM_TYPE Applet_Type(void)
  BEHAVIOR
    Unallocated(void; void) =
      create_applet . start_applet . Active();
    Active(void; void) =
      choice
      {
        signal_engine_on . Checking(signal_engine_on.success),
        signal_accelerator . Checking(signal_accelerator.success),
        signal_brake . Checking(signal_brake.success),
        signal_on . Checking(signal_on.success),
        signal_off . Checking(signal_off.success),
        signal_resume . Checking(signal_resume.success),
        signal_engine_off . Checking(signal_engine_off.success),
        stop_applet . Inactive()
      };
    Checking(boolean success; void) =
      choice
      {
        cond(success = true)  -> update . Active(),
        cond(success = false) -> beep . Active(),
      };
    Inactive(void; void) =
      choice
      {
        start_applet . Active(),
        destroy_applet . Unallocated()
      }
  INPUT_INTERACTIONS  SYNC  UNI create_applet; destroy_applet;
                                start_applet; stop_applet
  OUTPUT_INTERACTIONS SSYNC UNI signal_engine_on; signal_engine_off;
                                signal_accelerator; signal_brake;
                                signal_on; signal_off; signal_resume
```

As far as the instance of **Applet_Type** is concerned, its four input interactions
are related to user commands for starting/stopping the simulator. By contrast,
its seven **signal_** output interactions are related to user commands for the cruise
control system, hence they are attached to the corresponding **detected_** input
interactions of the instance of **Sensor_Type**.

Suppose we wish to verify whether the applet-based simulator is deadlock
free. From the topological viewpoint, the system is a cycle formed by four AEIs
(sensor, controller, actuator, detector) with an additional AEI (applet) attached
to one of them (sensor). Within the cycle there are no non-synchronous interactions, hence applying the modified interoperability check to the cycle boils down
to applying the original check. The outcome is thus known from [3]: the cycle
is deadlock free, because it is weakly bisimilar to the sensor and the sensor is
deadlock free (Thm. 2).

Now the sensor and the applet constitute a degenerate star, for which the original compatibility check is not appropriate due to the presence of semi-synchronous

interactions within the applet. By applying the modified architectural compatibility check, we see that the parallel composition of the closed interacting semantics of the applet and of the sensor is weakly bisimilar to the closed interacting semantics of the applet, where all the semi-synchronous interactions and the related exceptions have been hidden. Since the applet is deadlock free, we can conclude that the applet-based simulator is deadlock free (Thm. 1).

5   Conclusion

In this paper we have extended process algebraic ADLs by including semi-synchronous interactions – handled by means of suitable semantic rules – and asynchronous interactions – managed by adding implicit buffer-like components. Besides enhancing the expressiveness of a typical process algebraic ADL without compromising its usability, we have shown that architectural checks for acyclic and cyclic topologies – compatibility and interoperability – can be easily adapted to cope with the presence of non-synchronous interactions.

In the case of asynchronous interactions, the semantic model underlying a process algebraic architectural description may have infinitely many states because the additional implicit components behave like unbounded buffers. In order for the modified architectural checks to be effectively applicable in this case, one option is to allow users to limit the size of buffers statically. Another option is to derive sufficient conditions under which the state space is guaranteed to be finite. This will be the subject of future work.

References

1. Aldini, A., Bernardo, M.: On the Usability of Process Algebra: An Architectural View. Theoretical Computer Science 335, 281–329 (2005)
2. Allen, R., Garlan, D.: A Formal Basis for Architectural Connection. ACM Trans. on Software Engineering and Methodology 6, 213–249 (1997)
3. Bernardo, M., Ciancarini, P., Donatiello, L.: Architecting Families of Software Systems with Process Algebras. ACM Trans. on Software Engineering and Methodology 11, 386–426 (2002)
4. Canal, C., Pimentel, E., Troya, J.M.: Compatibility and Inheritance in Software Architectures. Science of Computer Programming 41, 105–138 (2001)
5. Carzaniga, A., Rosenblum, D.S., Wolf, A.L.: Design and Evaluation of a Wide-Area Event Notification Service. ACM Trans. on Computer Systems 19, 332–383 (2001)
6. Gelernter, D.: Generative Communication in Linda. ACM Trans. on Programming Languages and Systems 7, 80–112 (1985)
7. Inverardi, P., Wolf, A.L., Yankelevich, D.: Static Checking of System Behaviors Using Derived Component Assumptions. ACM Trans. on Software Engineering and Methodology 9, 239–272 (2000)
8. Magee, J., Kramer, J.: Concurrency: State Models & Java Programs. Wiley, Chichester (1999)
9. Milner, R.: Communication and Concurrency. Prentice-Hall, Englewood Cliffs (1989)
10. Oquendo, F.: π-ADL: An Architecture Description Language Based on the Higher-Order Typed π-Calculus for Specifying Dynamic and Mobile Software Architectures. ACM Software Engineering Notes 29(3), 1–14 (2004)

Stakeholder Perception of Enterprise Architecture

Bas van der Raadt[1], Sander Schouten[1], and Hans van Vliet[2]

[1] Capgemini, Global Financial Services / Architecture & Governance Improvement,
Papendorpseweg 100, 3528 BJ Utrecht, the Netherlands
{bas.vander.raadt,sander.schouten}@capgemini.com
[2] VU University, Department of Computer Science
De Boelelaan 1081a, 1081 HV Amsterdam, the Netherlands
hans@cs.vu.nl

Abstract. Enterprise Architecture (EA) is increasingly being used by large organizations to get a grip on the complexity and inflexibility of their business processes, information systems and technical infrastructure. Although seen as an important instrument to help solve major organizational problems, effectively applying EA seems no easy task. Efficient collaboration between architects and EA stakeholders is one of the main critical success factors for EA. The basis for efficient collaboration between architects and EA stakeholders is mutual understanding. In EA research, there has been much focus on the role of the architect; there is little research on the EA stakeholder. In this article we present the cognitive structure of four EA stakeholder groups, revealing how they expect the EA function to help them achieve their goals. With this we gain understanding of the EA stakeholder and provide the basis for better collaboration between architects and EA stakeholders.

Keywords: Enterprise Architecture, Organizational Function, Stakeholder Perception, Efficiency, Effectiveness.

1 Introduction

Each organization tries to be unique in order to distinguish itself from its competitors. However, many large organizations are not unique when it comes to the complexity they face regarding their business and IT structures, processes, systems and procedures. Organizations have different causes of this complexity – e.g., mergers & acquisitions [1], low maturity of the IT function [2], or high diversity between operating models of various business divisions [3] – but as a result typically face similar problems. For example, due to the complexity of the operational environment, maintenance becomes a managerial problem [4], which results in stability and continuity problems.

Large organizations use similar instruments to tackle these problems, one of which is *Enterprise Architecture* (EA). EA provides a means to get a holistic view of the organization's current state, a clear description of the target situation, and a road map to an integrated, well structured organization [5]. Hence, it acts as a means of abstracting current state complexity, making decisions about the future state of the organization, and provides a means of communicating those decisions taken [6], [7].

R. Morrison, D. Balasubramaniam, and K. Falkner (Eds.): ECSA 2008, LNCS 5292, pp. 19–34, 2008.

EA offers a model driven management approach to set the boundaries at enterprise and domain level for engineers, designers and software architects. EA ensures the delivery of solution designs which integrate well into the existing operational environment of the organization and contribute to achieving the organization's strategy [5]. EA provides a mechanism for the overall planning and structuring of organizations – by providing standardization, and setting a clear direction for the future to guide changes – covering the aspect areas: (1) business, (2) information, (3) information systems, and (4) technical infrastructure [8], whereas Software Architecture (SA) aims at creating one system or component within the information systems aspect area [5].

Although EA is an instrument for reducing organizational complexity, effectively applying EA is not without problems in many organizations [7]. For example, many EA delivery functions suffer from the ivory tower syndrome [9], delivering EA models that are too abstract and complex to be used in practice. This shows that the EA delivery function is often not well integrated into the organization. Collaboration between architects and EA stakeholders is often problematic.

In our view, the EA function reaches beyond *EA delivery* and also includes the stakeholders involved with *EA decision making* and *EA conformance* [5]. In order for the EA function to be effective, architects and EA stakeholders should effectively work together through formal (governance) processes, but more importantly informal (collaboration) processes [10]. The foundation for effective collaboration between architects and EA stakeholders is understanding of each other's perspectives in EA decision making [10]. EA stakeholders make decisions based on the objectives specific to their roles [11]. The willingness of EA stakeholders to participate in the EA function depends on their satisfaction with its performance, which is determined by the degree in which they perceive their expectations about the EA function to be met [12]. EA stakeholders expect the consequences of the EA function's products and services [5] to help them achieve their goals [13]. In order to effectively work together with EA stakeholders, architects should have a good understanding of those goals. Current EA literature provides limited insight into the expectations of EA stakeholders regarding the products and services the EA function provides, and how it helps them achieve their objectives.

In this article, we provide insight in the mindset of EA stakeholders, showing their expectations regarding the EA function's products and services, and goal-achievement. In order to build the EA stakeholders mind map, we used techniques taken from consumer research [13] to get an understanding of the way in which EA stakeholders see the EA function. This mind map allows architects to better understand the EA stakeholder's perspective and subsequently improve the collaboration with them. Additionally, architects may improve their quality of EA products and services based on the expectations of the EA stakeholders. This is no easy task, since we found that stakeholder objectives are potentially conflicting, and expectations regarding the EA function are extensive and hard to satisfy completely.

The article is structured as follows. In Section 2 we provide a brief description of the EA function (2.1), and give an overview of the EA stakeholder groups (2.2). Section 3 explains the two core elements of the theoretical framework of this study, namely stakeholder satisfaction (3.1) and cognitive structure (3.2), and introduces the interview and analysis techniques we used in creating the cognitive map of EA stakeholders (3.3). Section 4 describes the context and characteristics of the company we conducted this study in. In sections 5 and 6 we provide the approach and results of the data gathering and analysis. In Section 7 we discuss related work on EA stakeholders, and discuss the limitations of our research. In Section 8 we draw final conclusions, and provide recommendations for future research.

2 Stakeholders of the EA Function

2.1 EA Function

We define the EA function as: *The organizational functions, roles and bodies involved with creating, maintaining, ratifying, enforcing, and observing Enterprise Architecture decision-making – established in the enterprise architecture and EA policy – interacting through formal (governance) and informal (collaboration) processes at enterprise, domain, project, and operational levels* [5]. Based on their roles architects and other EA stakeholders focus on one or more aspect areas, such as business, information, information systems, or technical infrastructure [8].

The EA function consists of three core activities: (1) EA decision making, (2) EA delivery, and (3) EA conformance [5]. *EA decision making* involves approving new EA products or changes in existing EA products, and handling escalations and waivers regarding EA conformance. EA products (i.e., architectures and EA policies) describe the EA decisions taken, and provide a means for communicating and enforcing these decisions throughout the organization. *EA delivery* is responsible for creating and maintaining these products, and provides advice to guide EA decision making. EA delivery also validates projects and operational changes to see whether they conform to the EA, and provides support in applying EA products. Finally, *EA conformance* is responsible for implementing organizational changes through solutions described in the target architectures, complying with the EA policies, and provides feedback on the applicability of the EA products [5].

2.2 EA Stakeholders

EA stakeholders are individual or grouped representatives of the organization who are affected by EA products [14], either by providing input to EA decision making or having to conform to the EA products. Typical EA stakeholders are senior management, program and project managers, software architects, and enterprise architects. Based on their specific role within the EA function, the organizational level at which they operate, and the aspect area they focus on, EA stakeholders actively pursue specific objectives. These objectives are potentially conflicting [5], and may not help to meet the organizational objectives [10]. However, regarding the attributes of the products and the services of the EA function, each stakeholder expects these to help achieve their goals [13].

We used the key SA stakeholder roles described by Smolander et al. [15] as a basis to create a 4 by 4 matrix of EA stakeholders shown in Table 1. The columns represent the four EA aspect areas [8] and the rows represent the four organizational levels [5]. We omitted the architect role in Table 1, since we focus on the other EA stakeholders in this article. Architect roles exist at the various organizational levels, and have one or more aspect areas of responsibility – e.g., enterprise business architect or project application architect.

At *enterprise level*, general management is responsible for EA decision making regarding the target enterprise architecture. This involves creating a strategy for the aspect area these stakeholders are responsible for. The board, responsible for the enterprise business strategy, typically consists of the Chief Executive Officer (CEO), Chief Financial Officer (CFO) and the Chief Operational Officer (COO). The Chief Information Officer (CIO) is responsible for business and IT alignment [20], i.e. that IT supply meets business information demand. Therefore, the CIO is concerned with both information and IS aspect areas. The Chief Technology Officer (CTO) is responsible for decision making regarding technology components and platforms.

Table 1. Key EA Stakeholders, their aspect areas and organizational levels

	Business	Information	Information Systems (IS)	Technical Infrastructure (TI)
Enterprise	• CEO, CFO, COO	• CIO	• CIO	• CTO
Domain	• Head of BD/BU • Business change manager	• DIO • IT change manager	• DIO • IT change manager	• Platform manager • Platform subject matter expert
Project	• Business project manager • Business process designer	• Information analyst	• Software development project manager • Software designer/architect	• Infrastructure project manager • Infrastructure engineer
Operational	• Operational business manager • Business process engineer	• Data administrator	• Application management • Application administrator	• Data center management • Infrastructure administrator

Domain level EA stakeholders are typically domain owners and change managers that coordinate (i.e., portfolio manager) or manage (i.e., program managers) change programs within that domain. Within the business aspect area, a domain owner is the head of a Business Division (BD) or Business Units (BU), who is responsible for the operational performance of his/her domain. Like the CIO, the Division Information Officer (DIO) [10] is responsible for the business and IT alignment for a specific business domain, and therefore focuses on both information and information systems aspect areas. Within the TI aspect area, the platform manager is responsible for the operational performance of the platform or infrastructure domain. The platform subject matter expert guides all changes on that platform or domain.

At *project level*, EA stakeholders are responsible for running projects and implementing high impact changes into the operational environment [5]. For example, the business project manager is responsible for delivering, within fixed time and budget, a solution that fits the business requirements. The business process designer is responsible for determining the requirements and design of the solution. An information analyst determines the information requirements and creates a database design accordingly. The project managers in the IS and TI aspect areas manage the projects that develop the software applications and infrastructure components. The software designer creates a design that realizes the functional and non-functional requirements. The infrastructure engineer configures infrastructure components based on the infrastructural requirements of the software application.

EA stakeholders at *operational level* are responsible for the stability and continuity of the operational environment. The operational (business, application or data center) manager is responsible for day-to-day operation and reporting. Business process engineers and data, application, and infrastructure administrators perform day-to-day maintenance and improvement activities to optimize continuity and stability.

3 Theoretical Framework

3.1 Stakeholder Satisfaction

Customer satisfaction is defined as the degree in which the customer perceives the expectations regarding a specific product or service to be met [12]. In customer service literature there has been a lot of effort in investigating the concept of customer satisfaction, where the customer is seen as the main strategic stakeholder. For example, Voss et al. used theory and approaches from the customer service literature to measure the perceived service quality in higher education [16]. The concept of customer satisfaction has, to our knowledge, not yet been applied in EA literature.

3.2 Cognitive Structures

Cognitive structures reflect the sense-making structures of individuals [17]. In customer service literature, cognitive maps are used to study stakeholder expectations and to evaluate their satisfaction [16]. Personal cognitive structures typically show the sequence of conscious and unconscious acts directed toward goal achievement [13]. They contain hierarchically related sets of elements across levels of abstraction; high-visible, short-term goals and low-visible, long-term goals [18]. For example, the cognitive map of a student may reveal that the high-visible, short-term act of drinking coffee helps in achieving the low visibility, long term goal of obtaining a master degree; drinking coffee allows the student to stay awake, study longer, and get better grades [13]. Stakeholder groups typically differ in the goals they pursue, and therefore have different dominant logics and cognitive schemas [19]. Therefore, we expect that different EA stakeholder groups evaluate the EA function service delivery differently.

3.3 Means-End Chain Analysis and Laddering Technique

A well-known type of cognitive structure is the means-end chain. A *means-end chain* shows how a stakeholder associates, in its mind, consuming or using a product or service (the means) with achieving a valued state (the ends) [13]. The elements in a means-end chain know three levels: *attributes* (characteristics of a product or service), *consequences* (results directly related to the delivery of a product or service), and *values* (higher level ends the stakeholder wants to achieve) [16]. For example, "color" is an attribute of the product "car"; having a red car may help to get a car look more sportier. The objective with our study is to determine how EA stakeholders associate their ability to attain their goals and values (ends) with the qualities and attributes of the EA function during their participation in the EA function.

The *laddering technique* provides an approach for building means-end chains. There are two types of laddering techniques: (1) soft-laddering and (2) hard-laddering [16]. Soft-laddering involves in-depth interviews with respondents following, as far as possible, their natural flow of speech; the researcher seeks to understand the meaning of the given answers and to link them to the means–end model. Hard-laddering uses more standardized interview and questionnaire techniques. Because of the exploratory nature of our research we applied the soft-laddering technique. We wanted to leave room for the respondents to introduce their own attributes, and use further questioning to gain more understanding about those attributes, and how they connected these to consequences and values. The approach involves using semi-structured, qualitative, in-depth interviews during which the interviewer asks questions to reveal attribute–consequence–value chains by asking repeatedly questions why an attribute, consequence or value is important to the respondent. The interviewer takes the subject up a ladder of abstraction and follows a process of digging deeper by asking inquiring questions. The answer to a question is a starting point for further questioning [16].

Table 2 shows an example ladder were an EA stakeholder (i.e., change manager) mentions the attribute of the EA delivery function 'collaboration between architects'. He perceives high 'EA product quality' to be an outcome of proper 'collaboration between architects', which helps achieving the value 'monitoring' of changes.

Table 2. Attribute-consequence-value ladder of a change manager

Respondent: "It's important that domain architects reach consensus about the to-be situation."   Code: 'Collaboration between architects' (Attribute)
Interviewer: "Why do you consider that as important?"   Respondent: "Currently, they fail to reach consensus, which results in non-cohesive architectures."   Code: 'EA product quality' (Consequence)
Interviewer: "Why is that important to you?"   Respondent: "…insight in the to-be situation allows me to better monitor the ongoing changes."   Code: To-be insight (Consequence)   Code: 'Monitoring' of changes (Value)

4 Case Description

We conducted this study within a medium to large company. We do not mention the name of the company, but refer to it as company A, and have changed some characteristics of the company to keep the case description anonymous.

4.1 Organizational Context

Company A has four specific Business Units (BU), five generic domains, and one change organization (see Table 3). The BUs focus on different product lines or product-market combinations and make up the operational business units of the division. The five generic domains provide generic supporting services to the BUs.

The change organization guides and executes change activities in both BUs and generic domains. One generic change department is responsible for the changes within the generic supporting services domains. The four BU change departments each serve a specific BU as their 'customer', and have little interaction with stakeholders external to their own company. The Application Management (AM) department performs operational maintenance of all applications for BUs as well as generic domains. The staff department of the change organization contains the architecture department, and other staff departments. Company A uses an external Technical Infrastructure (TI) service provider to host its information systems and therefore has no in-house infrastructure engineering department, responsible for operational maintenance and change activities regarding the technical infrastructure.

Table 3. Organizational structure of company A

Business Units (BU)	Generic Domains	Change Organization
• Product Line 1	• Finance & Control	• BU Change Departments
• Product Line 2	• Marketing & Sales	• Generic Change Department
• Product Line 3	• Customer Relationship Management	• Application Management
• Product Line 4	• Delivery Channels	• Staff (Architecture, etc.)
	• Corporate & Performance Management	

4.2 EA Function

The EA function is primarily positioned within the change organization and consists of: (1) the EA interest group, (2) the architecture department, and (3) various roles within the change and application management departments.

The *EA interest group* consists of representatives of the change departments of each BU and generic domain, and of the application management department, with the mandate of the domain change managers to take decisions. Also, the manager of the architecture department resides in the EA interest group, which is chaired by a specific BU change manager. The responsibility of the interest group is to prepare EA decision making before it is introduced in the change organization management team (MT) meeting for final approval. Additionally, the EA interest group acts as a communication platform to "sell" enterprise level EA decisions to the specific BUs and generic domains.

The *architecture department* consists of three teams: (1) business and process architecture, (2) technical application and service architecture, and (3) technical infrastructure architecture. The department is responsible for supporting enterprise and domain level EA decision making, as well as creating target architectures and EA policies. Additionally, the architects are to provide support to the various stakeholders in the change departments and AM department in applying the EA products. Finally, the architects must ensure that the changes implemented as a result of the projects and application maintenance activities conform to the EA products.

The *various roles* within the change and AM departments are: the domain change manager, program manager, application manager, and project leader. Each role has specific responsibilities depending on their position in the organization (see Table 1).

The *change managers* are responsible for domain level EA decision making and coordination of all changes (implemented by programs and projects) within a specific BU or generic domain. Also, the domain change managers take part in the change organization MT meeting and are therefore also involved in enterprise level EA decision making where they represent the domain specific concerns. Outcome of enterprise level EA decision making is the enterprise target architecture, which is input for the yearly long-term planning cycle. Based on this long-term enterprise plan, each domain has to create their domain change implementation plan.

The *program managers* are responsible for running a change program within the constraints of the long-term plan. Running a program involves coordinating a set of change projects that share a common goal and business case. A program typically stays within a BU or generic domain, but it may have cross domain impact.

At project level, *project leaders* are responsible for implementing a solution within time and budget constraints of the program plan. *Application managers* coordinate the operational changes in the information systems implemented to ensure their stability and continuity.

5   Data Gathering

We created a list of topics to be addressed in the interviews. We first carried out 12 interviews with Capgemini architects to gain understanding of the world of an enterprise architect, and identify the types of stakeholders enterprise architects work with in practice. Next, we conducted preliminary interviews with 6 Capgemini consultants (2 project managers, 2 program managers, a business and an information analyst) experienced in cooperating with enterprise architects at client organizations. This allowed us to gain an understanding of how those stakeholders perceived their participation in the EA function. We used information thus gained to create a semi-structured interview form for EA stakeholders. The main objective of the interviews was to ask the respondents: What do you consider important regarding the service delivery of the EA function? And why is that important to you?

In total, we interviewed 21 stakeholders of the EA function at the national insurer (see Section 4): 4 change managers, 4 program managers, 3 project leaders, 5 application managers, 1 information analyst, 2 employees of the sourcing department, and 2 infrastructure architects of the external TI service provider. Interviewing these stakeholders was part of an integral assessment of the EA function. We also interviewed 8 architects and the EA delivery manager of the insurer to determine the maturity of the EA delivery function using our NAOMI approach [7]. We used the data from these interviews as background information in our study regarding the stakeholder's perception of the performance of the EA function.

Two interviewers, trained in applying the soft-laddering technique, conducted the interviews and took personal notes. The same scribe was present at all interviews to transcribe, as well as to double check whether the essential topics of the interview form were addressed. Afterwards, the interviewer checked the interview transcript with his personal notes and made necessary adjustments. A summary of the transcript was sent to the interviewees so they could check whether the highlights came across correctly. After having received feedback from the respondent, we completed the interview transcripts by making final adjustments.

6 Analysis

6.1 Attributes, Consequences and Values

We omitted five stakeholders in our analysis. Two of them, infrastructure architects of the external TI service provider, were external stakeholders with an architect role. We left them out because in this study we focus on non-architect roles. We omitted the information analyst role from our analysis, since we only had access to one such person. This was insufficient to get a complete enough perspective for that role. We also left out the two employees of the sourcing department, because they both indicated to have no role in the EA function. We used the interview transcripts of the remaining 16 respondents in our analysis.

Table 4. Attributes of the EA function as perceived by EA stakeholders

Attribute	Definition
Clear roles (13)	The demarcation and awareness of all roles within the EA function at the different hierarchical and functional levels within the organization.
Governance structure (12)	The responsibilities within the EA function assigned to formal (individual) roles and bodies (e.g., councils and management teams) regarding EA decision making and EA conformance.
Communication (11)	The individual skills and behavior of architects that makes communication with various stakeholders effective. Along with the content of architectural communication regarding architectural issues is be useful makes sense to stakeholders.
Proactive behavior (11)	Architects who act decisively and help stakeholders with applying EA products (architectures and policies).
Vision (10)	The architect having a long-term overarching view and a realistic opinion about the organization and the realization of its business and IT strategy.
Tenaciousness (10)	The architect being persistent and powerful regarding the architecture vision and principles, leading stakeholders to the planned direction.
Collaboration between architects (8)	A good cooperation within the architecture team/department in order to define clear directions for stakeholders. This includes discussing and sharing important knowledge.
Functional knowledge (7)	The architect's knowledge and insights in software packages/components and the functionality, and thus the way these packages/components and functionality can be used within the organization to support its business.
Think along (7)	The ability and willingness of the architect to think along with stakeholders and understand their goals and their problems in order to provide the best solution proposals.
Market trends (6)	The architects' knowledge and awareness of the current state of the art technology and innovations within the market regarding packages, tools and solutions.
Technological knowledge (6)	A broad and detailed knowledge about the technologies used within the organization and about the planned technological solutions that will be used in the future.
Governance processes (5)	The formal processes of decision making and the handling of architectural deviations and exceptions within the EA function.
Accountability (4)	Architects being responsible for their advises and the outcome of his/her work.
Communication structure (4)	The way in which communication within the EA function is formalized (e.g., reporting lines, intranet pages, etc.).

We analyzed the interview transcripts by labeling new categories and marking the quotes that indicated the recurrence of existing categories. This resulted in a set of labeled categories and accompanying quotes. We restructured and rephrased some categories to sharpen their definitions and to achieve one level of abstraction. We grouped the categories in *attributes* (desired characteristics of the EA function service delivery), *consequences* (pleasant results directly related to the EA function service delivery), and *values* (higher level ends the EA stakeholders want to achieve). Also, for each category we determined how many members mentioned that category in the interviews, which shows how important an attribute is perceived by stakeholders.

The four most important attributes show that stakeholders expect from the EA function to have 'clear roles' defined, and a clear 'governance structure' which defines the responsibilities corresponding to those roles. Regarding the architects, stakeholders expect them to have proper 'communication' skills and content, as well as 'proactive behavior' in providing support in applying EA products.

Table 4 lists all attributes of the service provided by the architects or the EA function deemed important by respondents. For each attribute, it shows the label, number of respondents who mentioned that topic in their interview, and our definition of the attribute. Some attributes are closely related – e.g., 'governance structure' and 'governance processes', as well as 'thinking along' and 'proactive behavior'. The three themes 'technological knowledge', 'functional knowledge' and 'market trends' indicate the expectations regarding the knowledge of architects.

Stakeholders perceive attributes as important, because they result in positive consequences (see Table 5). The importance of the consequences is more evenly distributed than the attributes. Every respondent mentioned 'EA conformance', either for architectures (designs) or for EA policies, as an important consequence. We found that the EA function is expected to deliver insight in 3 important aspects: current state ('as-is insight'), target state ('to-be insight'), and 'concrete EA plans' (the translation of strategic plans to concrete solutions outlines). Architects are also expected to

Table 5. Consequences of the EA function attributes as perceived by EA stakeholders

Consequence	Definition
EA conformance (16)	Assure that everyone works according the current architecture rules, standards and guidelines. And assure that change initiatives and plans are checked on their compliance with the to-be architecture.
Decision making (14)	A fast, effective and well supported decision making process either to define a to-be situation or to tackle implementation issues.
To-be insight (14)	Having insight and a holistic perspective of the long and mid-term, future situation.
As-is insight (13)	Knowledge of the current environment, its activities, the IT systems, infrastructure, business units and the coherence among them.
Close cooperation (13)	A frequent and close cooperation between architects and stakeholders based on a good business relation and aimed at constructively resolving problems.
Concrete EA plans (12)	The translation of strategic plans into specific implications and solution outlines to support definition and start-up of projects.
EA product quality (12)	A high quality design (to-be or as-is) or policy regarding the organization's business and IT assets. Quality attributes are: consistency, coherence, readability, comprehensibility and relevance.
Acceptance of changes (7)	A positive attitude towards the chosen to-be architecture among organizational members.

support 'decision making', and to formalize the EA decisions in documents with a high EA product quality'. Actively working towards the 'acceptance of changes' triggered by architecture is mentioned least. In order to achieve the other consequences, stakeholders realize 'close cooperation' with architects is required.

Stakeholders expect the consequences (lower level goals), shown in Table 5, to help achieve four distinct values (highest level goals), shown in Table 6. The 'realization of strategy' is seen as an important goal of creating and implementing the to-be architecture. Also, achieving 'horizontal alignment' between generic domains and specific BUs through standardization of change implementation is a key value that stakeholders aim to achieve with EA. Furthermore, stakeholders expect to use EA as an instrument for 'monitoring of changes' implemented by programs and projects, and to ensure 'operational continuity'.

Table 6. Values of the EA stakeholders

Value	Definition
Realization of strategy (12)	Achieving a situation which is as closely possible to the planned to-be architecture and the company's strategy.
Horizontal Alignment (12)	Coherent and consistent (standardized) implementation of changes among the different generic domains and specific BUs.
Monitoring of changes (10)	The overview of the current activities (projects and programs) within an organization to supervise change/project status and how these activities can result in a particular future state.
Operational continuity (6)	The assurance of the quality (e.g. continuity, stability) and effectiveness of the current core- and supportive operations, both business and IT.

6.2 Hierarchical Value Map

We analyzed how the interviewees related categories to each other by building attribute-consequence-value ladders (e.g., see Table 2). We used a software tool to analyze ladders and store the accompanying quotes. Figure 1 shows the results of our analysis as a Hierarchical Value Map (HVM). A HVM is a graphical representation of means–end chains. The HVM provides the aggregated cognitive map of the 16 respondents, summing up all the categories and ladders we found. It shows how the four EA stakeholder groups – Change Manager (CM), Program Manager (PM), Application Manager (AM), and Project Leader (PL) – expect the EA function's service delivery attributes to result into consequences that contribute to achieving their personal objectives (values).

The HVM consists of nodes which represent the categories perceived as most important by the respondents. The size of the nodes depicts their relative importance. To keep the labels readable, categories mentioned by fewer than 8 respondents have the same size. The nodes are represented as pie charts indicating the ratio of importance of each category between the four stakeholder groups. This ratio of importance is based on how many of each stakeholder group's respondents mentioned a specific category in the interviews. We took into account the differences in total respondents for each group, and corrected the ratio accordingly.

The lines between the nodes represent the positive linkages between the concepts as the respondents perceive them. The direction of the relations between the categories is from bottom to top. The thickness of the lines between categories indicates how often these categories have been related to each other. To keep the HVM comprehensible, but at the same time ensure its level of detail, we applied a cut-off level of 4 to filter out the less important categories and relations. The cut-off level determines the minimally required number of recurrence of categories and relations that will be showed in the HVM.

To illustrate how to interpret the HVM, Figure 1 shows that stakeholders perceive 'clear roles' within the EA function and 'proactive behavior' of architects to be the most important attributes that lead to 'close cooperation' between stakeholders and architects. Other attributes (i.e., 'communication structure' and 'think along') also contribute to 'close cooperation', but are perceived less important. A clear 'governance structure' indirectly results in 'close cooperation', because it enables a proper 'communication structure'. This shows that stakeholders expect low level attributes to help achieve higher level attributes.

Stakeholders perceive attributes of the services and products of the EA function result in consequences. There is also a stratification in consequences, with 'EA conformance' and 'EA decision making' as high level consequences that are achieved through lower level consequence fulfillment (i.e., 'to-be insight', 'as-is insight', 'close cooperation', 'concrete EA plans', and 'EA product quality').

Finally, consequences are perceived to result in achievement of values – e.g., 'to-be insight' results in improved 'monitoring' of organizational changes. 'Acceptance for changes' as described in the to-be architecture plays a minor role, but is the only consequence that directly links attributes of the EA function ('governance processes' and 'communication') to values of the stakeholders ('horizontal alignment' and 'realization of strategy').

Figure 1 shows that all stakeholders, including project leaders, perceive 'EA conformance' as the most important consequence that contributes to achieving their values. This is striking, because enforcing EA conformance is accompanied with putting up restrictions for projects through EA products. Therefore, we expected 'EA conformance' to be perceived as a negative consequence of the EA function, especially by the project leader stakeholder group. Apparently, stakeholders recognize that uniformity and coherency in implementing changes is a critical success factor for the organization, and see it as a positive consequence essential for achieving their high-level objectives (values).

As a result of our analysis, we concluded that stakeholders have high expectations regarding the EA function. In this case study, it seemed infeasible for the EA function to fulfill all expectations. We found that stakeholder satisfaction with the EA function's performance differed for each stakeholder group, depending on the level of perceived fulfillment of their expectations. Also, we saw a relation between the intensity and efficiency of the cooperation with architects and the level of satisfaction with the EA function's performance. For example, the change managers were little satisfied with the performance of the EA function, because EA did not help them in the 'monitoring of changes' and the architects did not have 'close cooperation' with them. The members of the application management department were not satisfied with the EA function, because the architects did not provide 'as-is insight' in their operational application landscape, and did not act as a gate keeper ensuring 'EA conformance' and thus 'operational continuity'. The project leader stakeholder group was relatively satisfied with the performance of the EA function, because the 'functional' and 'technical knowledge' of the architects helped them in project level 'decision making'.

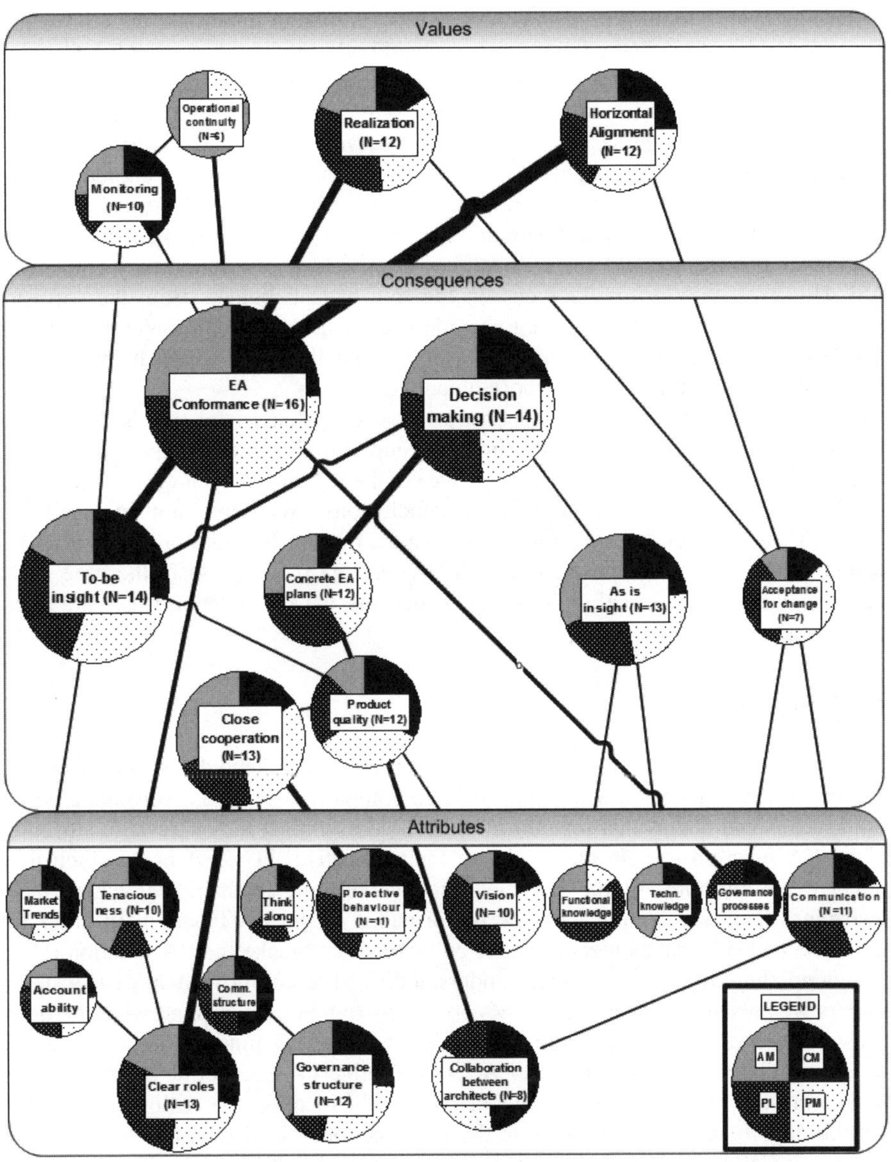

Fig. 1. The Hierarchical Value Map shows the attributes of the EA function as experienced by the EA stakeholders, and their relations with consequences and values as experienced by the EA stakeholders

7 Discussion

Related work on EA stakeholders by Lindström et al. describes how EA frameworks provide the CIO – as the primary EA stakeholder – a means for decision support, addressing his/her highest priority concerns [20]. Although important, the CIO is just one stakeholder of the many functions, roles and bodies that make up the EA function [5]. Clerc et al. describe the software architect's mindset, including some use cases that are stakeholder-centric and involve identifying stakeholders and communicating the architecture towards these stakeholders [21]. Even though they describe elements of importance for the collaboration between architects and stakeholders, they focus primarily on the software architect's perspective. Smolander et al. describe stakeholder participation in software architecture design, including their problems in relation to architecture, and the rationale for architecture description they emphasize [15]. However, they primarily focus on the role of stakeholders from the software architect's perspective. They do not provide insight in the specific objectives of EA stakeholder who are not architects themselves, and the way in which they expect architecture to help them achieve those objectives.

The study we present in this paper is exploratory. Reason for this is the limited number of respondents for each stakeholder group; 3 to 5 respondents per group is too small to draw detailed conclusions. Also, we conducted this study at one organization, which is insufficient to draw generic conclusions. We have not included the 'designer' and 'Chief Information Officer' roles, but the literature already provided insight in the relation of these roles with EA (e.g., [15], [20]). Also, the case study lacked stakeholders external to company A, because the EA function was quite internally oriented.

8   Conclusions

In this article we present the cognitive map of various stakeholder groups that take part in the EA function of a medium to large company. We used a soft-laddering to build means-end chains that reveal how stakeholders expect the observable attributes of the EA function to help them achieve their objectives. The extent to which they perceive the attributes of the EA function to contribute to their goal-achievement determines their satisfaction with the performance of the EA function. In order for architects and EA stakeholders to better collaborate and make the EA function effective, there should be proper mutual understanding. The cognitive map of EA stakeholders we present in this article allows architects to better understand what the other EA stakeholders expect from them. The attributes in the EA function we found form a basis for architects to improve their EA service delivery – e.g., define clear roles, and behave pro-actively in providing support. This will increase the willingness for EA stakeholders to actively participate in the EA function. Ultimately, this will improve EA function effectiveness, including the quality of the EA itself.

The cognitive map shows that different EA stakeholder groups pursue different objectives, related to their specific role within the organization. An important conclusion is that it is difficult to satisfy all stakeholders. Their objectives may be conflicting – e.g., the need of change managers for innovation and change versus the pursuit for operational continuity and stability of the operational manager. Based on this study, the architect is able to prioritize which stakeholder groups to serve, and determine a strategy accordingly. Completely ignoring a specific stakeholder group is not advisable. The EA function will only achieve maximum effectiveness when all stakeholders involved collaborate efficiently towards a shared goal.

Our sample of 16 interviews – with an average of 4 interviews for each stakeholder group – conducted at one organization is too specific and insufficient to draw general conclusions. This research is a first exploratory study of the stakeholders of the EA function. Up till now, there was little knowhow of stakeholder perception of the EA function. We are currently conducting research to get a more in-depth understanding of the expectations of the various stakeholder groups regarding the EA function. Our objective is to construct a standard customer satisfaction assessment approach, with which we can help client organizations become more effective with EA.

References

1. Pablo, A.L.: Determinants of Acquisition Integration Level: A Decision-Making Perspective. The Academy of Management Journal 37(4), 803–836 (1994)
2. Myers, B.L., Kappelman, L.A., Prybutok, V.R.: A comprehensive model for assessing the quality and productivity of the information systems function: toward a theory for information systems assessment. In information Systems Success Measurement. In: Garrity, E.J., Sanders, G.L. (eds.) Idea Group Information Technology Management Series, pp. 94–121. IGI Publishing, Hershey (1998)
3. Moore, G.A.: Strategy and your stronger hand. Harvard Business Review 83(12), 62–71 (2005)
4. April, A., Huffman Hayes, J., Abran, A., Dumke, R.: Software Maintenance Maturity Model (SMmm): the software maintenance process model. Journal of Software Maintenance and Evolution: Research and Practice 17(13), 197–223 (2005)
5. Van der Raadt, B., Van Vliet, J.C.: Designing the Enterprise Architecture Function. In: Fourth International Conference on the Quality of Software-Architectures (QoSA 2008) (March 2008) (to appear)
6. Van der Raadt, B., Soetendal, J., Perdeck, M., Van Vliet, H.: Polyphony in Architecture. In: Proceedings 26th International Conference on Software Engineering (ICSE 2004), pp. 533–542. IEEE Computer Society, Los Alamitos (2004)
7. Van der Raadt, B., Slot, R., Van Vliet, H.: Experience Report: Assessing a Global Financial Services Company on its Enterprise Architecture Effectiveness Using NAOMI. In: Proceedings of the 40th Annual Hawaii international Conference on System Sciences (HICSS 2007), p. 218b. IEEE Computer Society, Washington (January 2007)
8. Mulholland, A., Macaulay, A.L.: Architecture and the Integrated Architecture Framework. Capgemini (2006),
   `http://www.capgemini.com/services/soa/ent_architecture/iaf/`
9. Kruchten, P.: The Software Architect. In: Donohoe, P. (ed.) Software Architecture (WICSA1), pp. 565–583. Kluwer Academic Publishers, Dordrecht (1999)
10. Peterson, R.: Crafting Information Technology Governance. Information Systems Management 21(4), 7–22 (2004)
11. Nutt, P.C.: Types of Organizational Decision Processes. Administrative Science Quarterly 29(3), 414–450 (1984)
12. Zeithaml, V.A., Parasuraman, A., Berry, L.L.: Delivering quality service: balancing customer perceptions and expectations. The Free Press, New York (1990)
13. Gutman, J.: Means–End Chains as Goal Hierarchies. Psychology & Marketing 14(6), 545–560 (1997)
14. Boh, W., Yellin, D.: Using Enterprise Architecture Standards in Managing Information Technology. Journal of Management Information Systems 23(3), 163–207 (2007)

15. Smolander, K., Päivärinta, T.: Describing and Communicating Software Architecture in Practice: Observations on Stakeholders and Rationale. In: Pidduck, A.B., Mylopoulos, J., Woo, C.C., Ozsu, M.T. (eds.) CAiSE 2002. LNCS, vol. 2348, pp. 117–133. Springer, Heidelberg (2002)
16. Voss, R., et al.: Service quality in higher education: The role of student expectations. J. Bus Res. (2007)
17. Weick, K.E.: The social psychology of organizing. Addison-Wesley Pub. Co., Reading (1979)
18. Brewer, G.D.: Assessing Outcomes and Effects. In: Cameron, K.S., Whetten, D.A. (eds.) Organizational Effectiveness: A Comparison of Multiple Models. Academic Press, San Diego (1983)
19. Bettis, R.A., Prahalad, C.K.: The Dominant Logic: Retrospective and Extension. Strategic Management Journal 16(1), 5–14 (1995)
20. Lindström, Å., Johnson, P., Johansson, E., Ekstedt, M., Simonsson, M.: A survey on CIO concerns-do enterprise architecture frameworks support them? Information Systems Frontiers 8(2), 81–90 (2006)
21. Clerc, V., Lago, P., van Vliet, H.: The Architect's Mindset. In: Overhage, S., Szyperski, C.A., Reussner, R., Stafford, J.A. (eds.) QoSA 2007. LNCS, vol. 4880, pp. 231–249. Springer, Heidelberg (2008)

Web Services Orchestrations Evolution: A Merge Process for Behavioral Evolution

Sébastien Mosser, Mireille Blay-Fornarino, and Michel Riveill

University of Nice Sophia – Antipolis
CNRS, I3S Laboratory, RAINBOW team
Sophia Antipolis, France
{mosser,blay,riveill}@polytech.unice.fr

Abstract. Services Oriented Architectures preach loosely-coupled services and high–level composition mechanisms, using for example Web Services to define services and Orchestrations to compose them. But orchestration evolutions imply modification at source code level. This article shows how the orchestration paradigm itself can be used to support evolution of Web Services Orchestrations through a behavioral merge process. Using the same model to express orchestrations and evolutions, we expose formally and illustrate in this contribution a merging process helping WSOA administrators to deal with behavioral evolutions.

1 Introduction

Services Oriented Architectures (SOA) [1] use the concept of *service* as an elementary brick to assemble complex systems. Services are loosely–coupled by definition, and complex services are build upon basics ones using compositions mechanisms. The loose coupling methodology enables the separation of concerns and helps systems evolution.

Using Web Services as elementary services, and Orchestrations [2] as composition mechanism, Web Service Oriented Architectures (WSOA) provides a way to implement these loosely–coupled architectures. W3C define orchestrations as *"the pattern of interactions that a Web Service agent must follow in order to achieve its goal"* [3]. Specialized (*i.e. elementary*) code is written inside Web Services, and business processes are described as an orchestration of those Web Services.

Code manipulations, like the refactoring operation, help software evolution support. In [4], authors identify some challenges for future research on software evolution and focus on the abstraction need. Lehman identifies as his first *"Law of Software Evolution"* [5] that *"A program that is used must be continually adapted else it becomes progressively less satisfactory"*. As WSOA focus on business reactivity and eternal adaptation to fit with market and anticipate trends, this well–known law makes sense twenty four hours a day.

This contribution deals with WSOA orchestrations evolutions, focusing on behavioral evolutions. Our originality is to use the same model to represent the

R. Morrison, D. Balasubramaniam, and K. Falkner (Eds.): ECSA 2008, LNCS 5292, pp. 35–49, 2008.

behavior of orchestrations and evolutions. We propose a merging algorithm build upon this formal model helping integration of evolutions into orchestrations.

We identify in Sect. 2 the need of evolution capabilities inside orchestrations. Sect. 3 proposes a high level model for orchestrations supporting evolution reasoning and Sect. 4 shows how this model works on an example. Sect. 5 exposes validation of this work, Sect. 6 discusses related work about orchestrations evolution mechanisms. Finally, Sect. 7 concludes this paper and shows perspectives of our contribution.

2   Orchestration Behavioral Evolutions

Following the W3C definition, orchestrations can be represented as a *"white-box service"*: *"service"* because it basically defines a public interface (including data types) and *"white-box"* means that we can understand the behavior of such services, defined as the exchange of messages between other services.

Obviously, orchestrations can evolve in three ways: *(i)* interface, *(ii)* data type and *(iii)* behavior. This study focuses on static behavioral changes, *i.e.* the evolution process (presented here in Sect 3) handles orchestrations and evolution in a non–production state. Interface and data types evolutions are out of the scope of this paper, and refer more to refactoring [6] and model checking concepts.

In [7], authors sketched a taxonomy dealing with software changes and evolution. Using this taxonomy, we express in Tab. 1 the kind of evolutions this contribution deals with: our goal is to propose a partially–automated evolution process using a high–level reasoning abstraction.

Example: We consider here an application called SEDUITE, based on a WSOA. This software uses different atomic services as *information sources* and users access to information using an orchestration called `InfoProvider` (Fig. 1). It describes a basic business process: using an authorization `ticket` and a user `profile` as input data, it will return informations as `result` from a *source* called `News` in accordance with `profile`, if the given `ticket` is a valid ticket.

Table 1. WSOA evolution using [Buckley *et al*, 2005] taxonomy

Temporal Properties (*When*)			
Time of change:	*static*	**Change history:**	*parallel*
Change frequency:	*periodically*	**Anticipation:**	*unanticipated*
Object of Change (*Where*)			
Artifact:	*orchestration*	**Granularity:**	*coarse–grained*
Change propagation:	*traceable*	**Impact:**	*local*
Change Support (*How*)			
Degree of Automation:	*partially–automated*	**Change Type:**	*semantic*
Degree of Formality:	*partial*		–

Two kinds of evolutions commonly encountered[1] can be illustrated through the SEDUITE example:

- How to add a new source of information service into `InfoProvider` (*e.g.* a weather forecasting service, a calendar service, events notification, restaurant menu, TV shows, ...).
- How to ensure that a given input profile is correct (not empty, conform with current usage of the application, ...) before invoking sources ?

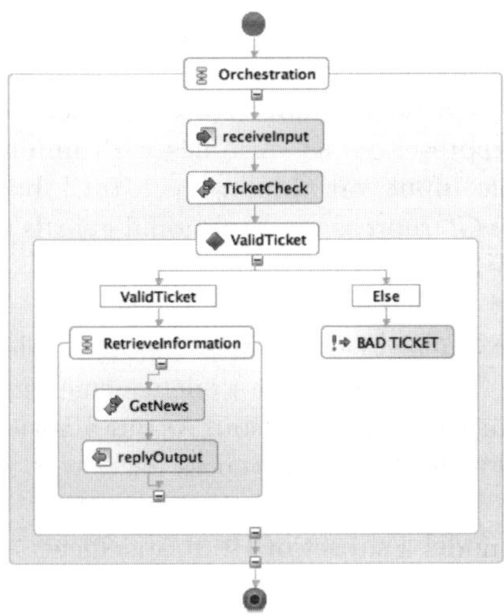

Fig. 1. `InfoProvider` orchestration using ECLIPSE BPEL Designer

Obviously, all these kinds of behavioral evolutions can be done at the orchestration language level by editing the source code (*e.g.* adding some activities, conditional statements, exceptions, ...) but this process is error-prone and off–putting.

Moreover, when the user wants to apply n different evolutions into the same orchestration (*e.g.* adding two new sources of informations), she can expect from the system some support mechanisms to ease the task. Our goal is to automate this process, providing an evolutions merging algorithm. This algorithm lets the user focus on evolution interactions and semantic. Next sections focus on these points, proposing an orchestration model able to merge evolutions.

3   A High Level Reasoning Model: "ADORE"

To perform high level composition and to allow reasoning on orchestrations and evolutions, we define a model called ADORE : *"Activity moDel suppOrting oRchestration Evolution"*. This section describes formally this model, and shows on

---

[1] More informations and use cases at `http://anubis.polytech.unice.fr/jSeduite`

the SEDUITE example how we can express an existing orchestration using it. It also describes the meaning of the *Merge* operation enabling our process.

3.1 ADORE Formalism: Orchestrations and Evolutions

Orchestration: An orchestration is a tuple $(A^\star, \prec^\star)$ representing a behavior. $A^\star$ is a set of *Activity* $\{a_1, \ldots, a_n\}$ and $\prec^\star$ a partial ordering between these activities.

Activity: An activity is a tuple $(uid, K, V_{in}^\star, V_{out}, G^\star)$. Each activity is unique inside an *Orchestration* and identified by *uid*. K refers to the *Kind* of this activity, $V_{in}^\star$ (resp. V_{out}) represent inputs (resp. output) *Variables* (identified by name). Constants are represented as variables with immutable content. An activity can take multiple input variables $\{in_1 \ldots in_n\}$ but returns exactly one result V_{out} (possibly $\emptyset$). $G^\star$ represents conditional guards and allows conditional expressions (`if/then/else`).

Partial ordering ($\prec$, precedence rules): Activities are ordered using an operator $\prec$. The expression $a_1 \prec a_2$ is called a precedence rule and means that a_2 must wait the end of a_1 to start its own execution. As our algorithm is based on acyclic behavior, we do not allow loop expressiveness for now.

Kind: We use in that model a subset of BPEL specifications [8]. We consider the following kind of allowed activity: *(i)* variable assignment ($assign(function)$), *(ii)* service invocation ($invoke(Service, Operation)$), *(iii)* message reception ($receive$), *(iv)* response sending ($reply$) and *(v)* fault report ($throw$). To deal with conditional statement, we add a *test* activity (a *test* activity evaluate a boolean predicate. It has exactly one output variable).

Guards: Guards refers to the expected *test* activity, and add a "true or false" semantic into our model. Adding $guard(a_t, true)$ as a guard on an activity a means that a will start only if a_t (which is a *test* activity) output is evaluated to true. Implicitly, it exists a precedence rule $a_t \prec a$.

Fig. 2 represents the `InfoProvider` orchestration using both textual and graphical formalisms (inspired by UML activity diagrams).

Evolution: An *Evolution* can be considered as a piece of orchestration which can be plugged into existing orchestrations. Evolution is therefore as a superset of orchestrations. $A^\star$ contains exactly one *hook* special activity which represent where the evolution will be connected into an orchestration.

Two special activities $\mathbb{P}$ and $\mathbb{S}$ refers to targeted orchestrations where they represent *hook* predecessors (resp. successors) in targeted partial ordering. Considering *Evolution* as a superset of *Orchestration* means that an orchestration cannot contains any *hook*, $\mathbb{P}$ or $\mathbb{S}$ occurrence. Fig. 3 represent graphically an evolution.

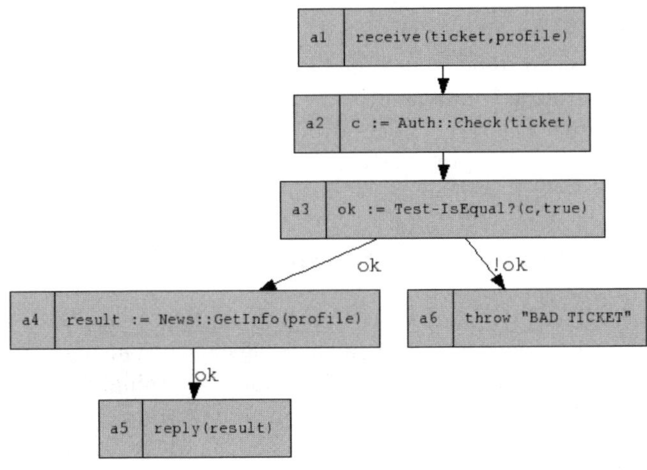

$$O = (\{a_1, \ldots, a_6\}, \{a_1 \prec a_2, a_2 \prec a_3, a_3 \prec a_4, a_4 \prec a_5, a_3 \prec a_6\})$$
$$a_1 \equiv (a_1, receive, \{ticket, profile\}, \emptyset, \emptyset)$$
$$a_2 \equiv (a_2, invoke(Auth, Check), \{ticket\}, c, \emptyset)$$
$$a_3 \equiv (a_3, test(isEqual), \{c, true\}, ok, \emptyset)$$
$$a_4 \equiv (a_4, invoke(News, GetInfo), \{profile\}, result, \{guard(a_3, true)\})$$
$$a_5 \equiv (a_5, reply, \{result\}, \emptyset, \{guard(a_3, true)\})$$
$$a_6 \equiv (a_6, throw, \{\text{``Bad Ticket''}\}, \emptyset, \{guard(a_3, false)\})$$

Fig. 2. $O \equiv$ `Infoprovider` orchestration using ADORE formalism

Substitution: Stickel defines a substitution σ in [9] as "a set of substitution components with distinct first elements, that is, distinct variables being substituted for". A substitution component is an ordered pair of two variables x and y (written as $x \rightarrow y$), denoting the replacement of the x by y (x cannot be a constant). Applying a substitution on an activity performs those replacements.

As boxes and arrows are more readable than huge sets of equations, we define a graphical syntax to represent ADORE entities. Inspired from the UML activity diagram formalism, each activity is represented as a box, and precedence rules using arrows between boxes ($a_1 \rightarrow a_2 \equiv a_1 \prec a_2$). Guards are represented as *labels* on arrows. To represent *hook* predecessors and successors, we use the *start/end* syntax from UML: • refers to $\mathbb{P}$, and ⊙ to $\mathbb{S}$.

3.2   Merging Process

Using the ADORE model, we define a merging process enabling the automatic integration of n evolutions into an orchestration. This process composes evolutions between each others, and then, merge the resulting evolution with the targeted orchestration.

Global overview: $Merge(\{e_1, \ldots, e_n\}, \{k_1, \ldots, k_m\}, o, b) \rightarrow o'$
The process takes as input a set of evolutions $\{e_1, \ldots, e_n\}$. As merge conflicts can occur, user can express some *knowledge* $\{k_1, \ldots, k_m\}$ to solve them. A knowledge k_i can be a substitution component σ_i, or new elements to add (activity, precedence rule or guard). The target of the evolution is an orchestration o and a binding $b \equiv bind(hook \rightarrow a_i)$ expresses where the evolution will be integrated inside o activities. The process results in a new orchestration o'. It does not have any side effects on existing orchestration or evolutions, as it works on a duplicated set of elements[2]. We consider it as a four steps process, described here.

1) $Merge(\{e_1, \ldots, e_n\}, \{k_1, \ldots, k_m\}) \rightarrow e'$ *("Evolution merge")*
As the global process does not have any side effect, all elements (activity, precedence) of $\{e_1, \ldots, e_n\}$ are duplicated before doing anything. This step produces a new evolution e', where all evolutions $\{e_1, \ldots, e_n\}$ are merged. From all hook points $\{h_1, \ldots, h_n\}$, we generate a new activity h' where input variables set is the union of h_i input variables set. The output variable is unified into a new one (using a σ). The partial ordering of e' is an union of existing partial ordering, taking care of hooks unification. Guards on h' are composed as a union of existing guards on h_i, and propagated to h' successors.

2) $DetectConflict(e') \rightarrow \{conflict_1, \ldots, conflict_n\}$ *("Conflict detection")*
At this step, we analyze the output of the previous step and detect if needed some merge conflicts[3]. Some constructions are not allowed in orchestration formalism, like *(i)*concurrent write access to a variable, *(ii)* multiple reply activities (under non–exclusive conditions), *(iii)* multiple throw activities (under non–exclusive conditions) or *(iv)* write access to a constant. To perform conflict resolution, we use an incremental approach [11]: the process automatically returns conflicts to the user, and she gives in response a knowledge (k_i, *e.g.* adding an order between two concurrent write access to a variable) to solve this conflict. The merging process is then recalled with this new knowledge.

3) $Merge(o, e', b, \{k_1, \ldots, k_m\}) \rightarrow o'$ *("Orchestration merge")*
Here, we consider that e' represents the merged evolution (output of step 2) without any conflicts. We now integrate e' into the original orchestration (following the binding specification $b \equiv \sigma(hook \rightarrow a_h)$) and produce a new orchestration o'. $\mathbb{P}$ and $\mathbb{S}$ are substituted with a_h predecessors and successors. We compute a unifying substitution where each *hook* variable (input, output) is bound to its equivalent in a_h. As in step 1, we perform guards union and propagate resulting guard set to a_h successors.

4) $DetectConflict(o') \rightarrow \{conflict_1, \ldots, conflict_n\}$ *("Conflict detection")*
This step is similar to step two except that a new kind of conflict based on evolution variables can be detected: all used variables must be declared and

---

[2] Duplication implies variable renaming to avoid conflicts and new *uids* for concerned activities.

[3] More information about conflict detection can be found in [10].

assigned before attempting to be read. Orchestration parameters are assigned as `receive` inputs (receiving a constant is considered as a conflict). Other variables are assigned when used as output of an activity.

As a conclusion, we can see that step 1 and 2 can be done in an abstract manner: they consist of composing evolutions, without any knowledge about target. The last steps imply real knowledge about the target, and business–specific skills. These two operations can be performed by two different users.

4   Illustrating Merge Process

This section illustrates the previously defined merge process. The first part explains on an example how activities duplication and unification works. The second part illustrates a full merge process, integrating three evolutions into the `InfoProvider` orchestration.

4.1   Activities Management: Duplication, Substitution and Unification

Guided by the SEDUITE description, we can imagine a frequent action for the administrator: "How to add a new source of information ?". To automate this action, an evolution E_s is expressed (Fig. 3). E_s invokes a `NewSource` service, and appends its result to the result of the *hook* activity.

E_s describes *abstractly* how to add a new source of informations. If an administrator wants to add a `Weather` source of information, she will specialize the semantic of this evolution using a substitution σ_x. Now, we consider two evolutions obtained by substitutions from the previous one (E_w adding a `Weather` source, and E_e adding an `Events` source) and focus on the first and second steps of the merge process, *i.e.* applying $E_{w\oplus e} \equiv Merge(\{E_w, E_e\}, \emptyset)$.

$$\sigma_w \equiv \sigma(\{NewSource \to Weather\}) \Rightarrow E_w \equiv \sigma_w(E_s)$$
$$\sigma_e \equiv \sigma(\{NewSource \to Events\}) \Rightarrow E_e \equiv \sigma_e(E_s)$$

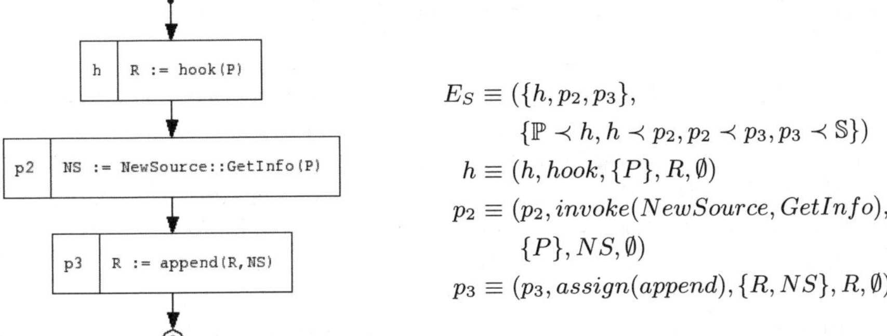

$$E_S \equiv (\{h, p_2, p_3\},$$
$$\{\mathbb{P} \prec h, h \prec p_2, p_2 \prec p_3, p_3 \prec \mathbb{S}\})$$
$$h \equiv (h, hook, \{P\}, R, \emptyset)$$
$$p_2 \equiv (p_2, invoke(NewSource, GetInfo),$$
$$\{P\}, NS, \emptyset)$$
$$p_3 \equiv (p_3, assign(append), \{R, NS\}, R, \emptyset)$$

Fig. 3. $E_s \equiv$ "How to add a new source of informations ?"

First of all, we duplicate each activity to avoid naming conflict (*uids*, *variable names*). The duplication produces the following result:

$$E_{E_w \cup E_e} \equiv rename(E_w) \cup rename(E_e)$$
$$\equiv (\{h^w, p_2^w, p_3^w, h^e, p_2^e, p_3^e\},$$
$$\{\mathbb{P} \prec h^w, h^w \prec p_2^w, p_2^w \prec p_3^w, p_3^w \prec \mathbb{S}, \mathbb{P} \prec h^e, h^e \prec p_2^e, p_2^e \prec p_3^e, p_3^e \prec \mathbb{S}\})$$
$$h^w \equiv (h^w, hook, \{P_w\}, R_w, \emptyset)$$
$$p_2^w \equiv (p_2^w, invoke(Weather, GetInfo), \{P_w\}, NS_w, \emptyset)$$
$$p_3^w \equiv (p_3^w, assign(append), \{R_w, NS_w\}, R_W, \emptyset)$$
$$h^e \equiv (h^e, hook, \{P_e\}, R_e, \emptyset)$$
$$p_2^e \equiv (p_2^e, invoke(Events, GetInfo), \{P_e\}, NS_e, \emptyset)$$
$$p_3^e \equiv (p_3^e, assign(append), \{R_e, NS_e\}, R_e, \emptyset)$$

The process will now perform merge of h^e and h^w into h. As R_w and R_e are output variables of a unified activity, they must be unified too in a R variable. The process does not have any knowledge k_i about inputs parameters P_w and P_e, and treat them as two different variables. This merge produces a substitution we apply onto the merged evolution to produce Fig. 4 result. The conflict detection step ($DetectConflict(E_{w \oplus e})$) will return a conflict, as there is no precedence rule between two different write into variable R.

To solve this conflict, we add a precedence rule between these two activities. If we consider that `Weather` information is more important than `Events` one, we can express a knowledge k_1 to represent it. Even if there is no conflict leading to it, we can also specify to the merging process using k_2 that the *hook* input variables have to be substituted to the same P variable.

$$k_1 \equiv augmentOrder(p_3^w \prec p_3^e)$$
$$k_2 \equiv \sigma(\{P_w \rightarrow P, P_e \rightarrow P\})$$

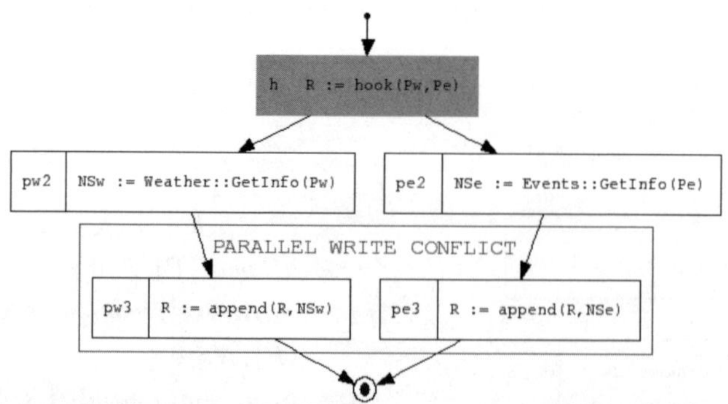

Fig. 4. $Merge(\{E_w, E_e\}, \emptyset) \Rightarrow ConcurrentWriteConflict(R, \{p_3^w, p_3^e\})$

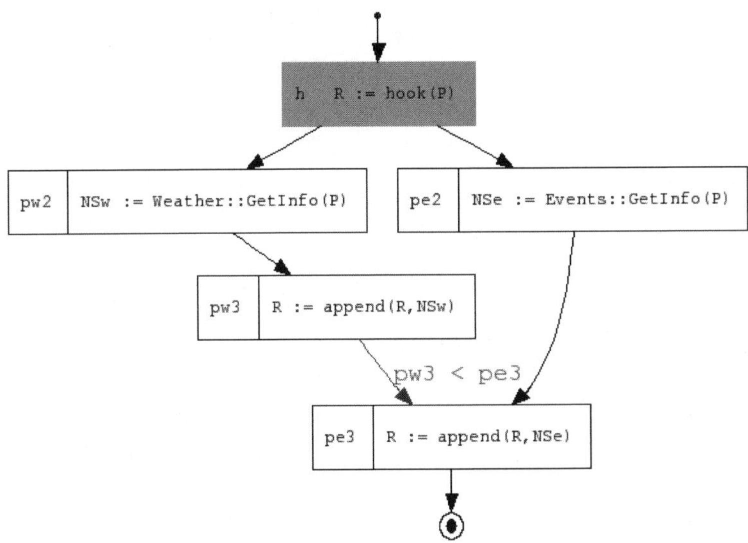

Fig. 5. $E_{w \oplus e} \equiv Merge(\{E_w, E_e\}, \{k_1, k_2\})$

These knowledge allow the merge process to perform full merge, and conflict detection returns an empty set of conflicts. We obtain as output a new evolution $E_{w \oplus e}$, Fig. 5.

4.2   Practicing the Merge Algorithm

In this section, we consider that the administrator wants to perform the following evolutions inside `InfoProvider` (Fig. 2): *(i)* add a weather source of information (E_w), *(ii)* add an events source of information (E_e) and *(iii)* check profile correctness before attempting to retrieve informations (E_p). E_p asks a service to verify the given profile, and throws an exception if this profile is not correct (Fig. 6).

As we attempt to merge E_w and E_p for a second time, we reuse the knowledge set $\{k_1, k_2\}$ from previous section and avoid the conflict detection step to clarify text. The administrator knows that all hook parameters should be unified, as they all refer to `profile`. She expresses this knowledge by adding a knowledge k_3 expressing this unification between hook parameters:

$$k_1 \equiv augmentOrder(p_3^w \prec p_3^e)$$
$$k_2 \equiv \sigma(\{P_w \to P, P_e \to P\})$$
$$k_3 \equiv \sigma(\{Q \to P\})$$

Following the merge algorithm, we perform $Merge(\{E_w, E_e, E_p\}, \{k_1, k_2, k_3\})$ and compute $E_{w \oplus e \oplus p}$ (Fig. 7) as a result of the first merge step. The guard on

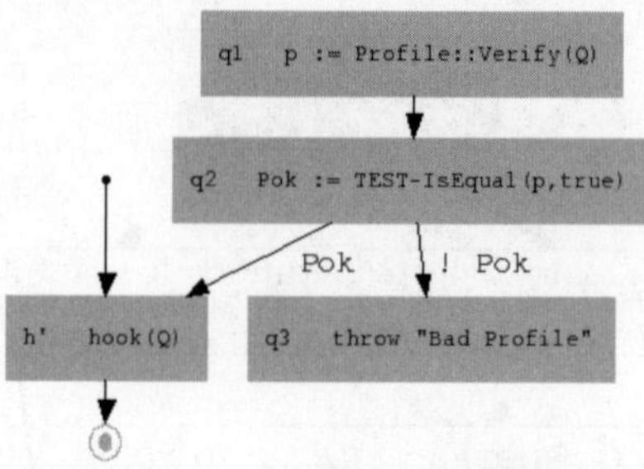

Fig. 6. $E_p \equiv$ Checking profile correctness evolution

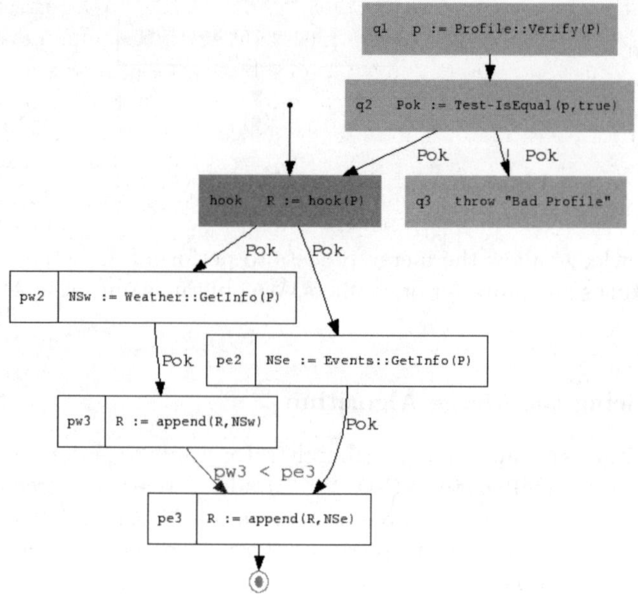

Fig. 7. $E_{w \oplus e \oplus p} \equiv Merge(\{E_w, E_e, E_p\}, \{k_1, k_2, k_3\})$

hook coming from E_p is propagated to successors of hook (now guarded by $guard(q_2, true)$). As there is no conflict detected at second step, we can perform the orchestration merge. Our evolution must be hooked on information retrieving activity in o, *i.e.* a_4.

When invoking $Merge(o, E_{w \oplus e \oplus p}, bind(hook \rightarrow a_4)\{k_1, k_2, k_3\})$ at third step, the merge process binds *hook* with a_4. We perform usual substitution of *hook* output variable with a_4 output variable, without any conflict. Moreover, as a_4 and *hook* activities have only one input variable, we can deduce a unification between these two variables. The activity q_1 interacts with a_1, and it generates an *UnassignedVariable* conflict (q_1 read **profile** content, but has no predecessors). As **profile** is an input of o, this assignment is performed by the **receive** activity

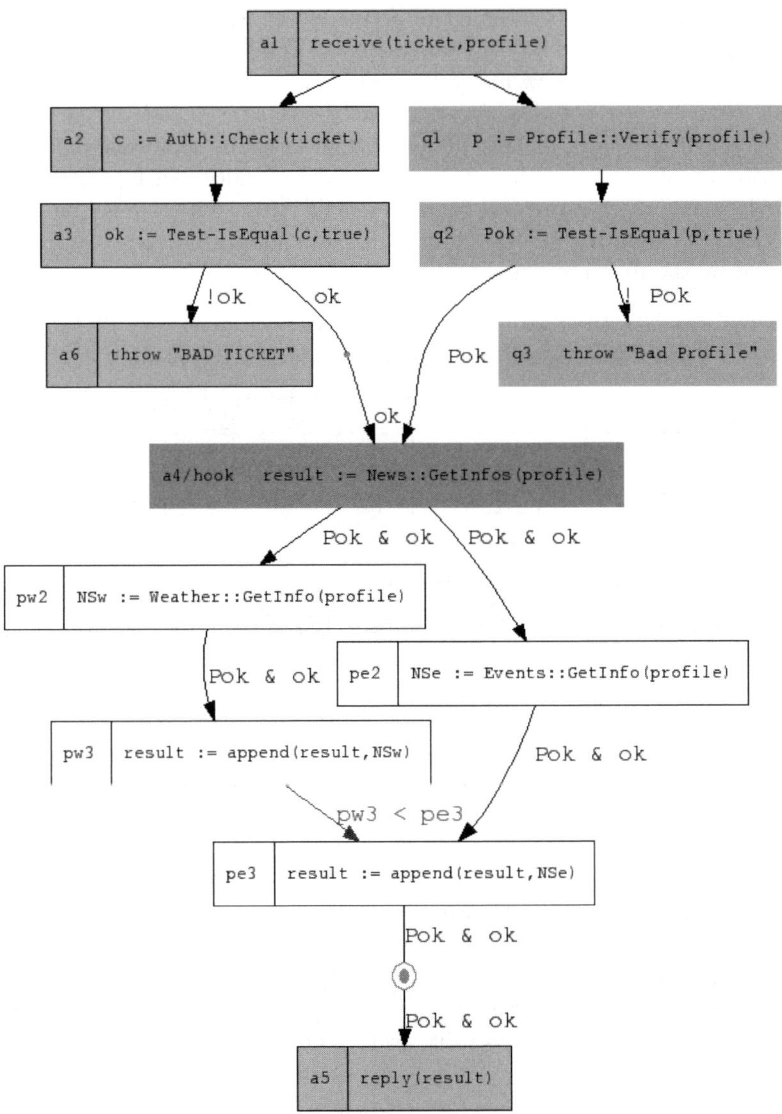

Fig. 8. $O' \equiv Merge(\{E_w, E_e, E_p\}, \{k_1, k_2, k_3\}, o, \sigma(hook \rightarrow a_4))$

a_1. We can automatically add a precedence rule $a_1 \prec q_1$ to solve this conflict. Fig. 8 represents the final orchestration o', result of the merge process.

5   Validation and Implementation

SEDUITE *example analysis:*   We can analyze the example shown previously using some metrics. We compare the obtained behavior with respect to three parameters: *(i)* $|Act|$ the cardinality of activities set, *(ii)* $|\prec|$ the cardinality of partial orderings and *(iii)* $|k|$ the cardinality of the knowledge set. We use the $|X_m|$ notation to express how many elements of $|X|$ were impacted by the merge process.

Tab 2 exposes results of this analysis. The last line analyzes the final orchestration o'. We can see that 93% of precedence rules can be automatically managed by the merge process. Moreover, 54% of activities must be adapted to be consistent with the evolution, and all these adaptations are automatically performed by the merge process.

Table 2. Measuring *Merge* impact on SEDUITE example

Behavior	$|Act|$	$|Act_m|$	$|\prec|$	$|\prec_m|$	$|k|$	$|k_m|$
$E_{w \oplus e}$	5	5 (100%)	7	6 (85%)	2	–
$E_{p \oplus w \oplus e}$	8	6 (75%)	10	9 (90%)	3	–
O'	13	7 (54%)	14	13 (93%)	4	1 (25%)

Implementation: the merge process is implemented using PROLOG. It allows partially–automated orchestration evolution. Based on EMF [12], we develop a model-driven software to deal with the merge process. A JAVA object front–end allows final user to interactively use the PROLOG merge engine in a user–friendly way. More information can be found on ADORE web-site[4].

The SEDUITE system is used to support research on user profiles management [13] and to validate a French national research project called FAROS[5], dealing with SOA reliability. The `InfoProvider` orchestration is implemented using the BPEL 2.0 standard. It runs over the APACHE ODE open–source orchestration engine. Seduite applications should be deployed in different academic institutions. We are working on a user-friendly environnment that supports controled evolutions. It 's the current validation for web services orchestrations evolution merging. More information about SEDUITE implementation can be found on SEDUITE web site[6]. Further validation is an ongoing work. We focus our experiments on large–scale work-flows from grid–computing research field.

6   Related Work and Discussions

In [14], Rémy Douence defines *Aspect Oriented Programming* (AOP) as:

> AOP *is a set of language mechanisms which enable the introduction of non anticipated functionalities in a base application. Without these mechanisms, the code of the base application should be modified in several locations.* AOP *enables to modularise these functionalities*

---

[4] http://rainbow.i3s.unice.fr/adore
[5] http://www.lifl.fr/faros (french only)
[6] http//anubis.polytech.unice.fr/jSeduite

Existent work [15,16] bind AOP concepts to Orchestrations. These approaches weave aspects inside the orchestration engine, and allow integration of unforeseen evolutions directly into the targeted orchestration. These approaches imply modifications of orchestration engines to add the aspect weaver inside it. Moreover, users will have to *(i)* implement their orchestrations using BPEL, *(ii)* use the aspect language to express new functionality and finally *(iii)* deploy orchestrations and weave aspects into an *ad'hoc* engine. Aspects interactions (*i.e.* different aspects woven at the same point) are solved by ordering aspect codes into block (this code will be executed before that one). AOP considers special keywords to decorate *pointcuts* with *advices* (*before, around, after*) and use **proceed** keyword to represent normal behavior of woven code. Considering the *hook* as a **proceed** and its binding as a *pointcut* selection, our approach supports the enhancement of the original behavior of an orchestration. As we reify and then merge behavior instead of expressing advice as black boxes and ordering them, we focus on parallel execution of distinct evolutions (we do not create order between evolutions unless it is necessary). Moreover, the ADORE behavior reification allows evolution to be composed in a quasi–automatic way, detecting conflits to ensure orchestration validity. Contrarily to AOP which can be dynamic, our approach only considers static evolutions. The evolution process is done at model level and then refined after success into BPEL code using usual models transformation tools. This approach does not require any specific orchestration engine. As soon as orchestration engines will support dynamic orchestration changes, our approach could be used at runtime.

Former work [17] defines an associative and commutative merge algorithm dealing with components interactions. As this approach is a superset of the previous one focused on orchestrations and WSOA, we can restrict the algorithm described here to ensure associativity and commutativity. If we consider evolutions always using a usual schema[7] and no conflict resolution rules, we can ensure theses properties. Proving associativity and commutativity in others cases is an ongoing work.

Similar to the UML templates, evolutions define generic orchestration view whose some variables (template parameters) need to be bound. The ADORE model is dedicated to orchestration merging and binding step implies automatic composition of elements. Knowldege is used to reduce the space adressed by an evolution or to solve a conflict during this automatic merging. It plays the equivalent role as composition directives as defined in [18] to compose models.

In conclusion, we claim that a high level reasoning model such as our merge algorithm helps composition mechanisms.

7   Conclusions and Perspectives

In this article, we addressed the problem of Web Services orchestrations evolution on behavioral part. After identifying some needs of evolution capability on a real case orchestration, we restrict our investigations to behavioral evolutions.

---

[7] $\mathbb{P} \prec hook \prec \mathbb{S}$.

A formal model called ADORE is proposed and we define a merge algorithm able to compose in a quasi–automatic way evolutions into orchestrations. We also show on an example how the algorithm works, detailing each steps of the merge process and focusing on non–trivial parts. Furthermore, we show how this process can help evolution composition and discuss our work with respect to related work.

The work presented in this paper collaborates with the WSOA administrator for resolving semantic choices. She will help variable unification and conflict resolution using her knowledge and skills on the system. As the knowledge domain is closed to enterprise system boundaries, we can imagine some semantic web mechanisms to express such knowledge and capitalize enterprise knowledge.

We only consider evolution processes as an enrichment of an orchestration. We never address the activities removal problem or activity substitution. AOP define a *delegate* keyword to substitute the original behavior with a new one [19]. The merge algorithm will have to be modified to take care of this kind of evolution. So far, we consider evolution removal as a very simple operation: we take the original orchestration and the set of wanted evolutions, excepted the removed one. Finer grain mechanisms can be envisaged to deal with evolution removal.

The merge algorithm presented here considers only one *hook* binding inside the original orchestration. But it could be useful to allow multiple bindings (*e.g.* selecting all `reply` activities inside an orchestration) at merge time. We also consider that a *hook* point is an atomic activity. But evolutions can be applied to a block of activities, adding scope concerns to the merge process [20]. These two considerations implies the composition of overlapping evolutions when such a situation occurs.

References

1. MacKenzie, M., Laskey, K., McCabe, F., Brown, P., Metz, R.: Reference Model for Service Oriented Architecture 1.0. Technical Report wd-soa-rm-cd1, OASIS (February 2006)
2. Peltz, C.: Web services orchestration and choreography. Computer 36(10) (2003)
3. W3C: Web service glossary. Technical report (2004)
4. Mens, T., Wermelinger, M., Ducasse, S., Demeyer, S., Hirschfeld, R., Jazayeri, M.: Challenges in software evolution. In: IWPSE 2005: Proceedings of the Eighth International Workshop on Principles of Software Evolution, Washington, DC, USA, pp. 13–22. IEEE Computer Society, Los Alamitos (2005)
5. Lehman, M.M.: Laws of software evolution revisited. In: Montangero, C. (ed.) EWSPT 1996. LNCS, vol. 1149, pp. 108–124. Springer, Heidelberg (1996)
6. Fowler, M.: Refactoring: improving the design of existing code. Addison-Wesley Longman Publishing Co., Inc., Boston (1999)
7. Buckley, J., Mens, T., Zenger, M., Rashid, A., Kniesel, G.: Towards a taxonomy of software change. Journal on Software Maintenance and Evolution: Research and Practice 17(5), 309–332 (2005)

8. Jordan, D., Evedmon, J., Alves, A., Arkin, A., Askary, S., Barreto, C., Bloch, B., Curbera, F., Ford, M., Goland, Y., Guízar, A., Kartha, N., Liu, K., Khalaf, R., Konig, D., Marin, M., Mehta, V., Thatte, S., Van der Rijn, D., Yendluri, P., Yiu, A.: Web services business process execution language version 2.0. Technical report, OASIS (2007)

9. Stickel, M.E.: A unification algorithm for associative-commutative functions. J. ACM 28(3), 423–434 (1981)

10. Nemo, C., Blay-Fornarino, M., Kniesel, G., Riveill, M.: Semantic Orchestrations Merging - Towards Composition of Overlapping Orchestrations. In: Filipe, J. (ed.) 9th International Conference on Enterprise Information Systems (ICEIS 2007), Funchal, Madeira (June 2007)

11. Mens, T., Van Der Straeten, R.: Incremental resolution of model inconsistencies. In: Fiadeiro, J.L., Schobbens, P.-Y. (eds.) WADT 2006. LNCS, vol. 4409, pp. 111–126. Springer, Heidelberg (2007)

12. Merks, E., Eliersick, R., Grose, T., Budinsky, F., Steinberg, D.: The Eclipse Modeling Framework. Addison-Wesley, Reading (2003)

13. Joffroy, C., Pinna-Déry, A.M., Renevier, P., Riveill, M.: Architecture Model For Personalizing Interactive Service-Oriented Application. In: 11th Iasted International Conference on Software Engineering and Applications (SEA 2007), Cambridge, Massachusetts, USA, Iasted, pp. 379–384. ACTA Press (2007)

14. Douence, R.: A restricted definition of AOP. In: Gybels, K., Hanenberg, S., Herrmann, S., Wloka, J. (eds.) European Interactive Workshop on Aspects in Software (EIWAS) (September 2004)

15. Charfi, A., Mezini, M.: Aspect-oriented web service composition with AO4BPEL. In (LJ) Zhang, L.-J., Jeckle, M. (eds.) ECOWS 2004. LNCS, vol. 3250, pp. 168–182. Springer, Heidelberg (2004)

16. Courbis, C., Finkelstein, A.: Weaving aspects into web service orchestrations. In: ICWS, pp. 219–226. IEEE Computer Society, Los Alamitos (2005)

17. Blay-Fornarino, M., Charfi, A., Emsellem, D., Pinna-Déry, A.M., Riveill, M.: Software interaction. Journal of Object Technology (ETH Zurich) 3(10), 161–180 (2004)

18. Reddy, Y.R., Ghosh, S., France, R.B., Straw, G., Bieman, J.M., McEachen, N., Song, E., Georg, G.: Directives for composing aspect-oriented design class models. In: Rashid, A., Akşit, M. (eds.) Transactions on Aspect-Oriented Software Development I. LNCS, vol. 3880, pp. 75–105. Springer, Heidelberg (2006)

19. Laddad, R.: AspectJ in Action: Practical Aspect-Oriented Programming. Manning (July 2003) ISBN-10: 1930110936, ISBN-13: 978-1930110939

20. Klein, J., Fleurey, F., Jézéquel, J.M.: Weaving multiple aspects in sequence diagrams. In: Rashid, A., Akşit, M. (eds.) Transactions on AOSD III. LNCS, vol. 4620, pp. 167–199. Springer, Heidelberg (2007)

Evaluating Domain Design Approaches Using Systematic Review

Ednaldo Dilorenzo de Souza Filho[1,2], Ricardo de Oliveira Cavalcanti[1],
Danuza F.S. Neiva[1], Thiago H.B. Oliveira[1,2], Liana Barachisio Lisboa[1,2],
Eduardo Santana de Almeida[2],
and Silvio Romero de Lemos Meira[1,2]

[1] Federal University of Pernambuco (UFPE)
{edsf,roc3,dfsn,thbo,lbl,srlm}@cin.ufpe.br
[2] Recife Center for Advanced Studies and Systems (C.E.S.A.R)
esa@cesar.org.br

Abstract. Software Product Lines are growing as a systematic way for achieving reuse in software companies. It involves three processes: *domain engineering, application engineering* and *management*. In domain engineering, assets that will be reused by products are developed, composing the core assets. In this context, the product line architecture, also called *Domain Specific Software Architecture* (DSSA), is an essential member in the collection of core assets. A good DSSA increases the probability of the success of applications that will be instantiated from it. In order to design a good DSSA, a process should be followed to manage domain's variability and commonality. On the other hand, companies that are moving from single system development to software product lines need systematic activities for taking advantage of existing assets to develop a DSSA. Thus, this paper presents a systematic review on domain design approaches, which can be useful for companies to understand the current scenario, and to choose a more suitable one or adapt them for their needs.

Keywords: Software Reuse, Software Product Line Architecture, Domain Engineering, Systematic Review, Software Design.

1 Introduction

Software companies are looking for ways to achieve an increase of productivity, and often software reuse is a viable approach to achieve this goal [5]. Software reuse has the purpose of increasing not only productivity inside software projects but also software quality, and cost reduction. Furthermore, currently, Software Product Line (SPL) engineering is the main method to achieve reuse at large, and suites very well for software companies working in a specific domain [5]. According to [21], the software product line engineering paradigm separate three major processes: *domain engineering, application engineering,* and *management.*

R. Morrison, D. Balasubramaniam, and K. Falkner (Eds.): ECSA 2008, LNCS 5292, pp. 50–65, 2008.

SEI [9] divides the SPL process in three activities (core asset development, product development and management) which in general, has the same idea. In this work, we consider Pohl's [21] definition, for the sake of simplicity.

The domain engineering process is responsible for establishing a reusable platform and defining what is common among the domain applications (commonality) and what varies in domain applications (variability) in a product line. The platform consists of all types of software artifacts (Core Assets). According to [21], the domain engineering process is composed of five key sub-processes: product management, domain requirements engineering, domain design, domain realization, and domain testing. In the domain design sub-process a common architecture is developed for all applications within the domain. This architecture is called Domain Specific Software Architecture (DSSA). The DSSA contains the core structure of all applications within a domain, representing its commonality and variability. Quality attributes from the applications in the domain may also be represented in the DSSA in order to make them present with the applications derived from it. A good DSSA is an important success factor in a software product line, however, according to [8] a deficient DSSA can bring problems to the products derived from it. Among them we can list multiple versions of the same asset, the increase of dependencies among assets, and the use of assets in different contexts from where they were designed. Thus, a well defined approach to achieve this architecture is very important.

Many companies have moved away from developing software from scratch for each product and instead focused on the commonalities among the different products, capturing those in a DSSA and an associated set of reusable assets [8]. For companies that are working on a specific domain and have developed assets, it is important to take advantage of these assets in order to improve the productivity in building a DSSA. This paper presents a systematic review on domain design approaches in order to understand and to summarize empirical evidence about their activities, identifying their directions, strengths and weaknesses. This review is systematically performed, following Kitchenhams guideline [15], which aids in assuring consistent results from individual studies (called primary studies).

The remainder of this paper is organizes as follows. Section 2 explains the planning phase of the systematic review, while the description of how data was extracted is described in Section 3. Section 4 details the selected approaches for this review. Section 5 presents the results of the research, in Section 6 are discussed the threats to validity. Section 7 describes the related work, Section 8 presents the systematic review summary and, finally Section 9 discusses the concluding remarks and directions for the future work.

2   Planning

2.1   Review Protocol

According to [18] a review protocol specifies the activities that will be used to undertake a specific systematic review and the most important activity is the research question. The research question comes from the need of aiding the approaches evaluation. The question addressed by this review is: **How existing domain design approaches are organized?**

This question is related to many aspects of the research, and thus it was further divided into several sub-questions (SQ) in order to improve this systematic review's clarity:

SQ1. Do the approaches use architectural views? The purpose of this question is to identify which approaches provide a reference for architectural views and which ones they work with, since these views are an important source of communication among the various stakeholders of the product line.

SQ2. What activities are adopted in the approaches for domain design in domain engineering? The objective of this question is to analyze which activities each approach follows in order to design the final DSSA.

SQ3. How do the approaches deal with variability? The purpose of this question is to evaluate which steps, identified in the previous questions are used for treating variability in the DSSA.

SQ4. Do the approaches adapt companies processes in order to treat domain design variability and commonality? The aim of this question is to analyze if the approaches adapt existing company process in order to develop a DSSA during the systems development, or if they define a separate process to develop a DSSA before the products development.

SQ5. Which models the approaches use to document the architecture? This question has the objective to identify which models the approaches use for documenting the architecture. This question has a strong relation with the question **SQ1**, because in the definition of architectural views, models are associated with each view in order to represent it.

SQ6. What are the strengths and weaknesses in the domain design approaches? The purpose of this question is to analyze the key points and drawbacks from each approach. This is relevant to decide if the evaluated approaches supply the need for development of DSSA from existing software. For aid in finding these key points and drawbacks, this question was divided in three sub-questions *SQ6.1*, *SQ6.2*, *SQ6.3* as follows.

SQ6.1. Were the approaches experimented? In what environments were the approaches experimented? This question has the purpose to discover where the approaches were experimented, if they were. It is very important because their experimentation can bring us evidence about its efficiency. Approaches being used in industry can bring us the maturity from the steps applied by it.

SQ6.2. Do the approaches provide guidelines for component development? This question has the intention of identifying if the approaches have guidelines to indicate to the architect how to develop software components to be used in the DSSA. Those guidelines should guide the architect on which components are needed to be defined for the domain, and what funcionalities they should have. The evidence that an approach has guidelines for component development can improve the chance of this approach be used since it avoids that architects define components based on their feeling.

SQ6.3. Do the approaches provide guidelines for architecture recovery? A good evidence for an approach that aims to support the development of DSSA's from existing assets is to provide guidelines for recovering existing architectures and translate them into a DSSA. Those guidelines should guide the architect on how to extract the architecture from existing systems source code.

The main purpose of these questions is to try to assess and evaluate steps, activities and, models developed in existing approaches addressing the fact that most companies start a software product line from existing systems [5] . In this systematic review, we followed Kitchenham's guideline [15], where it is proposed to discuss the main question from three viewpoints: *population*, which is the involved actors; *intervention*, the approach taken; and *outcomes*, i.e. the results of this approach:

Population: once this study focuses on identifying the approaches used for Domain Design, the population is composed by domain architects and system analysts;

Intervention: this review must search for indications that the domain design approach can be complete for developing DSSA from existing products; and

Outcomes: the main objective of this study is to understand and to sumarize empirical evidence about the evaluated approaches activities, identifying their directions, strengths and weaknesses.

3   Data Extraction

Primary studies are individual studies contributing to a systematic review. The search strategy is the plan for finding as many primary studies as possible meeting the aspects of the research question [15]. This strategy is divided in searching for primaries studies and identifying the inclusion and exclusion criteria and selecting the approaches.

3.1   Data Sources

The primary studies were searched scanning most relevant conference proceedings, journals, books and grey literature. The steps performed for the data extraction are described bellow:

- Main conferences in software reuse, software product lines, software architecture and, software engineering were analyzed and papers were selected according to their abstract, in order to verify the relation with a domain design approach.
- After that, the same research method was used for searching journals, looking for software reuse, software product lines, software architecture and software engineering, analyzing what the journal deals with.

- Web search engines were also used for searching papers and journals. This research was done through keyword matching *domain architecture approaches*.
- As next step, papers referenced by the authors of the found papers were also analyzed. Thus, it was possible to identify a new set of keywords, such as *modeling, design,* for the identification of other approaches. These new keywords lead to a new round of searches on the web search engines.
- Moreover, we analyzed all types of literature not available through the normal bookselling channels (grey literature), such as technical reports from research groups, specific books of software product line approaches, discussing the domain design phase and, Ph.D. theses. In the systematic review page[1], there are all the information about the conferences and journals searched.

3.2   Criteria

According to [15], it is necessary to define inclusion and exclusion criteria for the papers selection. The criteria should identify the primary studies, i.e. the ones identified during the research, which provide evidence about the research question. The inclusion criteria defined for this review were:

a) *Software product line and domain engineering approaching the design activity:* this criteria adds papers of software product line and domain engineering approaching the domain design activity in order to analyze their features.
b) *Comparison among domain design approaches:* papers comparing domain design approaches were searched in order to aid in this systematic review separating key aspects and drawbacks. These aspects were evaluated according to the personal experience.
c) *Approaches treating variability in DSSA:* some approaches addressing the variability in domain design were added to this systematic review for the evaluation of those practices in the context of a DSSA creation based on existing set of systems.

As exclusion criteria, we defined the following:

a) *Software product line and domain engineering approaches that do not treat domain design:* software product line and domain engineering approaches that do not address the domain design are not interesting for this survey. Approaches as FODA [14] that address mainly the requirements phase were discarded.
b) *Approaches for evaluating DSSA's:* even being very important to assure the DSSA's quality, approaches for evaluating them were out of the scope of this systematic review, because evaluating it and adding this step for a possible new approach for domain design would increase the scope of this work.

---

[1] `www.cin.ufpe.br/~edsf/sreview/conferences`

4   Approaches Selection

The approaches selection was performed by five M.Sc. candidates and two Ph.D. in conjunction with weekly discussions and seminars with the Reuse in Software Engineering (RiSE[2]) Lab.

At the end of the data source collection, 11 approaches were identified as possible choices for further analysis. Among these approaches were 5 books, 2 theses and 16 papers. The criteria was analyzed after a full text reading or just the title and abstract of those papers for which the content was clearly not related to the research question in the case of the papers. Books and theses were scanned in order to analyze if they were related with the criteria.

After the analysis, 10 approaches were selected (detailed in the next section). The selected approaches analysis were based on 11 papers, 2 theses and, 4 books.

4.1   Approaches Information

In this section, we present a brief description about the selected approaches in a chronological order.

FORM(1998). The Feature-Oriented Reuse Method (FORM) was developed in Pohang University of Science and Technology, Korea as an extension to the Feature-Oriented Domain Analysis (FODA) [18]. Its analysis was based on paper [13].

FAST (1999). The Family-Oriented Abstraction, Specification and Translation was developed at Lucent Technologies. It is a software development process focused on building families of systems. Its analysis was based on [22].

PuLSE (1999). The Product Line Software Engineering (PuLSE) was developed at Fraunhofer Institute for Experimental Software Engineering (IESE) with the purpose of enabling the conception and deployment of software product lines within a large variety of enterprise contexts. Its analysis was based on papers [11] and [6].

COPA (2000). The Component-Oriented Platform Architecting approach for Families of Software Intensive Electronic Products (COPA) was developed at the Philips Research Labs. The specific goal of the COPA approach is to achieve the best possible fit among business, architecture, process and organization of systems having the greatest level or reuse as possible. Its analysis was based on the papers [1], [20] and [18].

SEI's Framework (2000). The SEI's framework was developed in the Department of Defense at the Software Engineering Institute (SEI) in order to establish patterns for the Software Product Line practice. Its analysis was based on the book [9].

---

[2] www.rise.com.br/research

KobrA (2002). Komponentenbasierte Anwendungsentwicklung (KobrA) that is German for "component-based application development" [18] was developed at Fraunhofer Institute for Experimental Software Engineering (IESE). Its analysis was based on the papers [2], [4], [18], and the book [3].

QADA (2002). The Quality-driven Architecture Design and quality Analysis (QADA) approach was developed at VTT the Technical Research Centre of Finland. QADA claims to be a quality-driven architecture design approach. Its analysis was based on the papers [19] and [18].

PLUS (2005). The Product Line UML-based Software Engineering is a RUP based approach to software product line engineering. Its focus is on representing variability and product line concerns with UML. Its analysis was based on the book [12].

DECOM (2006). The DECOM approach was developed at Federal University of Rio de Janeiro (UFRJ), Brazil, as a Ph.D. thesis. It is an extension and update of ODYSSEY approach [7], developed at the same place. DECOM proposes a domain engineering process with domain engineering and component-based development methods, with the focus on domain design activities. Its analysis was based on the Ph.D. thesis [7].

RiDE (2007). The RiSE process for Domain Engineering (RiDE) was developed at Federal University of Pernambuco (UFPE), Brazil, as a Ph.D. thesis. It is based on the definition of a feature model (FODA) and the main purpose is to detail activities related with each phase of the domain engineering. Its analysis was based on the Ph.D. thesis [10].

For a better documentation of the approaches analysis, the available information about them can be seen in `http://www.cin.ufpe.br/~edsf/work.html`.

5   Results

In this section, we show the results of the systematic review, conducted with the objective of mapping how complete are domain design approaches. After the results of the SQs, a summary according to the main questions is presented in Table 1.

5.1   Use of Architectural Views

Analyzing the 10 approaches, we could identify that not all of them use architectural views. But approaches that do not use architectural views have different models for representing the DSSA.

FORM, FAST, KobrA, PuLSE, and DECOM do not mention the use of architectural views for describing the DSSA. Instead, they just use models and activities that will be described in Section 5.5.

The COPA approach defines 5 views: *customer view, application view, functional view, conceptual view* and *realization view*. These views can also be divided

Table 1. Summary of Systematic Review Questions of Software Product Line Approaches

Approaches	Activities				
	Apply Architectural Views	Adapt existing Process	Component Development Guidelines	Architecture Recovery Guidelines	Experimented in Industy
FORM (1998)		X			X
FAST (1999)					X
PuLSE (1999)					X
COPA (2000)	X				X
SEI (2000)	X	X			X
KobrA (2002)					X
QADA (2002)	X				
PLUS (2005)	X	X	X		
DECOM (2006)			X		
RiDE (2007)	X		X		

in two groups: commercial and technical, the first two views being defined as commercial views, the last two as technical views and the functional view as both commercial and technical. The *customer view* focuses on business modeling from the customer's viewpoint while the *application view* describes the applications that are important to the customer in the product line context. The *functional view* captures the system requirements of a customer application. The *conceptual view* includes the architectural concepts of the system and the *realization view* describes the realization technologies for building the system [18].

The QADA approach has the architectural representation divided in two groups: **conceptual architecture design** and **concrete architecture design**. Each group has the same set of views: *structural view, behavior view,* and *deployment view.* Conceptual views represent the architecture in a high level of abstraction, while concrete views in a more detailed level. The structural views are represented by components and the relationship among them, behavior views represent the messages exchanged by components and the responsabilities they have, and deployment views represent how components are phisically organized, in terms of hardware and software.

The PLUS approach deals with architectural views in the same way as Rational Unified Process (RUP): with the 4+1 model from [16].

The RiDE approach, as well as the SEI's framework, suggests the use of architectural views taking avantage of the 4+1 model as well, but they do not recommend any specific, letting the architect decide which view to use depending on the project's needs.

5.2 Activities Adopted for Design

In the approaches analysis, we could observe that all of them define their own steps to achieve the DSSA. All of them focus on the level of detail for the software

product line developers and have steps for a generic domain, needing just some customization for the domain change.

In the FORM approach, for each domain, a feature model is specified, with features from every system defined in the context phase. For the software DSSA, it has only the steps of defining the subsystem model, process model and module model. The FAST starts with the family design development, that will be reused to generate members of the family. The next step is to define traceability among specifications in Architecture Modeling Language (AML) and templates. The next step is to define the syntax and semantics of the AML.

The PuLSE approach also treats different contexts by instantiating the approach details for each specific environment. The first step of the domain design is to generate generic scenarios, that means architecturally significant scenarios for the software product line and property related scenarios, focusing on domain-indepent quality aspects such as couping and cohesion, based on functional and non-functional requirements, scenarios are sorted according to their architectural significance, which means that scenarios which hold important variability information should be considered first. Based on the sorted scenarios, the architecture is developed and refined to encompass more scenarios, after that, prototype of candidate architectures are developed for a better evaluation and it finishes with the architecture refinement by adding and satisfying another scenarios.

COPA approach is customized according to customer's needs and work products are derived from the commercial needs. Its first step is the *components identification*, that produces the conceptual DSSA by arranging it into components and subsystems, and the second, *aspect* design, that models the functions that are orthogonal to objects such as fault handling, diagnosis and debugging. For the SEI's framework, the practices related with the DSSA are added to an existing approach in business. It means that practices are dependent of context. The steps for achieving the DSSA were not evaluated because the framework just advises about practices but not about which steps should be followed. KobrA is divided in Komponent[3] *specification phase*, where the external properties of a Komponent are defined, and the Komponent *realization phase* that realizes the Komponent's specification. Analyzing QADA approach, we could observe that it has two main steps, the *conceptual architecture design*, where the conceptual components are defined, according to the functional and quality requirements, and *concrete architecture design*, where the components are specified in a lower level of abstraction.

In PLUS, activities take in consideration different viewpoints and needs for the whole SPL. Its framework is as generic as the Unified Process (UP), but has specific approaches to deal with variability in the context of SPL using UML. The architecture is designed addressing the main concerns about the DSSA to be built, such as choosing, using and documenting the architectural patterns that will satisfy the requirements of the software product line, documenting rationale and design decisions, and developing component-based architectures and distributing those components. DECOM approach defines a component creation

---

[3] Komponent is the notation for "KobrA component".

step, where components are created based on domain specific features and categorized in: business components, process components, utile components, and infrastructure components. After being created components are grouped according to messages changed among them and finally the architecture is assembled using architectural styles and taking quality attributes in consideration.

In RiDE approach, the modules are decomposed as the first step of the domain design, based on assets produced in domain requirements engineering, such as business goals, constraints, domain use case model, feature model, and scenarios. After the definition, the modules are refined choosing the architectural drivers that will be addressed by the architecture, choosing architectural patterns that can be applied, and allocating systems functionality to modules. The variability is represented in class diagrams, mapping the feature model with the suggested design patterns. Components are defined based on the messages changed among them and the DSSA is represented with the components defined in the previous steps.

5.3   Variability in Domain Design Approaches

Treating variability in software product lines is mandatory, since with variability many systems can be addressed and the variable aspects of the software in the domain can be documented.

In this sense, FORM, DECOM, and RiDE capture variability in domain requirements where a feature tree is developed, in FORM, these features are then associated with subsystems, processes, and modules (or components) regarding to the models of the domain design step. In DECOM, an extension of the feature models is used in order to achieve variability with the tracking with other models like, use case and class diagrams, and in RiDE, variability is represented with design patterns suggested by the approach with guidelines for each type of variability in feature model. FAST and KobrA approaches use decision models to capture and document the family aspects. The decisions are related to variability in domain.

PuLSE, as in KobrA, the variability is documented textually and taken in to consideration for each scenario built. COPA approach has specific processes for product family engineering and application engineering. Generic solutions are identified in the early stages of domain analysis and variability is represented along with the features, which are grouped in sets. SEI's framework suggests mechanisms such as inheritance, extensions and extension points, parameterization, configuration and module for addressing variability.

The QADA approach uses specific relations and notations, such aggregation, specialization of the UML modeling language for variability captured in requirements phase. In PLUS approach, the whole process and artifacts are intervened by the documentation of variation points, which addresses the variability concern.

5.4   Adaptation of Existing Processes

During the research, we could observe that some approaches try to minimize the business changes in start producing a software product line and this is done adapting the existing enterprise process. This is a good approach since it minimizes the companies cost and effort in this process adaptation. Other approaches have a specific method for developing a software product line requiring a bigger effort to have this kind of development, these approaches focus on preparing the core assets to be reused as a preliminary part of the softwares development.

In FORM's evaluation, we could observe that the feature models are used based on FODA, for supporting both engineering of reusable domain artifacts and development applications using these domain artifacts, representing the variability and commonality in the domain.

FAST, PuLSE, COPA, KobrA, QADA, DECOM, and RiDE define their own methods and steps not only for the domain design phase, but another phases from the domain engineering life cycle. Their purpose were not adapting a existing business process for achieving the DSSA but being a complete process for this activity.

SEI's framework is a set of guidelines essentially done to cover the variability issues in a common process. So its guidelines can be used for the adaptation of an existing process to achieve the DSSA.

PLUS approach defines a set of models for representing variability in DSSA based on RUP models. It brings us that existing companies processes based on RUP models can use PLUS models for the domain design as a way for achieving the variability across architecture.

5.5 Models for Architecture Documentation

For an effective product line engineering approach, the commonality and variability information that characterizes the members of a product family must be integrated into a single coherent description of the product line [5]. In order to have a good documentation, the set of models that the approaches define are very important to make development easier.

For the DSSA definition, FORM approach defines three models: the subsystem model, that defines the overall system structure by grouping functions into subsystems, the process model that represents the dynamic behavior of each subsystem (e.g., concurrency within a subsystem), and module models, where features at all levels of the feature model are used for defining reusable components.

The FAST approach does not state any specific model to represent the DSSA. It is based on the development of an Architecture Modeling Language defined during the product line development process. For PuLSE approach, the quality and functional scenarios, candidate architecture prototypes, configuration models, and DSSA descriptions are defined. Quality and functional scenarios are described as in SEI's ATAM approach for architecture evaluation [6]. Prototypes can be developed in any language, including the ones different from the aimed language for developing the products. The configuration model documents the decisions made during the DSSA development, such as alternative implementation strategies.

COPA approach documents the complete ABC (architecture business cycle). The customer view includes customer value drivers, customer business models and market models. The application view models entities and behavior of the product line. The functional view models the commercial decomposition of function features and options, price performance and dimensioning of the products planned. Conceptual view models product specific components, platform components, aspect-specific models, concurrency models, and deployability models written in UML.

KobrA defines three models: the *structural model* that describes classes and relationships by which a Komponent interacts with its environment, as well as any internal structure of the Komponent, which is visible at its interface. The *behavioral model* describes how a Komponent reacts in response to external stimuli and, the *functional model* of a Komponent that describes the externally visible effects of the operations that are provided by that Komponent, and the *decision models* that are used for the system architecture instantiation. These models are made in the framework engineering phase.

QADA approach has architectural elements and architectural languages for each of the views described in Section 5.1. For conceptual architectural view, conceptual structural components divide the system into functional blocks using UML elements as package diagrams. Its language describes the relation among these blocks. In conceptual behavioral view the architectural elements are components and their relationships. Its language defines these elements in an ordered sequence of actions, and for the conceptual deployment view elements defined are deployment nodes that are computing units and deployment units that are composed of one or more components. Concrete structural, behaviour and deployment views has the same purpose as in the conceptual, but it represents the components, interactions among them and their allocation in software and hardware in a higher level of detail.

For DECOM approach, class diagrams are used for expressing the variability found in identified classes, and component diagrams are used for expressing the variability and optionality of identified business, process, utile and infrastructure components. Sequence diagrams are used for identifing the messages changed among components and this will help to generate the DSSA.

RiDE, SEI's framework and PLUS are based on RUP for architecture representation using the $4 + 1$ models for each model defined in this methodology depending on the need for the models. In RiDE approach, the architecture is represented with class diagrams defining the classes that are related with the feature model representing its variability with the suggested design patterns. Classes defined for the feature model are allocated to components, these components are represented in a component diagram, and each component is configurable to implement its variability.

5.6 Approaches Key Points and Drawbacks

In this section, we evaluate the key points and drawbacks of the approaches reviewed based on sub-questions of the question 6.

Approaches Experimentation. As we can see in Table 1, FORM, FAST, PuLSE, COPA, SEI's Framework, and KobrA were experimented in industry.

However, in QADA, PLUS, DECOM, and RiDE, we did not find any evidences that they were experimented in industry. This can be true, because they are the most recent ones, and are probably in evaluation.

Guidelines for Component Development. With the information provided by Table 1, in PLUS, DECOM, and RiDE, we could find guidelines for component development. In PLUS, component development is based on the dependences between use cases and features. DECOM and RiDE approach takes in consideration the development of sequence diagrams and the messages changed by classes for the component definition and development.

Guidelines for Architecture Recovery. No guidelines for architecture recovery were found in this review. This review showed us that approaches are very well prepared for the development of a DSSA, but they do not take advantage of existing assets to improve its development.

6   Threats to Validity

The main threats to validity we identified in our review are described next:

Approaches selection: looking for studies from web search engines and key digital libraries do not assure that all domain design approaches were reviewed. Possibly, relevant approches were excluded from this systematic review, since some paper titles do not mention the key words defined for the research (*see Section 3*). In order to reduce this possibility, the selection of approaches was also based on identification of the key journals and conferences in software engineering in general, in software reuse, and software product lines, with a specilist analysis for the study's validation. We also analyzed the referenced works, including theses and technical report.

Data extraction: the lack of information available by approaches can make us to omit some relevant data about them. We tried to ensure validity by analyzing multiple sources of data, i.e. papers, technical reports, white papers and manuals, relating the similar information. The extracted data were compared to the research questions and later classified according to the objectives of the questions.

7   Related Work

Some studies were found in the same line of evaluating the existing software product line approaches. However, no one is performed through a systematic review.

Matinlassi [18] compared the design approaches KobrA, COPA, QADA, FAST and FORM. In her evaluation, she brings a brief description about the processes, and their related domains using a framework called NIMSAD. With this framework, she used four categories in the evaluation: context, user, contents and validation. Each category has its own questions to be addressed.

Similar to our work, Matinlassi presented the main characteristics of the described approaches. However, she concluded that they do not seem to compete with each other, because each of them has a special goal or ideology. Different from our work she does not bring the evaluation of some approaches such as PuLSE and since it was written in 2004, it does not bring recently developed approaches, such as RiDE, PLUS, and DECOM.

The AMPLE project [17] performed a survey on the State of the art in Product Line Architecture Design with a very detailed definitions about concepts from software product lines to software architecture, describing just how they represent the DSSA, different from our work, that shows other points of view from the Domain Design approaches. AMPLE project presented the approaches grouping them by their main characteristics. It describes approaches such as FODA, emphasizing the feature orientation characteristic, cites FAST, PuLSE, and KobrA, but it does not cite approaches such as COPA, QADA, DECOM, RiDE.

Moreover, it is important to highlight that our work performed this evaluation using a formal and defined approach. Thus, it can be more repeatable, e.g., for other researchers and research groups. In addiction, issues not defined in this review can be improved based on this version, since all the process is well defined and documented.

8   Systematic Review Summary

Analyzing activities, guidelines, and views, we could observe a set of good practices adopted by domain design approaches. The separation of architecture in views is considered a good practice since many stakeholders can see how the domain design will be implemented. The 4+1 model is easyly adaptable for software product lines that are RUP compliant since they must only extend the concept of variability for achieving the DSSA description. Other views described in this study are more specific according to the customer, the domain, and the business.

The activities defined by the approaches were very complex for analyzing, since each of them deals with different aspects from the DSSA perspective. The most interesting activities are related with the static modeling of the domain architecture, defining the variability among several levels of abstraction, such as components, classes, etc. In this review, we missed some activities for treating the quality attributes variability inside a DSSA, since it is a very important issue concerning the architecture definition. The addition of quality attributes in the DSSA can make it change in several components. An important activity verified was the component definition very well described in [10]. KobrA and FORM still presents suggestions on how to define components.

In the same way as in the architecture view/viewpoints, the models for describing a DSSA are very easier to understand when following the models described by 4+1 model. In some approaches, we could observe just the mention to use it, but not how to treat variability inside them. KobrA approach uses stereotypes from the UML language to define which assets from the domain are variable and which ones are common.Feature models are considered good models for represent variability inside a domain and to select which assets are going to be in a product from the features selection.

9   Concluding Remarks and Future Work

In this review, we analyzed and compared the domain design approaches, and discussed the strengths and weakness found in this context. The effort and quality data gathered by our review present interesting results that can be used as a documented important background in domain design development. The information listed in this paper provides valuable data for other researchers investigating domain design in academic or industrial settings. Futhermore, the common key points reviewed in approaches, can show what are the basic activities for the adoption of a domain design approach. Moreover, this review aids reseachers in collecting the key points each approach address in order to have a tailored approach.

The main problem addressed by this review, was the need for companies to develop a DSSA taking advantage of existing assets. As we could see, few approaches have guidelines available for the component development and no approaches have guidelines for achieving the DSSA from the assets available in software companies. This may lead us to develop an own approach addressing these issues in order to decrease the effort in the software product line adoption for companies that started development without a software product line approach. As future work, we are calibrating our study and starting the development of a full approach for domain design. This approach is strongly influenced by this paper and our industrial experience in the topic.

Acknowledgements

This work is sponsored by Brazilian Agency (CNPq process number: 475743/ 2007-5).

References

[1] America, P., Obbink, H., van Ommering, R., van der Linden, F.: Copam: A component-oriented platform architecting method family for product family engineering (2000)

[2] Atkinson, C.: Component-based product line development: The kobrA approach, pp. 289–309 (2000)

[3] Atkinson, C.: Component-based Product Line Engineering with UML. Addison-Wesley, Reading (2002)

[4] Atkinson, C., Bayer, J., Laitenberger, O., Zettel, J.: Component-based software engineering: The kobra approach (2000)

[5] Atkinson, C., Muthig, D.: Model-driven product line architecture (2002)

[6] Bayer, J., Flege, O., Knauber, P., Laqua, R., Muthig, D., Schmid, K., Widen, T., DeBaud, J.-M.: Pulse: A methodology to develop software product lines (1999)

[7] Blois, A.P.T.B.: A Component-based Architectural Design Approach in the Domain Engineering Context. PhD thesis, UFRJ (2006)

[8] Bosch, J.: Evolution and composition of reusable assets in product-line architectures: A case study (1999)

[9] Clements, P.: Software Product Lines - SEI Framework (2000)

[10] de Almeida, E.S.: RiDE - RiSE Domain Engineering Process. PhD thesis (2007)

[11] DeBaud, J.-M., Flege, O., Knauber, P.: Pulse-dssa a method for the development of software reference architectures (1998)

[12] Gomaa, H.: Designing Software Product Lines with UML: From Use Cases to Pattern-Based Software Architectures. Addison Wesley Professional, Reading (2004)

[13] Kang: Form: A feature-oriented reuse method with domain-specific reference architectures (1998)

[14] Kang, K.C., Cohen, S.G., Hess, J.A., Novak, W.E., Peterson, A.S.: Feature-oriented domain analysis (foda) feasibility study. Technical report, Carnegie-Mellon University Software Engineering Institute (November 1990)

[15] Kitchenham, B.: Procedures for performing systematic reviews (2004)

[16] Kruchten, P.: The Rational Unified Process An Introduction. Addison-Wesley, Reading (2000)

[17] Loughran, N., Sánchez, P., Gámez, N., Garcia, A., Fuentes, L., Christa, S., Kovacevic, J.: Survey on state-of-the-art in product line architecture design. Technical report

[18] Matinlassi, M.: Comparison of software product line architecture design methods: Copa, fast, form, kobra and qada (2004)

[19] Matinlassi, M., Niemela, E., Dobrica, L.: Quality-driven architecture design and quality analysis method, a revolutionary initiation approach to a product line architecture (2002)

[20] Obbink, H., Miller, J., America, P., van Ommering, R.: Copa a component-oriented platform architecting method for families of software-intensive electronic products (2000)

[21] Pohl, K., Backle, G., van der Linden, F.: Software Product Line Engineering Foundations, Principles, and Techniques. Springer, Heidelberg (2005)

[22] Weiss, D.: Software product-line engineering: a family-based software development process. Addison-Wesley Longman Publishing Co., Inc., Amsterdam (1999)

Characterizing Relations between Architectural Views

Nelis Boucké[1], Danny Weyns[1], Rich Hilliard[2],
Tom Holvoet[1], and Alexander Helleboogh[1]

[1] DistriNet Labs, K.U. Leuven, Belgium
{nelis.boucke,danny.weyns,tom.holvoet,
alexander.helleboogh}@cs.kuleuven.be
[2] Consulting software systems architect
r.hilliard@computer.org

Abstract. It is commonly agreed that an architectural description (AD) consists of multiple views. Each view describes the architecture from the perspective of particular stakeholder concerns. Although views are constructed separately, they are related as they describe the same system.

A thorough study of the literature reveals that research on relations between views is fragmented and that a comprehensive study is hampered by an absence of common terminology. This has become apparent in the discussion on inter-view relational concepts in the revision of IEEE 1471 as ISO/IEC 42010 (*Systems and Software Engineering — Architectural Description*).

This paper puts forward a framework that employs a consistent terminology to characterize relations between views. The framework sheds light on the usage, scope and mechanisms for relations, and is illustrated using several representative approaches from the literature. We conclude with a reflection on whether the revision of ISO 42010 aligns with our findings.

Keywords: architectural views, view relations, viewpoint, architectural descriptions, integration of views, consistency, models, IEEE 1471, ISO/IEC 42010.

1   Introduction

The architecture of a software system defines its essential structures, which comprise software elements, the externally visible properties of those elements, the relationships between them [3] and with their environment [21]. It is commonly agreed that an architectural description (AD) consists of multiple views. Views are used to achieve separation of concerns where each view describes the architecture from the perspective of related stakeholder concerns [21]. Although views can be constructed separately, they must be related in that they describe the same system.

Relying on implicit relations, e.g. relating elements having the same name and type, might be sufficient for simple architectures but is insufficient for more complex systems. An important part of the architect's job is to understand, describe and reason about how the different views relate to each other [8,40]. In this paper, we explicitly focus on the relations between architectural views; not on relations between elements within views.

Relations are essential for establishing consistency and for maintaining that consistency over time. Software architects need relations to manage the multitude of views. Developers need relations for an integrated picture of the architecture that is a prerequisite for detailed design and implementation. Other stakeholders need to see how their

R. Morrison, D. Balasubramaniam, and K. Falkner (Eds.): ECSA 2008, LNCS 5292, pp. 66–81, 2008.

concerns are realized and how these realizations relate to concerns of other stakeholders. Finally, relations provide the basis for automation in architectural tools of consistency checking, and integration or synchronization of multiple architectural views during design.

Problem Statement. In the architecture community, there is a common understanding of what an architectural view is. There are several seminal works on views, including Perry and Wolf [36] and Kruchten's 4+1 view model [26]. More recently, multiple views form the basis for approaches such as *Documenting Software Architectures* [8] and *Software Systems Architecture* [40]. Also, the concepts of architectural description and view have been standardized by ANSI, IEEE, ISO and IEC.[1]

Such common understanding however is lacking for relations between views. This lack of consensus became apparent in the recent discussions on the incorporation of relations between views in the ongoing revision of ISO 42010. A thorough study of the literature reveals that research on relations between views is fragmented and hampered by an absence of common terminology. Authors typically compare to approaches with similar purpose (e.g. automatic consistency checks). However, they tend to neglect other relations with similar technical characteristics but devised for another purpose (e.g. enforcing design decisions).

The fragmentation in research also becomes apparent through the myriad of terms in use for related or overlapping concepts. A sample of terms from recent research in this area illustrates the point: [30] uses *constraints, rules, standard constraints, extensions constraints, integration constraints* and *custom constraints*; [18] uses *design constraints, invariants* and *heuristics*; [28] uses *rule* and specializes rules in *constraints* and *obligations*; [14] additionally uses *policy constraints*; [4] uses *viewpoint correspondences*; [8] uses *relations* and *mapping*; [12] uses *refinement* and *overlap relations, relationships* and *consistency rules* that apply to the *relations*; [2] uses *relations* and *transformations* for the same thing; [38] uses *boolean rule, general design rule, constraints logic, dependency links, links, design rule* and *transformation rule*; [9] uses *links, relations, rules, correspondences* and *correspondence rules*; [43] uses *traceability links, dependency links, dependency relations, relations, trace relation*; etc. This makes it difficult to characterize and compare approaches for describing relations between views.

Contributions. The revision of ISO 42010 provides an opportunity to offer better guidance to architects for capturing relations between views within an architectural description. This paper contributes a proposed framework that structures approaches for explicit relations between views providing a common ground for relations. The framework is based on a thorough study of the literature and on our experience. The goal is to take a step to disentangle and bring clarification to the work on relations between views. The framework sheds light on the usage, scope and underlying mechanism. Application of the framework is illustrated with several representative approaches from the

---

[1] The abbreviation *ISO 42010* is used for the published version of ISO/IEC 42010:2007, *System and Software Engineering — Architectural Description* [24]. ISO 42010 is identical in content to ANSI/IEEE Std 1471-2000, *Recommended Practice for Architectural Description of Software-Intensive Systems* [21], and is currently undergoing revision. The abbreviation *42010 WD2* is used for the current working draft of this revision [22].

literature. Based on this, we reflect on whether view relations in the ISO 42010 working draft aligns with the findings in the literature.

Overview. To avoid confusion on terminology issues, section 2 introduces the basic architectural terminology used in this paper. Section 3 proposes the framework to characterize relations between views, and illustrates its use with representative approaches from the literature. Section 4 reflects on the proposal for view correspondences in 42010 WD2 with respect to the proposed framework. Finally, we conclude in section 5.

2   Basic Architectural Concepts

This section introduces the basic architectural concepts and terminology that we will use in the remainder of the paper. There are several known definitions of architecture and architectural views in the literature, the SEI [3,8], Siemens [20], ISO 42010 or RM-ODP [23]. We adopt the conceptual model of ISO 42010, to serve as a consistent set of basic terminology. This does not mean that our scope is limited to the standard; we studied a broad range of approaches in the literature.[2] ISO 42010 has two parts. The first part is a conceptual model for architectural descriptions. The conceptual model introduces and interrelates such concepts as *architectural description*, *concern*, *viewpoint*, *view* and *model*. The second part puts forward required content for any ISO 42010-conformant architectural description, independent of the specific architectural languages in use. Here, we only use the conceptual model.

Figure 1 shows a portion of the ISO 42010 conceptual model relevant for this paper. An *architectural description* (AD) is "a collection of products to document a specific architecture". An AD is organized into one or more *architectural views*, where a view is defined as "a representation of a whole system from the perspective of a related set of concerns". Each view is constructed according to an *architectural viewpoint*, defined as "the conventions for constructing and using a view; a pattern or template from which to develop individual views by establishing the purposes and audience for a view and the techniques for its creation and analysis".

One of ISO 42010's contributions was to explicitly distinguish between view and viewpoint, in this sense: A *viewpoint* is a way of looking at an architecture; the view is the result of looking at a specific system's architecture in this way.[3] First-class viewpoints first appear in Ross' Structured Analysis [39] and are elaborated upon by

---

[2] In 2007, IEEE 1471 was adopted by ISO as ISO 42010. At present, IEEE and ISO are jointly revising the standard.

[3] Not every architectural approach makes an explicit distinction between view and viewpoint. The term *viewpoint* appears in ISO RM-ODP [23], in a very similar fashion; although *viewpoint specification* is employed where IEEE 1471 uses *view*. In RM-ODP a *viewpoint specification* is defined as "the application of a viewpoint to a specific system". The book *Documenting Software Architectures* (DSA) [8] introduces *viewtypes* as "a viewtype defines the element types and relation types used to describe the architecture of a software system from a particular perspective." DSA further proposes there are three viewtypes: the module viewtype, the component-and-connector viewtype, and the allocation viewtype. In the present framework, these could be considered a three-way classification of viewpoints, in terms of their representational mechanisms (element and relation types).

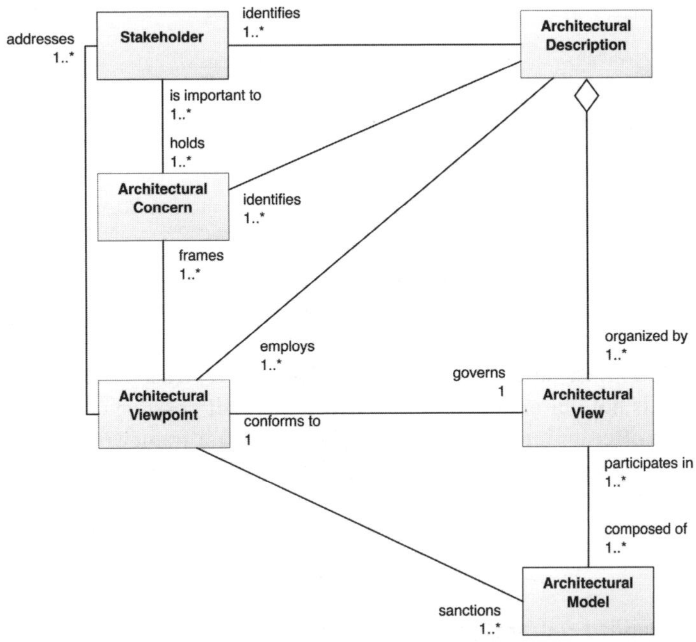

Fig. 1. A portion of the ISO 42010 conceptual model

Finklestein *et al.* [16]. In ISO 42010, viewpoints are intended to provide a representational approach for addressing specific architectural concerns: "those interests which pertain to the system's development, its operation or any other aspects that are critical or otherwise important to one or more stakeholders". A system stakeholder is any "individual, team, or organization (or classes thereof) with interests in, or concerns relative to, a system".[4] Each architectural view is composed of one or more *architectural models*. Each model contains a concrete description of architectural elements and relations, and obeys the conventions of the governing viewpoint with respect to the viewpoint language(s) and model type(s) employed therein. When a view is composed of multiple models, relations can arise between models within a view as well as between views.

The authors of ISO 42010 recognized the issue of view consistency, but did not specify a mechanism for enforcing that consistency except to require the recording any known inconsistencies. We return to the current proposal for introducing relations into the ISO 42010 working draft below section 4.

3   A Framework for Characterizing Relations between Views

Starting from a thorough study of literature and our experiences, we have identified several criteria to characterize relations between views. Each of the criteria emphasizes a particular aspect of view relations. Together, the criteria make up a framework that

---

[4] The standard uses *concern* in the sense of E. Dijkstra's *separation of concerns*.

Usage				Scope				Mechanism		
Consistency Checking	Composition	Tracing	Model Transformation	Intra vs. Inter Model Type	Level of Detail	Horizontal vs. Vertical	Metamodel vs. Model	Direct References	Tuples	Expression language

Fig. 2. Overview of the criteria for the framework in three orthogonal dimensions

allows structuring and comparing approaches for relations between views. Figure 2 shows an overview of the criteria. The criteria are grouped along three dimensions: Usage, Scope, and Mechanism.

In this section, we describe the criteria and discuss representative examples from the literature. It is not our ambition to be exhaustive in all possible criteria or references, but rather to offer an initial impetus towards defining a framework for characterizing relations between views. At the end of this section, we discuss possible extensions of the framework.

3.1   Usage

We have identified four main use cases for relations between views: (1) consistency checking; (2) composition; (3) tracing; and (4) model transformation. There is no one-to-one mapping between particular types of relations and their use; relations can be used for different purposes. Some of the use cases are not goals in themselves but can serve a further purpose. For example, tracing is typically used for backtracking of decisions and to allow easier changes to the architecture.

Consistency Checking. Consistency checking is about determining whether the information in several views does not conflict. We discuss three example uses of relations between views for consistency checking: general-purpose consistency checking, design constraint checking, and consistency checking of service compositions.

Nentwich et al. [30] put forward a general-purpose approach for automatic consistency checking of heterogenous and distributed software engineering documents. The approach uses constraints underpinned by a first-order logic specification. The associated xlinkit tool generates "inconsistency relations" between elements. A software architect can use the inconsistency relations to identify the elements that cause inconsistencies between several views,[5] and possibly alter particular elements to resolve inconsistencies. xlinkit is not limited to finding inconsistencies between architectural views. The approach has also been used for the identification of inconsistencies in distributed product catalogs [29], requirement specifications [31], UML diagrams [29], web service compositions [14].

Garlan et al. [18] use the Armani language to express design constraints in Acme and the associated AcmeStudio tool. Acme is a general-purpose, component and connector (C&C)-based ADL with particular support for architectural styles. Design constraints

---

[5] The authors do not distinguish between viewpoints and views. A view as defined in section 2 is called the viewpoint specification in their approach.

can be defined for architectural styles that impose restrictions on how an architectural design is permitted to evolve over time. For example, for a layered architectural style, the constraints will describe that a higher layer is allowed to use a lower layer but not the other way around.

Dijkman and Dumas [11] propose an approach for consistency checking in service composition between four interrelated views.[5] namely interface behavior, provider behavior, choreography, and orchestration. The views are formalized using Petri nets. By specifying relations between the views, the approach enables static verification of a web service composition.

Other examples of consistency checking are described by Boiten et al. [4] and Dijkman et al. [12] in the context of RM-ODP [23], Fradet et al. [17] use graphs and constraint expressions on these graphs, and Radjenovic and Paige [38] developed an ADL and consistency checking in the context of dependable systems. Radjenovic and Paige emphasize that to reach a strong sense of consistency between views, the number and complexity of the constraints increases significantly.

Other approaches deal with this issue of consistency in ADs without first-class relations. The ArchStudio tool for xADL [10] supports plug-ins to analyze an AD. The plug-ins can be used for automatic consistency checking over views. In this case, relations are programmed in the component. In *Software Systems Architecture* [40], Rozanski and Woods provide an extensive checklist of possible relations between different types of views. The list allows software architects to check whether an AD is consistent; however, the relations between views are described only informally.

Composition. Composition of views (sometimes also referred to "merging" or "integration" of views) allows the integration of information from several views. Composed views are useful to get a unified perspective, to understand the interactions between elements from different views, and to perform various types of analysis.

In his doctoral thesis, Egyed [15] presents a framework for integrating multiple heterogenous views. This framework exists of a set of integration activities, including the identification and cross-referencing of related model elements that describe overlapping and thus redundant pieces of information (called mapping). These relations are then used during the differentiation and transformation activities for integrating views with each other. The integrated views serve as a basis for several types of analysis, such as checking consistency.

Boucké et al. [6] introduce three types of relations (unification, refinement and composition) between structural views and demonstrate how these relations allow composition of structural views. Following the 'Having divided to conquer, we must reunite to rule' philosophy [25], the authors state that views can be used to describe concerns, but that relations and the associated composition are essential to bring the views together. Tool-supported composition allows one to easily generate overlays to understand and reason about the integration of several architectural views. The authors have integrated the relations in xADL and the ArchStudio tool suite [5].

Most composition approaches do not distinguish relations from compositions but program the relations directly in a composition algorithm or in composition operators. Abi-Antoun et al. [1] describe an algorithm and associated tool for differentiating and merging C&C views. The authors argue that architects often face the problem of reconciling different versions of architectural models, e.g. by using specific information from two versions to produce a new version that includes changes from both earlier versions. Sabetzadeh et al. [41] envision the use of explicit relations for merging views. Giese and Vilbig [19] present an approach to compose the behavior of several C&C models. The authors mention that views are related, but relations are not first class—instead programmed within the composition algorithm.

Tracing. Tekinerdoğan et al. [43] document explicit trace relations between architectural concerns, the architectural elements that address the concerns, and between architectural elements in general. In case the architectural elements related to a particular concern that are spread across different architectural views, the proposed trace relations span multiple architectural views. With respect to evolution of the software, one can follow the trace links to update and synchronize architectural views, keeping the software architecture consistent.

Model Transformation. A model transformation takes as input a model conforming to a given metamodel and produces as output another model conforming to a given metamodel. Model transformation is central to the domain of model driven architecture (MDA) [32]. We discuss two approaches using relations in the context of MDA: an approach using a refinement relation and another approach using relations for automatic transformation.[6]

Architectural stratification proposed by Atkinson and Kühne [2] combines the strength of separation of concerns and aspect-orientation with component-based frameworks and model-driven architecture. The goal of architectural stratification is to relate different architectural strata[7] so that they best represent a system's crosscutting concerns. Each stratum represents a software architecture on a certain level of abstraction. The authors use stepwise refinement to relate the strata. In each step, a refinement transformation is applied that refines connectors introducing a particular concern. Relations are thus defined as refinement transformations.

Cordero and Salavert [9] use relations on the metamodel level with the goal of automated transformation of architectural models. Example relations are: 'each module is related to a component' and 'each uses relation between modules to a connector'. The combination between the module view and the relations on the metamodel level allows one to automatically generate a component and connector view. The approach proposed by Dijkman et al. [13] is similar, but focuses on the RM-ODP views.

Recently, a standard for model transformation has been defined by the Object Management Group, the Meta Object Facility Query/View/Transformation Specification (QVT) [34]. QVT advocates explicit specification of relations before performing transformations. QVT provides a conceptual model and basic architecture for model-driven transformation tools. Because the standard is very recent, efforts are still on the way to conform approaches and tools to the QVT model.

---

[6] Alternatively model transformations could also be considered as a mechanism, where relations are implemented by transformations between models. We placed it under usage, as model transformations typically also embodies a process, and it is in this model transformation process that relations are used.

[7] An *architectural stratum* is a kind of architectural model as defined in section 2.

3.2 Scope

Scope refers to the extent or range of view relations. From the literature study, we identified four criteria for the scope of a relation: (1) intra vs. inter model type; (2) level of detail; (3) metamodel vs. model; and (4) horizontal vs. vertical.

Intra vs. Inter Model Type. Intra model type relations are relations between the same type of models. An example is a relation between two C&C models. Inter model type relations are relations that involve models of different types. For example, relations between a C&C model and a statechart model.

Several approaches we discussed in previous sections define relations between C&C models only. Examples are Garlan et al. [18], Atkinson and Kühne [2], and Boucké et al. [6]. Dashofy et al. [10] support inter model relations, in particular relations between types, structural elements, and component instances. xlinkit constraints [30] can be defined on any XML document, and as such also supports inter model relations.

Level of Detail. Relations can be described between complete views, between models, and between architectural elements inside views.

Clements et al. [8] use sibling and child relations to relate architectural models.[8] Sibling models document different parts of the same system. These models form a mosaic of the whole view, as if each partial view were a photograph taken by a camera that panned and tilted across the entire view. Child models document the same part of the system but in greater details. This is a coarse-grained kind of refinement. Sibling and parent/child relations are specified at the level of complete models; they do not allow specifying details about which particular architectural elements are related.

Architectural unification proposed by Melton and Garlan [27] supports fine grained specification of relations, up to the level of component interfaces and properties that are associated with the components.

Horizontal vs. Vertical Relations. The term *horizontal* is used for relations between views at the same level of abstraction. *Vertical* relations are either relations between views at different levels of abstraction (such as refinements) or relations with other representations (such as requirements, detailed design or even implementation). The terms *intra phase* and *inter phase* are also used in this context, for horizontal and vertical, respectively.

The approach to architectural stratification [2] is a good example of the use of vertical relations. The strata correspond to models at different levels of abstraction and are step-by-step refined via transformation. Both Nentwich et al. [30] and Radjenovic and Paige [38] propose approaches with explicit support for both horizontal and vertical relations. The latter propose transformation rules to capture relations between subsequent development stages. Muskens et al. [28] is a language-neutral approach that addresses intra and inter phase view relations.

Most other approaches do not define an explicit process to use relations in a vertical way. For example, Armani constraint relations are typically used to specify invariants

---

[8] The authors use the term 'view packets'; in the terminology of section 2, these can be considred architectural models.

over several models at one level. However, it is possible to define a process on top of Acme and Armani that uses constraints to support things like refinement.

Metamodel vs. Model. A metamodel is an explicit model of the constructs and rules to build specific models within a domain of interest. In the terminology of section 2, the metamodel refers to the part of the viewpoint language that defines an individual model type. View relations may be stated with reference to a metamodel or between metamodels.

A well-known example of metamodel relations are the constraints in the superstructure of the UML 2.0 definition [33]. The superstructure defines the language elements of UML 2.0 models and the constraints on how those language elements can be used within diagrams as well as across multiple related models.

Cordero and Salavert [9] require that each module is related with one component, and that each usage association is related with one connector. This enables automatic transformations between the models (section 3.1).

xlinkit constraints include expressions that reference specific points in an XML document [30]. Expressions can refer to elements at the model level as well as the metamodel level.

3.3 Mechanism

Support for relations between views requires constructs in the AD to represent those relations. We have identified three classes of mechanisms from the literature to describe relations between views, namely: (1) direct references; (2) tuples; and (3) expression languages.

Direct References. Elements from one view can refer directly to elements of another view. In this case, the description of the relations between architectural elements of different views is mingled with the view descriptions.

Dashofy et al. [10] use direct references between the architectural views of xADL. xADL allows several views, including a view specifying component types (types view), views showing the structure of the system by connecting component types (structural view) and views showing component instances (instance view). Components in a structural view can refer to their types. Component instances can refer to the structural components they adhere to and instances can refer to an internal structure (refinement) described in a structural view.

AADL [42] uses packages to structure architectural documentation. Packages group architectural elements (component types and instances) into logical blocks, so that there is a clear connection between the concepts of package and architectural view. The relations between the packages are directly described in the packages; i.e. a component instance can directly refer a component type in another package.

Tuples. In mathematics, a relation over sets is defined as a subset of the Cartesian product of the sets. Elements in the relational set are called tuples. Relations modelled as tuples are typically complex in the context of ADs. Architectural views typically contain several architectural models, each model defining several types of elements with possibly complex internal details. This may require one to annotate the tuple with more details of how the elements are related.

Documenting Software Architecture [8] introduces a 'mapping table' to describe the relations between views, as a part of the information "beyond" the views. Mapping tables define a set of tuples of elements from different views (one-to-many, many-to-many, many-to-one). Each table entry is annotated with a textual description to indicate whether the correspondence is partial and to provide additional details of the relation (such as corresponding interfaces). Tables can be used for any relation based on tuples.

Boiten et al. [4] also define relations between elements in a table, and annotate each entry with the type and the level of detail of the relation. The authors define relations between two RM-ODP Engineering views, and between the Engineering view and Computation view. Relations have a formal underpinning in ObjectZ. The details of the relations sometimes contain expressions as defined in the next section.

Expression Language. In general, an expression in mathematics is a combination of names and values, operators, grouping symbols (such as brackets), and possibly variables (free and bound) arranged in a meaningful way. Expressions containing variables may use quantifiers (such as $\forall$ and $\exists$). An expression language defines which expressions are well-formed, and therefore can be used and meaningfully interpreted. In the context of ADs, the expressions impose constraints or rules over (sets of) architectural elements. The complexity of the expression language may vary widely, depending on factors such as the formal system (e.g. first-order logic) on which it is based, the underlying viewpoint languages being related, etc.

The previously mentioned xlinkit tool [30] for automatic consistency checking between architectural views uses constraints. The tool processes XML documents, using a formal underpinning based on an extension of first-order logic. It is possible to describe things such as:

$$\forall c \in \text{'components'} \ (\exists m \in \text{'module'} \ (c.modulename == module.name))$$

The expressions 'components' and 'module' are XPath [44] expressions that select the sets of elements involved in the relation as a tree path in the XML document.

Muskens et al. [28] introduce a general approach for detecting inconsistencies between different views based on relational partition algebra. Its expression language includes named relations and operations such as inclusion, composition, intersection, union, inverse and transitive closure on those relations, but is quantifier-free. The approach introduces the interesting notions of prevailing vs subordinate views, that can be used in horizontal or vertical view relations. The distinction is used, for example, to report violations in the subordinate view, taking the content of the prevailing view as fixed. An example is a constraint between a message sequence diagram and a class diagram that requires that the dependencies between classes implied by the message sequence diagram are present in the class diagram. Checking this constraint is not trivial, since inheritance must be taken into account:

$$((CALLER; CALLEE^{-1}) \uparrow TYPE) \subset (DEPENDENCY \downarrow INHERITANCE*)$$

This rule states that all calls between caller and callee objects, lifted ($\uparrow$) to the types (leading to dependencies between the types of these objects), must be a subset of the dependency set of the class diagram, lowered ($\downarrow$) to inheritance (taking subclasses into account). The upwards arrow and downwards arrow are algebraic functions for respectively lifting or lowering the level of abstraction.

3.4 Discussion

Starting from a thorough study of the literature and our experience, we have proposed a framework for analyzing approaches to relations between views in three dimensions: usage, scope and mechanism. The illustrations from the literature provide a first indication of its usefulness, but the practical value of the framework for software architects remains to be proven. Although we believe that the framework adequately captures the existing work on relations between views, we do not claim that the framework is complete. One may discover additional use cases, and/or refine or extend the current dimensions.

An interesting criterion to add could be the way relations are formalized, and what underlying mechanism is used to support those relations. The nature of the formalization has implications on what analyses can be performed and what outcomes or results can be generated from those analyses (e.g. proofs of consistency, counterexamples, etc.). The underlying mechanism supporting relations can vary widely. Some approaches use first-order logic and a theorem prover to search for inconsistencies. Some establish consistency of two representations by formalizing them in ObjectZ and finding a common refinement.

4 Reflection on Relations between Views in ISO 42010

The revision of ISO 42010 provides an opportunity to capture common concepts and terminology in the area of views and relations between views. We first explain the proposal for relations in the current working draft of ISO 42010 (42010 WD2). Next, we compare the 42010 WD2 proposal with our findings about the literature, embodied in the framework outlined in the previous section.

4.1 Relations between Views in 42010 WD2

The working draft proposes a new concept: *view correspondence* (VC). A VC records a relation between two architectural views to capture: a consistency relation, a traceability relation, a constraint or obligation of one view upon another. Mathematically, a VC is a binary relation. The intent is that an AD might include several VCs to express one or more relations among its views.

> *Example*: Consider two views of a system, S, a hardware view, $HW(S)$, and a software component view, $SC(S)$. If $SC(S)$ includes software components, $e_1, \ldots e_4$, and $HW(S)$ includes hardware platforms, $p_1, \ldots p_4$, a view correspondence between $HW(S)$ and $SC(S)$, specifying which components execute on which platforms, might be:
>
> $$ExecutesOn = \{(c_1, p_1), (c_1, p_4), (c_2, p_2), (c_2, p_3), (c_3, p_3), (c_4, p_4)\}$$

In the context of the framework, this is a tuple-based specification between different types of models (inter model type). The level of detail is architectural elements: each item in the relation is a complete component or platform. *ExecutesOn* describes a horizontal relation between two concrete models.

In addition to VCs, 42010 WD2 introduces *viewpoint correspondence rules* (VCRs). A VCR expresses a required relation between two architectural viewpoints and is realized by VCs on views resulting from the application of those viewpoints within an AD.

> *Example*: Every software component, c_i, as defined by a software component viewpoint applied to system S, $SC(S)$, must execute on one or more platforms, p_j, as defined by a hardware viewpoint applied to that same system S, $HW(S)$.

$$ExecuteOnRule = \forall c_i \in SC(S) : \exists p_a \in HW(S) : (c_i, p_a) \in ExecutesOn$$

In the context of the framework, this is an expression with quantifiers in an expression language between different types of models (inter model type). The level of detail is architectural view elements: each variable is a complete component or platform. The rule describes a horizontal relation between two concrete models.

A VCR imposes the following requirements on VCs (in 42010 WD2):

- For each VCR that applies to an AD, there shall be a VC identified.
- A VCR *holds* in an AD if its associated VC can be shown to satisfy the rule.
- A VCR *is violated* in an AD if its associated VC can be shown not to satisfy the rule.

4.2 Comparison to Framework

Since 42010 WD2 is still a working draft, the effectiveness of the view correspondence proposal remains to be proven. In this section we compare the proposal with our findings in the literature, embodied in the framework of section 3. The discussion is structured according to the criteria of the framework.

Usage. 42010 WD2 contains an open list of possible uses, but stays neutral to what purpose relations are used, which is consistent with the method-neutral stance of the standard. However, a number of limitations which we have identified in the context of scope may imply restrictions on the possible use of relations. We describe these limitations next.

Scope: Model vs. Metamodel. There is a similarity between model and metamodel on the one hand and the concepts of VC and VCR on the other hand.

A VC is a relation between two views, often expressed as a relation at the model level. The similarity between a VCR and a metamodel relation is less obvious. Metamodels (or model types) are part of the viewpoint language and as such not explicitly represented in ISO 42010. A VCR is defined between viewpoints, expressed as a relation between viewpoint languages. From this point of view, a VCR can be considered as a relation at the metamodel level.

Notice that VCR and VC are tightly coupled concepts. Such coupling is typically less explicit between metamodel relations and model relations in the literature.

Scope: Inter vs. Intra. The use of inter vs. intra model type relations is less clear in 42010 WD2. In ISO 42010 a view is a representation of the *whole* system with respect to some concerns. Intra model type relations would be part of the same (viewpoint) language, and would therefore typically be models within the same view. Inter model type relations would be part of different (viewpoint) languages, which may or may not be models in the same view.

This contrasts with our observation of the literature: intra model relations are typically not limited to models that are in a single view. For example, it is quite common to have multiple C&C models in different architectural views.

Scope: Level of detail. VCs and VCRs are not restricted to a particular level of detail, and as such cover the different levels of detail of relations that we have seen in the literature.

Scope: Horizontal vs. Vertical. 42010 WD2 does not state anything about horizontal and vertical relations. The concepts of the standard can be applied in a horizontal or vertical manner.

Mechanism. A standard should be mechanism-neutral. 42010 WD2 does not make explicit statements about the mechanism to be used for view correspondences or viewpoint correspondence rules.

We give a side remark on the term "rule" in VCR, which may be confusing. The idea is that each VCR imposes an obligation on views that must be demonstrated by a VC. The term rule is often used for a specific mechanism to specify relations, suggesting the use of a mathematical expression in the sense of section 3.1. A VCR can just as well be represented as a direct reference or a tuple between language elements.

We have two other small remarks on the terminology. Firstly, the term 'correspondence' is used in the context of RM-ODP, but outside this scope the more neutral term 'relation' seems to be used more often. Secondly, the term *viewpoint* correspondence rule could lead to confusion, since the obligation is imposed on a view. *View* correspondence rule seems closer to the intent of the proposal.

In summary, the 42010 WD2 proposal largely aligns with our observations of the literature. Yet, there is some unclarity with respect to: (1) the advice that intra model relations are typically within a single view; (2) the role of model types; and (3) the terminology of view correspondences and viewpoint correspondence rules. It is hoped these can be clarified upon in future revision drafts.

5   Conclusion

Views and view relations have been studied for a long time. However, existing work on view relations is fragmented. The framework presented in this paper shows that there is a common ground for relations. There are strong arguments for making relations first-class concepts in ADs, treating them on equal terms as architectural views. As soon as an AD contains multiple views, these views are related since they describe the same system. Making the relations explicit improves the clarity of the architectural documentation. It forms the basis for consistency checking, for automatic analysis and verification of quality attributes and system wide properties, for tracing design decisions, etc.

An important observation is that existing ADLs, such as AADL, xADL, Acme, π-ADL [35], Fractal ADL [7] and AO-ADL [37] offer support for multiple types of architectural elements, but do not offer first-class support for architectural views in a way advocated by ISO 42010. ADLs lack facilities for *specifying* and *relating* several architectural views that cope with a diversity of architectural concerns. To the best of our knowledge, the AIM ADL for embedded systems [38] is the only notable exception. Imperative to exploit such view-based ADLs will be tool support. A tool can interactively suggest view relations based on particular heuristics, such as similar names and similar architectural patterns. Visual editors can simplify the specification of relations between views. On the fly generation and visualization of overlay views, or highlighting the elements involved in a relation, can improve the understanding and use of relations between views.

As a closing remark, a first-class concept of relations is just the start. A lot of work must be done to concerning practical problems like conflicts between views, integration of views, comparisons between different approaches in modeling the same views, and how to enforce consistency amongst views.

Acknowledgement

We are grateful to Christina von Flach, Peter Eeles, Bedir Tekinerdoğan, Hasan Sozer, Tomi Männistö, Thorsten Keuler and the other attendees of the Birds-of-a-Feather session on Relations between Views at WICSA 2008 for the interesting discussions. We also express our appreciation for the valuable input and feedback from Dimitri Van Landuyt, John Klein, Rich Paige and Steven Op de beeck.

This research is partially funded by the Interuniversity Attraction Poles Programme Belgian State, Belgian Science Policy, and by the Research Fund K.U.Leuven. Nelis is supported by the Institute for the Promotion of Innovation through Science and Technology in Flanders (IWT-Vlaanderen). Danny is supported by the Foundation for Scientific Research in Flanders (FWO-Vlaanderen).

References

1. Abi-Antoun, M., Aldrich, J., Nahas, N., Schmerl, B., Garlan, D.: Differencing and merging of architectural views. Automated Software Engineering 15(1), 35–74 (2008)
2. Atkinson, C., Kühne, T.: Aspect-oriented development with stratified frameworks. IEEE Software 20(1), 81–89 (2003)
3. Bass, L., Clements, P., Kazman, R.: Software Architectures in Practice, 2nd edn. Addison-Wesley, Reading (2003)
4. Boiten, E., Bowman, H., Derrick, J., Linington, P., Steen, M.: Viewpoint consistency in ODP. Computer Networks 34(3), 503–537 (2000)
5. Boucké, N.: xADLComposition: a tool for view composition in xADL, http://www.cs.kuleuven.be/~nelis/xADLComposition
6. Boucké, N., Holvoet, T.: View composition in multi-agent architectures. Special issue on Multiagent systems and software architecture, International Journal of Agent-Oriented Software Engineering (IJAOSE) 2(2), 3–33 (2008)

7. Bruneton, E., Coupaye, T., Leclercq, M., Quéma, V., Stefani, J.B.: The fractal component model and its support in java: Experiences with auto-adaptive and reconfigurable systems. Softw. Pract. Exper. 36(11-12), 1257–1284 (2006)
8. Clements, P., Bachman, F., Bass, L., Garlan, D., Ivers, J., Little, R., Nord, R., Stafford, J.: Documenting Software Architectures, Views and Beyond. Addison-Wesley, Reading (2003)
9. Cordero, R.L., Salavert, I.R.: Relating software architecture views by using MDA. In: Gervasi, O., Gavrilova, M.L. (eds.) ICCSA 2007, Part III. LNCS, vol. 4707, pp. 104–114. Springer, Heidelberg (2007)
10. Dashofy, E., van der Hoek, A., Taylor, R.: A comprehensive approach for the development of modular software architecture description languages. ACM Transactions on Software Engineering and Methodology (TOSEM) 14(2), 199–245 (2005)
11. Dijkman, R.M., Dumas, M.: Service-oriented design: a multi-viewpoint approach. International journal of cooperative information systems 13(4), 337–368 (2004)
12. Dijkman, R.M., Quartel, D., van Sinderen, M.J.: Consistency in multi-viewpoint design of enterprise information systems. Information and Software Technology (2007)
13. Dijkman, R.M., Quartel, D.A.C., Pires, L.F., van Sinderen, M.J.: An approach to relate viewpoints and modeling languages. In: Proceedings. Seventh IEEE International Enterprise Distributed Object Computing Conference, pp. 14–27 (2003)
14. Dingwall-Smith, A., Finkelstein, A.: Checking complex compositions of web services against policy constraints. In: MSVVEIS, pp. 94–103. INSTICC PRESS (2007)
15. Egyed, A.: Heterogeneous view integration and its automation. PhD thesis, Los Angeles, CA, USA, Adviser-Barry William Boehm (2000)
16. Finkelstein, A., Kramer, J., Nuseibeh, B., Finkelstein, L., Goedicke, M.: Viewpoints: a framework for integrating multiple perspectives in system development. International Journal of Software Engineering and Knowledge Engineering 2(1), 31–57 (1992)
17. Fradet, P., Le Métayer, D., Périn, M.: Consistency checking for multiple view software architectures. SIGSOFT Softw. Eng. Notes 24(6), 410–428 (1999)
18. Garlan, D., Monroe, R.T., Wile, D.: ACME: Architectural description of component-based systems. In: Foundations of Component-Based Systems. Cambridge University Press, Cambridge (2000)
19. Giese, H., Vilbig, A.: Separation of non-orthogonal concerns in software architecture and design. Software and Systems Modeling 5(2), 136–169 (2006)
20. Hofmeister, C., Nord, R., Soni, D.: Applied software architecture. Addison-Wesley Longman Publishing Co., Boston (2000)
21. IEEE1471. Recommended practice for architectural description of software-intensive systems (ANSI/IEEE-Std-1471) (September 2000)
22. ISO. Second working draft of Systems and Software Engineering – Architectural Description (ISO/IEC WD2 42010). Working document: ISO/IEC JTC 1/SC 7 N 000
23. ISO. ISO/IEC 10746-2 Information Technology – Open Distributed Processing – Reference Model: Foundations (September 1996)
24. ISO. ISO/IEC 42010 Systems and Software Engineering – Architectural Description (July 2007)
25. Jackson, M.A.: Some complexities in computer-based systems and their implications for system development. In: Proceedings of Comp. Euro. 1990. IEEE Computer Society Press, Los Alamitos (1990)
26. Kruchten, P.: The 4+1 view model of architecture. IEEE Software 12(6), 42–50 (1995)
27. Melton, R., Garlan, D.: Architectural unification. In: CASCON 1997: Proceedings of the conference of the Centre for Advanced Studies on Collaborative research, p. 18 (1997)
28. Muskens, J., Bril, R.J., Chaudron, M.R.V.: Generalizing consistency checking between software views. In: WICSA 2005: Proceedings of the 5th Working IEEE/IFIP Conference on Software Architecture, pp. 169–180. IEEE Computer Society, Los Alamitos (2005)

29. Nentwich, C., Capra, L., Emmerich, W., Finkelstein, A.: xlinkit: a consistency checking and smart link generation service. ACM Trans. Inter. Tech. 2(2), 151–185 (2002)
30. Nentwich, C., Emmerich, W., Finkelstein, A., Ellmer, E.: Flexible consistency checking. ACM Trans. Softw. Eng. Methodol. 12(1), 28–63 (2003)
31. Nuseibeh, B., Kramer, J., Finkelstein, A.: Expressing the relationships between multiple views in requirements specification. In: International Conference on Software Engineering, pp. 187–196 (1993)
32. OMG. Model Driven Architecture (MDA)
33. OMG. Unified Modeling Language 2.0: Superstructure (August 2004)
34. OMG. Meta Object Facility 2.0: Query/View/Transformation Specification (August 2007)
35. Oquendo, F.: Pi-adl: an architecture description language based on the higher-order typed pi-calculus for specifying dynamic and mobile software architectures. SIGSOFT Softw. Eng. Notes 29(3), 1–14 (2004)
36. Perry, D.E., Wolf, A.L.: Foundations for the study of software architecture. SIGSOFT Softw. Eng. Notes 17(4), 40–52 (1992)
37. Pinto, M., Fuentes, L.: Ao-adl: An adl for describing aspect-oriented architectures. In: Moreira, A., Grundy, J. (eds.) Early Aspects Workshop 2007 and EACSL 2007. LNCS, vol. 4765, pp. 94–114. Springer, Heidelberg (2007)
38. Radjenovic, A., Paige, R.F.: The role of dependency links in ensuring architectural view consistency. In: WICSA 2008: Proceedings of the Seventh Working IEEE/IFIP Conference on Software Architecture (WICSA 2008), pp. 199–208 (2008)
39. Ross, D.T.: Structured Analysis (SA): a language for communicating ideas. IEEE Transactions on Software Engineering SE-3(1), 16–34 (1977)
40. Rozanski, N., Woods, E.: Software Systems Architecture. Addison-Wesley, Reading (2005)
41. Sabetzadeh, M., Nejati, S., Easterbrook, S., Chechik, M.: A relationship-driven approach to view merging. SIGSOFT Softw. Eng. Notes 31(6), 1–2 (2006)
42. SAE: Society of Automotive Engineers. Architecture analysis and design language (AADL)
43. Tekinerdogan, B., Hofmann, C., Aksit, M.: Modeling traceability of concerns for synchronizing architectural views. Journal of Object Technology 6(7), 7–25 (2007)
44. W3C. XML path language (XPath), http://www.w3.org/TR/xpath

How Do Agents Affect Modifiability? A Comparison between Two Architectures for Intelligent Virtual Environments for Training

Gonzalo Méndez and Angélica de Antonio

Computer Science School
Technical University of Madrid
gonzalo@gordini.ls.fi.upm.es, angelica@fi.upm.es

Abstract. The use of agents is spreading as a means to develop different kinds of software systems, among which we can find Intelligent Virtual Environments for Training. The agent community has already started to pay attention to software engineering issues to develop agent-oriented systems, but they are mainly focused on methodologies and, to some extent, design patterns. However, not much attention has been paid to software architecture for the moment. We compare two agent-based software architectures for Intelligent Virtual Environments for Training that are intended to be easily extended and modified. The first one was designed using an organizational approach recommended by some agent oriented methodologies. The second one is a redesign of the first architecture using more formal principles and methods of software architecture design. A comparison between both architectures highlights the need to pay more attention to software architecture design in this field.

1 Introduction

An Intelligent Tutoring System (ITS) is an application of computer science to education that has a particular structure shown in Fig 1 [1,2]. They are different from other educational software in that they are *intelligent*, since their purpose is to adapt teaching to the abilities and characteristics of every student. In addition, their structure was thought to make it possible to easily change the teaching domain (expert module), the tutoring strategy (tutoring module) or the way students are modeled in the system (student module). However, the biggest success of ITSs is the fact that a great deal of researchers in educational software use the structure shown in Fig. 1, with research groups specializing in the development of each of the different modules.

Educational Virtual Environments are software systems that make use of three dimensional Virtual Environments (VEs) for education and training. Their development has a quite short history, dating from the mid-nineties, and in some cases they have evolved from the necessity to integrate a Virtual Environment with an ITS. The use of Virtual Environments in fields such as military or industrial training has proven to be a very promising application area, so part of

R. Morrison, D. Balasubramaniam, and K. Falkner (Eds.): ECSA 2008, LNCS 5292, pp. 82–97, 2008.

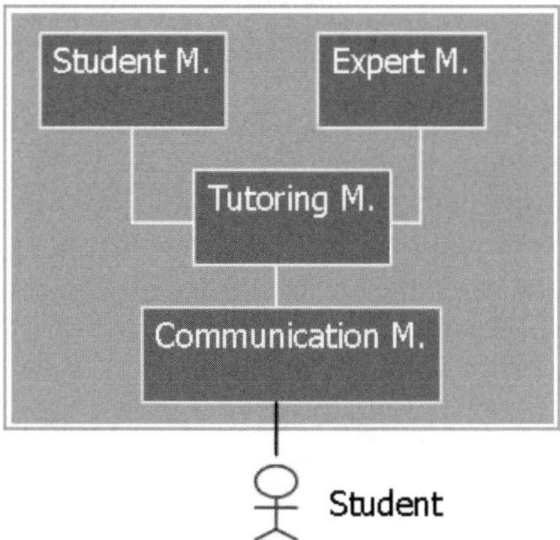

Fig. 1. Architecture of an ITS

the education community are making use of them to develop Intelligent Virtual Environments for Training (IVET), which are the conjunction of an ITS and a Virtual Environment for training.

The youth of the field, together with the complexity and variety of the technologies involved, have led to a situation in which neither the architectures nor the development processes have been standardized yet. Therefore, almost every new system is developed from scratch, in an ad-hoc way, with very specific solutions and monolithic architectures (even if they allegedly make use of the ITS structure), and in many cases forgetting the principles and techniques of the Software Engineering discipline [3].

The MAEVIF project (*Model for the Application of Intelligent Virtual Environments to Education*) was the result of several experiences integrating VEs and intelligent tutors [4,5] that served to point out the problems that commonly arise in such integrations. The objective of the MAEVIF project was to define a model for the application of intelligent virtual environments to education and training, which involved: the definition of a generic model for intelligent learning environments based on the use of virtual worlds; the definition of an open and flexible agent-based software architecture to support the generic model of an Intelligent Virtual Environment for Training; the design and implementation of a prototype authoring tool that simplifies the development of IVETs, based on the defined architecture; and the definition of a set of methodological recommendations for the development of IVETs.

In this paper we present two different approaches to the design of a software architecture for IVETs. The first one is the result of applying a specific Agent Oriented Software Engineering methodology, while the second is the result of applying more specific, architecture centric techniques. Our aim is to use our system as a case study for the application of general software engineering techniques to the development of agent-oriented software, since we believe the agent community is not making enough use of the knowledge produced by the software engineering community in general, and the software architecture community in particular.

In the remainder of the paper we briefly describe the first version of the architecture and the results of evaluating it (section 2). Then, we describe how the agent-based software architecture has been designed using software architecture principles (section 3) and how it is being evaluated (section 4). After that, we present some related work where agents have been used to develop IVETs (section 5). Finally, we present some conclusions and ongoing work (section 6).

2   An Agent-Based Architecture for IVETs

There are two main reasons why we have chosen agents to develop this system instead of a more traditional approach, either object or component oriented. The first reason, as described in [6] is the fact that, given the increasing complexity that the development of IVETs involves, agents represent a powerful tool to use abstraction as a way to face complexity. In addition, the fact that many agent platforms are developed on top of object oriented languages makes it possible to take advantage of all the possibilities provided by these languages (i.e. JADE and Java).

The second reason is that, although a widely accepted definition of agent does not currently exist, many authors agree on a set of features that agents must have, among which we can find both proactivity and situatedness. Given the fact that IVETs are a highly interactive kind of application, proactivity is a feature that is very well suited for their development, since it facilitates the design of tutors that interact with the students in a human-like way. In addition, training inside an IVET makes it necessary for the tutor to be aware of the structure and state of the environment where that training is taking place. Therefore, situatedness is a feature that makes it possible to manage that information in a more natural way.

This does not mean that the mere use of agents is the solution for all problems, but properly used they are likely to ease the design and implementation of a suitable solution.

2.1   A Hierarchical Approach

Taking the structure described in the previous section as a starting point, the next step was to decide which software agents were necessary to transform it into an agent-oriented architecture, which has been designed using the GAIA methodology [6]. In this methodology, the authors suggest the use of the *organizational metaphor* to design the software architecture, which requires the analysis of the real world organization in order to emulate its structure. This approach does not always work (depending on particular organization conditions), but in this case, considering the architecture of an ITS as the organization to reproduce, it is possible to imitate its structure to develop the architecture.

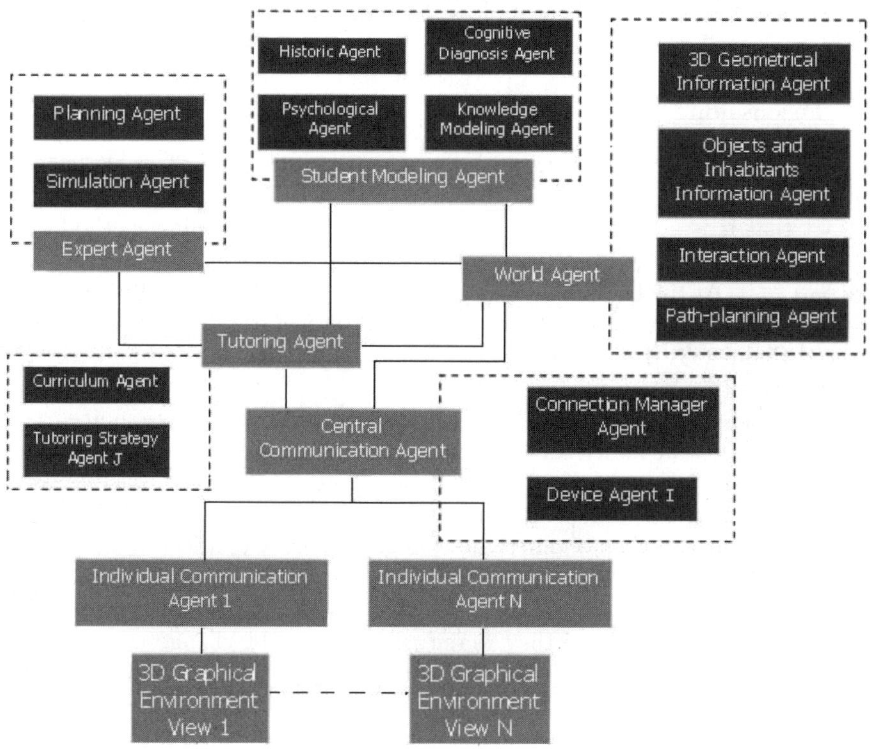

Fig. 2. Decomposition view of the agent-based architecture

There is an additional reason to use an ITS structure as a starting point: the ITS architecture shown in Fig. 1 is widely used by the educational software community. Therefore, if we aim at being able to exchange elements between different applications, making use of a widely used, well known structure is likely to facilitate this task.

The ITS architecture was transformed, from a modular point of view, into an agent-based architecture. It has five agents corresponding to the four modules of the ITS architecture plus an agent that represents the Virtual World: Communication Agent, Student Modeling Agent, Expert Agent, Tutoring Agent and World Agent.

Analyzing the responsibilities of these agents, some additional roles can be identified that point to the creation of new, subordinate agents that can carry them out, subsequently giving rise to a hierarchical multi-agent architecture. Each subordinate agent is in charge of managing some process and the information related to it, while each supervisor agent is in charge of coordinating its subordinate agents and communicating them with other subordinate agents through their respective supervisor. A decomposition view of this architecture can be seen in Fig. 2.

For more details about this architecture, we suggest reading [7] or a more detailed description in [8].

2.2 Discussion

All along the design and development of the architecture, one of the aspects that has had a bigger impact on it has been the planning process, since, due to the fact that it is a collaborative task, a change in the planning method or in the way that knowledge is represented may imply changes in all the agents that take part in it. At the beginning, a simple STRIPS planner [9] was implemented. However, trying to substitute it with one based on SHOP2 (Simple Hierarchical Ordered Planner 2) [10] showed that it was far more complicated and required more changes than expected.

Another aspect we tested was how easy it was to add new functionality to the IVET. To do this, we added an embodied tutor whose goal was to observe what happened in the VE and follow the student to supervise him. It was necessary to add two new agents and, although it was quite easy to make these changes, it soon became clear that any non-trivial change was likely to affect at least one of the supervisor agents (the one that supervises the modified agent) if not more. In addition, all the agents knew of the existence and identity of the agents they had to communicate with, so they were easily affected by changes.

There were some other factors that made us think that a redesign of the architecture was necessary, both at design and implementation levels. One of them was the poor performance the system offered when several students were taking part in a training session. Several tests pointed out that the agent platform presented a fairly good performance, and so did the VE. The problem arose when running both of them at the same time in different machines, which made us think of poor communication performance.

In addition, we were having problems when trying to add new functionality, since it was not clear whether some responsibilities were to be assigned to the expert agent or to the world agent, both of which started to be too coupled for the system to be modifiable. This is a problem that usually arises when establishing classifications and hierarchies: if the criteria used for classification changes or some elements dont fully fall under one of the categories, then the decomposition degrades quite quickly. This was the case with our architecture.

Finally, there were other facts that pointed out the unsuitability of the architecture. Among them, some are described in [11] as an indication of a poor design, such as the proliferation of agents to carry out small tasks, the difficulty to assign responsibilities to an agent or the existence of agents that carry out actions for which an agent is not needed. These problems were caused, at least partially, by the lack of an architectural design method in a not very mature field like IVETs.

3   Architectural Redesign

The main theoretical support to redesign the architecture has been the body of work on software architecture developed at the Software Engineering Institute (SEI) [12,13], such as Attribute Driven Design (ADD) and Architecture Tradeoff Analysis Method (ATAM). Their purpose is to design and evaluate a software architecture driven by the quality attributes desired for it, instead of only the functionality. A set of scenarios is used to help identify the quality attributes that are relevant for the architecture, based on the stakeholders interests, and to evaluate the architecture in order to identify potential risks.

The other important support has been provided by the use of *information hiding* [14]. The design decisions that are encapsulated in each module are related to the changes that are perceived to be likely over the system's life. The way to design is to use abstraction as a means to face complexity and facilitate changes.

Although we planned to use ADD as the architectural design method, we discarded it after a few design sessions because of two reasons. The first reason is the fact that ADD is based on a hierarchical system decomposition, and one that does not allow elements to have more than one father. After the experience gained with the previous architecture, we did not think a hierarchical structure was what we wanted to obtain. In addition, one of the problems we had with the first architecture was the fact that some agents were not clearly under the supervision of one of the five supervisor agents. The second reason has to do with the complexity of decomposing a module in more than four or five elements, which was likely to be the case (in the current design, the ITS consists of nine different kinds of agents).

We soon found two more grounded reasons to discard ADD as a design method. The first one is Parnas argument expressed in [15], where he clearly states that, although maybe desirable, information hiding and hierarchical structure do not always go together. On the contrary, we consider information hiding to be a design criterion, and not just a decomposition one. The other reason can be found in [16], where the author analyzes Simon's "Architecture of Complexity" and identifies the historical reasons that made hierarchical structure a predominant design mechanism.

Agent systems are intrinsically peer-to-peer (after all, they were born in the distributed artificial intelligence field), where each agent is a peer that makes use of services offered by other agents to carry out the responsibilities assigned to it. Therefore, this is the approach we have followed to design the new architecture.

Like ADD suggests, we have started by selecting the architectural drivers for our application, some of which were very well identified thanks to the analysis of the previous system. However, instead of following a decomposition approach, we have worked using an iterative an incremental approach.

If we think of a system we need to extend, we don't face this task by decomposing some part of the system. Instead, we usually try to make the new parts fit using the architectural mechanisms we used to design the existing architecture. Thus, this is the approach we have followed. We have started by designing a core architecture with a very small functionality, and we have proceeded by adding new functionality in each iteration.

As Haythorne states in [17], a system is only modifiable in the points that are designed to accept modifications, and we can have such a design only if we know the modifications we expect to happen. For the initial architectural design, we had a fairly clear idea of the modifications we were going to add (those corresponding to the functionality we wanted the system to have), so in each iteration we proceeded by adding one of the modules we had identified as likely to be substituted, along with what the existing modules would need to use from the new ones. Every time a feature had to be added, or a change had to be made, it was tested against the architectural drivers until a way was found to satisfy them. At that moment, the change was added to the architecture.

This approach to the architectural design has been useful in two ways. First, it has allowed us to make sure the architectural drivers have been taken into account or where and why they have not. Second, it has also made it possible to identify existing dependencies between agents, so we have obtained a list of possible changes we may have to make when substituting a specific agent.

In addition, this design method has allowed us to test the service oriented approach we have used to design the system (which we describe below) and we have been able to make sure that, with the information we have about the system and possible changes, the architecture may be easily modified to include them.

This is probably one of the issues ADD still has to address, since it is not always possible to face a new design or modification as a (hierarchical or not) decomposition.

3.1   Quality Attributes

The design started with the definition of a set of quality scenarios to establish what kind of changes were to be considered by the design. In general, this changes have to do with the ability to substitute an agent with a different one that provides a similar functionality, or to move some responsibility from one agent to another. This is required because one of the objectives of the system is to be used as a test-bed for teams developing just some of the elements of the ITS (e.g. the student modelling or the tutoring strategy).

Another kind of change is the possibility to turn off some functionality, such as supervision, so that the student can use the system in an exploratory way without the tutor interrupting him (although the system would continue registering his actions), or even disabling tutoring completely.

The system is also required to be easily extended, so that new agents that provide new functionality can be added without having to make changes in the existing ones (at least, in the ones that don't make direct use of the new functionality).

Taking into account that training is carried out in a VE, all these modifiability requirements cannot be an obstacle for the main objective of the system, which is to provide students with a training environment as similar as possible to the real one. For that, it is of utmost importance to keep performance close to real time. If not, training in the IVET may be somehow frustrating for the student, which may cause the training experience to be less efficient than other, more traditional, methods.

There is a usability attribute, adaptation to the user, that has not been considered explicitly because it is already included in the features of an ITS. The student modelling is used to personalize the training process to the student's abilities and needs, so it has not been necessary to consider it as an additional quality attribute to take into account.

3.2   Design Decisions

With the described modifiability objectives in mind, the approach we followed was to keep the agents as anonymous as possible, so that no agent directly knows which agents are carrying out the actions they need to successfully complete their responsibilities. To achieve this, during system startup, the agents announce in the system's yellow pages the services they are capable to provide to other agents. Thus, an agent does not know how many or what kind of agents there are in the system; they just know that there is an agent that can provide a certain service they need. This way, it is easier to change the agent that provides a service, as long as the service is provided in the same terms the original one was.

Once the agent finds the service it is looking for, it can act in two different ways. If the service involves frequent updates, the agent subscribes to an update list, so that every time an update arrives, it is immediately informed about it. If, on the contrary, the agent only needs to request the service at specific times, it annotates which agent it has to request the service to. In both cases, the decision is made at runtime, so changes in the design are easier to carry out. We considered the possibility of giving the chance to change the service provider any time during runtime, but we discarded it because it is not likely to happen in a system of this kind.

The agents communicate with each other exchanging FIPA ACL messages. Since it is a quite extended formalism, the difficulties may come from the communication protocol. We have designed a fairly simple communication protocol for a given agent to request a service from another agent. Agent A sends a request to agent B, who acknowledges the reception of the request. Then agent B carries out the required actions and sends agent A the result of the execution of the service (or a message with the reasons why it could not be carried out). Agent A acknowledges the reception of the result and the communication stops until another service request is required.

A similar mechanism has been used to communicate the agent platform with the VE, but with an even simpler communication mechanism. A communication centre has been designed where both the agent platform and the VE send their messages for other applications to receive them. Each application subscribes to the messages it is interested in receiving, so that, for example, different VEs or different versions of a VE only receive the messages they know how to handle.

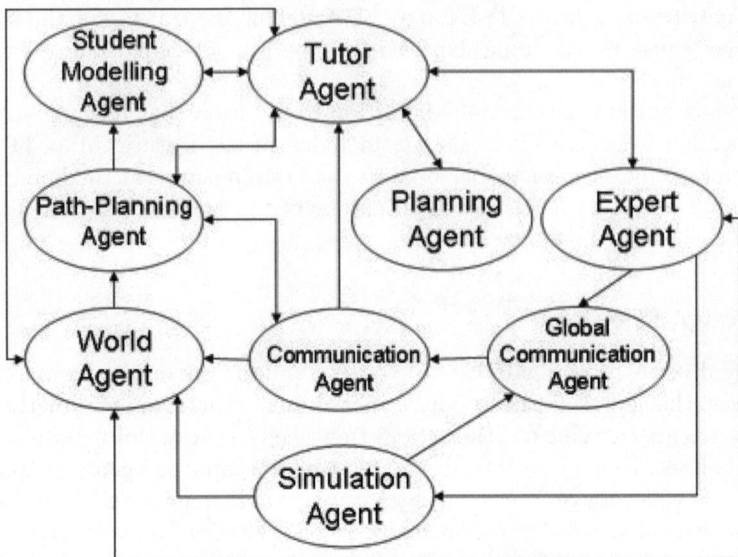

Fig. 3. Peer-to-peer view of the new architecture. Ellipses represent agents and arrows show communication channels.

We have used this possibility all along the development of the agent platform, so we could send the messages we wanted to test from a console instead of having to run the VE and carry out a specific procedure before the message we were interested in could be sent.

We have also made use of configuration files to set up the training session. Thus, the description of the procedures to be trained, the composition of the scenarios, the objectives of the activity, its participants or the parametrization of the tutoring strategy are all read from several configuration files, which allows changes in the way the system behaves without further changes in the design.

3.3 Resulting Architecture

The resulting architecture is the one shown in Fig. 3. The picture shows the structure of the architecture as it is currently designed, where all the agents are represented along with the communication channels (the yellow pages are not represented, since all the agents communicate with them).

During runtime, there is only one agent of each kind, except for the agents that are directly related with students: the Student Modelling Agent and the Communication Agent. This is so because, having several students, the system can handle the communication with them in parallel. In addition, if the agent platform needs to be distributed in different machines, the distribution can be made in terms of the number of students.

The main differences with the former architecture are:

- There is no hierarchical structure. Since the existence of the supervisor agents was due to modifiability reasons, and it was only achieved in a low degree, it has been considered preferable to use a peer-to-peer style.
- It uses a publish-subscribe style to offer a service oriented behaviour. Agents advertise their services in the yellow pages and other agents can subscribe to the services they are interested in. This is one of the mechanisms that introduces a higher degree of modifiability in the system.
- Task planning is not a collaborative task any more. The planning agent acts as a wrapper [18] for the planner, hiding details of its functioning to the rest of the system and enabling the change of the planing algorithm with a lower impact than collaborative planning had.
- Extended support for a simulator. Some systems such as the one described in [19] simulate environmental events that may be caused by external factors, such as changes in the state of a patient. In the cited system, events are directly simulated in the VE, but it may also be desirable to use an external simulator in cases where it has already been implemented or when it has a complex behaviour. The simulation agent can now simulate simple systems, but it can also receive information from a simulation running together with the VE or act as a wrapper of an external simulation.
- The tutoring strategy can be adjusted by changing some parameters that are read from a configuration file during the initialization of the system. These parameters are expected to change dynamically with the new design of the student modelling agent.
- The world agent is responsible for maintaining an ontology that stores the state of the VE. A simple reasoning engine has been added so that the world agent is able to provide richer answers to the student.
- A message centre is now used to communicate the different subsystems that form the training system. Each subsystem registers in the message centre and requests the kind of information it is interested in. Currently, in addition to the VEs and the ITS, a command line console can also connect to the message centre with debug purposes.

After the redesign, the implemented system has not shown any of the undesired properties the former one had. Performance is quite good, with no apparent latencies, two new agents and some new responsibilities have been quite easy to add and all agents seem to have well defined roles in the architecture. We have not been able to test the effects of changing the planner, since that change has not been required for the moment, although the evaluation we have run suggests it should not have a big impact on the architecture, given that it is now under the responsibility of a single agent.

There is one sensitivity point we have not been able to avoid, which has to do with the dependency there is between the tutoring agent and the student modelling agent. However, this dependency has to do with the original ITS architecture, and trying to solve it would require a completely different design approach that would probably make the substitution of these two agents a very problematic task.

4   Evaluation

In addition to the more formal design and documentation of the software architecture, we are currently evaluating the suitability of the architecture to our needs both at architectural and runtime levels.

At the architectural level, the evaluation requires the use of quality scenarios provided by the stakeholders to identify relevant quality attributes. We are trying to gather a thorough collection of scenarios that gives us a better understanding of the implications of the design decisions we have made. In order to do it, we have run an ATAM session and we are planing to run another one in the context of a 3-year research project, ENVIRA, that has already started in conjunction with two other research groups that will be using the multiagent system to develop their own training systems.

In the first session, the participants were the members of the development team, and we only made use of some steps of Phase 0 and of Phase 2 of ATAM, as described in [13], since all of them were familiar with the architecture. The main objectives of this session were to identify and evaluate *use case scenarios* and *growth scenarios*.

Given the composition of the group that took part in the evaluation, no significant results were obtained in terms of use case scenarios, although we have been able to check that the design decisions we made while designing the architecture were still valid. As for the growth scenarios, we were able to identify sensitivity points that we will have to cope with in the ENVIRA project. These sensitivity points have to do with the addition of a new student modelling scheme and a cognitive architecture for virtual characters managed by agents.

We have already scheduled a second ATAM session where the members of the other two research teams will also take part. In this session, we expect to get more results about growth scenarios related to their assignments in the project and a few exploratory scenarios provided by the members of the three research groups that are taking part in the ENVIRA project.

To test the system at runtime level, we are developing it in an iterative way. Each agent is being developed apart from the rest of the system, and the agents they need to communicate with have been substituted by 'dummy' agents. At the end of each iteration, the dummy agents are removed and substituted by the agents that are under development. This way, the development keeps focused on three aspects: adherence to the designed communication protocols; change of one agent by a different one, even if it is as simple as the dummy agents are; turning some functionalities on and off, with the aid of the dummy agents (although another mechanism is to be designed so that the dummy agents are not necessary to turn off functionalities).

There is already a functional application that offers much of the functionality that the previous version provided. For the moment, the student modelling is quite simple, as well as the simulation agent. In contrast, the tutoring agent is capable of supervising the student, providing different levels of hints and answers to the student's questions. The planning agent is already capable of planning a procedure and replanning alternatives in response to the student's actions, and the world an expert agents provide support to the tutoring agent, so that it can provide better assistance to the student according to the state of the environment and the characteristics of the procedure the student is training. Both the agent platform and the VE show an adequate performance when running at the same time in the same or different machines, either with one or two students. Further testing is needed to add more students, but with the current results we expect the system to behave better than the previous version.

5   Related Work

There are several projects aiming at the use of VR for education and training supported by intelligent agents. The first ones were developed over a decade ago, and the most representative among them are Steve [20], Adele [21], Cosmo [22], Herman the Bug [23] and Vincent [24]. What all of them have in common is the fact that the primary objective in all of them was to develop an embodied pedagogical agent to support education and training. Each of them tried to solve some of the problems that this emerging discipline posed.

None of these systems are structured as multiagent systems, but as a single agent that inhabits a particular virtual world, and each of them exhibits its own internal architecture. Even so, they have been the key to identify some of the issues that researches are still trying to solve in a satisfactory way.

There are some examples of multiagent systems that support education and training without using VEs. That is the case of FILIP, a multiagent system for training based on simulations [25] to provide training for air controllers. The system is composed by seven agents that cover the modules of an ITS: one for the student, one for the expert, three for the tutor (skill development, curriculum and instructor agents) and two other agents related to the communication with the learning environment and the user.

Baghera is another example of multiagent system used to teach geometry [26]. The aim of this system is to study emergent behaviours in multiagent systems. What makes this system more interesting is the fact that agents are organized in two levels, and the number of agents is not fix, but varies according to the number of students connected to the system. Each student is assisted by three agents: the personal interface agent, which monitors the student's actions, the tutor agent and the mediator agent. In addition, the tutor is assisted by two agents: the personal interface agent and the assistant agent. All these agents are supported by second level agents of four different kinds, which are in charge of evaluating the student's actions. This is made through a voting mechanism that causes the emerging behaviours that are the subject of study.

The systems that are closer to the one described in this paper are those that are based on multi-agent systems and make use of VEs to support training. A good example is MASCARET (Multi-Agent Systems to simulate Collaborative, Adaptive and Realistic Environments for Training) [27], an agent-based IVET that has been used to train firemen in operation management. In this system, agents are divided in organizations, each of which controls different aspects of the organization: physical, social, pedagogical, mediation, and human interaction.

The agents that integrate the pedagogical organization cover the four modules of an ITS, plus a fifth module that is in charge of controlling the mistakes an student may make. The expert agent communicates with the social and physical organizations to be able to know what to to and what objects and agents are involved in an action.

Lahystotrain is an IVET developed to train surgeons in laparoscopy and hysteroscopy interventions [19]. This systems contains five agents which help the student in the training process. One of them is the tutor, which supervises the student and registers his actions. An assistant agent provides explanations and interrupts him when he makes a mistake. These agents have an ad-hoc architecture tailored to suit their responsibilities. The other three agents take the role of an auxiliary surgeon, a nurse and an anaesthetist that play their role within the team. Their architecture is the same for all three, and it is a kind of BDI architecture with a perception module, a reasoning engine and an action control module. The student must learn what the role of these three agents is and how to coordinate them.

What most of these systems have in common is the fact that they have been developed to solve a specific problem, but only a few of them have been designed to be reusable, at least to some extent [20,28], and apparently none of them have taken advantage of the existing knowledge on software architecture. This is an aspect that was already put forward in [29], where three main problems are mentioned: the fact that most research groups develop only part of the systems, which does not give them a view about the whole design; systems are tailored to solve specific problems; and designs are not evolutive. They claim that an ITS can be developed as a set of independent agents that exchange messages in a predefined language, and they use the concept of federated architecture [30] to articulate their system GIA. To some extent, the architecture described in this paper follows those guidelines, although the federated architecture has been substituted by a service oriented approach and a more formal software engineering support has been used.

There are few examples of multiagent systems that have been evaluated using ATAM. Among these systems, we can highlight the work presented in [31], where the authors report a successful utilization of an ATAM workshop to evaluate an agent-based software architecture for an industrial transportation system. Although they do not explain the method that was used to design the architecture, they suggest they took quality attributes into account when designing it.

Another work reporting the use of ATAM is the one described in [32], which is the first reference we have found about the use of ATAM to evaluate a multiagent system. In this work, the authors put forward what they think to be relevant attributes in agent-based systems: performance predictability, security against data corruption and spoofing, resilience to modifiability of the environment and availability and fault tolerance. Although not all of them are applicable to the system presented in this paper, this work constitutes an important approach from agent-oriented software development to more traditional software construction.

6   Conclusions and Ongoing Work

It is getting common for Virtual Environments for Training to be designed as Multi-Agent Systems, since agents provide a higher level of abstraction than objects and this helps to face the increasing complexity that involves the development of these systems.

Many authors claim, without further proof, that their systems are flexible because they are using agents to build them, and to some extent we may have made the same mistake in our first version of the architecture. Although it had been designed with modifiability in mind, it soon became clear that successive modifications were making the architecture degrade quite quickly. That experience is one more example to show that the mere use of agents (or any other technology) does not guarantee that the application developed using them will have certain properties. On the contrary, the result may be even worse if the design decisions have not been made with care.

In the second version of the architecture, we have tried to take advantage of the growing experience in the field of software architecture, even if it is not specifically agent oriented – something that is not considered to be necessary at the architectural level [12] –. Even so, we have used agents in the architectural design because they involve the use of certain artifacts, such as yellow pages or asynchronous message passing, that are relevant in the architectural design.

However, we have not been able to use ADD for the architectural design, given the fact that a hierarchical decomposition does not seem to suit our needs. A review of the new version of ADD [33] shows it is based on the same design strategy, so we still need a different design approach that is not based on hierarchical structure and decomposition. Even so, designing with quality attributes as architectural drivers as ADD promotes has resulted in a design that, up to now, has proven to be more modifiable than the previous design was.

As for the use of ATAM, it is a valuable tool from which we still expect to obtain useful results as soon as the second workshop is carried out

We are already making changes to the system to test to what extent it can be modified, and they are being evaluated both on the architectural design and on the implemented system. In addition to the modification of the student modelling agent, there are two main changes that will prove the suitability of the architecture. The first one is the inclusion of a model of human-like perception [34] to use the student's attention as part of the student's model and as an additional source of information for tutoring decisions. The second one is the inclusion of a cognitive architecture that allows us to make use of virtual tutors and teammates with complex, emotional behaviours [35].

Acknowledgements. The research presented in this paper has been funded by the Spanish Ministry of Science through projects MAEVIF (TIC2000-1346), ICEVAPI (TIN2004-07946) and ENVIRA (TIN2006-15202-C03-01) and has been supported by the INTUITION NoE.

References

1. Sleeman, D., Brown, J. (eds.): Intelligent Tutoring Systems. Academic Press, London (1982)
2. Wenger, E.: Artificial Intelligence and Tutoring Systems. Computational and Cognitive Approaches to the Communication of Knowledge. Morgan Kaufmann Publishers, Los Altos (1987)
3. Munro, A., Surmon, D., Johnson, M., Pizzini, Q., Walker, J.: An open architecture for simulation-centered tutors. In: Proc. of AIED 1999: 9th Conference on Artificial Intelligence in Education, Le Mans, France, pp. 360–367 (1999)
4. Mendez, G., Rickel, J., de Antonio, A.: Steve meets jack: the integration of an intelligent tutor and a virtual environment with planning capabilities. In: Rist, T., Aylett, R.S., Ballin, D., Rickel, J. (eds.) IVA 2003. LNCS (LNAI), vol. 2792, pp. 325–332. Springer, Heidelberg (2003)
5. Mendez, G., Herrero, P., de Antonio, A.: Intelligent virtual environments for training in nuclear power plants. In: Proc. of the 6th Intl. Conf. on Enterprise Information Systems (ICEIS 2004), Porto, Portugal (2004)
6. Zambonelli, F., Jennings, N.R., Wooldridge, M.: Developing multiagent systems: The gaia methodology. ACM Transactions on Software Engineering and Methodology (TOSEM) 12(3), 317–370 (2003)
7. Mendez, G., de Antonio, A.: Training agents: an architecture for reusability. In: Panayiotopoulos, T., Gratch, J., Aylett, R.S., Ballin, D., Olivier, P., Rist, T. (eds.) IVA 2005. LNCS (LNAI), vol. 3661, pp. 1–14. Springer, Heidelberg (2005)
8. de Antonio, A., Ramirez, J., Mendez, G.: An Agent-Based Architecture for Virtual Environments for Training. In: Developing Future Interactive Systems, pp. 212–233. Idea Group (2005)
9. Fikes, R.E., Nilsson, N.J.: Strips: a new approach to the application of theorem proving to problem solving. Artificial Intelligence 2(3-4), 189–208 (1971)
10. Nau, D., Au, T., Ilghami, O., Kuter, U., Murdock, W., Wu, D., Yaman, F.: Shop2: An htn planning system. Journal of Artificial Intelligence Research (JAIR) 20, 379–404 (2003)
11. Wooldridge, M., Jennings, N.R.: Software engineering with agents: Pitfalls and pratfalls. IEEE Internet Computing 3(3), 20–27 (1999)
12. Bass, L., Clements, P., Kazman, R.: Software Architecture in Practice, 2nd edn. SEI Series in Software Engineering. Addison Wesley Professional, Reading (2003)
13. Clements, P., Kazman, R., Klein, M.: Evaluating Software Architectures. The SEI Series in Software Engineering. Addison-Wesley, Reading (2002)
14. Parnas, D.L.: On the criteria to be used in decomposing systems into modules. Communications of the ACM 15(12), 1053–1058 (1972)
15. Parnas, D.L.: On a 'buzzword': Hierarchical structure. In: Information Processing 1974, Proceedings of IFIP Congress 1974, pp. 336–339 (1974)
16. Agre, P.E.: Hierarchy and history in simon's "architecture of complexity". Journal of the Learning Sciences 12(3), 413–426 (2003)
17. Haythorn, W.: What is object-oriented design? Journal of Object Oriented Programming 7(1), 67–78 (1994)
18. Hayden, S., Carrick, C., Yang, Q.: Architectural design patterns for multi-agent coordination. In: Proc. of the 3rd Intl. Conf. on Agent Systems (Agents 1999) (1999)
19. los Arcos, J.L., Muller, W., Fuente, O., Orúe, L., Arroyo, E., Leaznibarrutia, I., Santander, J.: Lahystotrain: Integration of virtual environments and its for surgery training. In: Gauthier, G., VanLehn, K., Frasson, C. (eds.) ITS 2000. LNCS, vol. 1839, pp. 43–52. Springer, Heidelberg (2000)

20. Rickel, J., Johnson, W.L.: Animated agents for procedural training in virtual reality: Perception, cognition, and motor control. Applied Artificial Intelligence 13, 343–382 (1999)
21. Shaw, E., Johnson, W., Ganeshan, R.: Pedagogical agents on the web. In: Proceedings of the Third Annual Conference on Autonomous Agents, Seattle, WA, USA, pp. 283–290. ACM Press, New York (May 1999)
22. Lester, J., Voerman, J., Towns, S., Callaway, C.: Cosmo: A life-like animated pedagogical agent with deictic believability. In: IJCAI 1997 Workshop on Animated Interface Agents: Making them Intelligent, Nagoya, Japan (August 1997)
23. Lester, J., Stone, B., Stelling, G.: Lifelike pedagogical agents for mixed-initiative problem solving in constructivist learning environments. User Modeling and User-Adapted Interaction 9(1–2), 1–44 (1999)
24. Paiva, A., Machado, I.: Life-long training with vincent, a web-based pedagogical agent. International Journal of Continuing Engineering Education and Life-Long Learning 12(1) (2002)
25. Zhang, D., Alem, L., Yacef, K.: Using multi-agent approach for the design of an intelligent learning environment. In: Wobcke, W., Pagnucco, M., Zhang, C. (eds.) Agents and Multi-Agent Systems Formalisms, Methodologies, and Applications. LNCS (LNAI), vol. 1441, pp. 221–230. Springer, Heidelberg (1998)
26. Webber, C., Pesty, S.: A two-level multi-agent architecture for a distance learning environment. In: de Barros Costa, E. (ed.) Workshop on Architectures and Methodologies for Building Agent-based Learning Environments (ITS 2002), pp. 26–38 (2002)
27. Buche, C., Querrec, R., Loor, P.D., Chevaillier, P.: Mascaret: A pedagogical multi-agent system for virtual environments for training. International Journal of Distance Education Technologies 2(4), 41–61 (2004)
28. Evers, M., Nijholt, A.: Jacob - an animated instruction agent in virtual reality. In: Tan, T., Shi, Y., Gao, W. (eds.) ICMI 2000. LNCS, vol. 1948, pp. 526–533. Springer, Heidelberg (2000)
29. Cheikes, B.: Gia: An agent-based architecture for intelligent tutoring systems. In: Finin, T., Mayfield, J. (eds.) Proceedings of the CIKM 1995 Workshop on Intelligent Information Agents, Baltimore, Maryland (1995)
30. Genesereth, M.: An agent-based approach to software interoperability. Technical Report Logic–91–6, Logic Group Computer Science Department, Stanford University (1993)
31. Boucke, N., Weyns, D., Schelfthout, K., Holvoet, T.: Applying the atam to an architecture for decentralized control of a transportation system. In: Hofmeister, C., Crnković, I., Reussner, R. (eds.) QoSA 2006. LNCS, vol. 4214, pp. 181–199. Springer, Heidelberg (2006)
32. Woods, S.G., Barbacci, M.: Architectural evaluation of collaborative agent-based systems. Technical Report CMU/SEI-99-TR-025, CMU/SEI (1999)
33. Wojcik, R., Bachmann, F., Bass, L., Clements, P., Merson, P., Nord, R., Wood, B.: Attribute-driven design (add), version 2.0. Technical Report CMU/SEI-2006-TR-023, CMU/SEI (2006)
34. Herrero, P., de Antonio, A.: Keeping watch: Intelligent virtual agents reflecting human-like perception in cooperative information systems. In: Meersman, R., Tari, Z., Schmidt, D.C. (eds.) CoopIS 2003, DOA 2003, and ODBASE 2003. LNCS, vol. 2888, pp. 129–144. Springer, Heidelberg (2003)
35. Imbert, R., de Antonio, A.: Using progressive adaptability against the complexity of modeling emotionally influenced virtual agents. In: Proc. of the 18th Intl. Conf. on Computer Animation and Social Agents (CASA 2005) (2005)

An Architecture-Centric Development Environment for Black-Box Component-Based Systems

Gerald Kotonya

Computing Department, Lancaster University,
Lancaster LA1 4WA, UK
gerald@comp.lancs.ac.uk

Abstract. Component-based software system development typifies traditional engineering philosophy by promoting the construction of systems from pre-fabricated software components. Underlying this philosophy is the promise of accelerated, low cost development and reliable software systems. However, the development strategy is hampered by the lack of practical methods and tools that support the reuse-driven paradigm embodied in black-box components. Current methods and tool environments provide poor support for the challenges posed by developing systems from off-the-shelf black-box components. These include poor support for: component discovery and verification, modelling and mapping requirements to component architectures, negotiation, architectural design and composition, and managing change. This paper describes an architecture-centric approach and environment for formulating, integrating and deploying black-box component-based systems. Practical experience of using the approach is illustrated with a real case study.

Keywords: Development environment, black-box components, architecture.

1   Introduction

The last ten years has seen the advent of several commercial component technologies and a growing market of off-the-shelf components [1,2,3]. However, shift to developing large software systems using black-box components has been cautious [3,14]. One of the reasons for this is the lack of practical software engineering methods and tools that integrate key *development with reuse* activities (discovery, verification and negotiation) with practical system development [4,15,17].

This paper explores these development challenges and proposes a novel service-centred approach for developing component-based systems that is explicitly designed to support development with black-box components. Services are used to provide a framework for mapping between "ideal" requirements and available functionality, and form the basis for architectural design. At the heart of the method is a Component Architecture Description Language (CADL) [8] that provides mechanisms for:

- Partitioning services into abstract component architectures
- Searching and verifying plug-compatible black-box components

R. Morrison, D. Balasubramaniam, and K. Falkner (Eds.): ECSA 2008, LNCS 5292, pp. 98–113, 2008.

- Composing and adapting design-level components
- Visualising, mediating and validating component changes

Practical experience of using the approach is illustrated with a small industry case study. The rest of this paper is organized as follows: Section 2 discusses the challenges developing systems from black-box components. Section 3 describes the proposed COMPonent Oriented Software Engineering method (COMPOSE). Section 4 provides an overview of CADL. Section 5 describes development with COMPOSE using a real case study. Section 6 provides some concluding thoughts.

2 Challenges of Developing Systems from Black-Box Components

Developing software systems from black-box components poses five key challenges:

- *Component discovery and verification.* Off-the-shelf software components have to be discovered, understood and, sometimes adapted to work in a new environment. For the development process to be successful, it must provide mechanisms for discovering, verifying, adapting and 'wiring' plug-compatible components.
- *Balancing need and availability.* There is a conceptual gap between the way we articulate requirements in custom development and the reuse-driven paradigm embodied in black-box component-based system development. The features supported by commercial software solutions vary greatly in quality and complexity. This together with the variability in application contexts means that specifications delivered with black-box software are likely to be inadequate [5,13].
- *Architecting the system.* A typical component-based system architecture comprises a set of components that have been purposefully designed and structured to ensure that they fit together and have an acceptable match with a defined system context. However, poor support for negotiation and lack of effective techniques for defining, verifying, evolving and matching abstract designs to concrete components make this a difficult task.
- *Supporting diversity.* The increasing complexity and diversity of software systems means that it is unlikely that large systems will continue to be developed using a purely component-oriented approach. Rather, a hybrid model of software development is likely to emerge where components and other solutions such as web services co-exist in the same system.
- *Managing change.* Traditional system maintenance involves observing and modifying lines of code. However, in component-based development the main unit of construction is often a black-box component or service. This limited visibility to the component design presents fundamentally different change management tasks and has major implications for the way we manage and evolve composition-based systems [8].

There are several modelling tools and environments intended to support component-based development. Perhaps the best known is the Unified Modelling Language (UML) [10]. However, while the latest versions of UML offer some support with constructs for modelling component-based based systems, these are largely intended to support custom development (UML does not support the notion of component discovery and verification). UML component diagrams are not intended to provide a logical decomposition of a software system into reusable and combinable subsystems. In addition, UML modelling is largely domain-driven, which usually leads to designs based on domain objects and non-standard architectures. Lastly, UML provides no easy way of addressing "compositional mismatches".

Other component-based development environments are typified by WREN [7], model driven approaches such as ASF+SDF [9] and component tools for Networked Embedded Systems (NEST) [12]. WREN includes ability to locate potential components from component distribution sites, to evaluate the identified components for suitability to an application and to incorporate selected components into application design models. It is also possible to assemble selected components into the application. However, it does not support requirements formulation, pattern reuse, "glue-code" generation or negotiation, and provides no support for managing change. Model driven initiatives are based on the derivation of system models from which code can be automatically generated. They are often domain-specific and intended for developing reusable components, rather than systems from pre-existing components.

3 COMPOSE Method

COMPOSE (illustrated in Fig. 1) embodies a cyclical development process that integrates verification into every part of the process to ensure that there is an acceptable match between components and the system being built. It also includes negotiation in each cycle as an explicit recognition of the need to trade-off and accept compromise in successful component-based system development. This ensures that even the earliest stages of system development are carried out in a context of off-the-shelf component availability, user requirements and critical architectural concerns. The development phase comprises four stages: requirements definition, system design (service partitioning), composition and change management. The management stage cuts across the three early development stages. This paper is mainly concerned with

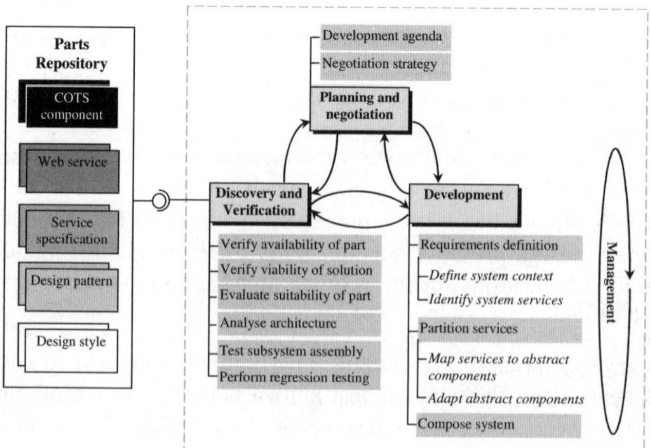

Fig. 1. COMPOSE Process

the system design and composition stages. The requirements and change management stages are described in detail elsewhere [5,6].

The requirements process in COMPOSE identifies a set of general requirements sources (actors and stakeholders) called *viewpoints*, which can be used as a starting point for identifying viewpoints specific to the system being developed [5]. Requirements are negotiated according to available off-the-shelf functionality and, where appropriate, traded to achieve the more acceptable or appropriate configuration in the circumstances. To address the gap between need and availability, functional and non-functional requirements are modelled as services and constraints, which represent the mapping between "ideal" requirements and what is available from identified components. Services are partitioned into abstract components (discussed in section 4). However, a service is not just an expression of required functionality, but also the result of verifying the suitability of the component selected. The flexible and implementation-independent nature of services means that the developer can explore different black-box solutions to compose abstract components. A service specification comprises the following elements [5]:

Required services   <Parameters required by the specified service >
Behaviour <Can be described at different levels of abstraction using predicates>
   Constraints <Description of constraints on service >
Search keywords< Keywords used for service discovery>
   Evaluation criterion <Tests that should be carried out to evaluate an off-the-shelf component's conformance with specified service>
   Trade offs < Aspects of original requirement not addressed by service and the possible conse-

The verification process assumes the existence of a repository of software part specifications (e.g. components, services and patterns). An integral toolset facilitates the incremental verification process (see in Section 5.3). At the requirements stage, context-based questions and logical filters are used to establish the availability and suitability of software components and services, and the viability of a reuse-driven solution [5]. At the design stage verification is concerned with ensuring the design matches the system context (i.e. system characteristics, valid architectural configurations and component interaction, constraints such as cost, schedule, operating and support environments, and business) [17]. CADL allows the developer to embed this information at different levels of abstraction in the system design, as *constraints*. The CADL compiler uses the information to verify valid architectural configurations and compositions (see example in Fig. 6).

4 Component Architecture Description Language - CADL

COMPOSE uses a constraint-based component architecture description language (CADL) [8] to partition services into design-level components which are then composed into concrete component configurations through a process of adaptation and negotiation. It is not possible to provide a complete description of CADL in the space of this paper; however, its key aspects are discussed. The experience of using CADL on a real system is discussed in section 5 and 6. The CADL component model is shown in Fig. 2. The model extends the ideas originally proposed by Ning [16], to specify a language that explicitly supports black-box component-based development.

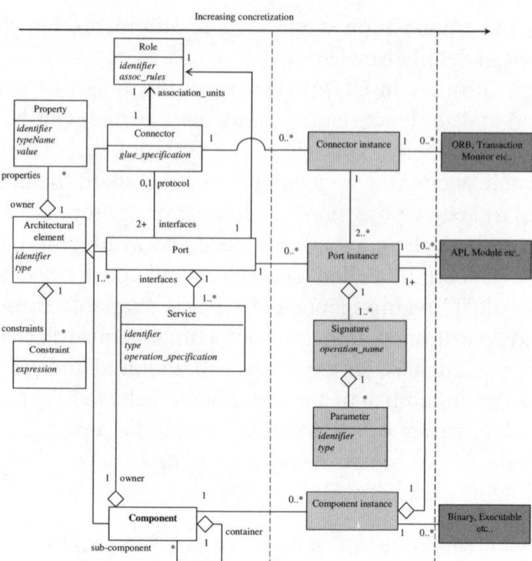

Fig. 2. CADL Component Model

The design-time component concepts are shown in clear (abstract components) and light grey (instances). The composition-time concepts are shown in dark grey. A component in the model is defined as an encapsulated, distributable and executable piece of software that provides and receives services through well-defined interfaces. A concrete component corresponds to the runtime manifestation of a component. In CADL, a component interface is made visible through a port. A port denotes the association of a port type to a component to make the services provided or required by the component externally visible. A port specifies named operation as part of its *signature*. A concrete interface denotes the runtime manifestation of an interface. A connector denotes the association of a connector type between the required and provided interfaces of components. A connector type denotes an abstract specification of a style of interaction among components. A concrete connector denotes the runtime manifestation of a connector. Each port and connector is associated with a role. A role defines the rules that a port and connector must conform to in order to be legal participants in a connection. CADL uses subtyping by inheritance together with constraints as mechanisms to "evolve" and "map" the specification of abstract design-level components, ports and connectors to concrete types. Subtypes are defined according to the following relation: $\forall x:subtype \bullet x \subseteq subtype$.

4.1 Modelling Component Architectures with CADL

A CADL architecture description comprises two main sections:

- The *element definition section* defines ports, connectors, properties and roles used in component definitions. Elements defined in this section are referred to by type and identifier in component definitions.
- The *component definition* section defines the components used in the architecture.

The general structure of the architecture is as follows:

```
architecture ::= [comment] {element_definition |component_definition}
element_definition::= defined_type |port_definition |connector_definition |role_definition
component_definition ::= subtype_component|component_instance |concrete_component
subtype_component::=
        component component_id extends component_type
              component_attributes
        end component_id
component_instance::=
        component component_id is component_type
              component_attributes
        end component_id
concrete_component::=
        component component_id is ComposerComponent
              [comment]
              {property_declaration}
              interface_definition
        end component_id
component_attributes ::= [comment] {property_declaration} [interface_definition]
              {constraint} [connector_list] [component_configuration]
              [component_mapping]
component composerComponent_id is ComposerComponent composes designComponent_id
        [comment]
        {property_declaration}
        interface_definition
        [port_correspondence]
end component_id
port_correspondence ::= {port identifier replaces identifier;} {port identifier replaces identifier;}
component_type ::= BasicComponent | identifier |ComposerComponent
interface_definition ::= interface port_id {, port_id};
connector_list ::= connectors [external] connector_id {, [external] connector_id };
```

A basic CADL component consists of a unique identifier and type. The component
may have a set of named ports, connectors, configuration, properties and constraints.
CADL defines four component types: *BasicComponent*, sub-type, instance, concrete.
BasicComponent denotes a primitive type from which all generic component types are
defined (by extension). A sub-type component corresponds to an extension of *Basic-
Component* or another sub-type. A component instance corresponds to a component
type whose parameters are assigned values. Component instances cannot be extended.
A concrete component corresponds to a runtime manifestation of a component in-
stance. The syntax for defining components is shown below:

CADL uses the "extends" keyword to evolve parameterised component types. The
"is" keyword is used to instantiate parameterised component types and "composes" to
associate component instances with concrete types. The "composes" keyword triggers
the CADL compiler to check a design-time component interface definition, properties
and the constraints defined over them against properties and interface definition in the
composer component definition for conformance. The *port_correspondence* property
is used to map composer component ports to designer component ports.

Component properties are specified as optional to provide the designer with
a mechanism for describing incomplete architectures. This flexibility is important
for experimentation and for incremental design. The designer can use this feature to

create "container" components. Constraints may represent non-functional requirements such as component cost, certification, memory and platform restrictions, or
dependability requirements such as security and availability. They may also represent
elements of interdependence that are introduced to allow services to meet certain
architectural considerations. Lastly, constraints may capture dependencies that are
introduced to make certain components choices acceptable in the current context.

4.2 Defining Component Interfaces

The interface section in a component definition specifies a set of ports through which
the component can interact with its environment. Ports may have properties and constraints defined on them that restrict the way they receive and provide services.
CADL incorporates a number of predefined ports. Ports are defined as shown below:

```
port_definition ::=  subtype_port | port_instance | composite_port| concrete_port
subtype_port ::=  port port_id extends standardPort_type
     port_attributes
end port_id
port_instance ::=  port port_id is standardPort_type
     port_attributes
end port_id
standardPort_type ::= BasicPort|predefinedPort|identifier
port_attributes ::= [comment] [role_attached] {property_declaration} {constraint} {service}
                    [signature_definition;]
composite_port ::= port port_id [is |extends] compositePort_type
     [comment]
     [port_membership;]
     {property_declaration}
     {constraint}
end port_id
concrete_Port::=
     port port_id is ComposerPort composes port_id
          [comment]
          {property_declaration}
          role_name
     end component_id
predefinedPort ::= RoutineCall|RoutineDef|RPCCall|RPCDef|StreamIn
     |StreamOut|Notify|Listen|FileWrite|FileRead
role_attached ::= role identifier;
compositePort_type ::= CompositePort|identifier
port_membership ::= portset port_id{; port_id}
```

4.3 Component Configuration

The configuration section in a component definition specifies the internal structure of
a component by specifying the nature of its composition. A component configuration
specifies the components that are used to construct the parent component, the connectors used to link them up, and the ports participating in the connections. It also specifies the desired constraints on the components making up the configuration. CADL
connectors follow a similar definition to ports. In addition, connectors can generate
"glue code" using introspection and "glue-code" specification.

component_configuration ::= **configuration** {use_list} {connection} {constraint}
use_list ::= **uses [external]** component_id {, **[external]** component_id };
connection::= **connects [external] (self|** component_id). identifier **to (self|** component_id). identifier
        using identifier;

4.4 Constraint Language

CADL incorporates an extensible constraint language to support service partitioning and component verification processes. Constraints in CADL are treated as *required* conditions that can be associated with properties of all the basic architectural elements and configurations. They are used to define desired component properties and acceptable interactions between components. The universal (*for all*) and existential quantifiers (*there exists*) are used to introduce global constraints that can be scoped.

constraint ::= **requires [global]** logical_exp |if_statement | quantifier_exp;
logical_exp::= [!] boolean_exp {logical_operator [!] boolean_exp}
boolean_exp ::= expression boolean_operator expression|component_part| "(" logical_exp ")"
expression ::= non_num_literal | arithmetic_expression {arithmetic_operator arithmetic_expression}
arithmetic_expression ::= component_exp| numeric_exp|" (" expression ")"
component_part ::= identifier {. Identifier}
component_exp ::= component_part | "(" component_exp ")"
numeric_exp ::= numLiteral | "(" numeric_exp ")"
if_statement ::= **if** logical_exp **then** logical_exp
quantifier_exp ::= (**forall** | **thereexists**) declaration_list : predicate_exp
declaration_list ::= identifier var_type {, identifier var_type}
     var_type ::= **component | port | connector**
predicate exp ::= logical_predicate_exp :: logical_predicate_exp | logical_predicate_exp
logical_predicate_exp ::= [!] boolean_predicate_exp {logical_operator [!] boolean_predicate_exp}
boolean_predicate_exp ::= expression boolean_operator expression
     | component_exp **[not] in** array_identifier | component_part | "(" logical_predicate_exp ")"
array_identifier ::= array
simple_value ::= non_num_literal|numLiteral
non_num_literal::= "null"|date_Literal|char_Literal |string_Literal|boolean_Literal
identifier_list ::= identifier {, identifier}

Examples of CADL constraint statements include:

1. **requires forAll** c **component**: (c.confidence >= 80);
2. **requires forAll** c **component**: (c.type= "IE"):(c.version >=5);
3. **requires thereExists** p **port**: (p.portSignature = "in: int, string out:int")
4. **requires forAll** c **component**: (c.identifier in [id1, id2, id3]): (c.version>5))
5. **requires forAll** c **component**: (c.identifier in [id1, id2, id3]): (c.id1= "web service" & c.id2= "custom" & c.id3= "COTS component"))

Explanation:
1. Requires that all components have a minimum confidence level of 80 (in percent terms). Confidence level is an organizational measure of the reliability of a component. This is likely to vary with organization and application
2. Requires that all components of type "IE" be version 5 or greater.
3. Requires that at least one port have the signature: "in: int, string out: int".
4. Requires that all components in the collection be of version greater than 5.
5. Requires that: component id1 be a web service, component id2 be a custom component and component id3 be a COTS component

5 Developing with COMPOSE

The development process in COMPOSE follows two modes:

- *Graphical.* This mode allows the developer to define and model applications using an extended UML graphical notation. The definitions can be automatically translated to syntactically correct CADL statements.
- *Textual.* An editor provides facilities to ease the writing of correct syntax (keywords colouring, templates, etc.). In this mode, the compiler verifies both syntactic and semantic correctness.

The toolset (Fig. 3) maintains dynamic synchronization of both representations making it possible to switch between the two.

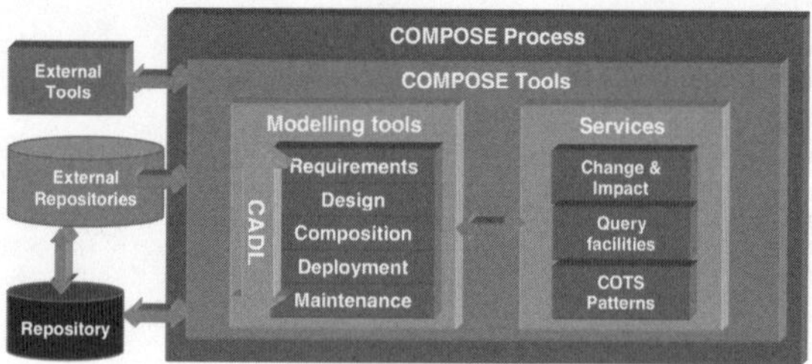

Fig. 3. COMPOSE Tool Architecture

The tools are distributed as three independent applications that share information via the *repository*:

- **Admintools:** These are utilities for repository management. The repository contains all the elements used in application development (components, services, architectures, etc.) as well as the knowledge gained during their development (intellectual assets). Every component is catalogued in the repository prior to its use in an application. Basic properties are predefined in the repository but the administrator can extend these to include specific business objectives. The repository is XML based and intended to communicate easily with other repositories. In addition, a package importer wizard allows to the administrator to automate the introduction of commercial software components specified according to existing standards (e.g. CCM) or standards defined by the administrator
- **VPManager:** Allows the developer to elicit requirements for a proposed system and specify them as services.
- **Modeller:** Allows the developer to model, verify, compose, deploy and manage component architectures. The modeller uses CADL and supports both a graphical and textual expressions of the system architecture.

5.1 Case Study

This case-study describes the results of a pilot project to extend a legacy system for a freight company to support an independent tracking and tracing system for one of their large customers. The existing tracking and tracing reporting system ran on an old VAX mini-computer. It only allowed the freight company customer service representatives to identify the delivery status of customer shipments on a booking by booking basis. If a customer provided the customer service representative with a particular booking reference, then they could use the existing system to identify whether or not it had been delivered. However, this type of reporting system did not adequately address the needs of the freight company's larger customers. Although the report consolidated all relevant customer information it still did not allow freight company customer representatives to answer questions responsively. To do this the report had to be imported into Microsoft Excel™ where a customer service representative could use Microsoft Excel's query tools.

This short-term solution overcame the limitations of the freight company's existing tracking and tracing reporting system. However, it failed to address two key problems:

1. The consolidated report was based on information that was a day old.
2. The customer service representatives had to wait 5 to 10 minutes every morning to load and format each customer's consolidated report in Microsoft Excel. A better solution was to provide a system that generated an up-to-date consolidated web-based report on demand. The customer service representatives could then produce the report at any time during the day by selecting the appropriate customer link.

The next sections describe a step-by-step process of how COMPOSE was used to extend the freight customer report system to support these requirements. The extended functionality is referred to as the *Tracker Report* system.

5.2 Defining Tracker Report Requirements

The first step in extending AS Freight's legacy system is defining the Tracker Report system context by identifying the viewpoints (domain entities) associated with it. Viewpoint requirements are realised by components through the service mapping process. Fig. 4 shows the viewpoints identified for the Tracker Report system and some of their requirements (left pane).

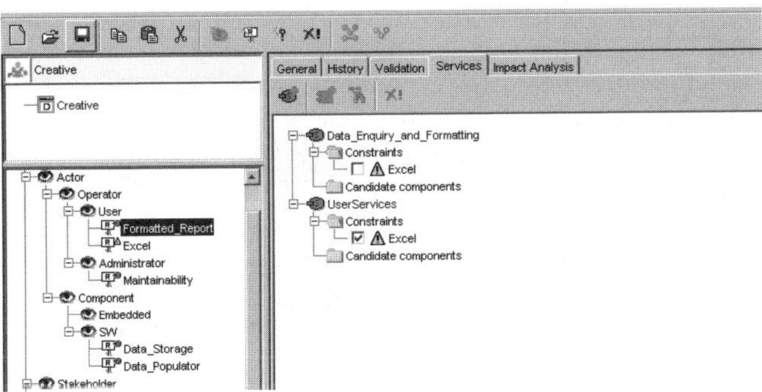

Fig. 4. Requirements definition in COMPOSE toolset

These requirements are associated with a number of services and constraints (right pane). The *SoftwareComponent* viewpoint represents the legacy system. It is important to mention that complete requirement descriptions include non-functional requirements [5]. Requirements ranking and negotiation process supported by COMPOSE are not shown in this paper.

5.3 Tracker Report System Architecture

The COMPOSE architectural design process starts with the partitioning of service descriptions into logical sub-systems. The process requires that all specified services be associated with either abstract or concrete components. Priority is given to essential services as these determine the viability of the COTS-based solution. COMPOSE supports the process of service groupings by providing several architectural styles that can be used as a starting point. CADL provides support for describing, verifying and composing abstract components. It is not possible to discuss the detailed description of the Tracker Report system design in the limited space of this paper. However, I will provide enough description of the case study to demonstrate the power of COMPOSE.

Architectural styles provide a good starting point for partitioning services. Fig. 5 shows the result of the using a 3-tier web architecture style to partition the *DBMS*, *Maintainability* and *UserServices* service. The design shows the concrete MS Excel component that already exists on the *user* viewpoint's client machine along with the unspecified Web Browser that will act as the container for the MS Excel report. The service responsible for generating the formatted report is the *Data_Enquiry_and_Formatting* service. In order to provide this service, a component has to be created that will read data from the DBMS and format it so that it can be displayed as an Excel document within the browser.

The web server must be able to activate individual instances of the Excel application. Three COTS component options were evaluated for the server: Microsoft's Active Server Page, HTML page and an ActiveX object.

The ActiveX object was found to provide the best solution because it registered itself on the user machine as a compiled in-process component allowing the web server to transparently activate instances of the Excel application. As the ActiveX

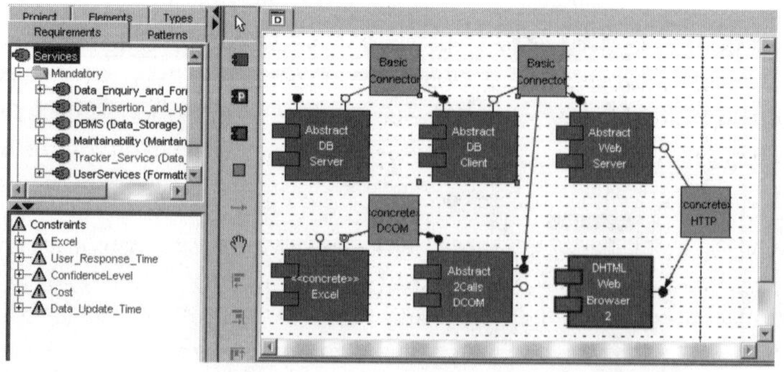

Fig. 5. System design with ActiveX component

component does not exist at this stage of the logical design it is modelled as an abstract component. The abstract component needs to have at least one DCOM output port so it can be called from the web browser page and at least two input ports (one DCOM input port for calling the Excel methods and one DCOM port for accessing the database's data). The abstract component is labelled Abstract_2Calls_DCOM. Once the Abstract_2Calls_DCOM component has been inserted into the modeller it can be linked to the Abstract_DB_Client (i.e. the obtained data will inserted into an Excel worksheet on the client computer prior to any formatting) and to the Excel component as shown in Fig. 5.

Mismatches between design component interfaces are verified and flagged by the CADL compiler. For example, signature mismatches between connected ports. Fig.6 is an example of a design-time verification report (in addition other errors, the Excel component has been deleted in this example).

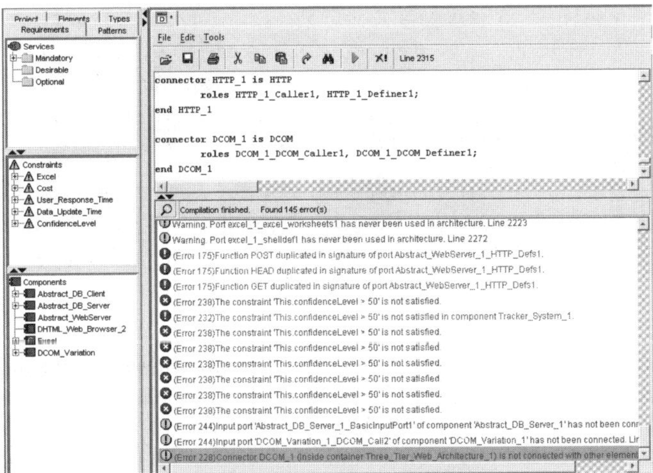

Fig. 6. Example of design-time verification

To address this problem, COMPOSE provides the designer with a tool to create glue-code connectors. The tool uses introspection to generate a basic connector whose internal logic can be modified to provide additional functionality.

5.4 Composing Components

The COMPOSE toolset provides four different ways to compose abstract components:

- *Searching*. This option uses a constraint-based query editor to help the developer locate suitable candidate components from the repository
- *Existing replacement*. This option uses the developer's existing replacement knowledge to facilitate rapid composition realisations
- *Private container*. This option replaces an abstract component with an empty container. To complete the composition, the maintainer must add components to it

110   G. Kotonya

- *Pattern*. This option provides the maintainer with a list of patterns that implement the abstract component service.

The CADL compiler verifies that the design is correct and that all the services are correctly associated with concrete components. The toolset allows the maintainer to create competing compositions to explore different solutions. Fig. 7 shows the composed system.

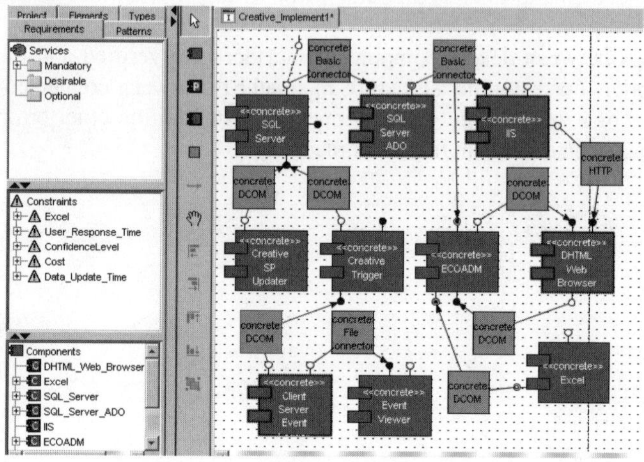

Fig. 7. Composition for the System

The toolset allows the developer to specify hardware deployment blocks needed for the different platforms that make up the legacy and extended system. Different producers ship commercial components in different formats (.jar, .war, .cab, .tgz etc) according to the intended target environments. The format of the assembly depends on the target environment (EJB, COM+, CCM, .NET etc). The deployment blocks generated for the *Tracker Report System* are shown in Fig. 8.

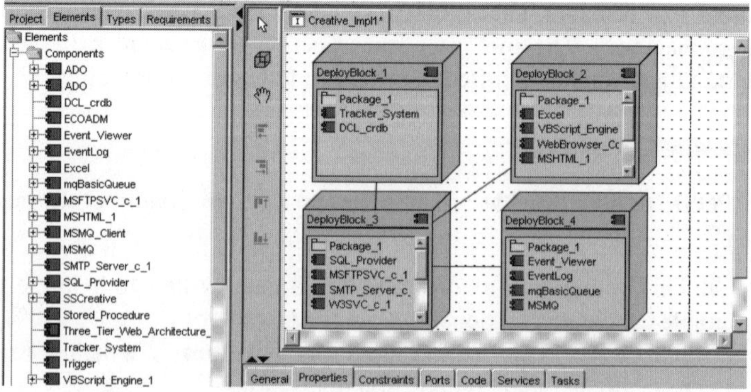

Fig. 8. Hardware deployment blocks for Tracker Report System

5.5 Traceability and Change Impact Analysis

It is recognized that Component-based systems generally exhibit structural degradation making it difficult to assess the impact of change; they also exhibit more troublesome incompatibilities. This means that the degradation is likely to manifest itself in the form of locally implemented patches, wrappers and increasingly complex "glue code". Fig. 9 shows how the COMPOSE impact analysis tool can be used to trace and visualise change impact from requirements through to components. The impact analysis shows, for example, that the *UserServices* service is currently associated with one abstract component called *Abstract_WebBrowser* (5th column, 3rd from top). In addition, however, the impact analysis shows that *Abstract_WebBrowser* is required to implement MS Excel, at specified cost and response time.

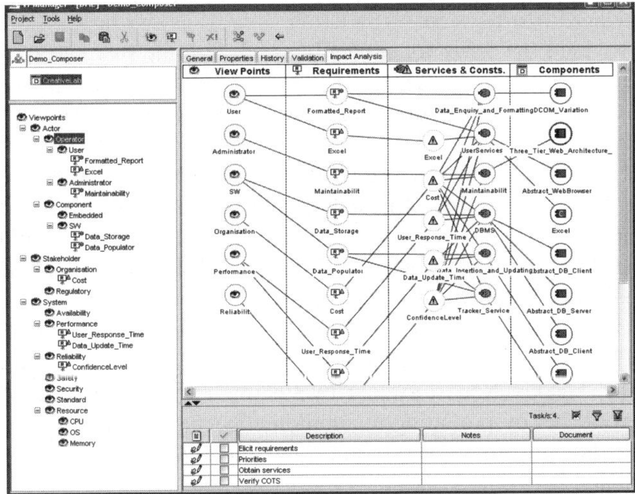

Fig. 9. Impact traceability

6 Conclusions

This paper has described an architecture-centric development method for black-box component-based systems. COMPOSE incorporates a mechanism for defining user requirements and a novel means for mapping "ideal" requirements to available component functionality. COMPOSE provides incremental support for modelling and evolving abstract component architectures to concrete systems. The process is supported by an extensible architecture description language, CADL, which provides support for searching and verifying plug-compatible components and other design artefacts. COMPOSE also provides support for impact analysis and the deployment of the composed system. The following section assesses the case study against the challenges outlined in section 2.

- *Component discovery and verification.* COMPOSE supports an extensible repository of well documented components, connectors services, patterns, architectural styles, workflow information and other reusable artifacts. Patterns and styles were frequently used in developing the legacy system extension to save time and enhance productivity. COMPOSE supports component and architecture verification through CADL.

- *Balancing need and availability.* COMPOSE provided us with an effective and practical mechanism for defining the Tracker Report system context through viewpoints and services. COMPOSE uses a predicate system to automatically match requirements with component properties and a process of negotiation [5].
- *Architecting the system.* In order to support the design of the Report Tracker system a mechanism was needed for mapping its requirements to off-the-shelf components and for defining its architecture. The mapping process was provided through services. Services served three important purposes:
  - o they were derived from viewpoint requirements, hence provided a link to initial Tracker Report system formulation
  - o they provided the basis for modelling and deriving test cases for the Report Tracker requirements. A service can be specified in a variety of notations
  - o they were the basis for partitioning the Tracker Report system into a set of abstract components.
  - o CADL provided the means for partitioning services into components.
- *Supporting diversity.* COMPOSE and its toolset allowed creation of competing compositions for the Tracker Report system. This is essential for addressing architectural, platform and implementation differences. However, COMPOSE provides only limited support for hybrid compositions.
- *Managing change.* Traceability is central to informed system evolution. In COMPOSE, services provided an efficient vehicle for documenting change decisions for the Tracker Report system by linking different development activities. They achieved this by providing a common concept for mapping requirements to components, documenting the system design and ensuring links between architectural design and later composition

COMPOSE represents a genuine attempt to address the problem of lack of practical environments for developing systems from black-box components. Initial thoughts, based on the enhancement of the legacy system are that COMPOSE is an improvement on other development approaches. However, further improvements to the approach are needed if it is to address complex development problems, particularly hybrid development. We are currently exploring ways to:

- provide productivity improvement aids for the maintainer
- provide better support for impact analysis. In particular we are exploring ways to support the visualization of quantitative "what if" analysis under conditions of uncertainty that allow designers and maintainers to develop and change scenarios to assess the impacts of different design and changes options
- provide interoperability support with other analysis tools
- provide support for hybrid system development, in particular we are exploring how CADL can be extended to support the dynamic aspects of service composition and integration in hybrid architectures.

Acknowledgements

I am grateful to the EU IST Programme for funding the ECOADM IST-1999-20771 project on which this work is based. I am also grateful to our project partners for their contributions.

References

1. Heineman, G., Crnkovic, I., Schmidt, H.W., Stafford, J.A.: Component-Based Software Engineering. In: Heineman, G.T., Crnković, I., Schmidt, H.W., Stafford, J.A., Szyperski, C.A., Wallnau, K. (eds.) CBSE 2005. LNCS, vol. 3489, pp. 14–15. Springer, Heidelberg (2005)
2. Ravichandran, T., Rothenberger, M.A.: Software reuse strategies and component markets. Communications of the ACM 46(8), 109–114 (2003)
3. Kim, S.D.: Lessons Learned From A Nationwide CBD Promotion Project. Communications of the ACM 45(10), 83–87 (2002)
4. Voas, J.M.: The Challenges of Using COTS Software In Component-Based Development. Computer 31(6), 44 (1998)
5. Kotonya, G., Hutchinson, J.: A Service-Oriented Approach for Specifying Component-Based Systems. In: ICCBSS 2005. LNCS, vol. 3412, pp. 150–162. Springer, Heidelberg (2007)
6. Kotonya, G., Hutchinson, J.: Managing Change in COTS-based Systems. In: Proceedings of 21st IEEE International Conference on Software Maintenance (ICSM), September 25-30, pp. 69–78 (2005)
7. Luer, C., Rosenblum, S.D.: WREN an environment for component-based development ACM. SIGSOFT Software Engineering Notes 26(5), 207–217 (2001)
8. Kotonya, G., Onyino, W., Hutchinson, J., Sawyer, P.: Component Architecture Description Language (CADL). Technical Report, CSEG/57/2001 Computing Department. Lancaster University (2001)
9. van den Brand, M.G.J., Heering, J., de Jong, H.A., de Jonge, M., Kuipers, T., Klint, P., Moonen, L., Olivier, P.A., Scheerder, J., Vinju, J.J., Visser, E., Visser, J.: The ASF+SDF Meta-Environment: a Component-Based Language Development Environment. Computational Complexity, 365–370 (2001)
10. Pilone, D., Pitman, N.: UML 2.0 in a Nutshell. O'Reilly, Sebastopol (2005)
11. Pilskalns, W., Williams, D., Andrews, A.: Defining Maintainable Components in the Design Phase. In: Proceedings of 21st IEEE International Conference on Software Maintenance (ICSM), September 25-30, pp. 49–58 (2005)
12. Volgyesi, P., Ledeczi, A.: Component-based development of networked embedded applications. In: Proceedings of 28th IEEE Euromicro Conference on Component-Based Software Engineering, September 4-6, pp. 68–73 (2002)
13. Vigder, M., Gentleman, M., Dean, J.: COTS Software Integration: State of the Art. Institute for Information Technology, National Research Council, Canada (1996)
14. Morisio, M., Seaman, C.B., Basili, V.R., Parra, A.T., Kraft, S.E., Condon, S.E.: COTS-based software development: Processes and open issues. Journal of Systems and Software 61(3), 189–199 (2002)
15. Hutchinson, J., Kotonya, G.: A Review of Negotiation Techniques in Component-Based Software Engineering. In: Proceedings of 32nd IEEE Euromicro Conference on Component-Based Software Engineering, pp. 152–159 (August 2006)
16. Ning, J.Q.: A Component Model Proposal. In: Proc. of 2nd International Workshop on Component-Based Software Engineering, pp. 13–15 (May 1999)
17. Medvidovic, N., Dashofy, E.M., Taylor, R.N.: Moving architectural description from under the technology lamppost. Information and Software Technology 49(1), 12–31 (2007)

Automating the Trace of Architectural Design Decisions and Rationales Using a MDD Approach

Elena Navarro[1] and Carlos E. Cuesta[2]

[1] Department of Computing Systems, University of Castilla-La Mancha,
Campus Universitario s/n, 020071, Albacete, Spain
`enavarro@dsi.uclm.es`
[2] Dept. Computing Languages and Systems II, Rey Juan Carlos University,
C/ Tulipán s/n. 28933 Móstoles, Madrid, Spain
`carlos.cuesta@urjc.es`

Abstract. The impact of architecture is not only significant in the final structure of software, but also in the development process. Architecture itself is assembled by a network of design decisions (DD) composing a design rationale. Such rationale has often been neglected; however it is essential to deal with future change. This is also the role of traceability, the crosscutting relationship describing the evolution of software. The methodology ATRIUM provides the method to manage traceability, by using a Model-Driven Development (MDD) approach where every model element maintains links to related elements in previous and further stages. This proposal defines how these links have been exploited to support the tracing of DDs and their accompanying design rationales (DRs), and study their propagation. We also present how ATRIUM tools support this proposal by introducing DD/DRs and their traceability links from requirements to the target architectural model. These are automatically generated by M2M transformations, avoiding the error-prone task of managing them by hand.

Keywords: Design Decision, Design Rationale, Model-Driven Development, Model-To-Model Transformation, CASE Tool, Traceability.

1 Introduction

Almost two decades have already passed since Perry and Wolf wrote their seminal paper [27] on the foundations of Software Architecture, an event which is considered as the beginning of the modern age of Software Architecture. Already in this pioneer paper, Perry and Wolf defined architecture as a model composed of *elements*, *form*, and *rationale*. The first item refers to the description of components and what would be later defined as connectors; the second item refers to constraints in their properties and relationships. Both of them have been integrated into practice long ago; but the third one has often been neglected. Rationale was defined as the *motivation* for the choice of style, form or elements, which explains why this choice satisfies the system requirements; but it has been scarcely considered until recently.

R. Morrison, D. Balasubramaniam, and K. Falkner (Eds.): ECSA 2008, LNCS 5292, pp. 114–130, 2008.

Just four years ago, a number of researchers including Bosch [1] highlighted this fact, and stressed the importance of overcoming this drawback. They noticed that many architectural designs still lack such an explanation, and that this limitation is a factor hindering further spreading and improvement in the area. They advocate for the insertion of additional first-class assets in architecture description, which explicitly document *design decisions* (DDs) being made.

This emphasis on the management of architectural knowledge has quickly achieved a great popularity, not only within the specific field but also outside it [10]. Much of the research in this topic has focused on the *internal* structure of design assets. For instance, for every asset we can at least separate the *decision* itself (DD) from the *rationale* (DR) for this decision. But their external (compositional) structure is even more interesting. The composition of the set of individual DD/DRs builds up the system's global rationale; and the structure of this *architectural rationale* is not only supported by the final architecture, but it also mimics the dynamic structure of the development *process* itself. The perspective is much richer when it is considered; then a *decision* is a choice, and this means a potential turn during the process. Every decision has the potential to be a *variation point* (VP) for the architecture. This also means that traceability relationships must also be considered.

However complexity grows exponentially in this case, and then automatic support becomes a necessity. Of course, if we are considering automation of the development process, and traceability relationships in particular, there is an obvious connection to MDA [28]. Model-driven tools (should) consider traceability as a basic relationship; therefore they already provide the basis to exploit decisions as described.

The proposal outlined in this article starts from this idea –*supporting architectural knowledge with a model-driven process*– and in doing so, it gathers every feature in research mentioned so far. Indeed, traceability will be the "spine" for the architectural rationale, which will reflect the structure of the process. This building process will be supported by (semi-)automatic model-driven tools, and by applying MDD techniques, one of the most important trends in current software engineering will be used.

Therefore, in this article a specific extension of ATRIUM (Architecture Traced from RequIrements applying a Unified Methodology) [22], a methodology which uses a model-driven approach to generate an architecture definition from the requirements, is presented. The extended version provides an explicit support to describe decisions, and to trace them back to requirements. This is also implemented in its specific tool, MORPHEUS [19], which has been also extended to support the management of additional information and its inclusion within the relevant M2M transformations. The result is explained by means of a concrete, real-world case study, and the support for automation provided by MORPHEUS is described. Finally this is related to the state-of-the-art in architectural knowledge proposals, and some consequences are extracted from this comparison, such as the consistency of the whole approach.

2   ATRIUM in a Nutshell

There are many compelling reasons about why it is necessary to include traceability throughout the process of software development process. Among them, the most accepted one is that traceability makes available the ability to deal properly with the

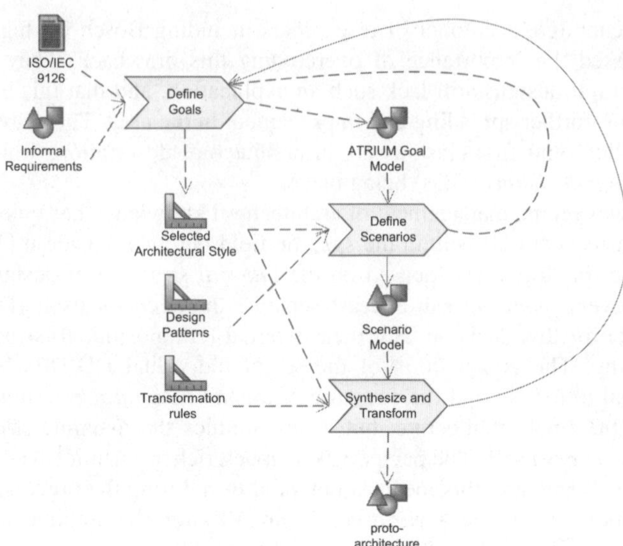

Fig. 1. An outline of ATRIUM

change as it appears, evaluating its impact, determining the affected elements, etc. Therefore, the exploitation of the traceability from the requirements stage towards the architectural specification (and code) arises as one of the necessary cornerstones to achieve the success of any software development process. In this context is where the methodology ATRIUM (Architecture Traced from RequIrements applying a Unified Methodology) [22] provides support. It is a methodology designed for the concurrent definition of Requirements and Software Architecture, defining the automatic/semi-automatic support for traceability throughout its application.

ATRIUM has been described following a MDD approach [28]. Fig. 1 shows its three main activities (described using SPEM [29]) that must be iterated over in order to define and refine the different Models and allow the analyst to reason about both the requirements and the architecture. These activities are described as follows:

- *Define Goals.* This activity allows the analyst to identify and specify the requirements of the system-to-be by using the *ATRIUM Goal Model* [23] (Fig. 4 describes an example). This model is based on KAOS [4] and the NFR Framework [2] proposals. During the specification phase, along with an informal description of the requirements stated by the stakeholders, the ISO/IEC 9126 quality model [11] is used as an instantiable framework in order to provide the analyst with an initial set of concerns of the system-to-be.

- *Define Scenarios.* This activity focuses on the specification of the *ATRIUM Scenario Model*, that is, the set of *Architectural Scenarios* that describes the system's behaviour under certain *operationalization* decisions. A process for its description [21] has been established, to facilitate the automatic analysis of alternatives. Therefore, each Architectural Scenario depicts the architectural and environmental elements that interact to satisfy specific requirements and their level of responsibility for achieving a given goal. It is worth noting that a profile has been defined to describe solutions, applying both to functional and non-functional requirements [22].

- *Synthesize and Transform.* This activity has been defined to generate the proto-architecture of the specific system. With this purpose, it synthesizes the architectural elements from the ATRIUM Scenario Model, building up the system along with its structure. This proto-architecture is used as a first draft of the final description of the system that can be refined in a later stage of the software development process. This activity has been defined by applying *Model-To-Model Transformation* techniques (M2M, [3]), specifically, QVT Relations [24]. The advantages are twofold. First, the Architectural Style selected during the *Define Goal* activity can be automatically applied so that the constraints imposed by the Style are satisfied. Second, the analyst can generate the proto-architecture he/she deems appropriate for his/her purposes.

It must be pointed out that ATRIUM is independent of the Architectural Metamodel used to describe the proto-architecture. The *Synthesize and Transform* stage has been defined using M2M techniques whereby the analyst only has to describe the needed transformations to instantiate the needed Architectural Metamodel. Currently, the set of transformations [22] to generate the proto-architecture instantiating the PRISMA Architectural Model [25] has been defined because a compiler to generate code from PRISMA Models already exists.

3   MDD for Tackling Design Decisions and Rationales

As stated above, ATRIUM has been defined following the MDD approach, so that every stage of the software development process is described by establishing clearly its associated Metamodels along with forward and backwards traceability links between them. To tackle the description of DDs and DRs, our proposal exploits these links throughout the application of ATRIUM by means of both their incorporation in each Metamodel and the establishment of mechanisms for their propagation through abstraction levels, as it will be presented in the following.

Fig. 2 shows how DDs and DRs are introduced from the very beginning of the software development process by means of its introduction at the requirement stage. *Operationalization* is one of the main concepts used to describe the *ATRIUM Goal Model*. An *Operationalization* is a description of an architectural solution, i.e., an architectural *design choice* for the system-to-be to meet the users' needs and expectations. They are called *Operationalizations* because they describe the system behaviour to meet the requirements, both functional and non-functional. For this reason, two key attributes are included while they are described: *designDecision* and *designRationale*. The former is in charge of describing DD architectural design solution and the latter describes why this decision has been made. The *Operationalizations* are related to *Requirements* by means of a relationship called *Contribution* whose main aim is to specify how an *Operationalization* contributes to/prevents the satisfaction of a *Requirement* facilitating the automatic analysis of architectural alternatives [22].

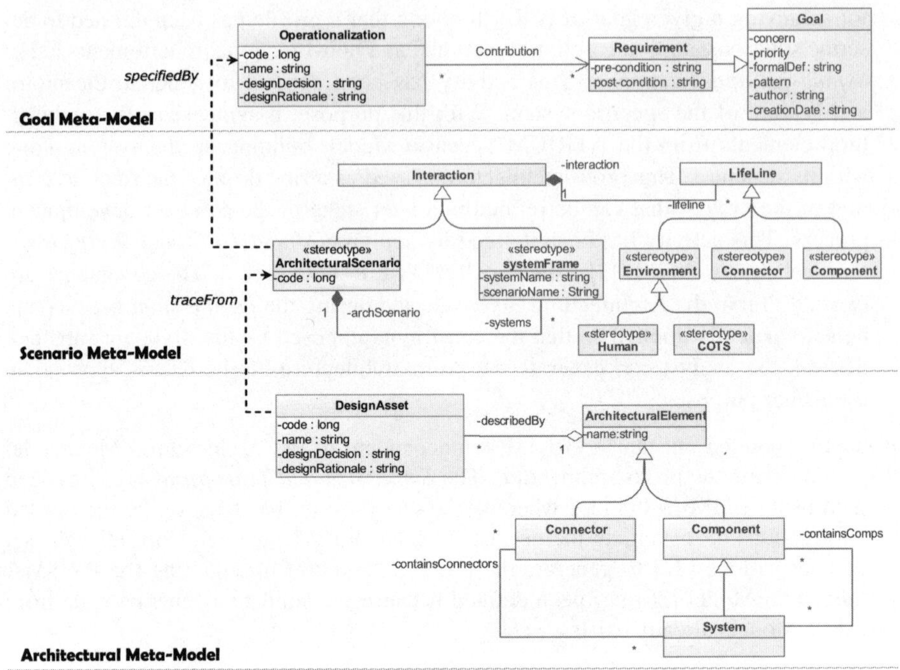

Fig. 2. Traceability Links between the main meta-elements of the involved Metamodels

Fig. 2 shows that *ArchitecturalScenario* constitutes one of the main concepts of the ATRIUM Scenario Metamodel. The *ArchitecturalScenario* is used to describe the system behaviour associated to one or several requirements and under a certain operationalization decision. Unlike proposals about classic scenarios, *Architectural Scenarios* specify interaction between architectural elements together with the environmental elements which play a role in that scenario. As depicted in Fig. 2, in ATRIUM *Architectural Scenarios* are traced from *Operationalizations* by means of a relationship known as *specifiedBy,* thereby stating clearly how (and why) every Architectural Scenario is specified. This relationship is specified by the analyst whenever a new *Architectural Scenario* is described, as it only emerges in the context of a specific *Operationalization.* For this reason, the relationship can be easily maintained thanks to the capabilities provided by MORPHEUS (see section 5).

Finally, at the Architectural Metamodel level, both DDs and DRs should be considered, to properly evaluate the impact of any change on the Architectural Specification. Therefore, the PRISMA Architectural Metamodel has been modified to introduce both of them at this level of abstraction. Fig. 2 shows a partial view of the PRISMA Metamodel, which has been extended to include a new element, the *DesignAsset,* in order to describe the DD and DR associated to each *ArchitecturalElement.* However, as stated above, this approach can be applied to any Architectural Metamodel. Another advantage of the proposal is that the *DesignAsset* could be linked to any other architectural element, when considered necessary, just by establishing properly the relationships inside the Metamodel and applying the process described in the following.

Fig. 2 also shows that *DesignAsset* has a relationship *traceFrom*, used to determine which ArchitecturalScenario originated the description of the Architectural Element. However, the task of specifying the relationship *traceFrom* could be cumbersome and error-prone if it was performed by hand. This has motivated the development of a proposal based on the use of M2M transformations, facilitating that both the *trace-From* relationship and the *DesignAsset* itself can be automatically generated in the target Architectural Model, as described in the following section.

3.1 Model-to-Model Transformations to Deal with Traceability Links

As indicated in Fig. 1, the *Synthesize and Transform* activity in ATRIUM is in charge of the generation of the proto-architecture. Considering that the Goal Model and the Scenario Model must be transformed into the target Architectural Model, the use of M2M transformation techniques emerges as the most adequate approach to describe a solution for this activity. Several existing languages, such as QVT [24] or GReAT [31], have been proposed as solutions to define M2M transformations that increase the productivity, capture traceability relationships between models, improve maintainability by consistently describing the traceability throughout the lifecycle, etc. These languages were analyzed in [22], where their suitability for ATRIUM was studied by considering their support for several required features, such as the capability to *incrementally* update the target Architecture in response to the evolution in the Scenario and the Goal Model, or the support for automatic *tracing* between the source and target models. This analysis led us to select *QVT Relations* as the most adequate language to describe the required transformations.

To describe how our transformation works, we have to introduce briefly the way in which QVT Relations operates. In this language, a transformation is defined between *candidate models* and specified as a set of *relations*. A candidate model is any model that conforms to some Metamodel referenced in the transformation declaration. Every *relation* describes the constraints to be satisfied by the elements of these candidate models; all relations must hold in order to successfully apply the transformation.

Table 1. Declaring the Transformation to Generate the Architectural Model

```
transformation ScenariosToArchModel(goals: GoalMetamodel,
    scenarios: ScenarioMetamodel, archModel:ArchitecturalMetamodel)
```

Consider, for instance, the transformation in Table 1, which generates the target Architectural Model from two inputs: the Goal Model and the Scenario Model. This transformation has three candidate models, namely: *goals*, a candidate model conforming to the ATRIUM Goal Metamodel; *scenarios*, a candidate model conforming to the ATRIUM Scenario Metamodel; and finally *archModel*, a candidate model which must conform to the target Architectural Metamodel (in our case, the chosen metamodel is that of PRISMA). Specifically, we are going to focus here on

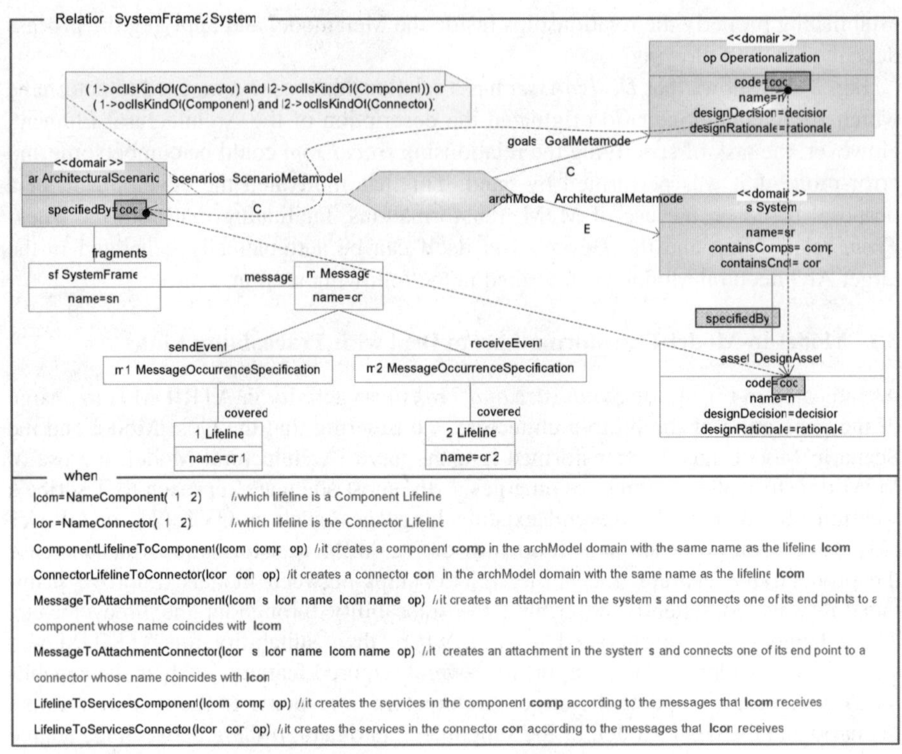

Fig. 3. Describing a Relation to Propagate the Design Decisions and Rationales

how *Operationalizations* and *ArchitecturalScenarios* are used in the generation of both *DesignAssets* and the *traceFrom* relationship in the target Model[1].

The structure of a *relation* is better exposed with an example. Consider the one in Fig. 3, *SystemFrame2System*, one of the relations which compose the transformation described in Table 1. This one was defined to generate "Systems" in the target Architectural Model. Every relation is defined by two or more domains (three in this case), identified by typed variables which must match some of the Metamodels in the transformation declaration. In Fig. 3, these are the same which were defined in the example in Table 1, namely: *goals*, *scenarios*, and *archModel*.

The relation imposes a pattern on every domain, describing the constraints to be satisfied by the elements of the involved model. When the elements contained in each candidate model *simultaneously* fulfill their corresponding patterns, then the matching happens and the relation is held.

In the example in Fig. 3, three patterns are described, using QVT graphical syntax: one for every domain (*goals*, *scenarios*, *archModel*). For instance, in the *goals* domain the relation establishes that every Operationalization (i.e. all elements of type *Operationalization*) must be retrieved to be used. But the pattern also imposes the condition which defines that the *code* of these Operationalizations gets bound to the variable *cod*. Simultaneously, in the *scenarios* domain, every Architectural Scenario

---

[1] Interest reader is referred to [22] to obtain the whole description of the transformation.

(i.e. all elements of type *ArchitecturalScenario*) has a variable *specifiedBy* which is bound to the same variable *cod*. Then, the dotted line in Fig. 3 highlights the matching which might happen between both domains; this means that only Operationalizations and Architectural Scenarios having the same value in these attributes will be used when the relation (or its container transformation) is applied. A similar pattern is also defined for the *archModel* domain, as can be seen in the Figure. In this case, not only the attribute *code* (which is again bound to the variable *cod*), but the rest of the attributes is also bound to those in the Operationalization.

The lower half of Fig. 3 contains the *when* clause, which describes a condition that must be held before the relation can be successfully applied. Within this example, the *when* clause contains the code required to invoke some additional relations.

In QVT Relations, the transformation can be defined either to *check* the models for consistency or to *enforce* the consistency by modifying one of the models, selected as target. Therefore, every pattern can be evaluated using two different modes: *checkonly* (marked with a *C* in Fig. 3), that just checks if the pattern is satisfied, reporting an inconsistency otherwise; and *enforce* (marked with an *E* in Fig. 3) which first checks whether the pattern is satisfied, and then creates, modifies or erases elements in the target model, as it is necessary to ensure consistency.

In the example in Fig. 3, we can observe that domains *goals* and *scenarios* are marked as *checkonly* but, on the contrary, *archModel* is marked as *enforce*. This means that when *archModel* is the target model, the proto-architecture is generated. The execution of the transformation checks whether there are elements in the target model that satisfy the relations, that is, the patterns described for its domain. If that was not the case, elements in the target model will be created, deleted or modified to enforce the consistency. This allows the analyst either to generate the proto-architecture, or to check whether inconsistencies emerge between the generated proto-architecture, the Goal Model, and the Scenario Model. Therefore, information about our DDs and DRs is automatically registered for Architectural Elements as the target Architectural Model is generated. For instance, in our proposal, every *System* in the target Architectural Model will be related to its corresponding *DesignAsset*, because the relationship *specifiedBy* between them will be automatically generated, as it has been defined in the relation described in Fig. 3.

Another advantage of using QVT Relations is that the language itself automatically generates a *Trace Class* for every relation, facilitating the registration of mappings between the elements in the involved Models, for instance those between elements in the proto-architecture and their corresponding elements in the scenarios and goals models. This means that the already described *traceFrom* relationship (see Fig.2) is automatically generated when the transformation is applied. This makes possible to easily maintain the traceability, both forward and backwards. Therefore, if some DD changes at the requirements stage, the set of architectural elements which will be affected can be determined automatically, and therefore the Architectural Model can easily be maintained up-to-date.

4 Case Study: Operationalizations in a Teachmover Robot

The proposal has been validated in a real case study associated to the European project EFTCoR (Environmental Friendly and cost-effective Technology for Coating

Removal) [9]. This project aims at designing a family of robots capable of performing maintenance operations for ship hulls. The system includes operations such as coating removal, cleaning and re-painting of the hull. Among the subsystems constituting the EFTCoR platform, our case study focuses on the *Robotic Devices Control Unit* (RDCU), which interacts with other robotic devices to obtain the required information to control the different devices (positioning systems and cleaning tools) to be used for maintenance tasks. The RDCU is in charge of commanding and controlling, in a co-ordinated way, the positioning of devices together with the tools attached to them. However, the use of a real system would be too complex in order to exemplify this proposal, so TeachMover [33], a simplified version of the EFTCoR will be used in the remainder of this article. The TeachMover is a durable, affordable robotic arm used for teaching robotic fundamentals. It has been specifically designed to simulate industrial robotic operations. Similarly to what was said for the EFTCoR, this work focuses on the RDCU in charge of controlling this robot.

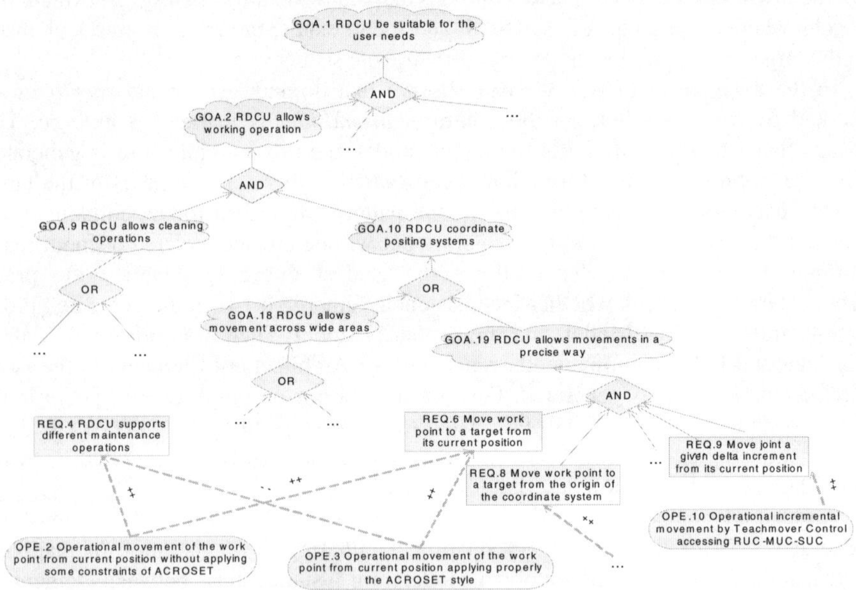

Fig. 4. Partial description of some of the *EFTCoR* requirements

Fig.4 shows a partial view of the Teachmover requirements that have been described using the ATRIUM Goal Model during the *Define Goals* activity. It depicts part of its functional requirements by refining the goal *Suitability*. It can be observed that the RDCU is expected to coordinate its movement, allow different cleaning operations in specific areas, and catch objects. These goals are refined into several goals, and finally into requirements. Fig. 4 also illustrates an example of how the requirement "REQ 6" is refined into two Operationalizations, namely:

- *"OPE.2 Operational movement of the work point from current position without applying some constraints of the ACROSET Style"*. The DD described in this

Operationalization is: "To perform the operational movement by allowing the direct access between systems RUC and SUC". The associated DR is: "The direct access facilitates an advantage in terms of the number of operations to be performed, because they are not only limited to the active tool";

- *"OPE.3 Operational movement of the work point from current position, applying properly the ACROSET style"*. The DD described along with OPE.3 is: "To perform the operational movement, by means of the interaction between the systems RUC-MUC-SUC". The related DR is: "This alternative is compliant with the ACROSET style; however, it exhibits problems because the number of operations that can be performed is only limited to the active tool".

Both the requirements and the operationalization are related by means of *contributions* relationships, that denote how the solutions contribute positively and/or negatively to meet the requirements. For example, it can be observed that the operationalizations "OPE.2" and "OPE.3" have a positive impact on the "REQ.6". However, the former has a positive impact on "REQ4" whereas the latter has a negative impact. It facilitates the analysis of which alternatives have less negative impact on the set of requirements. This example is used in the following to facilitate the comprehension of the presented work.

Associated to the *Operationalization* "OPE.2" an architectural scenario has been described, depicted in Fig. 5. It can be seen that the recommendations established by the DD have been followed, as the communication between the systems RUC and SUC has been directly established by means of components and connectors. When this scenario is described, the relationship *specifiedBy*, which defines its connection to the *Operationalization* "OPE.2", is established by the analyst that is shown as a contention relation in the Model Explorer situated on the left in Fig.5.

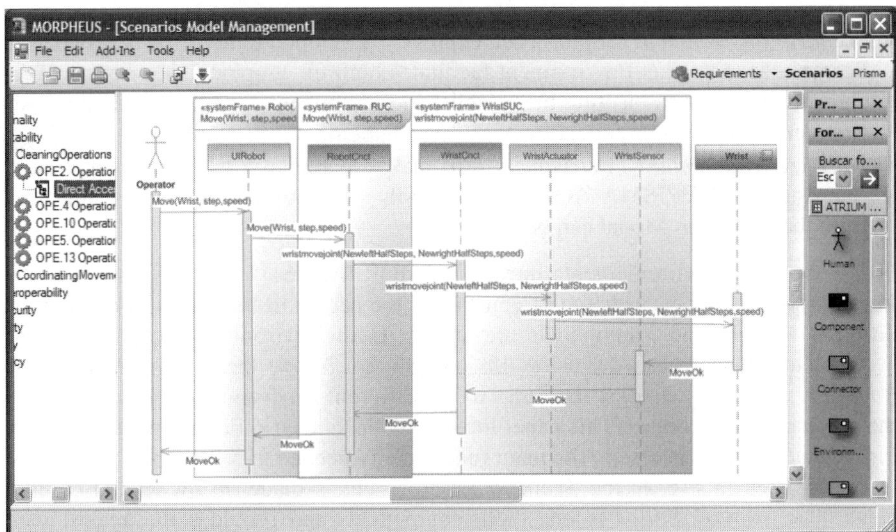

Fig. 5. Describing in the Scenario Environment an Architectural Scenario related to "OPE.2"

Once the Scenario Model has been described the activity *Synthesize and transform* can be applied to generate the proto-architecture. This activity can be performed when at least one scenario has been defined, and thanks to the *incrementality* feature of QVT as new architectural scenarios are defined the proto-architecture can be updated to introduce the necessary changes. It is during this activity that the *DesignAsset* and traceability links are generated as well. According to the example described above, a *DesignAsset* will be generated in the target Architectural Model that will be related to each one of the generated Architectural Elements; in this case, those are the elements Robot, RUC and WristSUC. The following section describes the way in which this activity is supported by MORPHEUS.

5 MORPHEUS: Supporting the Proposal

Nowadays, automation is becoming one of the principal means to achieve greater productivity and higher quality products. For this reason, its introduction in this proposal was compulsory, both to provide support for the meta-modelling and modelling processes and to assist as much as possible in their description and exploitation. This led us to the development of a tool called MORPHEUS, a graphical environment for the description of the different models, to provide the analysts with an improved legibility. ATRIUM entails three main activities, and this has caused that MORPHEUS[2] has also been structured in three different environments:

- *Requirement Environment* [19] provides analysts with a requirements meta-modelling work context for describing Requirement Metamodels customized according to the project's semantic needs. This Environment automatically provides another work context for the description and analysis of Requirement Models according to the active Metamodel.
- *Scenario Environment* [21] has been expressly developed to describe the ATRIUM Scenario Model. This Environment facilitates both the graphical description of architectural scenarios meeting the established requirements and their later synthesis to generate the proto-architecture of the system being defined.
- *Software Architecture Environment* [26] makes available a whole graphical environment for the PRISMA AO-ADL [25] so that the proto-architecture synthesized from the Scenarios Model can be refined.

Fig. 6 shows the main elements integrating MORPHEUS. As can be observed, the *RepositoryManager* is in charge of controlling the access to the repository where the different Models and Metamodels are stored. Each Environment described above accesses to the repository by using this component. Above these Environments, the *Back-End* allows the analyst to access to the different Environments, and to manage the projects he/she creates. This paper focuses on the Scenario Environment, shown in Fig. 5, that provides access to the main functionality needed to support the proposal.

As depicted in Fig. 6, the Scenario Environment is made up by several components. The *ScenarioEditor* is one these components and provides the analyst with

---

facilities for graphical modelling the ATRIUM Scenario Model. It must be high-lighted that the graphical description of the Scenario Models was a must for the design of this component. For this reason, several graphical components were analysed in order to select the one with more capabilities.

Eventually, as shown in Fig. 6, Microsoft Office Visio Drawing Control 2003[35] was selected, because it allows a straightforward management, both for using and modifying shapes. This feature is highly relevant for our purposes, because all the kinds of concepts that are included in our Scenario Metamodel can easily have different shapes, thus facilitating the legibility of the Model. Fig. 5 shows what MORPHEUS looks like when the *ScenarioEditor* is loaded. It also shows another element, the Model Browser, placed on the left, which allows the user to access the Scenario Model being defined. This browser loads, automatically, the *Operationalizations* defined during the *Define Goals* activity, along with their corresponding trace from the *Requirements*. In this way, the user can easily understand why the scenarios are being defined. In addition, the stencil placed on the right provides the user with all the concepts described in the Scenario Metamodel, so that he/she only needs to drag and drop the relevant concept on the graphical view to perform its description in the Scenario Model.

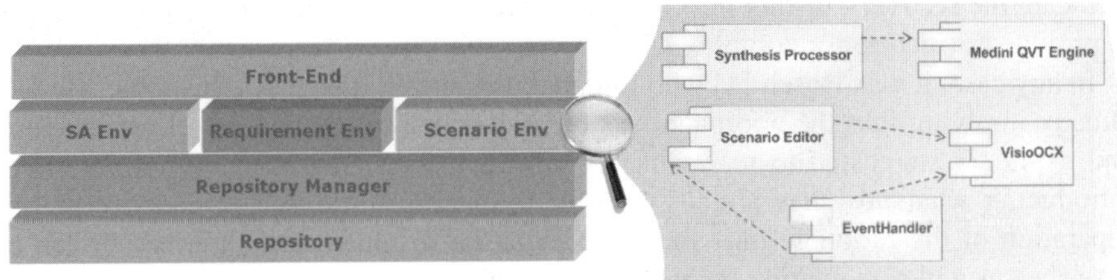

Fig. 6. An Overview of the MORPHEUS Architecture

Fig. 6 also shows that other component introduced in the development of the Scenario Environment was *SynthesisProcessor*, which applies the QVT Relations using a QVT engine called Medini [18]. With this purpose, it uses the Repository Manager to retrieve the active Goal Model and Scenario Model in XMI, and their respective Metamodels in ECORE. *SynthesisProcessor* provides Medini with them, and also with the name of the target Architectural Model and Metamodel, generating as a result a XMI file with the target Architectural Model. Once the Architectural Model has been generated, it can be loaded in the corresponding tool to be refined. If the user has chosen PRISMA as the target Architectural Metamodel to be instantiated, then MORPHEUS can be exploited to refine the Architectural Model, because it provides functionality to load such a description.

6   Related Work

As already explained in the Introduction, the specification of architectural rationales was an early requirement in the software architecture field, dating back to the very first article on the topic [27]. However, even in initial approaches, when architecture was considered largely as a way to document part of the system's design, the rationale was soon neglected. The reason was probably that at this early stage it was perceived basically as textual, unstructured documentation, and conceived as the kind of process information which was too often deemed as unimportant.

However, as software systems kept growing in size and complexity, architecture achieved ever more relevance; not only as a critical design asset, but also as a map or blueprint which would help to provide a global perspective of the system, and also to explain or describe the current stage during the software development process. Even in this context, DDs were still not explicitly documented, and hence all the assumptions and information about the design and its evolution, the *architectural knowledge*, was finally lost ("vaporized"). Indeed, if the architecture has a medium size, it is almost impossible to deduce the reasoning which led to the final structure, as the rationales behind concrete DDs are undocumented, and get ultimately forgotten. This is particularly unfortunate when considering evolution.

In recent times, Lago *et al* [16] were among the first authors in emphasizing the need to recover and maintain this information. Their proposal was not specifically constrained to the architectural level, but tried to include every design *assumption*, a term which would include our current architectural DDs, and which hinted towards an atomic, first-class specific module. Also, traceability was one of the reasons used to advocate the recovery of this information; however, it was not suggested to exploit it to provide a structure for complex DRs.

In any case, it was Bosch [1] who initiated the current interest in this topic. He was already implying that the approach was circumscribed to the context of architecture, and explicitly suggested to maintain this information as first-class *design decisions*, introducing what now has already become a specific term. A consequence of this separation of the rationale into small pieces is the resulting structure, which can be described as a plexus relating the whole architecture to the high-level rationale.

Some other initial works providing suggestions for this structure include Tyree and Akerman's [34], which proposes an ontology from an early industrial point of view, and the early survey by Tang, Babar *et al*, published in an evolved form in [32]. This survey also defines a framework to capture architectural knowledge, expressing the similarities between several approaches, and providing a first attempt to reconcile them. A different ontology is proposed by Kruchten *et al* [15], which divide the architectural knowledge into decisions, assumptions and context. This should be supported by tools, able to maintain also to eventually *evolve* this information.

Indeed, tool support has been one of the main interests in the area. There have been essentially two major approaches. The first one consists of describing DDs with some of the aforementioned structures, and then binding them to the architectural model, to provide an integrated perspective [14]. The other approach also describes those DDs, but it is more interested in defining platforms implementing strategies to share this knowledge between actors involved in the development process [7].

Garcia *et al* [8] use an aspect-oriented approach to tackle the description of architecture knowledge, namely describing DDs in a separate aspect [8]. In fact, this is reminiscent of our own approach, which also uses aspects. However, in ATRIUM aspects are not used just to describe DDs, but for almost everything; the process itself can be considered aspect-oriented, and in fact it covers every conceived *early aspect*, both at the requirements and at the architectural level.

Falessi *et al* [5] propose a goal-based, scenario-driven *decision model* to choose between alternatives, and to document the corresponding DR. They also detail some potential inhibitors which could hinder its use, and provide some hints towards their subsequent value-based approach [6]. Obviously, this has some points of contact with ATRIUM, a consequence of both being goal-oriented. But their proposal lacks both the automatic support and the integration within a MDD process, which provides the traceability relationship and defines the strengths of our approach.

Our approach also has some common points with the already mentioned proposal by Jansen and Bosch [12]. They also provide a decision model, and even an extended metamodel which includes explicit DDs. The latter is, to some extent, similar to the one presented in section 3. However in our own case the extension was mandatory; otherwise new concepts would not have been explicit, and our DDs could have not been considered inside the MDD process.

Indeed most of the similarities between these proposals and the extended ATRIUM are casual or simply due to their common origin. In fact, in the existing literature there are only two works with a close resemblance. In the first one, Sinnema *et al* [30] suggest to exploit the variability in the architecture to support the definition of DDs. In ATRIUM this is indeed a consequence, not the starting point; but this is still the closest suggestion ever done to (implicitly) support DDs on top of traces.

In the second one, Mattson *et al* [17] remind that capturing design information is a feature of any MDD approach; also, that architecture itself is not fully integrated into MDA. Therefore, they provide a basic architectural framework, and then propose to formalize design rules, which should be enforced by the MDD process. However no more details are provided; though this is the only paper suggesting using MDD in this context, it is far from being complete.

In fact, both Sinnema's and Mattson's are preliminary short papers, sketching some interesting ideas which have not yet being exploited by further research. Indeed, our approach fulfils many of the promises implicit in those papers; for example, in ATRIUM traceability links can be used to define a variation point in any part of the process, and bind it to any explicit decision; and both the architectural framework and the exploitation of traceability within the MDD process and transformations are much more complex than any previous suggestion.

7 Conclusions and Further Work

As just noted in the previous section, the extended ATRIUM methodology and the tool support provided by MORPHEUS provide a support for traceability which allows a complex and advanced framework for the definition of architectural knowledge. From this perspective, their capabilities exceed those of any existing proposal, at least in terms of automation, generation and tracing. The rationale is defined in a composite structure which can be related to architecture itself, defining an elaborate network of first-class DDs. The consequences of using this approach are also fairly unknown; it obviously supports the definition of complex structures, but the great potential they provide has yet to be investigated.

For instance, there is a line of research which intends to deduce undocumented processes from their architecture [13]. To do so, they must extract the *deltas* between different versions, and deduce the nature of the decisions made. In our approach, this is not necessary, even when DD/DRs have not been originally provided; instead of defining deltas by comparing different versions, MORPHEUS can be used to generate a whole new version starting from a single different decision. The potential to exploit variability is enormous, but it can be also applied to specific issues like this.

Compared to other tools in the field, MORPHEUS provides a lot of facilities and complex functionality. Most of the others try just to either describing or sharing some static information; only a few of them try to actually integrate the information in the process and let it play an active role [14][17][30]. This even transcends the limits of the specific subfield of architectural knowledge, to be applied for concerns involved in any aspect of the architectural process. In this regard, the presented approach not only fulfils its specific purpose, but also provides a core model which can be applied to fulfil some of the traditional requests in the architecture field.

In summary, the proposal described in this paper provides both the technology and the methodology to define and explicitly manage architectural knowledge; this is done in a consistent and principled way, and providing an optimal integration. But this does not *just* describe a model-driven variant of a known idea, or provides a particular tool to deal with it. In fact, the most important contribution of this paper is the outlining of the explicit relationship to *traceability*, the explanation of how this provides the basic structure for the architectural rationale, and the consequences of this approach.

Acknowledgments. This work has been funded by the Spanish Ministry of Education and Science under the National R&D&I Program, META Project TIN2006-15175-C05-01. Further funding comes from Rey Juan Carlos University and the autonomous Government of Madrid under the IASOMM Project URJC-CM-2007-CET-1555.

References

[1] Bosch, J.: Software Architecture: The Next Step. In: Oquendo, F., Warboys, B.C., Morrison, R. (eds.) EWSA 2004. LNCS, vol. 3047, pp. 194–199. Springer, Heidelberg (2004)

[2] Chung, L., Nixon, B.A., Yu, E., Mylopoulos, J.: Non-Functional Requirements in Software Engineering. Kluwer Academic Publishing, Boston (2000)

[3] Czarnecki, K., Helsen, S.: Classification of Model Transformation Approaches. IBM Systems Journal 45(3), 621–645 (2006)

[4] Dardenne, A., van Lamsweerde, A., Fickas, S.: Goal-directed Requirements Acquisition. Science of Computer Programming 20(1-2), 3–50 (1993)

[5] Falessi, D., Becker, M., Cantone, G.: Design Decision Rationale: Experiences and Steps Ahead Towards Systematic Use. In: SHARK 2006. ACM DL, New York (2006)

[6] Falessi, D., Cantone, G., Kruchten, P.: Value-Based Design Decision Rationale Documentation: Principles and Empirical Feasibility Study. In: 7th Working IEEE/IFIP Conf. on Softw. Architecture (WICSA 2008), pp. 189–198. IEEE CS, New York (2008)

[7] Farenhorst, R., Lago, P., van Vliet, H.: EAGLE: Effective Tool Support for Sharing Architectural Knowledge. Intl. J. Cooperative Information Syst. 16(3-4), 413–437 (2007)

[8] Garcia, A., Batista, T., Rashid, A., Sant'Anna, C.: Driving and Managing Architectural Decisions with Aspects. In: SHARK 2006. ACM DL, New York (2006)

[9] GROWTH G3RD-CT-00794: EFTCOR: Environmental Friendly and cost-effective Technology for Coating Removal. European Project, 5th Framework Program (2003)

[10] Harrison, N.B., Avgeriou, P., Zdun, U.: Using Patterns to Capture Architectural Decisions. IEEE Software 24(4), 38–45 (2007)

[11] ISO/IEC Standard 9126-1, Software Engineering- Product Quality-Part1: Quality Model, ISO Copyright Office, Geneva (2001)

[12] Jansen, A., Bosch, J.: Software Architecture as a Set of Architectural Design Decisions. In: 5th Working IEEE/IFIP Conf. on Softw. Architecture (WICSA 2005), pp. 109–120 (2005)

[13] Jansen, A., Bosch, J., Avgeriou, P.: Documenting After the Fact: Recovering Architectural Design Decisions. Journal of Systems and Software 81(4), 536–557 (2008)

[14] Jansen, A., van der Ven, J., Avgeriou, P., Hammer, D.K.: Tool Support for Architectural Decisions. In: 6th Working IEEE/IFIP Conf. on Software Architecture (WICSA 2007), p. 4. IEEE CS Press, New York (2007)

[15] Kruchten, P., Lago, P., van Vliet, H.: Building Up and Reasoning about Architectural Knowledge. In: Hofmeister, C., Crnković, I., Reussner, R. (eds.) QoSA 2006. LNCS, vol. 4214, pp. 43–58. Springer, Heidelberg (2006)

[16] Lago, P., van Vliet, H.: Explicit Assumptions Enrich Architectural Models. In: 27th Intl. Conf. on Soft. Engineering (ICSE 2005), pp. 206–214. IEEE CS Press, New York (2005)

[17] Mattsson, A., Lundell, B., Lings, B., Fitzgerald, B.: Experiences from Representing Software Architecture in a Large Industrial Project using Model-Driven Development. In: SHARK/ADI 2007. IEEE DL, New York (2007)

[18] Medini, QVT Relations, http://projects.ikv.de/qvt

[19] Navarro, E., Letelier, P., Gómez, A.: MORPHEUS: tool support to tailor requirements management to the specific project needs. Inf. & Soft. Technology (submitted, 2008)

[20] Navarro, E., Letelier, P., Ramos, I.: Requirements and Scenarios: playing Aspect Oriented Software Architectures. In: 6th Working IEEE/IFIP Conference on Software Architecture (WICSA 2007) (short paper). IEEE DL, New York (2007)

[21] Navarro, E., Letelier, P., Jaén, J., Ramos, I.: Supporting the Automatic Generation of Proto-Architectures. In: Oquendo, F. (ed.) ECSA 2007. LNCS, vol. 4758, pp. 43–58. Springer, Heidelberg (2007) (Best poster award)

[22] Navarro, E.: Architecture Traced from Requirements applying a Unified Methodology, PhD thesis, Computing Systems Department, UCLM (2007)

[23] Navarro, E., Letelier, P., Mocholí, J.A., Ramos, I.: A Metamodeling Approach for Requirements Specification. J. of Computer Information Systems 47(5), 67–77 (2006)

[24] OMG document ptc/05-11-01, QVT, MOF Query/Views/Transformations. Final adopted specification (2005)

[25] Pérez, J., Ali, N., Carsí, J.A., Ramos, I.: Designing Software Architectures with an Aspect-Oriented Architecture Description Language. In: Gorton, I., Heineman, G.T., Crnković, I., Schmidt, H.W., Stafford, J.A., Szyperski, C.A., Wallnau, K. (eds.) CBSE 2006. LNCS, vol. 4063, pp. 123–138. Springer, Heidelberg (2006)

[26] Pérez, J., Navarro, E., Letelier, P., Ramos, I.: A Modelling Proposal for Aspect-Oriented Software Architectures. In: 13th IEEE Int. Conference and Workshop on the Engineering of Computer Based Systems (ECBS), pp. 32–41. IEEE CS, New York (2006)

[27] Perry, D.E., Wolf, A.L.: Foundations for the Study of Software Architecture. ACM Software Engineering Notes 17(4), 40–52 (1992)

[28] Selic, B.: The Pragmatics of Model-Driven Development. IEEE Soft. 20(5), 19–25 (2003)

[29] OMG, Software Process Engineering Metamodel (SPEM), Version 1.1 formal/05-01-06 (2005), http://www.omg.org/cgi-bin/doc?formal/2005-01-06

[30] Sinnema, M., van der Ven, J., Deelstra, S.: Using Variability Modeling Principles to Capture Architectural Knowledge. In: SHARK 2006. ACM DL, New York (2006)

[31] Sprinkle, J., Agrawal, A., Levendovszky, T., Shi, F., Karsai, G.: Domain Model Translation Using Graph Transformations. In: 10th IEEE International Conference on Engineering of Computer-Based Systems (ECBS 2003), pp. 159–167. IEEE CS, New York (2003)

[32] Tang, A., Babar, M.A., Gorton, I., Han, J.: A Survey of Architecture Design Rationale. Journal of Systems & Software 79(12), 1792–1804 (2007)

[33] TeachMover,
`http://www.questechzone.com/microbot/teachmover.htm`

[34] Tyree, J., Akerman, A.: Architecture Decisions: Demystifying Architecture. IEEE Software 22(2), 19–27 (2005)

[35] Visio (2003),
`http://office.microsoft.com/es-es/FX010857983082.aspx`

Development of Fault-Tolerant Software Systems Based on Architectural Abstractions

Patrick H.S. Brito[1,*], Rogério de Lemos[2], and Cecília M.F. Rubira[1,**]

[1] Institute of Computing – State University of Campinas (Unicamp)
{pbrito,cmrubira}@ic.unicamp.br
[2] Computing Laboratory – University of Kent
r.delemos@kent.ac.uk

Abstract. The incorporation of fault tolerance into systems normally increases their complexity, which consequently makes their analysis more difficult. This paper discusses how architectural abstractions can be effective in developing fault-tolerant software systems. Depending on the fault model and the resources available, different abstractions can be employed for representing issues that are related to fault tolerance, such as error detection, and error and fault handling. These architectural abstractions, and their internal views, can be instantiated into concrete components and connectors for designing fault-tolerant software architectures. Since structural and behavioural properties associated with these abstractions are formally specified, the process of verifying and validating software architectures can be automated. In this paper, we show how appropriate architectural abstractions and a recursive process can facilitate the architectural modelling and analysis of fault-tolerant software systems. The feasibility of the proposed approach is demonstrated in the context of a critical real-time application.

1 Introduction

Fault tolerance is the ability of a system to continue its normal operation despite the presence of faults [2]. Since fault tolerance has a global system scope, it should be related to both architectural elements (components and connectors) and architectural configurations. However, the incorporation of fault tolerance into systems normally increases their complexity, making their analysis more difficult. One way of handling the inherent complexity of fault-tolerant systems is to adopt architectural abstractions. These are able to hide system complexity, and provide the means for analysing how errors are propagated, detected and handled, and how faults in the system are handled [3].

The provision of fault tolerance relies on the existence of redundancy, which can be incorporated either implicitly or explicitly at the architectural level. An

---

* Supported by Fapesp/Brazil, grant 06/02116-2 and CAPES/Brazil, grant 0722-07-3.
** Cecília M.F. Rubira is partially supported by CNPq/Brazil, grants 301446/2006-7 and 484138/2006-5.

R. Morrison, D. Balasubramaniam, and K. Falkner (Eds.): ECSA 2008, LNCS 5292, pp. 131–147, 2008.

example of implicit redundancy is the usage of exception handling for supporting error recovery. If special care is not taken when structuring the system, the normal and abnormal specifications can be entangled thus increasing system complexity. Explicit redundancy is an inherent aspect of strongly-structured systems [15], i.e., systems in which the structuring of redundancy is part of the actual system, thus restricting the impact of faults. Examples of explicit redundancy are N-version programming and recovery blocks, which are two software fault tolerance techniques. In our previous work, we have defined an architectural abstraction, the idealised fault-tolerant architectural element (iFTE), an implicit redundancy approach based on exception handling, that provides the means for structuring abnormal behaviour in software architectures [4,5,10]. In that work, we have focused on the formal modelling of the architectural elements and their configurations using B-Method and CSP, including the representation of exception types.

In this paper, we present, first, how architectural abstractions can be effective when developing fault-tolerant software systems, applying both implicit and explicit redundancies, and second, how a general process can enforce the role of architectural abstractions in the specification, verification and validation of fault-tolerant software systems. In particular, how this process is able to support different abstractions, according to the design decisions, failure assumptions, and availability of resources. The process will be presented in the context of two architectural abstractions. First, the idealised fault-tolerant architectural element (iFTE), which provides the means for promoting error confinement and supporting fault tolerance at the architectural level. And second, the halt-on-failure architectural element (HoFE), which is an abstraction that assumes crash failure semantics, provides the basis for incorporating explicit redundancy when designing fault-tolerant systems. Depending on the fault model and the availability of resources, the appropriate architectural abstraction should be used. For obtaining fault-tolerant software architectures, these abstractions are instantiated into architectural components and connectors, which are then configured depending on the interaction constraints dictated by their structural and behavioural properties. These architectural abstractions are presented in the context of a general process that together with the use of formal languages allows, first, the automatic verification of architectural models for identifying and removing design faults, and second, the generation of architectural-based test cases that are able to identify and remove implementation faults that are related to the architectural design of the system.

The aim of this paper is to show that the appropriate architectural abstractions and a simple component-based development process can facilitate the architectural modelling and analysis of fault-tolerant software systems. Compared with previous publications [4,5,10], the contribution of the paper is twofold. First, we show how architectural abstractions should be defined in terms of structural and behavioural properties to be used to guide the specification, verification and validation of the system, and for that, we have defined a new architectural abstraction based on explicit redundancy (HoFE). Second, we show how a recursive component-based development process can be tailored to accommodate different types of architectural abstractions. The proposed process supports the specification, verification and validation of fault-tolerant software architectures, and supports the prevention and removal of faults at different stages of the development process [3]. Since the internal structure of the architectural elements can be recursively detailed, the software architecture can be hierarchically specified, verified and validated, which helps to master the additional complexity associated with the provision of fault tolerance. Moreover, since the software architecture is verified in the context of specific behavioural scenarios, it scopes the model to be verified, which, consequently, reduces the state-space of the model, thus improving its scalability. The rest of this paper is organised as follows. Section 2 presents two architectural abstractions for developing fault-tolerant systems. Section 3 discusses how architectural abstractions can be integrated into a development process of fault-tolerant software systems. Section 4 evaluates the feasibility of the overall approach using a critical real-time application as an example. Section 5 presents some related work. Finally, Section 6 provides some concluding remarks and future directions of research.

2   Fault-Tolerant Architectural Abstractions

The architectural abstractions presented below are used to structure software architectures of fault-tolerant systems. The first one (Section 2.1) implements error handling based on the exception handling mechanism, while the second one (Section 2.2) is based on crash failure. The components are described in terms of provided and required interfaces, to which operations are associated.

2.1   Idealised Fault-Tolerant Architectural Element

The idealised fault-tolerant architectural element (iFTE) is an architectural abstraction for structuring fault-tolerant systems. This abstraction enforces the principles associated with the concept of the idealised fault-tolerant component [2], and incorporates mechanisms for detecting errors, as well as propagating and handling them in a structured way.

The iFTE abstraction provides an explicit separation of concerns between two types of behaviour: (i) the normal behaviour, which realises the services of the application, and (ii) the abnormal (exceptional) behaviour, which realises the detection, propagation and handling of errors. In order to provide this separation, the iFTE abstraction defines four types of interfaces, which are presented in Figure 1: (i) I_iFTE_PN is a provided interface that defines a set of fault-tolerant operations; (ii) I_iFTE_PA is a provided interface that defines a set of exceptions that the iFTE signals to the external environment; (iii) I_iFTE_RN is a required interface that specifies a set of operations used for implementing its normal behaviour and for handling exceptions; and (iv) I_iFTE_RA is a required interface that specifies the external exceptions that the iFTE is able to handle. In other words, while the I_iFTE_PN and I_iFTE_RN are responsible for the normal behaviour, I_iFTE_PA and I_iFTE_RA are responsible for the abnormal behaviour.

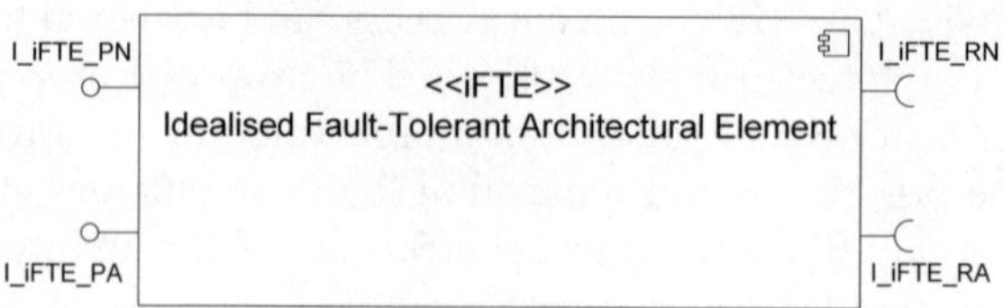

Fig. 1. iFTE Abstraction

iFTE External Behaviour. The external behaviour of the iFTE is defined through behavioural scenarios related to its external interfaces. A scenario is a sequence of events expected during the system operation [17]. In the context of this paper, a scenario is defined as a sequence of events triggered by the request of an operation of the I_iFTE_PN interface, including operation responses, other operation requests and signalling of exceptions. A total of nine different scenarios were identified for the iFTE. The scenarios are derived from the interaction rules existing between the interfaces of the iFTE. These rules involve requests of external services, the reception of the respective returns (normal or abnormal), raising of new exceptions, propagation of received exceptions, and masking of exceptions for tolerating software faults.

Internal View of the iFTE. The internal view of the iFTE (Figure 2) is composed of five architectural elements: (i) the Normal component implements the normal behaviour of the iFTE; (ii) the Abnormal component handles the exceptions raised by the Normal component, and those propagated from the environment of the iFTE; (iii) the Provided component acts like a bridge between the services provided by the iFTE and its environment, including the signal of exceptions; (iv) the Required component also acts like a bridge, but between the required services of the iFTE and its environment; and (v) the Coordinator connector coordinates the interaction between the four internal components. It is important to stress that the iFTE also supports the resolution of architectural mismatches. This high-level adaptation is carried out by the Provided and Required components present in Figure 2.

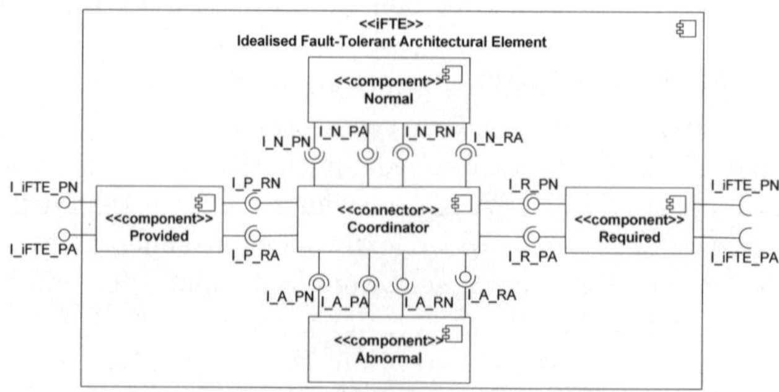

Fig. 2. Internal View of the iFTE

The **Normal** component can be either implemented by scratch or by reusing an existing component. When reusing an existing component, it is necessary to adapt the interfaces of an existing component to the external interfaces of the **Normal** component. This can be done in terms of two adapters: one responsible for converting all the provided interfaces of the existing component, and the other responsible for converting all the required interfaces of the existing component.

iFTE Internal Behaviour. Analysing the internal details of the iFTE, it is possible to distinguish some interactions between the internal elements, which characterise new scenarios when compared with the external view [4]. As a whole, we have identified four new scenarios involving the masking of internal exceptions, and the other scenarios of the external view.

2.2   Halt-on-Failure Architectural Element

The halt-on-failure architectural element (HoFE) is an architectural abstraction for the provision of error confinement and fault tolerance, and which enforces the principles associated with the *crash failures* fault model [16]. When an HoFE fails, it fails silently without producing any error signal. The HoFE abstraction defines two types of interfaces, which are presented in Figure 3: (i) I_HoFE_Prov defines a set of operations provided by the HoFE; and (ii) I_HoFE_Req specifies operations required by the HoFE for implementing its behaviour. It is assumed that an HoFE is able to detect failures on other architectural elements from which requests operations, e.g., by associating *time-outs* with the I_HoFE_Req interfaces.

HoFE External Behaviour. The external behaviour of the HoFE architectural abstraction is defined through five basic scenarios: (i) *internal normal execution*, when an HoFE provides the requested services without requesting external services; (ii) *internal erroneous execution*, when an HoFE fails before requesting external services; (iii) *external normal execution*, when an HoFE provides the requested services after receiving the requested external services; (iv) *external erroneous execution 1*, when an HoFE fails after receiving the requested external services; and (v) *external erroneous execution 2*, when an HoFE fails after failing to receive the requested external services. Based on these scenarios, one can describe more complex scenarios of fault-tolerant software architectures that are based on the HoFE architectural abstraction.

Internal View of the HoFE. The internal view of the HoFE can be implemented using different strategies for detecting errors, usually involving explicit

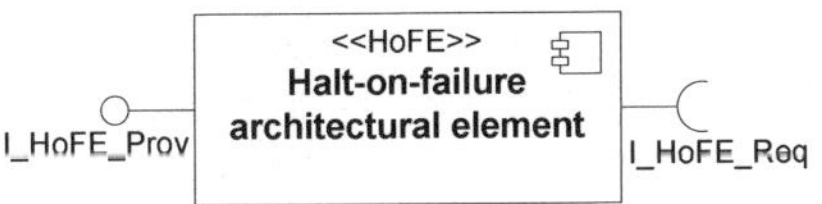

Fig. 3. HoFE Abstraction

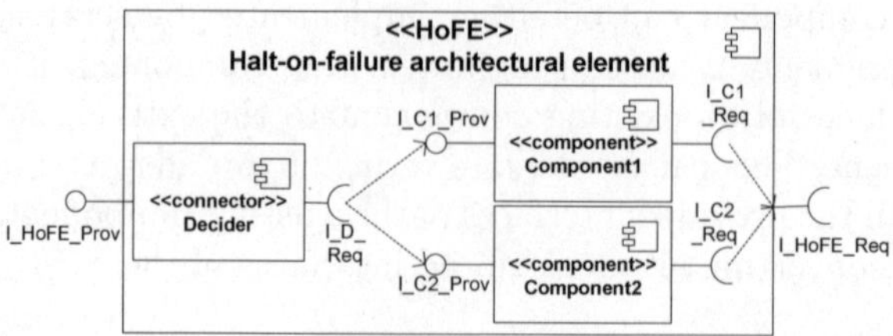

Fig. 4. Implementing a HoFE Using Redundant Components

redundancy. Figure 4 presents a possible implementation using two redundant components. In this approach, the error detection is conducted by the Decider, which evaluates the results of the two executing versions of components. If there is no consensus between them, the result is considered unreliable. Since the error detection depends on both components, this implementation of the HoFE does not provide internal fault tolerance and is not able to recover from internal errors. However, if redundant HoFEs are used, fault tolerance can be implemented at the architectural level.

3   A Rigorous Development Process Using Architectural Abstractions

In our approach, architectural abstractions are first-level units, guiding the development from the architectural specification to the implementation of the application. We propose an iterative, recursive and incremental process for developing fault-tolerant software architectures. Figure 5 presents an overview of the proposed approach. Activity 1 specifies the software architecture, which can be done graphically using a CASE tool. From the system requirements, the architect should first choose an architectural abstraction based on the fault model of the application and the available resources for implementing redundancy. Then, two artefacts should be specified: a UML component diagram representing the structure of the software system, and a set of UML sequence diagrams representing the architectural scenarios related to fault tolerance. The scenarios are represented as sequence of events describing how a specific system behaves in presence of errors for the purpose of tolerating faults. These specific scenarios should be consistent with those defined for a particular architectural abstraction. Activity 2 formally specifies the software architecture (architectural configuration and scenarios). This activity consists on an automatic model transformation from UML (XMI files) to B-Method and CSP. Activity 3 is the formal verification of the architectural elements for identifying design faults related to behavioural inconsistencies that might exist when taking as a reference the scenarios associated with a particular architectural abstraction. So, a different set of predefined properties is used according to the adopted architectural abstraction. For example, in the context of the iFTE (Section 2.1), the verification focuses on the consistency related to scenarios of exception handling (e.g., exception raising, exception masking). When the architectural element is based on the HoFE (Section 2.2), the focus of verification concerns the scenarios of error detection (e.g., same result - *normal*, accepted divergence - *normal*, unaccepted divergence - *abnormal*). A complete list of properties verified for the iFTE abstraction is presented elsewhere [4]. Activity 4 consists of the generation of unit test cases for assessing the implementation of architectural elements. The unit test cases are generated based on the verified formal models of the architectural elements.

Activity 5 verifies the architectural configuration, in order to assess the consistency of interactions between architectural elements. Depending of the architectural abstractions, different properties of interest are verified. For example, in the context of the iFTE, the focus of verification is the consistency of the exception control flow and handlers, while the HoFE focus on the verification of scenarios of error detection and halting. A complete list of properties verified for architectural configurations based on iFTEs is presented elsewhere [5]. Activity 6 uses the verified formal model of the architectural configuration for generating integration test cases. This high-level integration test cases aim to assess the existence of architectural mismatches. Beyond the mismatches regarding the compatibility of required and provided operations, in the case of iFTE, it is particularly necessary to assess mismatches of exception types at propagation scenarios. Activity 7 specifies the internal structure of the architectural elements, according to the internal structure of the chosen abstraction (see Section 2). This activity consists on the recursive execution of the whole process (rigorousProcess), starting in Activity 1. Recursion is used to provide scalability in terms of an unlimited internal refinement of architectural elements. After the system (or detailed architectural element) has been properly verified and the test cases already generated, Activity 8 consists on the implementation of the system, which ideally should be automatically executed. In order to provide a mapping between the software architecture and the implementation, we suggest the use of a component implementation model such as COSMOS [8]. Even considering current trends on Model-Driven Development [20], our approach is motivated by the fact that there are no full guarantees that the source code is an accurate implementation of its software architecture. So, in Activity 9, the source code should be validated against its specification through the execution of unit and integration test cases, which were previously generated. Finally, if faults are identified during the test execution, they should be fixed in Activity 10, otherwise, the source code is considered deployable. Since each recursion implies in a deliverable source code artefact, the proposed process is also considered incremental for delivering the system in parts. Moreover, the iterative characteristic of the process allows the detection of errors in different stages of the software development, specification (Activities 3 and 5) and implementation (Activity 9).

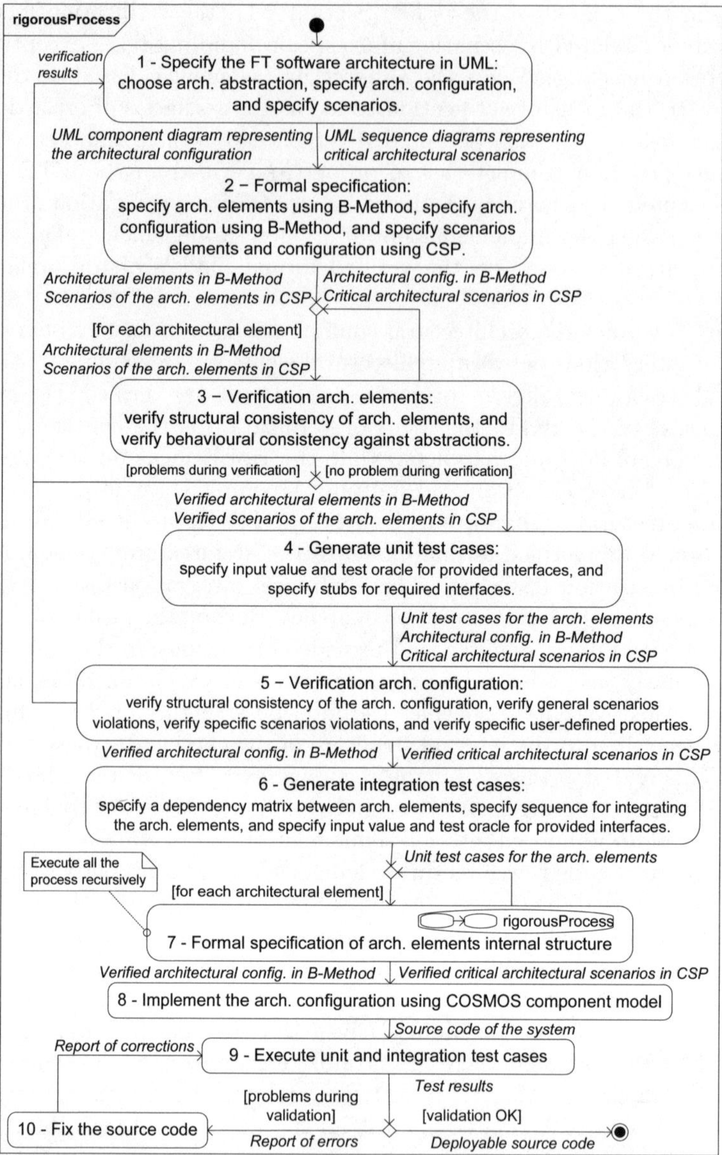

Fig. 5. A Rigorous Method for Developing Fault-Tolerant Software Architectures Using Architectural Abstractions

4 Case Study: Mining Control System

4.1 Description of the Target System

The mining control system [18] has been adopted as a case study for showing the feasibility of the proposed approach when developing fault-tolerant software architectures that are based on the two architectural abstractions presented in Section 2. In this case study, the extraction of minerals from a mine produces water and releases methane gas. In addition to extracting minerals, the mining control system is used to drain water from the sump, and to remove air from the mine when the methane level becomes high. The system is composed by three main sub-systems: MineralExtractorController, which controls the extraction of minerals, PumpController, which controls the level of water, and AirExtractor-Controller, which controls the level of methane. When the water reaches a high level, the pump is turned on and the sump is drained until the water reaches a low level. A water flow sensor is able to detect the flow of water in the pipe. However, the pump is situated underground, and for safety reasons it must not start, or continue to run, when the amount of methane in the mine exceeds a safety limit. For controlling the level of methane, there is an air extractor controller that monitors the level of methane inside the mine, and when the level is high an air extractor is switched on to remove air from the mine. The whole system is also controlled from the surface via an operator console that should handle any emergencies raised by the automatic system.

In the following, we present two software architectures for the mining control system that were obtained by using the two architectural abstractions previously introduced, namely, the iFTE, which is based on exception handling, and the HoFE, which is based on crash failure semantics. Which architectural abstraction is more appropriate depends on the fault model being adopted, and this decision should be influenced by the type of resources available in the system.

4.2   Description of the Case Study

The main goal of the case study was to evaluate the feasibility of the proposed approach, as well as the advantages of employing an abstraction-based development process. In order to analyse the advantages of the process, we have specified the mining control system presented in Section 4.1 using the two architectural abstractions presented in Section 2: (i) the iFTE architectural abstraction, which is a fault-tolerant abstraction based on implicit design diversity; and (ii) the HoFE architectural abstraction, which implements error detection through explicit design diversity. The execution of the case study is composed of three steps. First, we have executed the process presented in Section 3 choosing the iFTE architectural abstraction (Section 4.3). Second, we have executed the same process choosing the HoFE architectural abstraction (Section 4.4). Finally, we compare the two executions of the process, analysing qualitative aspects, such as separation of concerns, control of complexity, and evolvability of the software architecture. Sections 4.3 to 4.5 detail the three steps of the case study. Then, Section 4.6 summarises the overall evaluation.

4.3   Choosing the iFTE Abstraction

In Step 1 of the case study, we have chosen the iFTE abstraction for specifying the software architecture of the mining control system (Activity 1 of Figure 5).

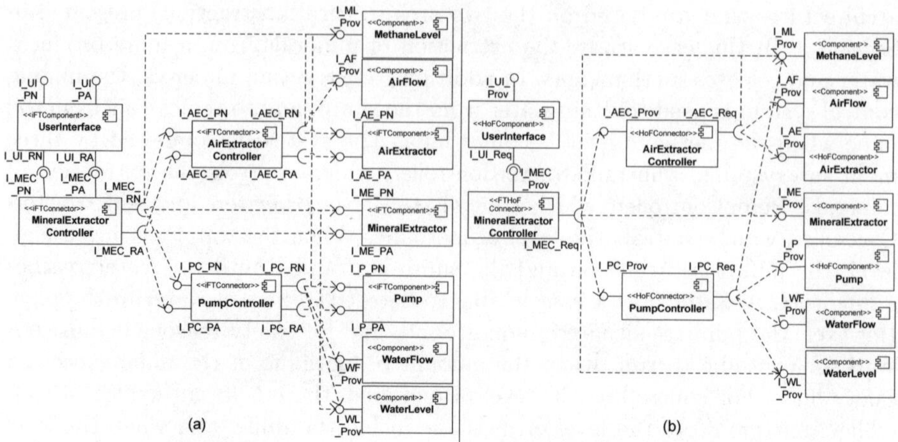

Fig. 6. Two Versions of the Mining Control System Software Architecture

The resulting software architecture is presented in Figure 6 (a) using the UML 2.0 notation. The software architecture is composed of 11 architectural elements, four of them are sensors: (i) MethaneLevel, which detects the level of methane inside the mine; (ii) AirFlow, which detects the flow of air inside the pipes; (iii) WaterLevel, which detects the level of water inside the mine; and (iv) WaterFlow, which detects the flow of water inside the pipes.

The identified controllers (MineralExtractorController, AirExtractorController, and PumpController), have the role of architectural connectors. Each controller is responsible for dealing with the normal behaviour of the system, and handling any exceptions that are propagated by the components. Depending on the state of the sensors, one of the controllers will always be activated: (i) water low & methane low ⇒ MineralExtractorController; (ii) water high & methane low ⇒ PumpController; and (iii) methane high ⇒ AirExtractorController. In case there is a failure that cannot be handled by the system, the AirExtractorController signals an exception to notify the UserInterface element that such a failure has occurred.

For this architectural configuration, a total of 13 architectural exceptions were identified related to errors in the system architecture. For exemplifying the flow of exceptions, in the following, we consider the case when an error is detected inside the AirExtractor, and an internal exception is raised [10]. If AirExtractor fails to handle this exception locally, it propagates an exception to the AirExtractorController. Again this architectural element attempts to handle the exception once it is catched, but if it fails, it propagates the exception to the MineralExtractorController. If the concentration of methane is high and the AirExtractor has failed, there is nothing that MineralExtractorController can do, except to propagate an exception to its collaborating architectural elements. Upon receiving this exception, the MineralExtractor, the PumpController and the AirExtractorController should shut down their activities, and the UserInterface should raise an alarm for the operator to take the appropriate measures.

As indicated by the development process, the verification of the software architecture follows two activities. First, the architectural elements were verified against the restrictions specified by the iFTE. Each element was verified through 22 properties of interest assessing exception signalling and masking. Second, for the software architecture, we have specified a total of 17 properties, focusing the attention on the scenarios considered critical to the application. These scenarios occurs when the Pump is turned on, and the MethaneLevel components informs that the level of methane is high. In this case, the only sequence of operations that should be possible is turn the Pump off, and turn the AirFlow component on. If these operations are successfully executed, the system continues working. In any other case, an alarm should be raised into the UserInterface.

Executing the process recursively (Activity 7 of Figure 5), the internal structure of the iFTEs were detailed according to the iFTE abstraction. Figure 7 presents the internal details of two of the architectural elements: PumpController and Pump. The Required component of the PumpController and the Provided component of the Pump are responsible for enabling the interaction, adapting the received requests (Provided), and the respective return values (Required). Note that the reuse of the internal structure of the iFTE represents a high-granularity reuse and a consequent reduction of cost.

Regarding the generation of test cases, we have specified two kinds of tests: (i) unit test cases were generated for each software architectural element (Activity 4 of Figure 5); and (ii) integration test cases were generated for assessing the existence of mismatches between the architectural elements (Activity 6 of Figure 5). Table 1 summarises the number of unit test cases generated for the iFTEs. Regarding integration testing, test cases were generated for each pair of elements that interact each other, focusing especially in the flow of exceptions between architectural elements. We have specified a total of 48 test cases. The criteria adopted for the integration test was to coverage all the critical scenarios specified for the application (involving error detection and risk of death). To assess the error detection, we have tried to identify both *false positives*, which are limit situations of the normal behaviour that could be wrongly interpreted as an error, and *false negatives*, which are limit situations of the abnormal behaviour

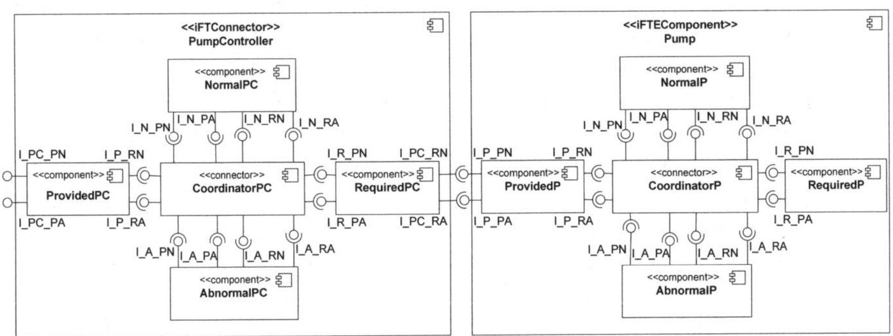

Fig. 7. Part of the Detailed View of the Mining Control System Architecture (iFTE)

Table 1. Number of unit test cases for the iFTEs

Arch. Element	#	Arch. Element	#
UserInterface	6	MineralExtractorController	38
AirExtractorController	19	PumpController	22
AirExtractor	6	MineralExtractor	6
Pump	6		

that could not be detected by the application. Details about the execution of test cases (Activity 9 of Figure 5) are available elsewhere [4,5].

4.4   Choosing the HoFE Abstraction

In Step 2 of the case study, we have chosen the HoFE abstraction during the specification of the software architecture of the mining control system (Activity 1 of Figure 5). The resulting software architecture is presented in Figure 6 (b). The use of the HoFE abstraction has considerably reduced the number of architectural elements, since the mechanism of error detection is hidden inside the architectural elements, and noticed only at the second level of recursion. The HoFE-based architecture is composed of 11 architectural elements, four of them are sensors: (i) MethaneLevel, which detects the level of methane inside the mine; (ii) AirFlow, which detects the flow of air inside the pipes; (iii) WaterLevel, which detects the level of water inside the mine; and (iv) WaterFlow, which detects the flow of water inside the pipes. It is assumed that in this system all the architectural elements are HoFEs, except for the four sensors (AirFlow, MethaneHigh, WaterLow, WaterHigh) and the MineralExtractor component, which are assumed to be free of faults.

The three identified controllers (MineralExtractorController, AirExtractorController, and PumpController), have the role of architectural connectors (≪HoFConnectors≫). Each controller is responsible for dealing with the normal behaviour of the system, but they will stop once an internal error is detected. For example, if there is a fault that prevents the air to be extracted, the AirExtractor detects it and halts. After that, the AirExtractorController, which cannot operate without the AirExtractor working, halts to inform the MineralExtractorController that there is a problem. Finally, when the MineralExtractorController halts, the UserInterface detects it and raises a warning alarm.

Regarding the verification of the HoFE architectural elements (Activity 3 of Figure 5), each element was verified through 10 properties of interest predefined by the abstraction. For verifying the architectural configuration (Activity 5 of Figure 5), we have specified a total of 21 properties, focusing the attention on the scenarios considered critical to the application. There are two kinds of critical scenarios: (i) scenarios involving error detection, which occur when the internal redundancies of the HoFE diverge on their results; and (ii) scenarios involving risk of death, which occur when the Pump is turned on, and the MethaneLevel components informs that the level of methane is high. During the verification, no property have been violated. To test the verification mechanism, we have

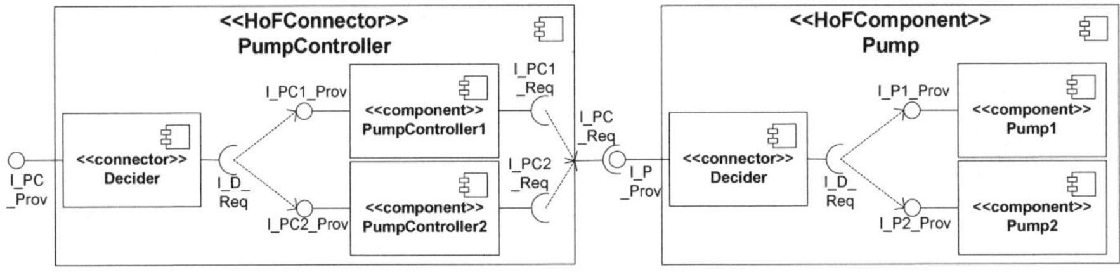

Fig. 8. Part of the Detailed View of the Mining Control System Architecture (HoFE)

forced a failure in the model, allowing the **AirExtractor** component to continue working after a previous halt. In this case, two properties have been violated: *violation of the halt-on-failure principle*, related to the HoFE abstraction, and *invalid architectural scenario*, related to the architectural configuration.

Executing the process recursively (Activity 7 of Figure 5), the internal structure of some architectural elements were detailed according to the HoFE abstraction. Figure 8 illustrate the recursive decomposition of two of the architectural elements: **PumpController** and **Pump**. For verifying the internal details of the HoFEs, other 15 properties have been used.

Regarding the generation of test cases, we have specified two kinds of tests: (i) unit test cases were generated for each HoFE (Activity 4 of Figure 5); and (ii) integration test cases were generated for assessing the existence of mismatches between the architectural elements (Activity 6 of Figure 5). Table 2 summarises the number of unit test cases generated for the HoFEs. Regarding integration testing, test cases were generated for each pair of elements that interact each other, focusing especially in the error detection, and the respective impact of it in the execution flow. We have specified a total of 38 test cases. We have adopted the same coverage criteria used for the UML abstraction.

4.5 Case Study Evaluation

Regarding the qualitative analysis of the case study, we notice that the use of specific architectural abstractions has provided a gain of separation of concerns, control of complexity, and evolvability of the software architecture. Moreover, the use of architectural abstractions made explicit some important design decisions regarding software fault-tolerance. In the iFTE-based architecture, presented in Figure 6 (a), it is explicit that **iFTComponents** and **iFTConnectors** are

Table 2. Number of unit test cases for the HoFEs

Arch. Element	#	Arch. Element	#
UserInterface	3	MineralExtractorController	15
AirExtractorController	7	PumpController	9
AirExtractor	3	Pump	3

responsible for detecting errors and tolerating faults through implicit design diversity using exception handlers. In the hoFE-based architecture, presented in Figure 6 (b), the HoFComponents and HoFConnectors are responsible for detecting errors through explicit design diversity using redundant components. The control of complexity was improved in three complementary ways: (i) reduced number of architectural elements; (ii) reduced number of dependencies between architectural elements; and (iii) simplicity of architectural scenarios, which in the case of the HoFE, abstract away the behaviour of error detection. The internal decomposition of the abstractions and their respective behavioural refinement, has enabled a stepwise development of the system, which simplifies the overall system model, and improves its understandability. Finally, regarding the evolvability of the software architecture, the use of abstractions facilitates the addition of new non-functional requirements. For example, if we would like to evolve the HoFE-based architecture to also tolerate faults (not only to detect errors), the architecture presented in Figure 6 (b) would be almost the same, changing only the architectural abstraction to a Fault-Tolerant-HoFE, which encapsulates two HoFEs and a switcher.

4.6   Overall Evaluation

The claim of this paper is that the use of dependable architectural abstractions can be effective when developing fault-tolerant software systems. Firstly, the explicit consideration of key issues related to fault tolerance, such as, error detection, reduces the chance of neglecting essential decisions during the system design. Secondly, system verification has also benefited from using architectural abstractions. The properties of interest associated with a dependable architectural abstraction can be used as a basis for verifying the architectural elements and their composition. Moreover, the process of verifying, first, a software architecture based on the architectural abstraction, and then on its detailed model, proportionates an incremental verification process that promotes the identification and correction of faults at earlier stages of software development. Finally, regarding the system validation, the adoption of an architectural abstraction allows the test cases for the architectural elements and their configurations to be gradually refined.

5   Related Work

In this section we review selected publications related to architectural abstractions for structuring software systems.

Some contributions have proposed graph-based notations for representing structural constraints of software architectures [11,12]. The simplicity of their notations is achieved through the use of an architectural abstraction for representing high-granularity architectural elements. Moreover, Denford et al. [11] uses the concept of architectural refinement, which allows the modularisation and internal decomposition of the architectural elements. The similarity between the latter and our work concerns the focus on modelling the software architecture in different levels of abstraction, considering the internal structure of the high-granularity architectural elements. However, the architectural abstractions considered in our work also focus on the representation of behavioural constraints, in such a way that it is possible to verify and validate properties related to software fault-tolerance.

Regarding the formal representation of software architectures, there are several contributions of architectural languages that support refinement, such as, SADL [13]that supports structural refinement, and π-ARL [14] that supports both structural and behavioural refinement. Differently from those notations, our solution does not define a new description language. Instead, we have defined formal templates in B-Method [1] and CSP [6] to represent the structure and behaviour of the software architecture, respectively. This is particularly convenient for representing different types of exceptions (in B-Method), and scenarios of exception propagation and fault tolerance (in CSP).

Regarding the definition of specific architectural abstractions for dealing with software fault-tolerance, the idealised C2 component (iC2C) [9] is a structuring technique based on the idealised fault-tolerant component [2], which focus on software systems compliant with the C2 architectural style [19]. The internal protocol followed by the internal elements of an iC2C enforces error confinement and makes it possible to define multiple exception handling contexts at the architectural level. Later work by Castor et al. [7] defined and implemented an architectural level exception handling mechanism based on the concept of iC2C. The iFTE abstraction presented in this paper can be seen as an extension of the iC2C for a broader class of software architectures that adhere to the peer-to-peer architectural style. Moreover, the solution presented in this paper also provides the proper support for verifying and validating the system based on the abstractions' constraints.

6 Conclusions and Future Work

This paper has shown that the development of fault-tolerant software system can be more effective if architectural abstractions are employed. These are able to abstract away from system details while providing the means for analysing how errors are propagated, detected and handled, and how faults are handled. Since the provision of fault tolerance depends on the system resources and their fault model, we have presented two distinct architectural abstractions from which fault-tolerant software systems can be built: the idealised fault-tolerant architectural element (iFTE), which is based on exception handling, and the halt-on-failure architectural element (HoFE), which assumes a crash failure semantics. Associated with these abstractions, we have defined a rigorous development process for the formal specification, verification and validation of software architectures. The effectiveness in building fault-tolerant software systems based on these architectural abstractions a simple component-based development process was demonstrated in the context of the mining control system case study.

The proposed approach would benefit considerably if tools were available that could automate the activities related to the integration of formal specification, verification and architectural-based validation. An example of such activity where a tool could be applied is the automatic extraction of test cases from the software architecture, taking as a reference the architectural scenarios. In addition to the two architectural abstractions presented in this paper, the development process, or parts of it, could be with other architectural abstractions for obtaining fault-tolerant software architectures.

References

1. Abrial, J.-R., et al.: The B-Method. In: Proc. of the 4th Int. Symp. of VDM Europe on Formal Sof. Devel., vol. 2, pp. 398–405 (1991)
2. Anderson, T., Lee, P.A.: Fault Tolerance: Principles and Practice, 1st edn. Prentice-Hall, Englewood Cliffs (1981)
3. Avizienis, A., et al.: Basic concepts and taxonomy of dependable and secure computing. IEEE Trans. on Dependable and Secure Computing 1(1), 11–33 (2004)
4. Brito, P.H.S., et al.: Architecture-centric fault tolerance with exception handling. In: Bondavalli, A., Brasileiro, F., Rajsbaum, S. (eds.) LADC 2007. LNCS, vol. 4746, pp. 75–94. Springer, Heidelberg (2007)
5. Brito, P.H.S., et al.: Verification and validation of a fault-tolerant architectural abstraction. In: Proc. of the Workshop on Architecting Dependable Systems, pp. 1–6 (2007)
6. Butler, M.J., Leuschel, M.: Combining CSP and B for specification and property verification. In: Fitzgerald, J.S., Hayes, I.J., Tarlecki, A. (eds.) FM 2005. LNCS, vol. 3582, pp. 221–236. Springer, Heidelberg (2005)
7. Castor Filho, F., et al.: An architectural-level exception-handling system for component-based applications. In: de Lemos, R., Weber, T.S., Camargo Jr., J.B. (eds.) LADC 2003. LNCS, vol. 2847, pp. 321–340. Springer, Heidelberg (2003)
8. da Silva Jr., M.C., et al.: A Java component model for evolving software systems. In: Proc. of the 18th IEEE Int. Conf. on Automated Soft. Eng., pp. 327–330 (2003)
9. de Castro Guerra, P.A., et al.: A fault-tolerant software architecture for component-based systems. In: de Lemos, R., Gacek, C., Romanovsky, A. (eds.) Architecting Dependable Systems. LNCS, vol. 2677, pp. 129–149. Springer, Heidelberg (2003)
10. de Lemos, R.: Architectural Fault Tolerance Using Exception Handling. In: de Lemos, R., Gacek, C., Romanovsky, A. (eds.) Architecting Dependable Systems IV. LNCS, vol. 4615, pp. 142–162. Springer, Heidelberg (2007)
11. Denford, M., et al.: Architectural abstraction as transformation of poset labelled graphs. Journal of Universal Computer Science 10(10), 1408–1428 (2004)
12. Fahmy, H., Holt, R.C.: Software architecture transformations. In: Proc. of the Int. Conf. on Software Maintenance, pp. 88–96 (2000)
13. Moriconi, M., Riemenschneider, R.: Introduction to sadl 1.0 a language for specifying software architecture hierarchies. TR SRI-CSL-97-01, SRI International (March 1997)
14. Oquendo, F.: π-ARL: an architecture refinement language for formally modelling the stepwise refinement of software architectures. SIGSOFT Softw. Eng. Notes 29(5), 1–20 (2004)

15. Randell, B.: Turing memorial lecture facing up to faults. Computer Journal 43(2), 95–106 (2000)
16. Schlichting, R.D., Schneider, F.B.: Fail-Stop Processors: An Approach to Designing Fault-Tolerant Computing Systems. Computer Systems 1(3), 222–238 (1983)
17. Siau, K., Halpin, T.A. (eds.): Unified Modeling Language: Systems Analysis, Design and Development Issues. Idea Group (2001)
18. Sloman, M., Kramer, J.: Distributed systems and computer networks. Prentice Hall International, Englewood Cliffs (1987)
19. Taylor, R.N., et al.: A component- and message- based architectural style for GUI software. In: Proc. of the 17th Int. Conf. on Soft. Eng., pp. 295–304 (1995)
20. Thomas, D., Barry, B.M.: Model driven development: the case for domain oriented programming. In: Companion of the 18th Annual ACM SIGPLAN Conf. on Object-oriented Programming, Systems, Languages, and Applications, pp. 2–7 (2003)

Towards Interoperability in Component Based Development with a Family of DSLs

Ileana Ober, Ali Abou Dib, Louis Féraud, and Christian Percebois

IRIT – Université Paul Sabatier Toulouse
118, route de Narbonne 31062 Toulouse- France
{aboudib,feraud,ober,perceboi}@irit.fr

Abstract. In this paper we address interoperability between components specified using various languages within a same family of DSLs. Our approach consists in applying results of the category theory in order to merge the languages
into a unification one, automatically obtained. For this, we use the category of
formal specifications of each DSL in the family. Using colimits on the category
of algebraic specifications that implements the semantics of the DSLs in the
family, we construct a language that unifies the family. Additionally we obtain
translation morphisms from individual DSLs to the resulting unified one. By
application of the translation morphisms, one can translate each component
specifications into a specification written in the unification language. Moreover,
properties established in the context of a DSL are transferred to the unifying
language. In this paper, we illustrate the unification and the preservation of a
property on an example.

Keywords: heterogeneous components, interoperability, domain specific language (DSL), formal semantics, category theory, Specware.

1   Introduction

It has always been the vision of software engineers to have reliable methods to produce correct software. The rise of domain specific languages (DSL), as opposed to
general purpose languages, highlights the need for interoperability between components specified in various DSLs.

The work we present here is triggered by a case study that we developed with col-
leagues from the French Space Agency (CNES). The case study revealed the need to
deal with a set of related – yet different – DSLs in remotely controlled satellites. In
this paper, we propose a rigorous method to deal with heterogeneity in this context:
both at the level of language definition and at the level of component specification.

We consider the category of algebraic semantics of DSLs. Classical results in category theory allow us to obtain *by construction* the formal semantics of a *unification
language* and translators from the source DSLs to this *unification language*. The fact
that we also obtain translators from the original languages to the unified one allows its
transparent use. This is essential since one major benefit of a DSL is its accessibility
by domain experts unfamiliar with programming.

R. Morrison, D. Balasubramaniam, and K. Falkner (Eds.): ECSA 2008, LNCS 5292, pp. 148–163, 2008.

An interesting point in our approach is that properties established in the context of DSLs and expressed as invariants in the algebraic structure can be transferred to the unification language.

Our approach is based on the use of already existing tools: Specware [10] that gives us the framework to reason on categories and the prover Isabelle [16] that is already connected with Specware. We use it to transfer properties in the context of the unification language.

This paper is organized as follows: Section 2 gives an overview of the issue of interoperability between components described using related DSLs. In Section 3 we detail our approach. In Section 4 an example is given. Section 5 presents a discussion of our approach, with an overview of some related approaches.

2   Components Specified with Related DSLs

The issue of interoperability [9] is not a new one in computer science and it holds at several levels: software interoperability, modeling / development language interoperability and theory interoperability. These levels are strongly related. In this paper we refer mainly to language interoperability within a set of components specified using DSLs of a same family.

The starting point of our work is a case study issued from joint work with the National French Space Agency (CNES). One major critical issue in this case study is how to precisely handle the differences existing between languages dedicated to the definition of procedures for space system testing and operations. Indeed, different space agencies or equipment builders use different languages to remotely control the satellites: Pluto [6] for the European Space Agency, Stol by NASA, and Elisa by EADS/Astrium.

These languages are imperative and contain constructs to deal with algorithmic constructs, task scheduling, remote commands, and measures, but still they are distinct. In spite of the need to occasionally use them jointly; several attempts to impose a unique language have failed, for both economical and political reasons. The various languages of a family are similar; nevertheless a full interoperability between agencies and user organizations is necessary for the development of a mission infrastructure.

DSLs are specific to a domain or to a family of applications. They offer the correct level of abstraction over their domain, together with accessibility for domain experts unfamiliar with programming. DSLs focus on doing a specific task well and on being accessible for domain experts, often less competent in programming. For each DSL it exist development environments of variable complexity.

The obvious main advantage of using a DSL is that it provides the right vocabulary and abstraction level for a given problem. The price of this is a Tower of Babel of languages and the risk to have costly and less powerful development environments.

DSLs are not only dependent on their application domain. Their usage is often tailored on an enterprise's culture, personal programming, or modeling style. As a result, a domain is often represented by a family of languages.

A family of languages is a *set of related languages* that offer *similar functionality* at an *equivalent level of abstraction*. Nevertheless, the different languages of a family *differ by syntax and semantics.* Indeed, some differences may exist between the *semantics* of similar constructs in various languages.

Within a family of domain specific languages the issue of interoperability consists of identifying the best techniques that allow using the different languages in a coherent manner: *i.e.,* continue to use the environments and tools specific to each language, while being able to switch easily between them. This issue was already highlighted in [11] in the particular case of two related telephony languages.

3 Automating the Unification of a DSL Family

As mentioned, our study was triggered by a common work with the French Space Agency on the use of related though different languages (such as Pluto, Stol and Elisa) to remotely control satellites. Each of these is an example of a DSL: it is designed to best address the needs of remotely controlling satellites, and with no concern for generality or completeness.

We are therefore in the context of a family of DSLs that often need to be used jointly, for instance, in the case of missions using equipment from various providers.

Our approach is based on the use of well-established results in Category Theory [6]. Before entering into more details about our approach, let us start by a brief overview of the concepts we use.

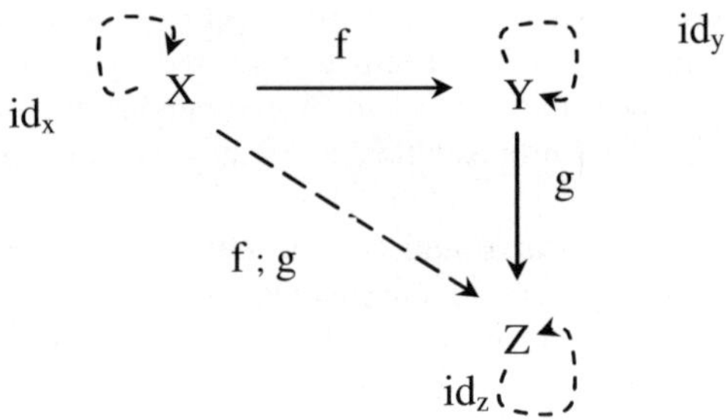

Fig. 1. Category of three objects and two morphisms

3.1 Category Theory ABC

Category theory provides abstract mechanisms to deal with structures (called *objects*) and their relationships (called *morphisms*). One can visualize a category as an oriented graph with a composition law on edges and an identity on each node.

For instance, the category depicted in Figure 1 is defined by the objects X, Y, Z and the morphisms $f : X \rightarrow Y$ and $g : Y \rightarrow Z$. Additionally, the category implicitly contains *identities* on objects and the composition ";", so that $f ; g : X \rightarrow Z$.

Within a category, it is possible to obtain *amalgamated* sums of objects by *pushout*: given the morphisms: $f_1: X \rightarrow Y_1$ and $f_2: X \rightarrow Y_2$, the *pushout* of these two morphisms is *an object Z* and *two morphisms* g_1 and g_2, for which the diagram in Figure 2 *commutes* (i.e. $f_1 ; g_1 = f_2 ; g_2$) and the pushout *(Z, g1, g2)* is *minimal* with respect to this diagram (Figure 3).

The pushout construction can be generalized to a collection of objects and morphisms as a "colimit". For more details see [7].

We use the following additional results, summarized in [7]:

Definition (co-complete category): A category is (finitely) co-complete if all (finite) diagrams have colimits.

Proposition: A category $\mathscr{C}$ is finitely co-complete *iff* it has initial objects (there exists a morphism from this object to each object in the category) and pushouts of all pairs of morphisms with a common source.

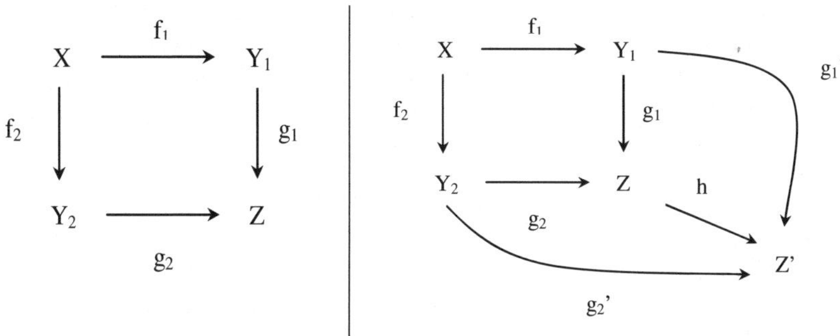

Fig. 2. Pushout commutativity   **Fig. 3.** Pushout: uniqueness constraint

3.2 Algebraic Specifications of DSLs

Our approach is based on the use of the formal specifications of DSLs. From the plethora of formal specification techniques available, we choose the algebraic specification [23]. An algebraic specification captures both the syntax and the semantics of a language. The semantics is expressed in terms of: sorts (value domains), operations (on the given sorts), and axioms (to specify properties in this context).

This formalism is often used in the context of combining specifications [17], mainly because of the interesting results on them: *the algebraic specification forms a finitely co-complete category* [8], *i.e.,* in the context of algebraic specifications the pushout exists, and the colimit computation can be made in terms of pushouts.

3.3 The Category of Formal Specifications of the DSLs of a Family

The theoretical ground of our research is the *category of algebraic specifications of DSLs.* This approach has already proved its relevance in industrial contexts, such as the one overviewed in [23]. According to [21], a set of algebraic specifications can constitute a category. The *co-completeness* results on this category ensure that the *colimit* exists. The formal specification of each DSL is an *object* in this category. Our goal is to be able to obtain *automatically* the formal specification of a unification DSL. The unification can be obtained as a *colimit* in the category of algebraic specifications of the DSLs. In order to have all the premises needed for computing the colimit, we need to additionally define a *"boot"* object and a set of *initialization* morphisms to each of the individual DSL objects, that ensure the existence of the *common source* mentioned in the proposition in Section 3.1. In the particular case of only two languages in a family, we are in a framework similar to the one in Figure 2:

1. Y_1 and Y_2 each correspond to the formal specification of a DSL in the family;
2. X is a "boot" object to be defined, in order to make explicit correspondences that exist between related elements of Y_1 and Y_2;
3. f_1 and f_2 are *"initialization"* morphisms to be defined;
4. Z corresponds to the unification object, obtained by pushout;
5. g_1 and g_2 are the morphisms that allow the *translation* from each original object to Z, *i.e.*, to pass from each individual DSL to the unification DSL.

In the case of a DSL family with *n* members, we have: *n* objects ($Y_1,.. Y_n$); *n* initialization morphisms ($f_1,... f_n$) and we obtain *n* translation morphisms ($g_1, ... g_n$).

The rationale behind the *boot* object and the *initialization* morphisms is to ensure that the obtained unification object goes beyond the set union of the language concepts present in the various languages. We have to express somewhere the correspondence between related constructs that exist in various languages in order to minimize the perpetuation of related concepts. Therefore, the *boot* object is a first-level abstraction of the DSLs in the family and it contains the *formal specification* of the *constructs* that exist in the various languages.

The *boot* object X used in the colimit $Y_1 \xleftarrow{\ i\ } A \xrightarrow{\ j\ } Y_2$ can be obtained following the newt steps [18]:

1. define the *disjoint union* of all sorts and operators of Y_1 and Y_2
2. define equivalence relations on these symbols.

The common symbols (sorts, operators, and axioms) – up to a renaming – form the *boot* object X.

The actual *mapping between* the *concepts in the boot object* and their *correspondents in the specific DSLs* is captured by the *initialization morphisms* that define each DSL in terms of refinements of the boot object elements.

The colimit operator gives the *unification object* and the translation morphisms. In our setting, the *colimit* object contains the formal specification of a unification language. A major interest of this approach is that the object is automatically obtained, *i.e.*, the unification language is *implicit*, and its definition *unifies* the concepts present in the various languages.

3.4 Applying the Framework to a Set of Component Specifications

The previous section describes how it is possible to depart from the set of formal semantics of DSLs in a family to *obtain* the formal semantics of a unifying DSL as well as translation morphisms from each DSL to the one newly obtained. We exploit this in the context of a set of components described in various languages of the family. Our solution to achieve interoperability consists in calculating the unification language of a family, as described in the previous section, and translating all component specifications into this language.

If the formal specification of a language is *set* based, the concrete specification of a program specified in that language is most likely defined as *initializations* of the various sets defined in the formal specification.

Suppose we have a set of m components described in a set of n DSLs that are members of the same family (where $m \geq n$):

$$C^1_{DSL_{k_1}}, \cdots, C^m_{DSL_{k_m}}, \quad \text{with } k_1, \ldots, k_m \in \{1, \ldots, n\} \tag{1}$$

Using the unification DSL and the translation morphisms obtained by means of the approach described above, the set of components (1) can be translated into the set of components:

$$C'^1_{DSL^\mu}, \; C'^2_{DSL^\mu}, \; \cdots, C'^m_{DSL^\mu} \tag{2}$$

DSL^μ denotes the *unification DSL* of the family $\{DSL^1, DSL^2, \ldots, DSL^n\}$, and

$$C'^i_{DSL^\mu} \;=\; g_j \left(C^i_{DSL_j} \right), \text{ with } i \leq m \text{ and } j \leq n \tag{3}$$

where g_j is the automatically obtained *translation morphism* from DSL_j to DSL^μ

Therefore, the original set of m components described in the various DSLs as shown in (1) can be translated into a set of m components described using one language.

In [20], the authors overview various techniques used for component classification. In our case, once the components are translated into a same language, the use of the composition techniques remains unconstrained. If we refer to the original case study that triggered our work, there the composition is based on the use of scripting languages. However, this choice is determined by other factors and it is independent of the heterogeneity of the various components.

3.5 Openings to Verification and Validation

In the context of the algebraic specification, we can define theorems corresponding to properties of individual DSLs. Moreover, from the axioms corresponding to the formal semantics of a DSL **D** it is possible to prove a property **P** given in an equational form, as a first order logics predicate, if **P** is a theorem over **D**'s axioms.

P is transferred to any other DSL, called **E**, connected to **D** through morphisms: the image of a theorem of **D** is a theorem of **E** *by construction* [8]. So, *the colimit of a DSL family preserves the equational properties of the family members.*

This gives the opportunity to verify properties separately in the context of DSLs and to transfer them in the context of the unification DSL.

4 Experimental Framework

As mentioned before, this work was initiated by a case study where the major issue is the interoperability between components specified using various DSLs in a same family dedicated to the remote control of the satellites. The different languages existing are imperative and contain constructs to deal with algorithmic constructs, task scheduling, remote commands, and measures, still they are distinct languages.

To illustrate our approach we extract a subset of this case study.

4.1 DSL Family Overview

In our example we use a family composed of two languages with a similar power of expression. The list of concepts they contain is not completely overlapping:

DSL α handles conditions and events exchanged between the remote system and the local application.

DSL β contains control structures that allow the decomposition of various activities into independent steps encapsulated within the procedures.

The main concept, present in both α and β, is the notion of *procedure* describing a goal to attain. In α, it materializes into the notion of *block,* while in β, it gets into a *module*. The main parts of a procedure are:

- the *activation* conditions (called check in α and condition in β);
- the *body* that describes the steps to be taken by the execution.

Before we actually proceed to a procedure's execution, its *activation* is evaluated. This can result either in the abortion of the procedure execution if the activation condition is not satisfied, or in the normal sequential execution of the procedure *body*.

In both α and β, activations may contain logical expressions. Additionally, α contains a *wait* construct which allows the testing of event occurrences. In this setting, the events are generated by the environment and are stored in a wait queue managed using a FIFO policy. When the *wait* clause of an activation fails the procedure is aborted.

In the DSL β, the activation contains the evaluation of a *contingency* on the status of the input queue. The contingency offers a connection point to hardware sensors.

4.2 Unifying the Languages Using Existing Tools

One of the goals of our study is to be able to exploit tools that already exist. The framework we set up for experimentation is based on using **Specware** [12][10][20]. This tool has been successfully used in the context of industrial projects [23] and it allows the manipulation of algebras and computation of pushouts. Specware permits the formal specification refinement into executable code by stepwise refinement. Coupled with theorem provers such as Isabelle [14] (see below), Specware guarantees that the final executable code is provably correct. In the context of Specware, it is possible to specify proof obligations with Higher Order Logic (HOL) which cover our formal requirements.

Our case study takes as an input the formal semantics of the languages α and β, in terms of abstract types. First, we focus on the language definition level. Figure 4 illustrates the concepts we handle at this level and their relationship with Specware. One can see that, besides the formal semantics of the languages we need to identify a *boot* object and the *initialization* morphisms, by using the process mentioned in Section 3.3.

In the formal specification of DSLs α and β, we use the notion of *environment* (modeled by the sort *Environment*) that is the set of variable-value pairs corresponding to all the variables local to the procedure in DSLs α and β. Additionally, in α, the *environment* contains an event queue.

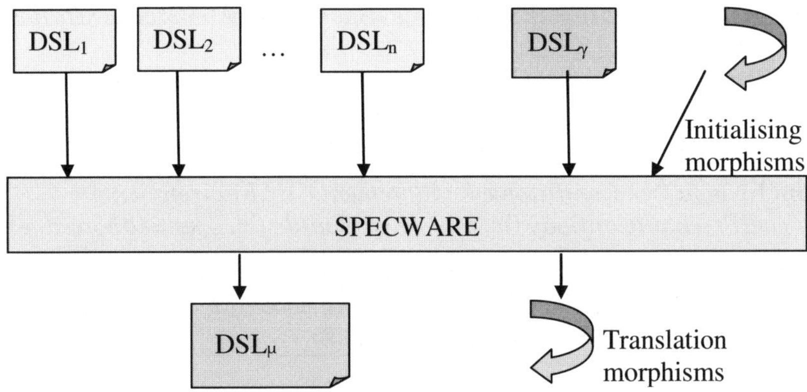

Fig. 4. Overall picture of the constructs handled at language definition level

In DSLs α the evaluation of a block activation (the block is modeled by the sort *Block)* may contain a check in the context of the environment. This is modeled with the aid of the operator *evalBlock* whose evaluation affects the environment:

> **op** *evalBlock : Checks $\times$ Block $\times$ Environment $\rightarrow$ Status $\times$ Environment*

In addition to this general activation evaluation, **in DSL α** there may be a *check variable clause* in the activation. This is to say that the block evaluation can only proceed if the variables evaluate to true:

> **op** *checkVariables :Checks$\times$Block$\times$Environment$\rightarrow$ Boolean $\times$ Environment*

To capture the fact that the evaluation to false of the variables leads to the abortion of the block we have the following axiom[1]:

> **axiom** a1 **is** *fa (c: Checks, b: Block, e: Environment)*
>   *~checkVariables(c,b) => evalBlock(c, b, e) = (aborted, e)*

Moreover, the following axiom characterises the variable evaluation[2], for which the sort *Environment* is refined as *Environment = Context $\times$ Queue*. The same environment definition same exists in β.

> **axiom** a3 **is** *fa (c : Checks, e : Environment) checkVariables (c, e) =*
>   *checkExpressions (c.1, e.1) && waitStatements (c.2, e.2)*

Similar to a *Block* in α, in the **DSL β**, we have the notion of *module*. A module evaluation is captured by the operation *evalModule*. A module evaluation can be completed only if its precondition is satisfied and the contingency status is ok. The following operators and axioms capture this:

---

[1] In these axiom *fa* stands for the universal quantifier *for all* ($\forall$).
[2] For a product type, $T = T_1 \times \ldots \times T_n$, for $l \in T, l.i$ refers to the projection on T_i.

> **op** *evalModule:Conditions×Statements×Environment → ModuleStatus ×
> Environment*
> **op** *evalPreconditionBody : Conditions × Environment → Boolean*
> **op** *evalBooleanExpressions : List (Expression) × Context -> Boolean*
> **op** *evalContingency : Environment → Boolean*
>
> **axiom** b1 **is** *fa* (lc : *Conditions*, s : *Statements*, e : *Environment*)
>   ~ *evalPreconditionBody* (lc, e) => *evalModule* (lc, s, e) = (*aborted*, e)
>
> **axiom** b2 **is** *fa* (lc : *Conditions*, e : *Environment*)
>   *evalPreconditionBody* (lc, e) = *evalBooleanExpressions* (lc.1, e.1)
>   && *evalContingency* (e.2)

In order to be able to unify the languages α and β, we have to identify corresponding concepts and to encapsulate into the boot object. After analysing the specification of the languages DSL α and DSL β, we realize that several concepts are similar up to a renaming. For instance, the notions of *Block* (α) and of *Module* (β) can be unified into a notion of *Procedure* which we include in the boot object γ. We apply a similar analysis of the other parts of the language, which leads us to the definition of the boot language. Here are some elements of its specification (to easy the reading we qualify these names with γ):

> **op** *evalProcedure$_\gamma$: Conditions × Steps × Environment →*
>   *ConfirmationStatus × Environment*
> **op** *evalPrecondition$_\gamma$: Conditions × Environment -> Boolean*
> **op** *evalExpressions$_\gamma$: List (Expression) × Context -> Boolean*

To clarify the relationships between the various operators and sorts of γ, and their counterparts in α and β, we define correspondences between them. These correspondences constitute the initial morphisms[3]:

> *gamma_to_alpha* = **morphism** gamma → alpha{
>
> *Conditions* +→ *Checks,   Steps* +→ *Block, ConfirmationStatus* +→ *Status,*
> *evalProcedure* +→ *evalBlock, evalPrecondition* +→ *checkVariables,*
> *evalExpressions* +-→ *checkExpressions*}
>
> *gamma_to_beta* = **morphism** gamma → beta{
> *Steps* +→ *Statements, ConfirmationStatus* +→ *ModuleStatus,*
> *evalProcedure* +→ *evalModule, evalPrecondition* +→ *evalPreconditionBody,*
> *evalMainBody* +→ *evalSequenceSection,*
> *evalExpressions* +→ *evalBooleanExpressions*}

Specware provides several techniques for combining specifications. In particular using the *translate* operation one can rename a (set of) sorts in the specification, similar to morphism definitions (such as those presented above). In our case study we do not use the *translate*, as we need to do more than simply renaming some terms.

---

[3] In Specware a +→ x is a notation to specify that a morphism takes a into x.

The boot object γ contains not only the common sorts and operations, but also an abstraction of the common part of the axioms of the different languages (here α and β). The following axiom factorizes the axioms a1 (α) and b1(β) presented above:

> **axiom** g1 **is** fa (lc : Conditions, ls : Steps, e : Environment)
>   ~ evalPrecondition (lc, e) => evalProcedure (lc, ls, e) = (aborted, e)

All the elements are ready for pushout calculation. At the implementation level, we do it in Specware. The pushout is an algebraic specification, i.e. it contains sorts, operators and axioms that unify those from α, β, and γ. This algebraic specification corresponds to what we called the *unification language* μ. This language contains sorts corresponding to the sorts refined from γ (i.e. having counterparts in α and β), plus sorts specific to α and β. In the pushout we keep track of the origins of sorts and operators called differently in the context of the other languages.

In the example below, the sort definitions (1) and (2) correspond to sorts originating from a term unification in α, β, and γ. The sort definitions (3) and (4) correspond to terms that exist and have the same name in α, β, and γ. In addition, the sort definition (1) has been refined from γ with the same type product both in α and β.

type *{Checks, Conditions}* $= List\ (Expression) \times List\ (Event)$	(1)
type *{Block, Statements, Steps}*	(2)
type *Expression*	(3)
type *Event*	(4)
type *Queue* $= List\ (Event)$	(5)

The same happens in the case of the operators: they are either unified from various languages, or copied from a single language (otherwise). For example, the operator described below is unified form α, β, and γ:

> **op** *{evalBlock, evalModule, evalProcedure}* :
> $Conditions \times Steps \times\ Environment\ \rightarrow ConfirmationStatus \times Environment$

The pushout also unifies the axioms. The axioms specific to α, β, or γ are translated as such. Therefore, the pushout will contain the axioms a1, a3, b1, b2, g1, described above. More than a mechanical copy, the transfer on the axioms in the context of μ is also ensuring that no contradictions exist between them. Therefore the specification of μ is coherent.

4.3 Preserving Properties

One key issue in this approach is that it can unifies properties established in the context of individual DSLs. In order to do this, we follow the schema presented in Figure 5.

In α, let us consider the following property **P**: *at the evaluation of an activation that contains a wait clause over a set of events, if the input queue contains fewer events, then the activation evaluation fails <u>and</u> the procedure execution is aborted.*

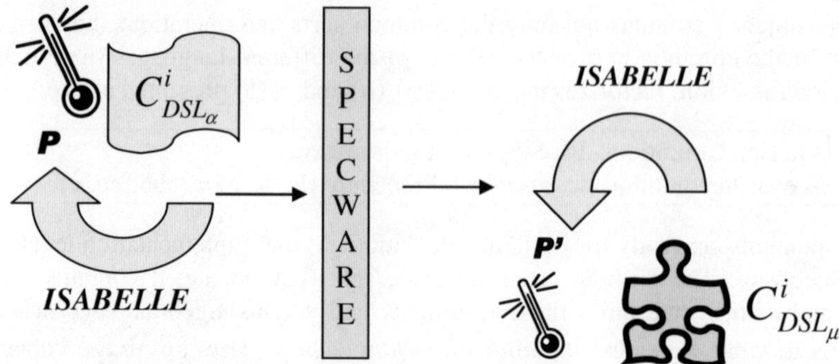

Fig. 5. Property transfer from an arbitrary DSL to the unification context

We express it as a property, through two theorems in α (one for each part of the conjunction in the property):

> **theorem** t0 **is** *fa* (le : *List (Event)*, q : *Queue*)
>   length (le) > length (q) $\Rightarrow$ ~*waitStatements* (le, q)
>
> **theorem** t1 **is** *fa* (le : *List (Event)*, q : *Queue*)
>   length (le) > length (q)
> $\Rightarrow$ *fa* (l : *List (Expression)*, c : *Context*) ~*checkVariables* ((l, le), (c, q))

To prove this result, we use a bridge offered by the Specware environment to the proof assistant Isabelle [14]. We apply the prover successfully on the previous example in the context of α, thus the **P** property holds, i.e. *t0* and *t1* are provable theorems.

If we add this property to the DSL α specification, when Specware calculates the pushout, it transposes this property in the context of the unification language. This leads to a property **P'**. In our case, the two properties are written identically. Note however that even though **P** and **P'** are syntactically identical; they do not represent the *same* property as they are expressed in the context of different sets of axioms. According to [8], *by construction* **P'** is a theorem in the context of μ.

However, as the case study is extracted from a domain where strong qualification is needed and in order to convince the industrial partners about the soundness of this property, we need to prove it again in the new context. Using Isabelle, the validity of **P'** in the context of μ is established also. Note that the proof of **P'** capitalizes the experience obtained with the proof of **P**: we use the same proof tactic, and similar intermediary lemmas.

One interesting feature of Specware that we have not yet used, as it is a component specification level feature, is the fact that we can get from the formal specification (*e.g.*, equivalent to a component specification) to executable code through stepwise refinement. Moreover, Specware may guarantee that the final executable code is provably correct, with respect to the original specification.

5 Discussion

In this paper we present an approach to deal with interoperability within a set of components specified in DSLs from a same family. Our approach is based on the exploitation of basic results in Category Theory in order to *construct* the unification DSL of the family.

One of the most important benefits of this approach is that it uses the category of *formal specifications* of the languages in the family. Depending on the level of detail present in the formal specification, this allows the treatment of both syntactic and semantic interoperability issues, thus *we go beyond purely translational approaches.*

Our approach allows *to obtain* the specification of the unification language of the family. An interesting feature that results, is that *end users do not have to interact with it.* One of the main advantages of DSLs is that it allows domain experts (not necessarily computer scientists) to write specifications. It is important to keep it like this, and that the interoperability does not come at the price of additional requirements from the users.

The unification language depends on the set of DSLs in the family. This means that different sets of DSLs would probably lead to various unification language definitions. The unification language of a set of DSLs is the best representative for that set and its definition is based on *usage* and *need* rather than on a best guess on the list of features present among the family.

Another key advantage of our approach, which we illustrated in our example, is that it preserves/translates properties established in the context of individual DSLs. This is particularly interesting in a domain where verification and validation are major concerns.

In order to meet the hypothesis of colimits application we need to provide *a boot language* and one initialization morphism per language in the family to unify. We have to express somewhere the correspondence between related constructs from various languages, in order to avoid the multiplication of similar concepts. The boot object and the initialization morphism play precisely this role.

The experience we have with the definition of these elements shows that the effort needed to define them is reasonable. Note that as the size of the boot object is reduced, defining the initialization morphisms is inherently simpler than defining translators from language to language.

One of the paths we plan to develop in the future concerns improving the methodology for defining the boot object.

Why applying this approach on a <u>family</u> of languages and why on <u>DSLs</u>?
One feature that is present in most DSL definitions [5] is the fact that they have a narrow application scope and contain a limited set of constructs. Moreover, DSLs are specification languages that are often close to the algebraic specification. These observations plus the constraint on dealing with *related* languages have an impact on the definition of the *boot* language and of the *initialization* morphisms. For a set of DSLs the boot language contains a limited number of constructs. Moreover, if the languages are *related* it is in principle easier to identify common points and to properly define their mapping to concepts in each of the languages.

5.1 Related Work

Many efforts were devoted to achieve component interoperability. We know of few approaches that concern, in particular, with the interoperability between components described in a family of DSLs.

As far as we know, the approach closest to ours is [4], in which the authors address the issue of building translators between the languages present in a DSL family. As it happens, the authors work on a similar family of DSLs as their study seems to be triggered by the same concerns of working with a family of DSLs used to program a satellite operations procedure. The resemblance of the two approaches ends here. In [4], the authors exploit the similarities between those languages to semi-automatically build a transformation schema between them, through the use of an annotated grammar. The result is a schema based on language-to-language translations, whereas we use an automatically generated unification language. Note that the number of translators needed is $O(n2)$ on the size of the family, which in the case of large families may be important. Moreover, in [4] the authors focus on the syntactic level, whereas we focus on the semantics also.

In [2] the authors describe an approach for using DSL to realize component composition. Therefore the authors propose the use of DSL as a substitute for scripting language in component composition. In our case, the components themselves are described using DSLs, and our approach consists in translating them into a same language.

In [11], the authors use AMMA [13] to bridge specific DSLs. This work goes beyond a simple language translation, as the AMMA environment allows for some genericity and reuse in a different context. However, this is also a language-to-language translation approach focusing on the syntactic level.

Finally, none of these approaches tackle the "transformation" of properties from a language to another, while our approach allows us to exploit properties established in the context of individual languages.

In [17] the authors solve the composition of modular specifications by means of colimits of the category diagrams. In the context of algebraic specifications such as Clear, pushouts allow to gather two specifications that share a common point. We extend this idea: consider a set of DSLs that can be modeled by a modular specification, whose common part has to be identified through the boot specification.

One traditional approach to deal with heterogeneity is to pass through a *pivot* language, which can be visible or internal. The pivot language technique was used in various contexts, and in principle it has the advantage of minimizing the number of translators needed, as it is linear with the size of the set of languages $O(n)$. With respect to such an approach, ours has a higher abstraction level. It has the advantage that the translators we have to define (from the boot object to the various DSLs) are simpler to define and the drawback that we have to additionally define the boot object. Other advantages are that we focus on syntax, semantics, and that we can exploit properties. For the moment, we do not know of any approach that uses a pivot in a family of DSLs.

In [11], the authors present an approach for using domain specific modeling throughout the system development. The issues dealt with in this approach concern the definition of the syntax and semantics of domain-specific modeling languages, plus techniques to deal with models and model transformations. We share the same concern of software specification through a set of components described in domain specific languages. However we focus on finding a solution to the heterogeneity issue, whereas [11] is less concerned with this point, and takes a higher level view.

In [22], the authors promote the use of domain specific modeling for system development. The authors propose meta-tools to be tailored to the needs of specific domains. Although we share the interoperability concern, our approach is different.

Most of the research conducted around DSLs concerns the identification of techniques that allow to obtain (more or less automatically) frameworks for extending or working with DSLs [3], some of them in a visual setting [19]. In [13], authors propose to apply MDE as support techniques when building DSL frameworks. Our work does not concern any of these issues related to DSL frameworks.

Our work is intrinsically related with the approaches that use Specware, for instance, to combine specifications [10] or to perform model driven reverse engineering [19].

In this paper, we present a continuation of the work started in [1], in particular with respect to the identification of the objects corresponding to the formal semantics of the DSL, with respect to the application of the results on property preservation as well as with respect to its application on component based development.

6 Conclusions

In this paper, we present an approach to handle the heterogeneity within a set of components specified by using a family of domain specific languages. This study started from the concrete case study of procedural languages used to remotely control satellites at the French Space Agency.

Our approach is based on the use of the category of algebraic specifications of the DSLs in the family. By colimit, we obtain the algebraic specification of a unification language and morphisms that allow specification translations from DSLs to the unification language. Moreover, properties established in the context of original DSLs are transferred to the unification context.

In order to investigate the feasibility of our approach, we apply it on a family of two DSLs. By using Specware we obtain the unification language of the family and the translating morphisms needed to pass from the two DSLs to the unification DSL.

To illustrate the verification facet of our approach, we consider a property specified in the context of a DSL. By use of the Isabelle prover integrated in Specware, we prove the validity of this property. Moreover, we transfer this property (by means of Specware) into a property in the context of the unification DSL.

In a long run, this work opens the way to several research paths:

- Find *heuristics* or define a *methodology* to assist the definition of the *boot language*, that follow the preliminary ideas we already presented in Section 5 and Section 3.3.
- Work on *properties* established in the context of the *concrete specifications*. Until now, the properties we described (as the ones presented in this paper) are defined at the language definition level. In the future, we will investigate the

propagation of properties established in the context of particular components. This would correspond to application specific properties.

- Work on sets of concrete languages to *study the impact of various parameters on the obtained results* (large size families, languages with a close core but still containing unrelated features).
- Work on the *extension of our approach* from the use of algebraic specifications to the wider context of *institutions* [8]. Indeed, some of the results we used to set up our approach hold in the context of *institutions*, it would be interesting to adapt our approach to the use of *institutions*, and to study the benefit in terms of the flexibility in the DSL specification.
- Study which composition technique fits better to our approach. For the moment we did not tackle this issue. In our experiments we considered that the composition uses scripting languages.

References

1. Abou Dib, A., Féraud, L., Ober, I., Percebois, C.: Towards a rigorous framework for dealing with domain specific language families. In: ICTTA 2008 Proceedings of the 3rd IEEE International Conference on Information & Communication Technologies: From Theory to Applications. IEEE Computer Press, Los Alamitos (in press, 2008)
2. Anlauff, M., Kutter, P.W., Pierantonio, A., Sünbül, A.: Using Domain-Specific Languages for the Realization of Component Composition. In: Maibaum, T.S.E. (ed.) FASE 2000. LNCS, vol. 1783, pp. 112–126. Springer, Heidelberg (2000)
3. Batory, D., Lofaso, B., Smaragdakis, Y.: JTS: Tools for Implementing Domain-Specific Languages. In: Proceedings of the 5th International Conference on Software Reuse, June 02-05, p. 143 (1998)
4. Ordonez Camacho, D., Mens, K., van den Brand, M., Vinju, J.J.: Automated Derivation of Translators From Annotated Grammars. Electr. Notes Theor. Comput. Sci. 164(2), 121–137 (2006)
5. Consel, C., Latry, F., Réveillillere, L., Cointe, P.: A generative programming approach to developing DSL compilers. In: Glück, R., Lowry, M. (eds.) GPCE 2005. LNCS, vol. 3676, pp. 29–46. Springer, Heidelberg (2005)
6. ECSS-E-70-31A - Space Engineering Standard - Ground Systems and Operations - Monitoring and Control Data Definition standard
7. Fiadero, J.L.: Categories for Software Engineering. Springer, Heidelberg (2005)
8. Goguen, J.A., Burstall, R.M.: Introducing Institutions: Abstract model theory for specification and programming. Research Report ECS-LFCS-90-106, University of Edinburgh (1990)
9. Hoare, C.A.R., Misra, J.: Vision of a Grand Challenge project, Verified Software: Theories, Tools, Experiments (VSTTE). In: IFIP 2005, ETH (July 2005)
10. Hongge, G., Weyman, J.: An Approach to Automation of Fusion Using Specware. In: Proceedings of the Second International Conference on Information Fusion, pp. 109–116 (1999)
11. Jouault, F., Bézivin, J., Consel, C., Kurtev, I., Latry, F.: Building DSLs with AMMA/ATL, a Case Study on SPL and CPL Telephony Languages. In: ECOOP Workshop on Domain-Specific Program Development (DSPD) (2006)
12. Kestrel. Specware documentation, `http://www.specware.org/doc.html`

13. Kurtev, I., Bézivin, J., Jouault, F., Valduriez, P.: Model-based DSL frameworks. OOPSLA Companion, pp. 602–616 (2006)
14. Lapets, A.: Algebraic Semantics of Domain-Specific Languages Thesis, Harvard (2006)
15. Mernik, M., Heering, J., Sloane, A.M.: When and how to develop domain-specific languages. ACM Comput. Surv. 37(4), 316–344 (2005)
16. Nipkow, T., Paulson, L.C., Wenzel, M.T. (eds.): Isabelle/HOL. LNCS, vol. 2283. Springer, Heidelberg (2002)
17. Oriat, C.: Étude des spécifications modulaires: constructions de colimites finies, diagrammes, isomorphismes. PhD thesis (in French), INPG, Grenoble (1996)
18. Pavlovic, D., Smith, D.R.: Software Development by Refinement. In: Aichernig, B.K., Maibaum, T.S.E. (eds.) Formal Methods at the Crossroads. From Panacea to Foundational Support. LNCS, vol. 2757, pp. 267–286. Springer, Heidelberg (2003)
19. Rugaber, S., Stirewalt, K.: Model Driven Reverse Engineering. IEEE Software 21(4), 45–53 (2004)
20. Schneider, J.-G., Nierstrasz, O.: Components, scripts and glue. In: Software Architectures - Advances and Applications, pp. 13–25. Springer, Heidelberg (1999)
21. Smith, D.: Composition by Colimit and Formal Software Development. In: Futatsugi, K., Jouannaud, J.-P., Meseguer, J. (eds.) Algebra, Meaning, and Computation. LNCS, vol. 4060, pp. 317–332. Springer, Heidelberg (2006)
22. Sprinkle, J., Karsai, G.: A domain-specific visual language for domain model evolution. Journal of Visual Languages & Computing 15(3-4), 291–307 (2004)
23. Williamson, K., Healy, M., Barker, R.: Industrial Applications of Software Synthesis via Category Theory—Case Studies Using Specware. ASE Journal 8(1), 7–30 (2001)
24. Wirsing, M.: Algebraic specification languages: An overview. In: Reggio, G., Astesiano, E., Tarlecki, A. (eds.) Abstract Data Types 1994 and COMPASS 1994. LNCS, vol. 906, pp. 81–115. Springer, Heidelberg (1995)

Modeling Architectural Patterns' Behavior Using Architectural Primitives

Ahmad Waqas Kamal and Paris Avgeriou

Department of Mathematics and Computer Science
University of Groningen, The Netherlands
a.w.kamal@rug.nl, paris@cs.rug.nl

Abstract. Architectural patterns have an impact on both the structure and the behavior of a system at the architecture design level. However, it is challenging to model patterns' behavior in a systematic way because modeling languages do not provide the appropriate abstractions and because each pattern addresses a whole solution space comprised of potentially infinite solution variants. In this paper, we advocate the use of architectural primitives for systematically modeling architectural patterns in the behavioral view. These architectural primitives are found among a number of architectural patterns and serve as the basic building blocks for modeling patterns' behavior. The main contribution of this work lies in the discovery of architectural primitives, defining architectural primitives using UML, and capturing the missing pattern semantics by using UML's stereotypes.

Keywords: Architectural Patterns, Architectural Primitives, Modeling, UML.

1 Introduction

Architectural patterns provide solutions to recurring design problems that arise in a specific context [1] [2]. These patterns propose a particular structure and behavior that can be tailored to the specific needs of the problem at hand [3] [4]. The solution of an architectural pattern is a model; applying the pattern results in incorporating that model into the software architecture of a specific system. One of the most significant aspects of modeling architectural patterns is the patterns' behavior, which are mostly represented as scenarios that define the run-time actions of the patterns [4]. Such a run-time behavior is vital for the pattern implementation as it shows the way 'pattern participants' collaborate and communicate with each other to express a pattern. We use the term 'participants' to mention the modeling elements that work in association to express architectural patterns. Unfortunately, modeling architectural patterns' behavior in a systematic way remains a challenging task mostly due to the following reasons:

a) Pattern participants do not match the architectural abstractions of commonly used modeling languages.

b) Architectural patterns' behavior can potentially be modeled in infinite different ways to balance the forces related to the problem at hand.

R. Morrison, D. Balasubramaniam, and K. Falkner (Eds.): ECSA 2008, LNCS 5292, pp. 164–179, 2008.
© Springer-Verlag Berlin Heidelberg 2008

Architecture Description Languages (ADLs) (e.g. ACME [5] or Wright [6]) and UML [7] have traditionally been used for modeling architectural patterns. Few of these languages focus specifically on modeling patterns' behavior while few others provide general architectural abstractions that can be extended to express patterns. UML is one such widely known modeling language that offers a generalized set of interaction elements to describe behavioral aspects of software architecture. However, both ADLs and UML provide only limited support for modeling patterns [8] because the architectural abstractions provided by these languages do not match the pattern participants and because they do not provide mechanisms for modeling the infinite variability of pattern behavior.

In our previous work, we have identified a set of *architectural primitives* in the Component-Connector view [9] and the Process Flow view [10]. We consider the primitives as key participants in modeling patterns and use them as the fundamental modeling elements to express a pattern in system design. These primitives offer reusable modeling abstractions that can be used for systematically modeling pattern variants. In this paper, we extend our work by focusing on architectural primitives in the behavioral view. We show how few primitives, which are already used for modeling patterns in the structural view, can be used for modeling patterns in the behavioral view as well. We illustrate our approach by presenting how the behavior of three typical architectural patterns can be modeled with the help of these new primitives. Furthermore, since primitives alone do not capture the entire semantics of the patterns, we show how to identify the missing semantics and express them through a vocabulary of pattern-specific objects and messages.

The remainder of this paper is structured as follows: in Section 2, we motivate our choice of selecting UML's collaboration diagram for modeling patterns' behavior. In Section 3, we present our approach for representing patterns and primitives as modeling abstractions using an extension of the UML. Section 4 gives detailed information of the primitives discovered during our work. In Section 5, we use primitives and a vocabulary of design elements, for modeling three selected patterns. Section 6 elaborates on related work and Section 7 discusses the future work and concludes this study.

2 The Unified Modeling Language in the Behavioral View

Although any modeling language can be used for modeling architectural primitives as long as the selected modeling language supports an extension mechanism to handle the semantics of the primitives, the UML is our choice in this work. The motivation behind the selection of UML is: a) UML is a widely known de facto modeling language; b) UML provides explicit extension mechanisms; and c) UML supports a variety of diagrams for describing the behavioral aspects of software architecture, such as Use case, Sequence, Collaboration, Statechart, and Activity. Each of these diagrams serves specific purposes to describe software design, which at times overlap with each other. These diagrams use particular UML modeling elements, which can be extended to meet the specific needs of modeling a system. In this paper, the requirements that we consider for modeling patterns' behavior are as follows:

- *Pattern elements operations:* The operations performed by pattern participants show the true essence of pattern behavior. The operation parameters, return values, and operation type should be represented in the design.
- *Relationships among pattern elements:* The relationships define the nature of interactions performed by the objects, such as the order of occurrence of the operations, multiplicity, and direction of flow etc.
- *Pattern behavior in response to user/system interaction:* Capturing the behavior of pattern participants that can explain the major dynamics of the pattern when a specific event or user/system action takes place.

Depending on the purpose, the UML supports a variety of diagrams for modeling different aspects of system behavior. A brief description of each UML diagram for modeling system behavior and their comparison to the requirements listed above is given as follows:

- *Use Case Diagrams* describe the interaction between actors – who initiate the action – and the system. The interaction is usually described using a sequence of steps. Use cases are usually defined at a higher level where the system design is considered as a black box, and emerges from the requirements used for designing the system. The use case diagrams, being at a higher level of abstraction, are not a close match to the requirements listed above because our focus lies on detail level interactions and operations among pattern participants.
- *Sequence diagrams* use objects, events, and arrows to depict scenarios by exchanging messages between objects when a specific event occurs. They usually show the execution of a typical example. Sequence diagrams are a close match to the requirements listed above as they show the sequence of operations entailed by the architectural patterns, occurrence of events to invoke specific operations, and use messages to show the interaction among pattern participants.
- *Statechart diagrams* show interactions with other objects inside or outside the system. A state shows the execution of a specific function when an event occurs. State diagrams are more focused on transition of states among objects while our focus lies on interaction among objects, which makes these diagrams a weak option for modeling patterns' behavior in context of the requirements listed above.
- *Collaboration diagrams* depict scenarios as flow of messages. Collaboration diagrams are very similar to sequence diagrams. However, an obvious difference is that collaboration diagrams show the teamwork of messages while sequence diagrams shows the stepwise execution of messages. Similar to the sequence diagrams, we consider collaboration diagrams as a close match to our work since collaboration diagrams can show the operations taking place between the pattern participants, the relationship, and occurrence of specific events.
- *Activity Diagrams* show an operation that is invoked when a specific event occurs. The activity diagram focus on using threads for the transfer of control and data among objects and hence more often used for synchronization checks [7]. These diagrams too are not a close match to the requirements listed above, as activity diagrams do not explicitly show the relationships and interactions among pattern participants.

Thus, we focus on capturing the interaction mechanism between pattern participants using either the sequence diagrams or collaboration diagrams. While sequence diagrams are more restricted to time-bound occurrence of events, the collaboration diagrams are the best choice in this work, which rely on interactions and relationships among objects in a time-independent manner. However, both types of these diagrams are comparative in nature and can be converted from one form to the other.

3 Extending UML to Represent Patterns and Primitives

UML is a widely known modeling language and is highly extensible [7]. There are two approaches for extending UML: extending the core UML metamodel or creating profiles by extending metaclasses. Our work focuses on the second approach, i.e. we create profiles specific to the individual architectural primitives. To capture the missing patterns semantics and to express the discovered architectural primitives, we extend the UML metaclasses using UML profile mechanism. That is, we define the primitives and pattern participants as extensions of existing metaclasses of UML using stereotypes and constraints as follows:

- *Stereotypes:* We use stereotypes to extend the properties of existing UML metaclasses. For instance, the Message metaclass is extended to generate a variety of primitives and specialized messages between pattern participants.
- *Constraints:* We use the Object Constraint Language (OCL) [11] to place additional semantic restrictions on extended UML elements. For instance, constraints can be defined on associations between objects, navigability, direction of communication, etc.

a. The UML 2 Metamodel

For the primitives presented in this paper, we mainly extend or use the following metaclasses of the UML 2.0 interaction metamodel to express the primitives:

- *Messages* are used to perform operations on the objects. Messages define a specific kind of communication in an interaction and connect the MessageEnds, which store references to the adjacent objects that need to be connected.
- *Interaction* provides connection between connectable elements using message ends. It uses namespace to store the sequence of operations taking place in the collaboration diagrams.
- *MessageEnd* connects the source object to the target object, where the source and target objects own the message ends.

We have also used the following UML metaclasses in order to express the constraints on UML metamodel:

- *EventOccurence* is a specialization of the MessageEnd. The message operations use the MessageEnds to send and receive events.
- *ExecutionOccurence* is represented by two event occurrences, the start event occurrence and the finish event occurrence.

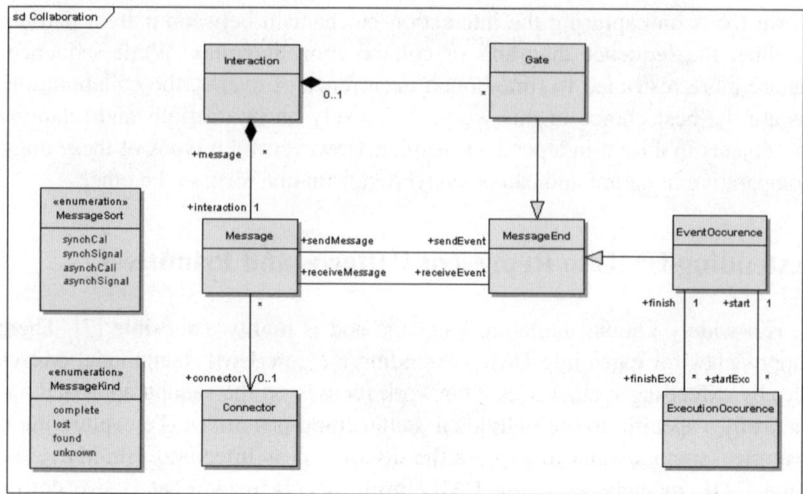

Fig. 1. Part of the UML Interaction metamodel used for defining primitives

4   Architectural Primitives

This section presents a continuation to our previous work where we have listed several architectural primitives in Component-Connector view [9] and the Process Flow view [10]. In this section, we present seven primitives discovered in the behavioral view that are repetitively found as abstractions in a number of patterns. The aim of our work is to capture common recurring solutions at an abstraction level that can be used to model architectural patterns' behavior, hence providing a better reusability and systematic support to model patterns. Following, we list the primitives discovered during our work and present the UML profile elements as a concrete modeling solution for expressing these primitives.

4.1   Documenting an Architectural Primitive: Push-Pull

Textual Description: Push, Pull, and Push-Pull structures are common abstractions in many software patterns. They occur when a target object receives a message sent by a source object (Push), or when a receiver receives information by generating a request (Pull). Both structures can also occur together at the same time (Push-Pull).

Known uses in patterns

  - In the Model-View-Controller [4] pattern, the model pushes data to the view, and the view can pull data from the model.
  - In the PIPE-FILTER [4] pattern, filters push data, which is transmitted by the pipes to other filters and even pipes can request data from source filters (Pull) to transmit it to the target filters.
  - In the PUBLISH-SUBSCRIBE [4] pattern, data is pushed from the framework to subscribers and subscribers can pull data from the framework.

- In the CLIENT-SERVER [4] pattern, data is pushed from the server to the client, and the client can send a request to pull data from the server.

Modeling Issues: Semantics of the push-pull structure is missing in UML diagrams. It is difficult to understand whether a certain operation is used to push data, pull data, or both. A major problem in modeling the above listed patters in UML is that although a Push-Pull structure is often used to transmit data among objects, it cannot be explicitly modeled using UML interaction diagrams.

Modeling Solution: To capture the semantics of Push-Pull properly in UML, we propose a number of new stereotypes for dealing with the three cases: Push, Pull, and Push-Pull. Figure 2 illustrates these stereotypes according to the UML 2.0 interaction model.

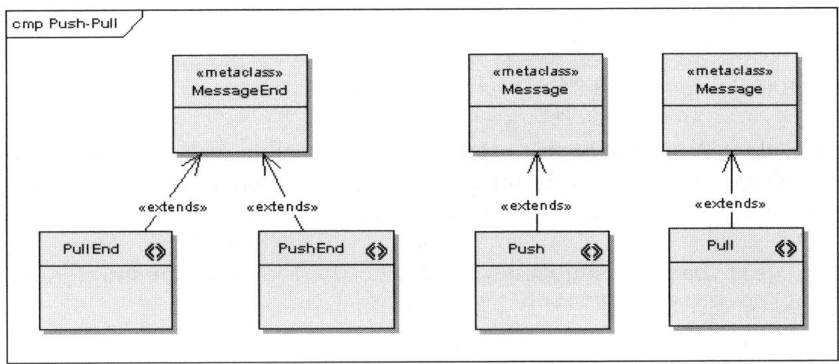

Fig. 2. UML Stereotypes For Modeling the Push-Pull Structure

<<Push>>: A stereotype that extends the 'Message' metaclass and attaches to message ends that connect adjacent objects.

-- A Push message has only two ends

```
inv: self.baseMessage->size() = 2
```

-- A Push message should be represented by a directed Message only

```
inv: self.baseMessage.type.MessageEnd->select(
Message = Core::MessageKind::directed).class->any(true)
```

-- The following constraint specifies the presence of interaction link between connected elements

```
inv: self.enclosingInteraction->select(
oclAsKindOf(Message)->exists(I:Interaction | I.PushEnd)
```

<<Pull>>: A stereotype that extends the 'Message' metaclass and owns Message Ends that connect adjacent objects.

-- A Pull message has only two ends

```
inv: self.baseMessage.end->size() = 2
```

-- A Pull message should be represented by a directed Message only

```
inv: self.baseMessage.type.MessageEnd->select(
Message = Core::MessageKind::directed).class->any(true)
```

-- The interaction contains the message ends owned by the adjacent objects

```
inv : self.enclosingInteraction-> se-
lect(oclAsKindOf(Message)->exists(I:Interaction | I.PullEnd)
implies
select(oclAsKindOf(Message)->exists(I:Interaction |
I.PushEnd)
```

<<PullEnd>>: A stereotype that extends the MessageEnd metaclass and contains a number of operations that serve the purpose of Pull operations between connected elements.

```
inv: self.baseMessageEnd->forAll(i:Core:: MessageEnd |
PullEnd.baseMessageEnd->exists (j | j=i)
```

<<PushEnd>>: A stereotype that extends the MessageEnd metaclass and contains a number of operations that serve the purpose of Push operations between connected elements.

```
inv: self.baseMessageEnd->forAll(i:Core:: MessageEnd |
PushtEnd.baseMessageEnd->exists (j | j=i)
```

4.2 More Architectural Primitives

Due to space restrictions, we do not go into the detailed definition for the rest of the architectural primitives discovered in this work. Instead, we present a shortened modeling solution.

I.   Callback

Textual Description: In a callback interaction between objects, an object B invokes an operation on object A, where object B keeps a reference to object A. Usually the callback function is invoked when a run-time event happens.

Known Uses in Patterns: MODEL-VIEW-CONTROLLER [4], OBSERVER [4], PUBLISH-SUBSCRIBE [4]

Modeling Issues: A major problem in modeling these patterns in UML is that even though callback is an active participant in the patterns, it can not be semantically represented in the interaction diagrams. A UML interaction diagram can depict the presence of a callback structure but it cannot be distinctively identified. It is hard to distinguish between many operations taking place between objects and the callback-specific operations.

Modeling Solution: To capture the semantics of callback primitive properly in UML, we use the following stereotypes: <<Callback>>, <<EventEnd>>, and <<CallbackEnd>>.

The <<Callback>> extends the Message metaclass while the <<EventEnd>> and <<CallbackEnd>> extend the MessageEnd metaclass. A callback invocation is always preceded by an event occurrence and the callee object must have subscribed itself to the caller object beforehand. In this case, the kind of message communication must be of signal type [7] where the EventOccurence takes place at the sender object (EventEnd) while the EventExecution takes place at the receiver end (CallbackEnd).

II.   Forward-Request

Textual Description: Forward-Request primitives are used to depict the presence of a request forwarding mechanism. Forward-Request messages decouple the underlying system from the external objects.

Known Uses in Patterns: PEERS [2], BROKER [4], CLIENT-SERVER[9], FORWARD-RECEIVER [2], MARSHALLER [2]

Modeling Issues: A Forward-Request typically differs from simple function calls, return calls, and other forms of communications among objects. The Forwarder object decouples the underlying system implementation from external function calls and converts incoming data into matching data format without introducing further dependencies. Moreover, in certain cases, the forwarder objects can receive return values that are forwarded to the source objects. However, UML elements cannot structurally express the presence of Forward-Request operations in software design.

Modeling Solution: To capture the semantics of Forward-Request properly in UML, we propose the following new stereotypes: <<Forward-Request>>, <<ForwardEnd>>, and <<ReceiverEnd>>. The <<Forward-Request>> extends the Message class and uses the <<ForwardEnd>> and <<ReceiverEnd>> to connect the adjacent objects. Both the <<ForwardEnd>> and <<ReceiverEnd>> extend the MessageEnd metaclass and are owned by the forwarder and receiver objects respectively. To execute an operation,, the <<ForwardEnd>> invokes the sendMessage operation, which is intercepted by the receiver object using the <<ReceiverEnd>>.

III.   Command

Textual Description: Calling a method in the target object typically involves invoking a specific method or procedure in the target object. The invocation operation is usually carried out on the occurrence of a specific event.

Known Uses in Patterns: MODEL-VIEW-CONTROLLER [4], PRESENTATION-ABSTRACTION-CONTROL [2], LAYERS [4]

Modeling Issues: A command typically differs from data, events, and other forms of communications among objects. However, UML elements cannot structurally distinguish the presence of command operations in software design.

Modeling Solution: To capture the semantics of Command primitive properly in UML, we propose two new stereotypes: <<Command>>, and <<CommandEnd>>. The <<Command>> extends the Message class and uses the <<CommandEnd>> to invoke command on the target object when a specific event occurs. The <<CommandEnd>> extends the MessageEnd metaclass and is owned by the command invocation object.

IV. Asynchronous Message

Textual Description: In an asynchronous communication, the message sender continues with its operation without waiting for any reply from the message receiver.

Known Uses in Patterns: PIPE-FILTER [4], CLIENT-SERVER [2], BROKER [4]

Modeling Issues: The patterns listed above often use Asynchronous messaging. UML supports the invocation of asynchronous messages when a specific event occurs. However, it does not enforce any constraints in distinctively recognizing the asynchronous operations. Various architectural patterns use degrees of asynchrony in their operations. In the most common form of asynchronous communication, the sender's data is buffered in queues without waiting for the recipient to pick the data. The current UML collaboration diagrams support the Asynchronous messaging; however, there are two major issues:

- Even though the UML diagrams have a support for Asynchronous messaging, they do not differentiate between the return values from the target objects. It is an ambiguous 'hint' to determine whether the return value is merely a notification event about the receipt of message or the actually processed data.
- Asynchronous messages are often buffered in queues until the target object notifies about its availability using events, often much later in the time. Such a structure cannot be un-ambiguously determined in UML interaction diagrams where a number of operations among objects are taking place at the same time.

Modeling Solution: We use the <<AsynchMessage>> stereotype along with the existing UML interaction diagram functions for modeling the asynchronous communication among the objects. The <<AsynchMessage>> extends the Message metaclass and uses the existing MessageSend and MessageReceive operations to guarantee that the invocation flag is active whenever an operation is invoked. We further constrain the Asynchronous communication to ensure that the method that invoked the operation is not bound to receive the results and only a notification event can inform the receipt of message.

V. Synchronous Message

Textual Description: In a synchronous communication, the sender waits till the receiver finishes the activated operation.

Known Uses in Patterns: PIPE-FILTER [4], CLIENT-SERVER [2], BROKER [4]

Modeling Issues: The patterns listed above often use Synchronous messaging. UML denotes a synchronous message with a solid arrowhead. We specify additional constraints on UML synchronous messages to provide a clear depiction of synchronous message.

Modeling Solution: We add a simple extension to the UML metamodel by proposing the <<SynchMessage>> stereotype for modeling the synchronous communication between objects. The <<SynchMessage>> extends the Message metaclass and uses the existing UML synchmessage operations to ensure that: a) a synchronous message is always represented with a directed association; b) an end-to-end connection is established with the target object, which owns the EventEnd and returns a flag each time a data processing is completed; and c) a return operation is mandatory for the synchronous communication to update the status of the operation that invoked the synchronous communication.

VI. Call-Slave

Textual Description: The objects called slaves provide sub-services on behalf of a master object. The master also keeps reference to all the slave components.

Known Uses in Patterns: MASTER-SLAVE, PRESENTATION-ABSTRACTION-CONTROLLER [2], WHOLE-PART [2]

Modeling Issues: The call-slave structure is a key participant in modeling patterns when a task is delegated to a number of sub-objects. In such a case, the dependent objects work as slaves and usually do not invoke any operations on the surrounding elements. UML interaction diagrams can depict such a structure but cannot express the semantics in the diagrams.

Modeling Solution: We propose the following stereotypes to model the Call-Slave primitive: <<CallSlave>>, <<Slave>>, and <<Master>>. The <<CallSlave>> extends the Message metaclass and provides a selfMessage operation to invoke operations that further call upon slave objects. Both the <<Slave>> and <<Master >> represent the objects with further constraints such that only the <<Master>> object can access the <<Slave>> objects.

5 Modeling Architectural Patterns Using Primitives

In this section, we use the primitives described in the previous section to model known variants of three selected architectural patterns: Pipe-Filter, Model-View-Controller (MVC) and Client-Server. As aforementioned in the introduction, primitives capture only part of the semantics of the patterns, since there are semantics specific to individual patterns and not recurring in several patterns. Therefore, in order to complete the behavioral modeling of patterns, we need to find the missing pattern semantics and express them through a stereotyping scheme. Due to space limitation, we only provide detailed OCL constraints for the Pipe-Filter, while we omit the OCL code for the MVC and Client-Server.

5.1 Pipe-Filter

The Pipe-Filter pattern consists of a chain of data processing filters, which are connected through pipes. The output of one filter is passed through pipes to the adjacent filter. The elements in the Pipe-Filter pattern can vary in the functions they perform. For instance, pipes can buffer data, form feedback loops or fork/join structures, filters can be active or passive etc. Each such function can be described with a specific scenario to depict the behavior of the pattern. The primitives discovered so far address many such variations. We select the Push, Pull, and Synchronous Message primitives from the existing pool of primitives. The rationale behind the selection of these primitives is as follows:

- The Push and Pull primitives are used to express the pipes that transmit streams of data between filters.
- Data is sent from one filter to the next filter in the chain using synchronous operations.

Missing Pattern Semantics: Despite the reusability support offered by the selected primitives, the Pipe-Filter pattern semantics cannot be fully expressed in design because the feedback, pipe, and filter structure are still missing. We apply the Feedback stereotype on the Push primitive to capture the presence of feedback loop in the Pipe-Filter pattern. Such a structure represents data being pushed from one filter object to another filter object using the feedback loop. The original Push primitive, as described in section 4, extends the UML metaclasses of Message and MessageEnd. The feedback stereotype further specializes the Push primitive by stereotyping it as Feedback without introducing new constraints.

<<Feedback>>: A stereotype that is applied on the Push primitive for expressing the Feedback operation in the Pipe-Filter pattern. The semantics of a feedback operation are similar to Push and Pull data streams operation.

The second stereotype named 'Filter' that we use from the existing vocabulary of design elements is defined as follows:

<<Filter>>: A stereotype that extends the Object metaclass of UML and owns message ends.

-- A Filter object owns the MessageEnds of the associated pipes such that within an interaction, it owns the receiver end of source pipe and the sender end of next pipe in the chain

```
inv: self.enclosingInteraction->
select(oclAsKindOf(Object)->exists(I:Interaction |
I.MessageOut) implies self.enclosingInteraction->
select(oclAsKindOf(Object)->exists(I:Interaction |
I.MessageIn)
```

<<MessageOut>> A stereotype that extends the MessageEnd class and owned by the filter objects

```
inv: self.enclosingInteraction->select(
oclAsKindOf(Message)->exists(I:Interaction | I.MessageOut)
```

<<MessageIn>> A stereotype that extends the MessageEnd class and owned by the filter objects

```
inv: self.enclosingInteraction->select(
oclAsKindOf(Message)->exists(I:Interaction | I.MessageIn)
```

The fifth stereotype that we use from the existing vocabulary of design elements is the 'Pipe' that is defined as follows:

<<Pipe>>: A stereotype that extends the Message metaclass of UML and attaches the MeesageEnd of source object to the MessageEnd of the target object.

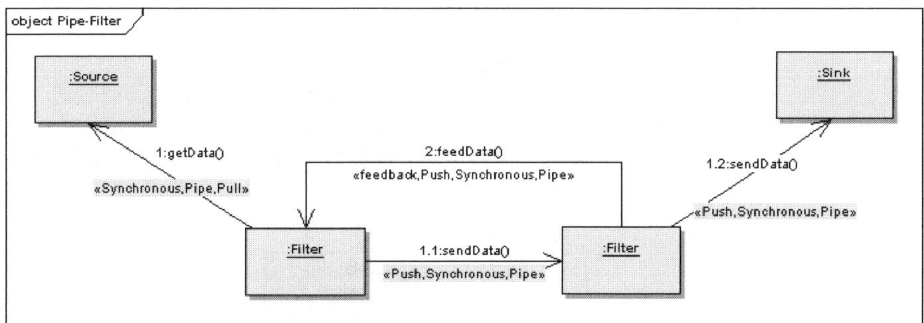

Fig. 3. Modeling Pipe-Filter Pattern Using Primitives and Design Elements

As shown in the figure above, the first filter object pulls data from the source object, and after processing pushes this data to the next filter in the chain. The second filter sends data back to the first filter using feedback pipe for further processing, and sends the final processed data to the sink.

5.2 Model-View-Controller

The behavior of MVC pattern relies on the functions performed by the following elements: Model, View, and Controller. The Model provides the functional core of the application and notifies views about data changes. Views retrieve information from the model and display it to the user. Controllers translate events into requests to perform operations on the view and model elements.

As a first step, we map the MVC pattern to the list of available primitives. We select the callback and command primitives for modeling the MVC pattern. The rationale behind the selection of these primitives is as follows:

- The view subscribes to the model to be called back when some data change occurs.
- Controller issues a command request on the model and view objects when some event occurs.

Missing Pattern Semantics: However, not every aspect of the MVC pattern can be modeled using the existing set of primitives. For instance, the Model, View, and Controller objects are not mapped to any primitives discovered so far. Keeping in view the general nature of these objects and their mandatory use in modeling different variants of the MVC pattern, we include the <<Model>>, <<View>> and <<Controller>> stereotypes in the existing vocabulary of pattern elements, as described below.

<<Model>>: A stereotype that extends the Object metaclass of UML and owns message ends for interaction with Controller and View objects.

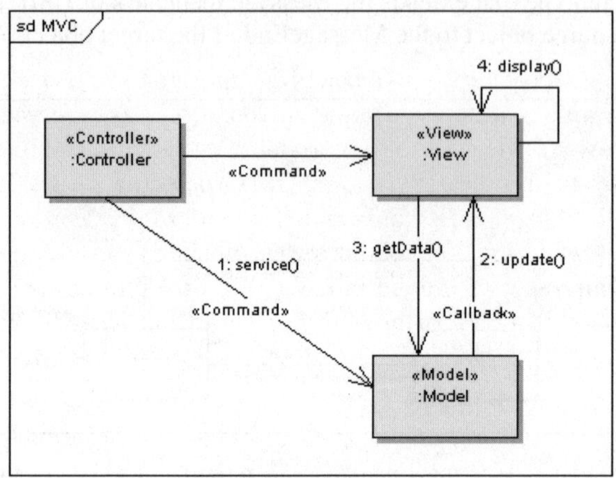

Fig. 4. Modeling the MVC Pattern Using Primitives and Design Elements

<<Controller>>: A stereotype that extends the Object metaclass of UML and owns message ends for interaction with Model and View objects.

<<View>>: A stereotype that extends the Object metaclass of UML and owns message ends for interaction with Model and Controller objects.

5.3 Client-Server

In a typical Client-Server pattern variant, the server offers operations that are accessed by the clients and even clients can perform domain-specific operations at their own. Usually a broker pattern is used to establish connections between client and server. The client sends request to the broker asking to fulfill a specific task. The broker in response looks for the appropriate server and assigns the task to the server. The server provides the functional core of the application and uses the broker to send information back to the clients.

As a first step, we map the Client-Server pattern to the list of available primitives. We select the forward-request, asynchronous, and command primitives for modeling the Client-Server pattern. The rationale behind the selection of these primitives is as follows:

- The Server issues a command request to the clients when some event occurs.
- The Client and Server side proxies synchronously forward requests to other objects.

Modeling Pattern Semantics: However, not every aspect of the Client-Server pattern can be modeled using the existing set of primitives. For instance, the Client, and the Server objects are not mapped to any primitives discovered so far. Keeping in view the general nature of these objects, we provide reusability support by making these two pattern participants available in the existing vocabulary of design elements.

<<Client>>: A stereotype that extends the Object metaclass of UML and owns message ends for interaction with Server and mediator objects.

<<Server>>: A stereotype that extends the Object metaclass of UML and owns message ends for interaction with Client, surrounding objects, and mediator objects.

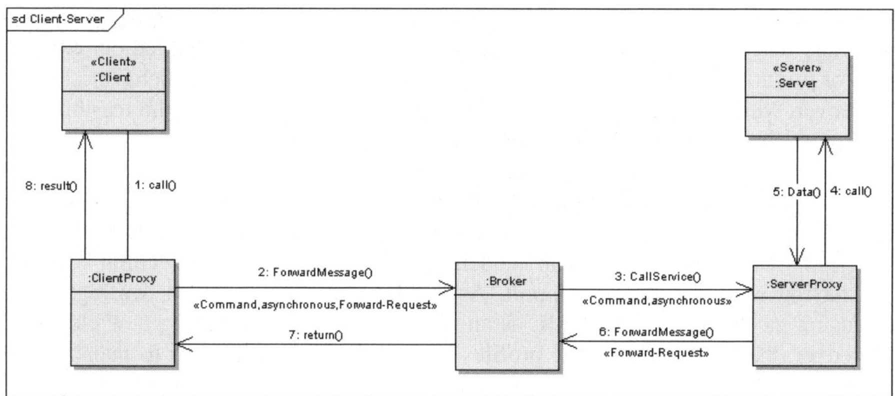

Fig. 5. Modeling the Client-Server Pattern Using Primitives and Design Elements

6 Related Work

The work described in this paper is based on our previous work [9] where we present an initial set of primitives for modeling architectural patterns in the component-connector view. However, the idea to use primitives for software design is not novel and has been applied in different software engineering disciplines [12]. The novelty of our work lies in the use of primitives for systematically modeling the behavior of architectural patterns.

Using different approaches, other researchers have been working actively on the systematic modeling of architectural patterns. Garlan et. al. [13] propose an object model for representing architectural designs. They characterize architectural patterns as a specialization of object models. However, each such specialization is built as an independent environment, where each specialization is developed from scratch using basic architectural elements. Our approach significantly differs as our focus lays on reusing primitives and pattern participants, which are defined as specializations of UML elements.

Werner et. al. [14] uses message sequence charts to propose a language that is capable enough to fully express the behavioral specification of systems using use cases and scenarios. Their work focuses on the execution of scenarios when different kinds of events occur for message calls of type e.g. asynchronous message, synchronous message. In our approach, we also use messages as a base for interaction but our focus revolves around modeling patterns where we use primitives and pattern participants' definitions as reusable abstractions.

7 Conclusion and Future Work

The combination of architectural primitives and the vocabulary of design elements offers a systematic way to model patterns' behavior in system design: the primitives and the design elements are reusable architectural abstractions in the form of extended UML elements; the semantics of the primitives and subsequently of the patterns can be validated by checking the OCL constraints; the patterns can be manually or automatically detected in the system design. In this paper, we have extended our existing pool of primitives with the discovery of seven more primitives in the behavioral view. Moreover, with the help of some example patterns, we demonstrated the feasibility of our approach for modeling architectural patterns using primitives.

To express the discovered primitives and design elements vocabulary, we have used UML2.0 for creating profiles. Compared to earlier versions, UML2.0 has come up with many improvements for expressing architectural elements. However, we still find UML a weak option in modeling many aspects of architectural patterns, e.g. having weak messaging support. As a solution to this problem, we regard the extension mechanism of the UML as an effective way for describing new elements. Moreover, the application of the profiles to the primitives allows us to maintain the integrity of the UML metamodel. By defining primitive-specific profiles, we enable the user to apply *selective* profiles in the model.

As future work, we would like to advance the automation of our approach by developing a tool, which supports modeling pattern variability, documenting design decisions, analyzing the system quality attributes, consistency checking between the structural and the behavioral views, and source code generation. We believe that in different architectural views, more primitives will be discovered in the near future, which will provide a better re-usability support to the architects for systematically expressing architectural patterns.

References

[1] Avgeriou, P., Zdun, U.: Architectural Patterns Revisited - A Pattern Language. In: Proceedings of the 10th European Conference on Pattern Languages of Programs (EuroPLOP), Irsee, Germany, pp. 1–39 (2005)

[2] Buschmann, F., Henney, K., Schmidt, C.D.: Pattern-Oriented Software Architecture: On Patterns and Pattern Languages. John Wiley & Sons, Chichester ISBN 978-0-471-48648-0

[3] Harrison, N., Avgeriou, P.: Pattern-Driven Architectural Partitioning – Balancing Functional and Non-Functional Requirements. In: First International Workshop on Software Architecture Research and Practice (SARP 2007), Silicon Valley, USA, p. 21. IEEE, Los Alamitos (2007)

[4] Buschman, F., Meunier, R., Rohnert, H., Sommerlad, P., Stal, M.: Pattern Oriented Software Architecture: A System of Patterns. John Wiley & Sons, Chichester (1996)

[5] Garlan, D., Monroe, R., Wile, D.: ACME: An Architecture Description Interchange Language. In: Proceedings of CASCON 1997, Toronto, Ontario, pp. 169–183 (1997)

[6] Allen, R., Garlan, D.: A Formal Basis For Architectural Connection. ACM Transactions on Software Engineering and Methodology 6(3), 213–249 (1997)

[7] Unified Modeling Language: Superstructure, version 2.0, Final Adopted Specification, ptc/03-08-02, http://www.omg.org/cgi-bin/doc?formal/05-07-04

[8] Kamal, A.W., Avgeriou, P.: An evaluation of ADLs on modeling patterns for software architecture design. In: 4th International Workshop on Rapid Integration of Software Engineering Techniques, Luxembourg (2007)

[9] Zdun, U., Avgeriou, P.: Modeling Architecture Patterns using Architecture Primitives. In: 20th annual ACM SIGPLAN conference on Object oriented programming systems languages and applications, pp. 133–146 (2005)

[10] Zdun, U., Avgeriou, P., Hentrich, C., Dustdar, S.: Architecting as Decision Making with Patterns and Primitives. In: Proceedings of the Third Workshop on Sharing and Reusing architectural Knowledge (SHARK), pp. 11–18. ACM, New York (2008)

[11] Object Constraint Language Specification versions 1.1, OMG standard, http://umlcenter.visual-paradigm.com/umlresources/obje_11.pdf

[12] Mehta, N.R., Medvidovic, N.: Composing Architectural Styles from Architectural Primitives. In: Proceedings of the 9th European Software Engineering Conference held jointly with 10th ACM SIGSOFT international symposium on foundations of software engineering, Helsinki, Finland, pp. 347–350 (2005)

[13] Garlan, D., Allen, R., Ockerbloom, J.: Exploiting Style in Architectural Design Environments. In: Proceedings of the ACM SIGSOFT 1994 Symposium on Foundations of Software Engineering, New Orleans, LA, pp. 175–188 (1994)

[14] Damm, W., Harrel, D.: LSCs: Breathing Life into Message Sequence Charts, Formal Methods in System Design. Kluwer Academy Publishers, Dordrecht (2001)

Approach for Dynamically Composing Decentralised Service Architectures with Cross-Cutting Constraints

Varvana Myllärniemi[1], Christian Prehofer[2], Mikko Raatikainen[1],
Jilles van Gurp[2], and Tomi Männistö[1]

[1] Helsinki University of Technology, P.O. Box 9210, 02015 TKK, Finland
[2] Nokia Research Center, P.O. Box 407, 00045 NOKIA GROUP, Finland
{varvana.myllarniemi,mikko.raatikainen,tomi.mannisto}@tkk.fi,
{christian.prehofer,jilles.vangurp}@nokia.com

Abstract. The emergence of open, composable Internet services and mashups means that services cannot be composed in a centralised manner. Despite this, cross-cutting constraints might exist between services, stemming from, e.g., security. Especially when used with mobile devices, these service compositions need to be constructed at runtime. This paper proposes a knowledge-based approach for dynamically finding and validating decentralised service compositions while taking into account cross-cutting constraints. The approach is exemplified with a case of a shopping mall portal.

1 Introduction

The emergence of various second-generation Web technologies enables the creation of increasingly complex new services by composing multiple services from multiple Internet locations [1]. For example, mashups combine data or services from multiple sources into one integrated user experience. At the same time, the emergence of personal mobile devices for Web browsing sets new requirements for service compositions. On the one hand, adapting to the user's context and personal preferences requires that compositions need to be changed dynamically. On the other hand, security and privacy issues create constraints in how services can be composed. Thus service compositions should be able to address dynamism, decentralisation and cross-cutting constraints.

The first requirement, dynamism, means that service compositions cannot be predefined, but must be created and recomposed at runtime. In some cases, even the number or the identities of the services cannot be predefined prior to runtime. The second requirement, decentralisation, stems from the fact that services participating in the composition are distributed in the Internet. However, decentralisation is not only about distribution, but it implies that there is no central, trusted party that can manage and govern composition. The third requirement, existence of cross-cutting constraints, means that there are dependencies between services that must be taken into account in order to achieve

R. Morrison, D. Balasubramaniam, and K. Falkner (Eds.): ECSA 2008, LNCS 5292, pp. 180–195, 2008.

a meaningful composition. Often such constraints are related to non-functional properties, especially security.

Together, dynamism, decentralisation, and cross-cutting constraints make the composition much more difficult. Because of the decentralisation, security constraints cannot be decided by one centralised party. Because of the dynamism, relationships between decentralised services cannot be established beforehand. Despite this, existing literature typically addresses these issues separately.

This paper addresses service compositions with dynamism, decentralisation, and cross-cutting security constraints. We describe a knowledge-based approach that enables finding and validating decentralised service compositions at runtime. Validating a composition means ensuring that the architecture or constraints set by different parties are not violated. The approach describes required knowledge, activities, and responsibilities; however, going through these in detail is beyond the scope of the paper. Instead, this paper lays out requirements and first solutions for required knowledge, activities, and responsibilities. We exemplify this approach using a case of a personalised search service inside a shopping mall.

The rest of the paper is organised as follows: Section 2 presents the case; Section 3 presents the approach; Section 4 compares the approach to previous work; Section 5 discusses the results; and Section 6 concludes the paper.

2   Case

The example case in this paper is a shopping mall that provides a Web-based portal through which the customers inside the mall premises can access and personalise the services via mobile devices. Using a browser for consuming mobile services is argued to offer superior portability and scalability [2]. Further, customers are familiar with various Web-based portals, which can be personalised by the user, and can encompass services provided by third parties. Popular examples of such Web sites include Facebook and MySpace. However, such service portals can be enhanced by tying them to particular physical places, and augmenting them with information on the user's location, for example.

To concretise a small slice of the service composition in the shopping mall portal, this paper concentrates on the following running example inspired by the search feature in [3]. The running example is a personalised search over available shops in the mall portal. Using the search service, users can search for, e.g., campaigns, offers, and information. The search can be performed over all available shops, or over a restricted set of shops. The search service is composed of several services (Fig. 1): mall search interacts with the user interface and collects search results from shop search services.

In the following, we discuss the dynamism, decentralisation and cross-cutting constraints in the case.

Firstly, service compositions in the case must be formed dynamically. In the shopping mall, each user may wish to personalise the portal, subscribe to services, and have different device capabilities. Naturally, completely new services may be published and old services removed. Consequently, service compositions cannot be decided beforehand; instead, one service composition represents those services

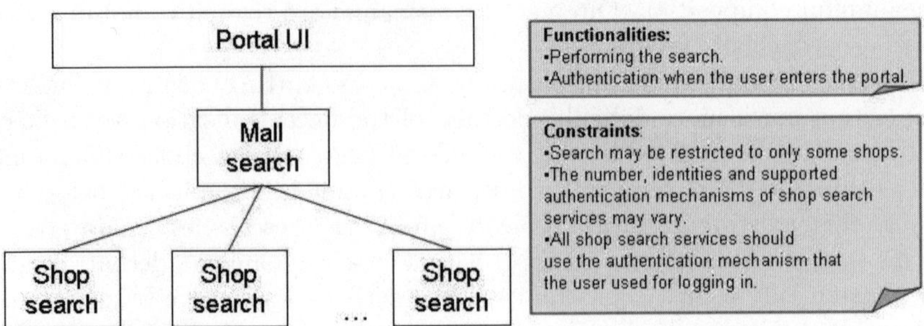

Fig. 1. Running example consists of a composed search service

that can be accessed by one user during one session. In the running example, there are several factors affecting the composition that cannot be decided before runtime (see informal explanations in Fig. 1). The number and identity of the shop searches depend on the available services, on the possible restriction to cover only certain shops, as well as on the authentication mechanism that the user used for logging in.

Secondly, the case illustrates how service compositions can be decentralised. Some of the services may be provided by the mall itself, while some may be provided by the shops or third parties; in some cases, even customers can act as service providers. In the running example, the decentralisation stems from the fact that some of the shop search services are provided by the shops themselves, not by the mall. This also means that the shop search services may reside on completely different hosts. To utilise, e.g., past purchase history for personalising the search, shop search services may require that users authenticate to the services provided by the shops (see Fig. 1).

Thirdly, there are several cross-cutting constraints that are mostly due to security and privacy considerations. Providing any kind of personalised service inherently involves handling sensitive information, such as a customer's location or personal preferences. Therefore, there may be a need to authenticate users of the mall portal. There are several mechanisms for authentication: customers can use an anonymous login, traditional passwords, or OpenID [4] as a decentralised, single sign-on (SSO) digital identity framework. However, in the running example, not all authentication mechanisms are supported by all shop search services. The shopping mall has decided to set a constraint that all participating shop search services must share the authentication mechanism used by the customer. However, this shared authentication mechanism cannot be decided before runtime, since it is established when the user logs in to the mall portal (see Fig. 1).

To summarise, the case as well as the running example portray a decentralised service composition in which there are cross-cutting security dependencies in how services can be composed. Further, the compositions for one particular user session cannot be decided beforehand, but they must be constructed at runtime. This calls for support in finding and validating a service composition dynamically. Our solution for tackling this particular problem is described next.

3   Approach

The overall goal of our approach involves finding a valid service composition. A valid composition adheres to the preferences and constraints of service providers, service consumers, and service aggregators, from structural, functional, and security points of view. The task of finding and validating the composition should be performed dynamically, as services and requirements for the service compositions evolve. Further, the approach should not assume any centralised party that can govern the composition. Finding a valid service composition can be accomplished in several ways. Compared to composition by trial and error, or to composition through autonomous interacting agents, our approach relies on capturing architectural knowledge based upon which service compositions can be found and validated.

In this section, we describe how our approach accomplishes this overall goal in terms of architectural knowledge, activities that produce and process the knowledge, and responsibilities and roles related to the knowledge.

3.1   Architectural Knowledge

In general, the architectural knowledge for service compositions should satisfy the following requirements. The knowledge should:

1. support automated finding and validation of service compositions;
2. be captured as models of Web-based services and their interfaces;
3. support modelling cross-cutting constraints and structural rules in how services can be composed;
4. support dynamically changing services; and
5. support distribution of the services as well as the knowledge itself.

To capture the knowledge, we propose a technology-independent conceptualisation that borrows concepts from WSDL [5] and many architectural description languages, for example, Koala [6] and UML 2.0. Fig. 2 illustrates a graphical representation of the running example. Besides this graphical representation, an XML-based language has been defined for capturing the knowledge shown in Fig. 2; due to space limitations, this XML language is not described here.

In the following, we discuss each of the above requirements. Our focus here is on bringing all of these aspects together in a consistent and simple way. As some of the above items are very general problems, we cannot cover each of these items in all possible ways, but rather propose basic concepts to model these aspects.

The first requirement states that the service composition should be found and validated with automated tools. In order for this to be possible, our approach distinguishes between two kinds of knowledge: composition model and composition configuration. *Composition model* depicts the participating service types, their interfaces and characteristics; it specifies the structural rules and cross-cutting constraints that govern how services can be composed. In contrast, the architecture of one particular service composition is called *composition configuration*. If composition model specifies the rules, composition configuration is the target that is composed from and checked against those rules. In order to support automated finding and validation, our composition model conceptualisation has been built to be compatible with metamodelling language Nivel with formal semantics [7]. This enables the use of *smodels* [8], which is a general-purpose inference tool based on the stable model semantics of logic programs. Using *smodels*, one can check the composition model for validity, as well as check the composition configuration for consistency, for completeness, and to deduce consequences.

Running example. For the search scenario, the composition model defines rules on how valid service compositions can be formed for different customer sessions within the shopping mall. The composition model, as well as an example composition configuration, is shown in Fig. 2. The composition model captures the service architecture and constraints, illustrated informally in Fig. 1. Further, the composition model states session parameters as options; in this case, an option is the method that the user used for logging in to the portal. In contrast, the composition configuration represents those services that are available for one particular user session at a time.   □

The second requirement states that the knowledge should be captured as models of Web-based services and their interfaces; thus the models represent the architectural knowledge. For this purpose, our approach uses the concept of a service type for composition model and a service instance for composition configuration. A service type describes a set of service instances with similar properties. Similarly to, e.g., WSDL [5], a service interacts with other services through its interfaces only; hence a service exists only as a placeholder of interfaces. An interface type consists of a number of operations, whereas an interface is an instantiated interface type in a particular service instance. To attach an interface to a service, a service type can define an interface definition. Similarly to, e.g., Koala [6], an interface definition is either required or provided; provided interface definition means that the instantiated service provides the operations for others to be accessed, while required means that the service instance depends upon other services for providing these operations. To support varying interactions for the service, the interface definition can define several possible interface types as well as the minimum and maximum number of instantiated interfaces.

Running example. The composition model in Fig. 2(a) defines a service type called *MallSearchService* with a provided interface definition *search* of type *DoSearch*. Although not illustrated here, *DoSearch* consists of one operation that takes the search term as an input and returns the results as an output. The example composition configuration in Fig. 2(b) shows the corresponding *MallSearchService* service instance with the provided *DoSearch* interface. To illustrate the possibility of defining varying capabilities for services, service type *MallSearchService* defines a provided interface definition named *login*, which can be either of type *LoginOpenID* or *LoginPasswd*, or it can optionally be left out altogether. This means that all service instances of *MallSearchService* must implement these interfaces, and when the composition is constructed, the interface

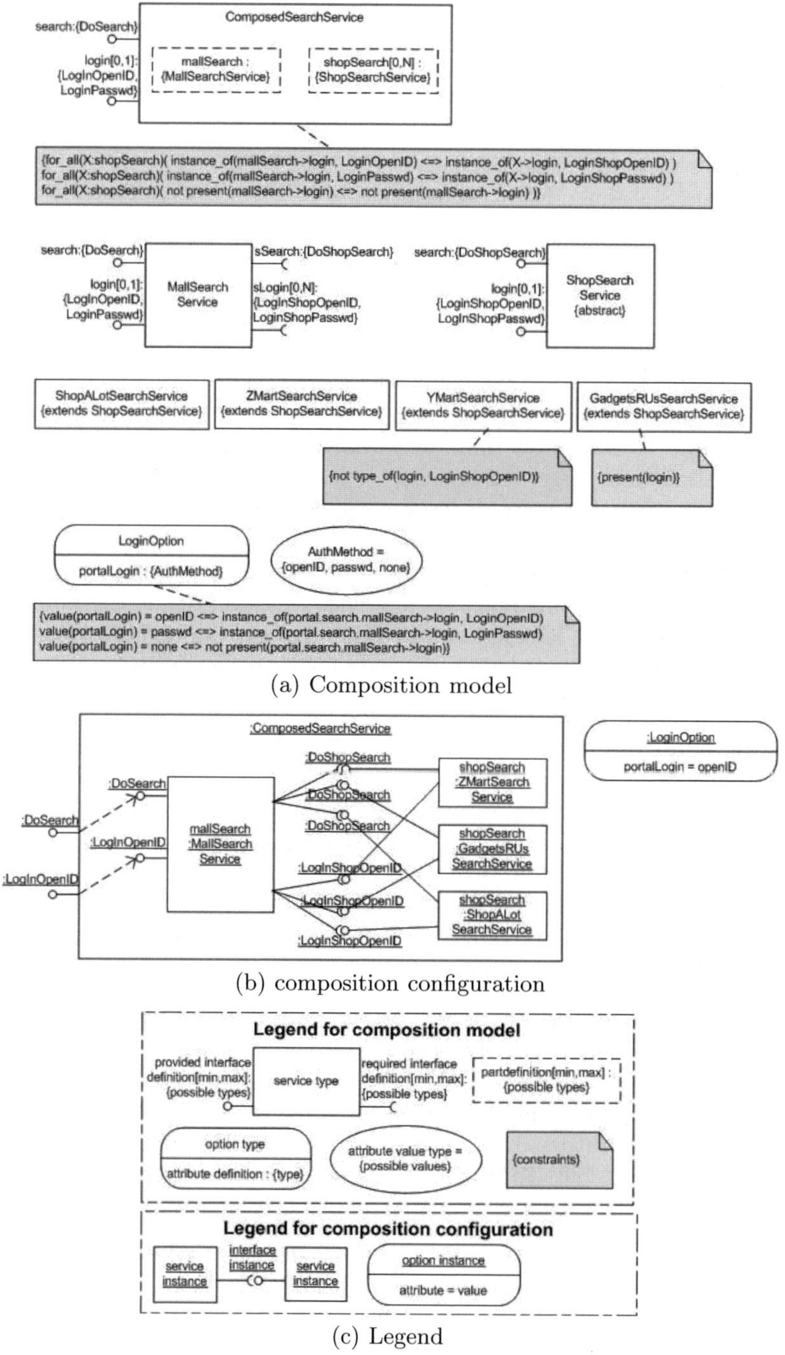

(a) Composition model

(b) composition configuration

(c) Legend

Fig. 2. Graphical representation of the knowledge describing the service compositions of the running example

Table 1. Constraint language in the running example

present(ref)	true if an instance referenced by ref is in the composition
instance_of(ref, type)	true if ref is an instance of type
value(ref, attr)	the set of values that instances referenced by ref have by the name attr
for_all(X:ref)	universal quantifier $\forall$
and, or, not	$\wedge$, $\vee$, $\neg$
<=>, =>	equivalence $\Leftrightarrow$, implication $\Rightarrow$
=, !=	equals, does not equal

type is selected to match the needed authentication mechanism. In Fig. 2(b), the interface has been instantiated as *LoginOpenID* interface. $\square$

The third requirement states that the knowledge should support adding cross-cutting constraints and structural rules for how services can be composed. The proposed conceptualisation provides three mechanisms for this purpose: composite services, constraints, and options.

A simple mechanism for stating how services can be composed is to model composite services. For this purpose, a service type can define the number and types of services that it is composed of using a construction called part definition. A composite service can then delegate calls to some of its interfaces to its constituent services.

Running example. The composition model in Fig. 2(a) defines one composite service type known as *ComposedSearchService*. Through part definition *mallSearch*, it states that any *ComposedSearchService* instance contains exactly one *MallSearchService* service instance. Since the number of the participating shop search services can vary, part definition *shopSearch* states that any *ComposedSearchService* instance contains from zero to N *ShopSearchService* instances. The corresponding composite service instance *ComposedSearchService* is shown in Fig. 2(b). $\square$

Besides composite services, more fine-grained and cross-cutting constraints can be defined by composition models stating constraints that restrict the instances in composition configurations. The supported constraints can consist of references to service instances, predicates on these references, boolean conjunctions, and comparison operators. Due to space limitation, the entire constraint language is not shown, but Table 1 lists those constructs that are used in the running example.

Running example. *ComposedSearchService* defines a constraint that states that all shop search service instances must have the same authentication mechanism. Further, *YMartSearchService* defines a constraint that denotes it cannot support OpenID as an authentication mechanism, whereas *GadgetsRUsSearchService* defines a constraint which denotes that it must always use some authentication mechanism, either OpenID or traditional password. $\square$

There might also be constraints between services and other options of the session. These options can relate to the user's device, or to the context or the session itself.

Running example. The authentication method that the user used to log in to the portal affects the service composition. Fig. 2(a) illustrates how the composition model specifies an option type *LoginOption*. *LoginOption* has one attribute definition *portalLogin*, with possible types defined by an attribute value type *AuthMethod*. Further, the *LoginOption* type defines a constraint that relates the login mechanism to service composition. It states that authentication mechanism provided by the composite search service must be the same as the user used for logging in.   □

The fourth requirement states that the knowledge should support dynamically changing and discoverable services. Since service types are defined independently of each other in the composition model, newly discovered services can be added to the model. However, it should be possible to state constraints on these dynamically changing services, even if their identities are not yet known. This is supported by providing abstract service types, which can be inherited by other service types. An abstract service type can be used as a representative of a set of concrete service types; all interfaces and constraints defined in an abstract service type are applicable to the inherited service types as well.

Running example. Since the identities of the participating shop search services may evolve over time, they are represented with an abstract *ShopSearchService* type in the composition model in Fig. 2(a). This way, it is possible to state constraints on the interfaces of all shop search services without knowing their identities beforehand. Inherited shop search service types can then state further constraints: for example, *YMartSearchService* adds a further constraint that excludes OpenID.   □

The fifth requirement states that the knowledge should support distribution of the services as well as the knowledge itself. The distribution of services can be captured in the composition models by stating the location of concrete service types. The distribution of the knowledge itself is again supported by the possibility of defining service types independently and then combining this knowledge to derive composition configurations.

Running example. Concrete shop search service types, such as *YMartSearchService*, are attributed with location information including protocol, address and port. Further, concrete search service types can be defined independently of the model, excluding information on abstract service type *SearchService*. The detailed process of how this definition is conducted in described in Section 3.2.   □

3.2   Activities

Fig. 3 illustrates the activities that create and process the architectural knowledge described in Section 3.1. Activities numbered from 1 to 4 create and process composition model, while activities 5 and 6 create and process composition configuration.

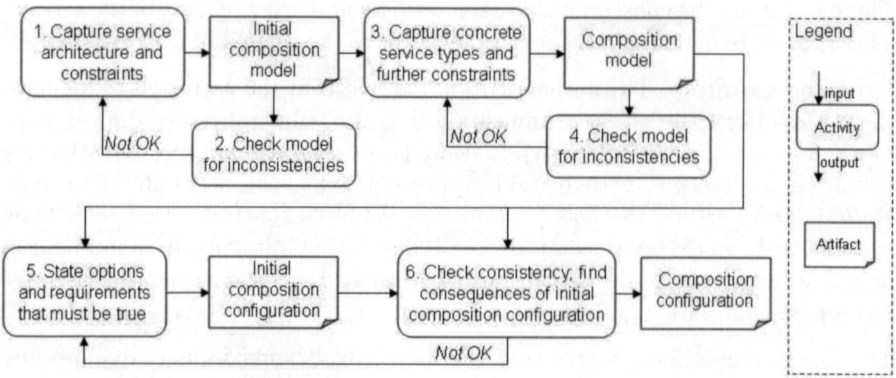

Fig. 3. Activities related to the approach

The first activity involves capturing the overall service architecture, architectural cross-cutting constraints, and global options. This activity utilises abstract service types to group together services with known interfaces and constraints; thus this activity can be performed without any references to the identities of concrete service types. Typically, this activity requires understanding the domain, and hence cannot be fully automated. As a result of the first activity, an initial composition model is created. Already at this stage, it is possible to check whether there are any inconsistencies in the initial composition model, for example, due to inconsistent constraints. This checking comprises the second activity.

Running example. The first activity involves defining service types *Composed-SearchService*, *MallSearchService*, and *ShopSearchService*; interface types; and relevant constraints, as well as option type *LoginOption* with its constraints. Since neither the number nor the identity of the participating shop search service types is known before runtime, they can be grouped together as an abstract *ShopSearchService* service type.   □

The third activity in Fig. 3 continues from the initial composition model by listing concrete service types that can participate in the composition; new constraints can also be added. The concrete service types may fill the roles in the service architecture by inheriting abstract service types defined in the initial composition model. This activity may be performed automatically, as part of service discovery or service registration. Depending on the decentralisation, there may be several of such registries (see Section 3.3). Again, the fourth activity checks the inconsistencies in the model.

Running example. The third activity involves registering concrete shop search service types *ZMartSearchService*, *ShopALotSearchService*, *GadgetsRUsSearch-Service*, and *YMartSearchService*. They are marked to inherit the abstract *ShopSearchService* type and all its interface definitions. Further, they can specify further constraints, e.g., *YMartSearchService* can specify that it does not support OpenID authentication. The third and fourth activities are done automatically when registering new services to the mall. □

After the composition model has been constructed, composition configurations can be found and validated. This is begun by stating those session options and requirements for the composition that are known; this is activity number five in Fig. 3. These known requirements and options are captured in an initial composition configuration. The final activity in Fig. 3 involves validating the initial composition configuration against the composition model, and filling in the consequences to obtain the final service composition configuration. In this case, a valid composition configuration is such that it does not violate the rules or the constraints specified in the composition model. Since activities five and six rely on an existing composition model, they can be fully automated. Typically, for one composition model, activities five and six can be repeated whenever there is a need to find or validate compositions.

Running example. The fourth activity starts by identifying the authentication mechanism that the user used for logging in, as well as possible user-set restrictions on the shops participating in the search. If the user had logged in using his or her OpenID identity, without any restrictions on the shops, the sixth activity would involve finding and validating a composition configuration that aggregates all shops providing an OpenID authentication mechanism. □

Again, the activities in Fig. 3 can be evaluated from the point of view of cross-cutting constraints, dynamism, and decentralisation.

The first aspect, support for cross-cutting constraints, is realised by providing the possibility to model and check such constraints in activities one through four. Inevitably, the division between the first and the third activity depends on the availability of top-down architectural information. In a fully bottom-up service composition, the first activity can be omitted altogether, by relying on modelling concrete services in the third activity. This way, the division aims at balancing between bottom-up composition of services and top-down, typically cross-cutting architectural constraints.

The second aspect, the level of dynamism, is mainly determined by the time when the activities are performed. The more activities are performed at runtime, the higher the level of dynamism. Therefore, dynamism is not just about composing services dynamically, like is suggested in the taxonomy of composing adaptive software [9]. Instead, it should be separated whether also composition model knowledge is created and processed dynamically. In the simplest dynamic case, the initial and final composition configurations are created at runtime (activities five and six in Fig. 3), but composition models are created before runtime. However, in a very dynamic case, both the composition model as well as composition configurations are created at runtime.

Running example. The first and second activities in Fig. 3, which model and check the service architecture, are performed at design-time. In contrast, available services and related constraints can be added and removed at runtime, as part of the service registration; this implies that the third and fourth activities

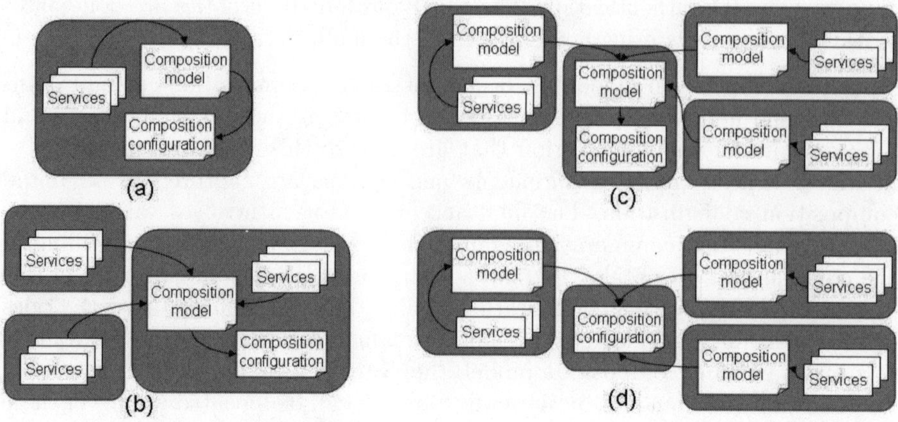

Fig. 4. Some example ways of allocating responsibilities of creating and managing knowledge. Each rounded rectangle represents one realm of responsibility for one actor.

are performed dynamically. Finally, the fifth and sixth activity are performed dynamically when the user starts a new session, subscribes to new services, sets personal preferences, or otherwise changes the options or requirements affecting the required service composition.   □

The third aspect, the support for decentralisation, depends on how different parties participate in performing the activities, and how the resulting knowledge is managed. This is discussed further in the next section, which covers the roles and responsibilities related to the activities.

3.3   Responsibilities and Roles

In addition to the architectural knowledge (Section 3.1) and activities (Section 3.2), it should be established who is responsible for managing the knowledge and performing the activities. Fig. 4 illustrates four different ways of allocating responsibilities between different actors. Fig. 4(a) corresponds to a fully centralised situation in which both composition model and composition configurations are governed by one party. Fig. 4(b) corresponds to a situation in which some services are governed by separate parties, but composition models and compositions are collected by one actor. Fig. 4(c) depicts a situation in which several parties govern some parts of the composition model knowledge, but this knowledge is integrated into one in order to find and validate composition configurations. Finally, Fig. 4(d) illustrates a situation in which different parties do not trust each other enough to share any composition knowledge, but composition configuration is found and validated against fragments of composition models.

Running example. The search scenario corresponds to Fig. 4(c); some services and their composition model knowledge are created and managed by separate shops. However, because of the existence of the central shopping mall, it makes sense to collect an integrated composition model to the shopping mall. The benefit of such centralised knowledge is that one can validate all composition configurations against this centralised model. The composition model is collected to the portal server. When new shop services are registered to the mall, composition model fragments are also registered, which describe the registered service types, their interfaces, and relevant constraints. □

The division of responsibilities can be evaluated against dynamism, decentralisation, and cross-cutting constraints. Firstly, dynamism affects how relationships between different roles can be established. If new actors can emerge dynamically, there must be a mechanism for discovering those actors, and consolidating their possible composition model fragments. In our running example, this is implemented with new shop services being registered to the mall portal. Secondly, the level of decentralisation mainly determines how responsibilities are divided. The more the responsibility for performing the activities and managing the knowledge is distributed, the higher the level of decentralisation. Finally, the division of responsibilities affects how cross-cutting constraints are managed. If most cross-cutting constraints can be defined by one party, like in our running example by the mall portal, it is easier to manage them as part of the composition model. In contrast, handling cross-cutting constraints in Fig. 4(d) can only rely on specifying the properties of other services through their interfaces.

4   Comparison to Previous Work

This section compares the approach described in Section 3 to existing literature. The comparison evaluates the literature from the points of view of dynamism, decentralisation, and cross-cutting (especially security) constraints.

There are a wealth of studies on runtime architectural adaptation and adaptability. In general, software adaptation can be categorised to be either parameterised or composed [9]; typically architectural adaptation addresses the latter. Studies on composed adaptation stem from architectural description language studies [10], software product families and software variability [11,12,13], or from adaptive software in general [14,15]. Typically, these approaches adapt an existing architecture based on an adaptation model that has been defined pre-runtime; hence they do not address whether adaptation models are also adapted dynamically. In some cases, e.g., in [12], the dynamism is limited to selecting among predefined compositions resolved before runtime. Some of these dynamic approaches address also decentralisation. For example, [16] provides an overview of dynamic evolution of distributed, component-based systems. However, decentralisation typically means that composed elements are distributed; further, some kind of centralised adaptation model still exists to govern the composition.

In many respects, [17] is close to our approach, since it addresses dynamic adaptation and distributed systems, and it provides a mechanism for constraining compositions using utility functions, which are matched to the adaptation needs of the system, compared to explicit constraints in our approach. However, this approach is oriented more towards adapting single systems for one user with possibly distributed resources, not towards adapting truly decentralised systems. Further, such component-based approaches require special middleware to be present in the adapting system.

A study that applies software product family techniques for dynamic Web personalisation with varying privacy constraints has been presented in [18]. Similar to our approach, it addresses personalising the Web experience, while using simple boolean constraints to specify privacy concerns. However, their aim is to find an architecture consisting of User Modeling Components, which encapsulate personalisation methods, e.g., used recommendation algorithms. In contrast, our aim is to find and validate an architecture consisting of Web-based services.

Essentially, the principles of service-oriented architecture (SOA) and service-oriented computing (SOC) promise to deliver distributed, independent services that can be discovered and composed dynamically [19]. However, most approaches do not address truly dynamic, adaptive compositions, but different dynamic and adaptive aspects of service compositions are still research challenges [20].

For decentralisation, SOC does not assume anything about the location of the services participating in the composition. However, many facets of SOC still rely on having centralised knowledge, based on which compositions can be formed. For example, business process notations, such as BPEL, that orchestrate one service composition, are typically created statically and governed by a centralised engine. An example of a more dynamic approach for composing services using process descriptions is proposed in [21]. However, this approach does not discuss the decentralisation of the required knowledge, nor the possibility for cross-cutting constraints.

The artifacts in our approach have been described using a notation that resembles WSDL [5]. At the abstract level, WSDL describes message types, port types and operations; port types roughly correspond to interface types in our solution. However, there are several differences. WSDL is oriented more towards describing properties of a single service. Therefore, it cannot be used for expressing constraints among services that cross-cut many services. Further, our approach is more explicit in describing varying rules of combining elements in the services. Further, Web Services are much more complicated compared to the simple request-response operation mode of Web-based services in our case example. Finally, WSDL does not separate between composition model and composition configuration, but describes services only at the level of a composition model.

The tenets of SOA highlight the importance of flexibility and autonomous services. Therefore, imposing cross-cutting security constraints becomes a challenge. Security solutions for SOA have been categorised to comprise of message-level security, security as a service, and policy-driven security [22]. Out of these, policy driven security, such as WS-Policy and WS-SecurityPolicy for Web Services, resembles our approach for declaratively specifying constraints. Although implementing security as a service could encapsulate security constraints across many services, it is limited to certain scenarios. Message-level security, with WS-Security extension for Web Services, is mainly interested in protecting service-to-service communication.

Finally, current composition support in SOA is complicated for end users when building their own applications [23]. Consequently, mashups have emerged as a light-weight method of composing Web-based services. Several composer tools aimed at easy composition of Web-based services have emerged, including Marmite [24] and YahooPipes [25]. Marmite and YahooPipes both support a data flow architecture, where data is processed by a series of operators in a manner similar to Unix pipes. Thus both are suitable for manipulating and combining, e.g., Web feeds. However, while visual mashup composers provide a more user-friendly approach for service composition than SOA techniques, they still require the user to construct and validate the composition herself. Within our approach, the finding and validation of a composition is made completely invisible to the end users, since these activities can rely on the rules set in the composition model. Finally, current mashup composers do not address security, nor provide means for specifying cross-cutting security constraints.

5   Discussion

The following discusses the approach and lays out future work items.

Section 3 described the knowledge as well as the activities required for automating compositions. A tool suite for the automation should consist of the following three tools. Firstly, a graphical modelling tool is needed to produce and check initial composition models in XML. Secondly, a tool is needed to register concrete service types at runtime and consequently check the validity of the resulting composition model. Depending on the decentralisation, several instantiations of such a tool can be deployed at a time. Thirdly, a tool is needed to find and validate composition configurations at runtime; this tool should utilise *smodels* [8] inference engine.

Another issue that is not addressed is instantiating and executing the service composition after the composition configuration has been found. In general, this requires the integration between composition process and used technologies. However, compared to dynamically adaptable component-based approaches, there is no need to shut down or start up components in order to deploy the composition, since services are already deployed and running. On the downside, executing the service composition must not rely on the availability of the services in the composition, since previously available services may not be available at the time of execution. Thus, in an extreme case, dynamism does not cover only service composition, but also services in the composition can appear or disappear dynamically.

The activity six in Fig. 3 could be elaborated further to take into account a situation in which there are several competing services and thus several competing composition configurations that match the options and requirements stated in activity five. The running example in this paper was such that all search services that did not violate against the authentication constraints could be included in the composition. However, there could be several mutually exclusive alternative services, among which selection should be made. If activity six in Fig. 3 results in several possible composition configurations, the approach can be augmented with a selection or optimisation algorithm.

This paper addressed security as a non-functional property to illustrate cross-cutting concerns. Security constraints often cross-cut many services in the architecture, therefore requiring them to be considered during the composition. The constraints in this paper were rather functional; this is typical for security. However, in order to address quality properties expressed in numeric metrics, such as availability or performance, the approach could be extended. Firstly, the conceptualisation should be able to capture numerical quality properties of interfaces and services. Secondly, the approach could include a means of evaluating the overall quality property of the composition based on the quality properties of constituent services; this can utilise existing methods available for, e.g., predictable assembly [26].

Finally, our approach does not address the semantics of modelling constructs. The more knowledge is decentralised, the more semantic issues are bound to rise. Within the field of service-oriented computing, semantic issues have been studied. However, such considerations are out of the scope of this paper.

6 Conclusions

In this paper, we presented an approach for dynamically finding and validating decentralised service compositions with cross-cutting security constraints. The approach is knowledge-based in the sense that it relies on capturing architecture and rules of the compositions and then utilises the collected knowledge to find and validate compositions. For our approach, we presented the knowledge that needs to be captured, the activities that create and manage knowledge, and responsibilities related to knowledge and activities. Although there has been considerable work regarding distributed, dynamic, and cross-cutting constraints in architecture modeling, the issue has not been sufficiently covered in our view. As our related work survey shows, most related works address one of these aspects; for instance, our running example could not be fully covered by state of the art works. However, the approach is still lacking tool support as well as integration with service implementation technology. As a future work item, we aim to build tool support that utilises existing inference engine *smodels* [8] for validating the compositions.

References

1. Murugesan, S.: Understanding Web 2.0. IT Professional 9(4) (2007)
2. Bosch, J.: Service orientation in the enterprise: Towards mobile services. IEEE Computer 40(11) (2007)
3. van Gurp, J., Prehofer, C., di Flora, C.: Experiences with realizing smart space Web service applications. In: Proc. of Consumer Communications and Networking Conference (CCNC) (2008)

4. OpenID: `http://openid.net/`
5. WSDL: `http://www.w3.org/tr/wsdl`
6. van Ommering, R., van der Linden, F., Kramer, J., Magee, J.: The Koala component model for consumer electronics software. IEEE Computer 33(3) (2000)
7. Asikainen, T., Männistö, T.: Nivel: A metamodelling language with a formal semantics. Software and Systems Modeling (to appear)
8. Simons, P., Niemelä, I., Soininen, T.: Extending and implementing the stable model semantics. Artificial Intelligence 138(1–2) (2002)
9. McKinley, P.K., Sadjadi, S.M., Kasten, E.P., Cheng, B.H.: Composing adaptive software. IEEE Computer 37(7) (2004)
10. Magee, J., Kramer, J.: Dynamic structure in software architectures. SIGSOFT Software Engineering Notes 21(6) (1996)
11. Lee, J., Kang, K.: A feature-oriented approach to developing dynamically reconfigurable products in product line engineering. In: Proc. of Software Product Line Engineering Conference (SPLC) (2006)
12. Gomaa, H., Saleh, M.: Feature driven dynamic customization of software product lines. In: Morisio, M. (ed.) ICSR 2006. LNCS, vol. 4039, pp. 58–72. Springer, Heidelberg (2006)
13. van der Hoek, A.: Design-time product line architectures for any-time variability. Science of Computer Programming 53(3) (2004)
14. Ye, J., Loyall, J., Shapiro, R., Neema, S., Abdelwahed, S., Mahadevan, N., Koets, M., Varner, D.: A model-based approach to designing QoS adaptive applications. In: Proc. of Real-Time Systems Symposium (RTSS) (2004)
15. Floch, J., Hallsteinsen, S., Stav, E., Eliassen, F., Lund, K., Gjørven, E.: Using architecture models for runtime adaptability. IEEE Software 23(2) (2006)
16. Fung, K.H., Low, G., Ray, P.K.: Embracing dynamic evolution in distributed systems. IEEE Software 21(2) (2004)
17. Alia, M., Hallsteinsen, S., Paspallis, N., Eliassen, F.: Managing distributed adaptation of mobile applications. In: Indulska, J., Raymond, K. (eds.) DAIS 2007. LNCS, vol. 4531, pp. 104–118. Springer, Heidelberg (2007)
18. Wang, Y., Kobsa, A., van der Hoek, A., White, J.: PLA-based runtime dynamism in support of privacy-enhanced Web personalization. In: Proc. of Software Product Line Engineering Conference (SPLC) (2006)
19. Erl, T.: Service-Oriented Architecture: Concepts, Technology, and Design. Prentice-Hall, Englewood Cliffs (2005)
20. Papazoglou, M., Traverso, P., Dustdar, S., Leymann, F.: Service-oriented computing: State of the art and research challenges. IEEE Computer 40(11) (2007)
21. Vuković, M., Kotsovinos, E., Robinson, P.: An architecture for rapid, on-demand service composition. Service Oriented Computing and Applications 1(4) (2007)
22. Kanneganti, R., Chodavarapu, P.A.: SOA and Security. Manning Publications (2007)
23. Xuanzhe, L., Yi, H., Wei, S., Haiqi, L.: Towards service composition based on mashup. In: Proceedings of IEEE Congress of Services (2007)
24. Wong, J., Hong, J.: Making mashups with Marmite: Towards end-user programming for the Web. In: Proc. of Computer/Human Interaction Conference (2007)
25. Trevor, J.: Doing the mobile mash. IEEE Computer 41(2) (2008)
26. Crnkovic, I., Schmidt, H., Stafford, J., Wallnau, K.: Anatomy of a reseach project in predictable assembly. In: Proc. of 5th Workshop on Component-Based Software Engineering (2002)

Architectural Prototyping in Industrial Practice

Henrik Bærbak Christensen and Klaus Marius Hansen

Department of Computer Science, University of Aarhus
Aabogade 34, 8200 Århus N, Denmark
{hbc,klaus.m.hansen}@daimi.au.dk

Abstract. *Architectural prototyping* is the process of using executable code to investigate stakeholders' software architecture concerns with respect to a system under development. Previous work has established this as a useful and cost-effective way of exploration and learning of the design space of a system, in addressing issues regarding quality attributes, in addressing architectural risks, and in addressing the problem of knowledge transfer and conformance. Little work has been reported so far on the actual industrial use of architectural prototyping. In this paper, we report from an ethnographical study and focus group involving architects from four companies in which we have focused on architectural prototypes. Our findings conclude that architectural prototypes play an important role in resolving problems experimentally, but less so in exploring alternative solutions. Furthermore, architectural prototypes include end-user or business related functionality rather than purely architectural functionality. Based on these observations we provide recommendations for effective industrial architectural prototyping.

1   Introduction

In practice, software architecture [21,3] design is a complex design process in which technical requirements (e.g., in the form of functional and quality requirements or technology platform constraints) needs to be balanced with organizational reality (e.g., stakeholder needs and concerns or organizational constraints). Often this must take place within an iterative and incremental development process where requirements and constraints may change frequently and fundamentally. The architect has numerous techniques at his disposal that we may categorize as follows:

- *Theoretical techniques.* These techniques support software architecture design, evaluation, or implementation through *argumentation* that tries to convince stakeholders of a specific *theory* (which could, e.g., be a specific architectural design that tries to resolve specific quality attribute requirements). Theoretical techniques abound, examples being quality attribute scenarios [3], architectural patterns [4], view-based documentation techniques [16], and scenario-based evaluation methods [14].
- *Experimental techniques.* These techniques involve some form of *demonstration* to stakeholder of software architecture to inform their decision making.

R. Morrison, D. Balasubramaniam, and K. Falkner (Eds.): ECSA 2008, LNCS 5292, pp. 196–209, 2008.

This can be, e.g., either through demonstration of the final system or through demonstration of aspects of the architecture. Examples of such techniques include simulation [8], prototyping [1,2], and scenario-based methods with explicit stakeholder involvement [14].

Both types of techniques are important, but arguably for development processes that involve a high degree of uncertainty and change, experimental techniques (in general) have increasing importance since tangible demonstrations to stakeholders are needed throughout the project [17,11].

For most techniques, few studies have been made of their (industrial) practical use. In this paper, we focus particularly on the experimental technique of *architectural prototyping*, providing new insight into the practical, industrial use of this technique. Architectural prototyping may be defined as:

> An *architectural prototype* consists of a set of executables created to investigate architectural qualities related to concerns raised by stakeholders of a system under development. *Architectural prototyping* is the process of designing, building, and evaluating architectural prototypes [1].

This definition is rendered as an ontology in Figure 1. Bardram et al. [1] provided

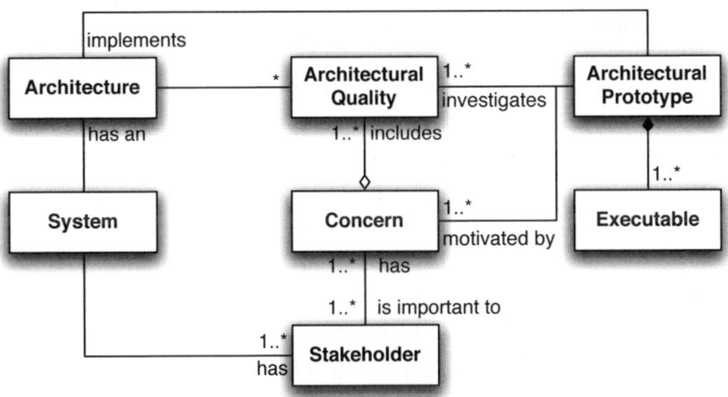

Fig. 1. Architectural prototype ontology (adapted from [1])

examples of architectural prototypes and (following [10]) classified architectural prototypes in terms of objective of construction[1]:

- *Exploratory* architectural prototypes are constructed in order to explore the architecture design space. Often, several alternatives are constructed, analyzed, and executed in order to come up with a solution to a posed problem
- *Experimental* architectural prototypes are constructed in order to evaluate a specific architectural decision. Often, a single prototype is constructed and evaluated

---

[1] In practice, of course, the construction of a specific architectural prototype may have several types of objectives

- *Evolutionary* architectural prototypes are constructed as a series of prototypes in which each prototype build upon the previous. Often, such a prototype leads to a skeleton system in which little functionality is present, but where a software architecture design is implemented that is used as a basis for producing a final system[2]

Furthermore, architectural prototypes may be characterized as

1. *being constructed for exploration and learning of the architectural design space*, i.e., they are constructed to learn about the effect of architectural decisions largely ignoring the intent of the system,
2. *addressing issues regarding quality attributes*, i.e., a main motivation for building an architectural prototype is often to measure (or observe) the quality implications of a decision,
3. *not providing functionality per se*, i.e., little or no business and end-user functionality is implemented,
4. *addressing architectural risks*, i.e., the driver for architectural prototyping is often an attempt to address or mitigate a risk in architectural design, and
5. *addressing the problem of knowledge transfer and architectural conformance*, i.e., architectural prototypes may be used after construction to ensure that developers learn about the architecture and that knowledge about the architecture is transferred through code [1].

In [1], these claims were validated through the case study of a set of research architectural prototypes. In this paper, we investigate the characteristics and extent of architectural prototyping through an investigation of current architectural practice.

Paper Outline

The rest of this paper is structured as follows: First, we describe the research project, SA@Work, involving software architects from four companies, in which the work reported here has taken place (Section 2). Next, we present accounts of architectural prototyping based on field studies (Section 3) and on focus groups (Section 4). These accounts are then analyzed (Section 5) and finally we discuss related work (Section 6) and conclude (Section 7).

2   The SA@Work Project

The research has been carried out in the context of the SA@Work project; the project has been further described in [6,7]. The SA@Work project is a one and a half year project that started August 2007. It involves software architects from four Danish companies chosen among others because they represent a diversity of application domains. In the following, we briefly describe each company:

---

[2] This is, e.g., what the Rational Unified Process advocates [15].

1. *Bang & Olufsen (BeO)* produces high end audio products, television sets, and telephones. The company was founded in 1925, in Struer, Denmark. Since the beginning the company has focused on creating quality products. The IT-organization of B&O consists of offices in Struer and Århus (Denmark) and a subsidiary in Estonia, furthermore they work with a consultancy company in India.
2. *DSE A/S* was established in 1981 in Horsens. The present company is divided into two divisions, Test and Airport, with respective markets. We have followed architects in the airport division that employs approximately 18 persons. The DSE Airport Solutions division supply IT-based solutions for Danish and international airports including ATC (Air Traffic Control) and CNS (Communication, Navigation and Surveillance) /ATM (Air Traffic Management).
3. *Jyske Bank (JB)* is the second largest independent Danish bank, employing some 4,000 people in 119 Danish branches. The IT organization of Jyske Bank is the largest in Jutland, designing, implementing, and running the systems of Jyske Bank in addition to processing central-government payments and operating a payroll system for the Danish counties.
4. *Systematic Software Engineering (SSE)* is Denmark's largest privately owned software company. It was founded in 1985 and has since grown to over 400 employees, 50 of these employed in the UK and USA. SSE is certified in process maturity at CMMI level 5. The main business areas are mission critical systems for the defense and healthcare sectors.

The SA@Work project has two phases:

Phase 1 Fields studies of architectural practice. In this phase we have followed architects in their work for one and a half to two weeks using ethnographical techniques to observe and record actions, collaborations, artifacts, etc. The observations have been complemented with interviews and document analysis.

Phase 2: Collaboration between practicing architects and researchers. During this phase particular aspects of architectural work are identified that could be improved, and collaboration executed (intervention).

In the following sections, we report from both these phases with particular focus on architectural prototyping. Section 3 relates findings made during field studies of software architects and Section 4 relates finding made during focus groups with practicing software architects.

3   Field Studies of Architectural (Prototyping) Practice

In the first phase of the project we did a bottom-up, ethnographically-inspired study of software architects. Concretely, each company designated a software architect that we would follow, observe, and interact with. Specifically, we applied "participatory observation" in which we engaged with the software architects as necessary and did this akin to Miluk's "rapid applied ethnography" process [19].

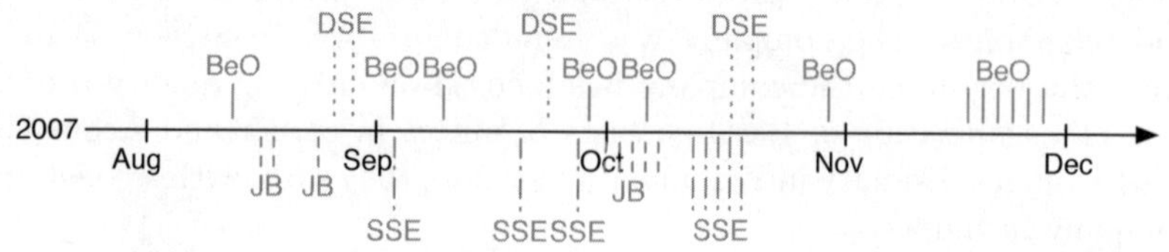

Fig. 2. Schematic overview of observations and interviews in SA@Work

The reason for using observations in this phase was two-fold: 1) we wanted to be as open as possible in our conception of actual architectural practice (while acknowledging, though, that we had prior knowledge of the filed and that the presence of an observer changes what is being observed. In the analysis of observations, the presence of the observer thus has to be taken into consideration as noted in, e.g., Hammersley's and Atkinson's "reflexive realism" [12]). 2) retrospective accounts such as interviews are often inaccurate because interviewees may not remember details about their work practice and may also not know what is important or relevant for researchers to know.

Figure 2 shows a timeline of the Phase 1 interactions with software architects covering both observations and interviews. The exact timing and extent of the observations at the individual companies depended on the availability of architects and researchers, but we aimed at having five days of observation at each company.

One striking commonality between work practices of the architects was that the daily activities of software architects are very diverse and may change frequently according to project needs. This also means that specific architectural techniques were often only glimpsed, something that is also true for architectural prototyping. We only observed direct programming and/or execution of architectural prototypes in a few cases, but through the observation and followings interviews, we tentatively concluded the following:

— *Architectural prototypes are important.* In all companies, critical architectural decisions (such as the choice of a user interface platform or a remote procedure call middleware) had been taken based on the construction of architectural prototypes. However, architectural prototypes complement other, theoretical, architectural techniques more than being an essential technique in its own right. It was however not clear to which extent architectural prototypes were used and what were their precise characteristic?
— *Architectural prototyping needs opportunistic planning.* All companies in our study used an iterative and incremental development approach in which the activities of the software architect did not fit well [7]. Architectural prototyping was often initiated due to uncertainties or risks in the activities that were part of the iterative process, meaning that architects often had to take time out of their schedule to do prototyping (or even do them at home). One issue that was not clear was in which phase (e.g., inception, elaboration, construction, or transition as in [15]) architectural prototyping was most useful?

– *Architects (and developers) code architectural prototypes.* In most cases, the software architects themselves programmed architectural prototypes (often because they were the experts of the (technical) domain being investigated); at other times, architects specified the architectural prototype and a (lead) developer would code the prototype. How the construction of architectural prototypes fitted into the rest of the system construction was, however, not clear?

Among others to investigate these issues further, we initiated two focus groups with software architects on architectural prototyping. The results of these are presented next.

4   Case Studies of Architectural Prototyping

The case studies were presented on two focus group workshop. For practical reasons, architects from three of the companies were present at one focus group workshop and architects from the last company were present at a separate focus group workshop. The architects were in both cases given a homework assignment: they had to review their past use of coding practices in their architectural work to identify between three and four instances of using experimental, code-based, analyses or techniques in their architectural work. Furthermore, they were asked to present one of the instances in technical detail at the focus group. They were also given the paper "Architectural Prototyping: An Approach for Grounding Architectural Design" by Bardram et al. [1] as part of the initial assignment.

The first focus group seminar lasted about six hours and the last lasted about two hours. In both cases, it consisted of an introduction by the authors, describing the definition and characteristics of architectural prototype based upon the aforementioned paper. Next, the companies presented the instances of using architectural prototypes and questions and clarifications were asked by researchers as well as the attending architects. The seminar ended by an analysis of the primary cases of architectural prototypes. This analysis was lead by the authors. The analysis went through each primary case study from the companies and clarified whether the aspects and characteristics set forth in [1] were applicable or not.

Below the main case study of each company is presented.

4.1   Bang and Olufsen

The Bang and Olufsen software architect described a "vertical demo" for a media library browser for a new line of audio-visual products. This new line is based upon a product-line architecture that is presently being developed. The device must enable users to have a high quality browsing experience of a centrally stored library of available audio and video streams including images and text.

Several architectural aspects were planned to be explored in the prototype:

– verification of the communication channel (the connectors) between the various devices, including media server, connections, and the device

- analysis of the response times in the system under various scenarios
- analysis of power management and experimentation and verification of the present architecture for this aspect
- analysis of discovery protocol behavior in various scenarios like device out-of-range and radio signal shut down
- analysis if the selected technologies "plays well together"

As e.g. audio sources are browsed by showing album covers the prototype included full graphics to verify rendering quality and performance.

4.2   Jyske Bank

The architect from Jyske Bank described a large experimental effort to prototype the layering aspects of a novel service oriented architecture that at the moment is being introduced at the enterprise level to supplement and partially replace the present architecture. The layering is a traditional three-tier layering with data, business, and presentation layers but using a service oriented approach.

The architectural aspects to be investigated were:

- verification and exploration of proper layering in the architecture with emphasis on achieving loose coupling and low maintenance costs
- verify that adequate performance was still attainable
- verify the security aspects could be implemented in the layered SOA model
- analyze with respect to stability and 24/7 service

The infrastructure was prototype developed along with an example application of using it. The example application is a Jyske Bank internal teaching example, KAOS, that is course administration system. The KAOS system is well known to the entire bank's IT staff as they have all gone through the same internal training.

4.3   Systematic Software Engineering

A Systematic Software Engineering software architect presented a "frontier run" (Danish: "Frontløb") which is the company's term for executables that explore technological or architectural issues. The application explored how to add a hand-held personal digital assistant (PDA) to the company's Columna product which is an electronic patient record (EPR) infrastructure.

The purpose for the prototype was:

- exploration of technical challenges of WiFi communication with PDAs using a proprietary RMI system with large data objects
- exploration of the Windows CE programming model
- analysis of how to make a SOA architecture on Windows CE
- exploration of how to make web services on the Columna server

The process actually started as two disjoint prototypes, one experimenting with Windows CE and the other experimenting with SOA. As they evolved and architectural decisions matured and stabilized, the two prototypes grew into a single one. The architecture prototype code was after the process thrown away but the architectural learning lead into adopting the architecture as the reference model for SOA for Columna.

4.4   DSE

The software architect from DSE presented VERDI that is an ongoing project to upgrade an existing map application for the Danish authorities' readiness to handle natural disasters. The upgrade was to provide vastly more detailed maps that put high demands on data transfer and especially graphical map rendering performance.

Several prototypes were crafted in an exploration phase for:

- risk analysis as it was not obvious whether to take on the project at all as the existing legacy application ran on ten year old frameworks and hardware.
- assessment of whether the developed technologies/components as well as the learning outcome would enrich the company's portfolio of products as the application was somewhat outside the current set.
- exploring Microsoft WPF (Windows Presentation Foundation) technologies to replace the rendering engine.
- explore performance and optimization issues with respect to rendering speed to support usability.

The process included prototypes for learning and experimenting with reading and rendering a new vector-based map data format and next a whole series of disjoint prototypes to assess rendering performance using various WPF techniques. Next several prototypes were constructed as bit mapped maps were included and a rewrite of the rendering engine as WPF could not handle the performance requirements.

5   Analysis

In this section, we will present how the characteristics of architectural prototypes (see Section 1) were matched against the concrete cases described above.

Ad 1: Exploration and Learning

This characteristic was considered essential for all case studies by their architects. This was perhaps especially true for the Systematic Software Engineering Columna PDA scanner system where the architect and the development team faced a device (PDA) and a technological platform (Windows CE) that was more or less unknown. DSE also faced new technology for the rendering engine in VERDI and several prototypes were made to find a WPF technique that could handle the performance issues. Bang and Olufsen stressed that using Remote Method Invocation (RMI) systems in the prototype was a relatively new issue to be explored.

Ad 2: Quality Attributes

The software architects all agreed that analysis of the quality attributes were a primary driver for their architectural prototyping. This is also evident from the motivation for the prototypes as outlined in the previous section: Bang and Olufsen analyzed performance metrics like response time and power management; Jyske Bank explored maintainability and availability metrics like layering and 24/7 service; Systematic Software Engineering explored performance and buildability aspects like SOA performance and Windows CE learning issues; and DSE assessed the same qualities, buildability and performance, in the VERDI prototype set.

Ad 3: No Functionality Per se.

In our previous work we have postulated that architectural prototypes do not include non-architectural functionality such as business logic, end-user interfaces etc., but only contains code central for the quality attributes being evaluated. As an example, in two of the cases the architects stressed the need to see "data flowing from end-to-end": Bang and Olufsen needed to see album data getting from the media server to the device within the allowed response time while Jyske Bank needed to see data flowing from the databases all the way "to the glass" (i.e., the user interface) even in the face of handling three million database rows. But for instance in the Bang and Olufsen case there was no need to graphically render cover images nor even have the media server containing real data. If response time is the issue it would suffice for the hand held device simply to measure round-trip times between issuing a request and receiving an appropriately sized chunk of data.

However, all prototypes contained quite a lot of non-architectural functionality. The Bang and Olufsen prototype media server contained real album data and the device rendered graphics. The Jyske Bank prototype contained user interface functionality, and the Columna PDA Scanner did scan real medicine bar codes. For the two first prototypes, the architects stressed that they were used also for demonstration to (business) stakeholders, not just for architectural evaluation. Nevertheless, they were in no way fully functional systems, but the important point here is that they did include non-architecturally relevant code.

The DSE case is perhaps a bit special in this respect because a primary concern was the risks associated with the technology update and the rendering performance. Thus one can say that the architectural challenge indeed was the graphical functionality.

Ad 4: Risks

The case studies presented by Bang and Olufsen and Jyske Bank were both examples of architectural prototypes constructed after a period of theoretical architectural analysis, that is, brain storming, reviews, discussions, and other techniques that rely on abstract artifacts like UML diagrams, rich pictures, architect's experience and gut-feeling, etc. Therefore many alternative architecture proposals had already been weeded out before the architectural prototyping processes were initiated. Therefore these prototypes have the flavor of skeleton systems. Nevertheless both companies considered the prototype building a way to assess and control risk. For instance, Jyske Bank mentioned their concern whether the new layered architecture would perform adequately when "processing three million rows?" and the prototype was used to answer this important question. Bang and Olufsen stated that the prototype's properties decided the "go/no-go" commitment for the proposed architecture.

The PDA prototype described by the architect from Systematic Software Engineering was more exploratory in that the company had little experience with the Windows CE platform on PDA devices and therefore even less idea about how to architect SOA on it. Therefore the prototype building was essential both to achieve confidence in programming the technological platform as well as exploring SOA. Therefore it was a crucial risk management tool.

Finally, the DSE VERDI architectural prototyping effort was most certainly driven by risk assessment as the company reserved the right to decline taking on the project if the result of the prototyping process would indicate too high risks and too little gains from the company's perspective.

Ad 5: Knowledge Transfer and Conformance

Also in this respect the architects generally agreed on the important property of communication with developers. For instance the Jyske Bank layering prototype was constructed using the KAOS course management system as instantiation instead of the real goal, namely banking. One important property of KAOS is that it is used for the internal training courses that the entire IT staff goes through—therefore the KAOS domain is well known to all and it is very easy to introduce the new architecture on the simpler KAOS domain. Another important property was that a lot of template code emerged from the prototyping process that is used by developers to ensure conformance with the intended architecture.

Systematic Software Engineering's PDA prototype code was trashed after the process and thus not used as conformance technique—however the key point of the exercise was the knowledge gained for the architect and the development team.

Bang and Olufsen stressed this property less but found that the architectural prototyping process worked to increase knowledge transfer in the team.

The VERDI prototype set from DSE did not squarely fit this characteristics. On one hand a lot of knowledge had been gained in the division regarding WPF with respect to programming model and performance issues but on the other hand it is less a matter of transferring architectural knowledge from the architect to the developers. Also the final "prototype" did match the performance requirements and is therefore close to a product quality finished component.

Table 1. Characteristics of the cases. '+' indicates that the given architectural prototype exhibits the identified characteristics, '–' the opposite, while '(+)' indicates that the characteristics is only partially present.

	(1) (2) (3) (4) (5)
BeO: Content browser	+ + – + (+)
JB: SOA and application Layering	+ + (+) + +
SSE: Columna PDA Scanner	+ + (+) + +
DSE: VERDI	+ + (+) + –

5.1 Discussion

The results concerning reported architectural prototype characteristics are summarized in Table 1. We conclude that four out of the five postulated characteristics are supported by the empirical data whereas the fifth characteristics, *no functionality per se*, is not always true for the observed cases. For instance the Bang and Olufsen content browser prototype did include a working user interface and it was real cover and album data that was delivered in the system. One might argue that from a purely performance assessment perspective this is a waste of implementation resources as performance conclusions could be made by just pushing realistically sized byte arrays with nonsense data over the connectors and simply measure at what pace they arrived. This would lower the implementation burden as no real data should be put into the system and no GUI implemented and thereby reduce costs. However, one property not stressed in our previous work but stressed by several architects is the importance of *demonstration to stakeholders*, typically business decision makers. As one architect stated: " 'Have a look' is the best argument." If decision makers have conflicting or impossible demands but cannot be persuaded, sometimes prototypes are simply made to make it evident that they require the impossible. Thus additional investments in implementation effort are made to make them into working demonstrators.

Another classification of architectural prototypes as either *explorative, experimental,* or *evolutionary* is concerned with the architects' focus on quality attributes (cf. Section 1). While this distinction makes sense from a theoretical stand point, the distinction appeared blurred in industrial practice. Most of the prototypes selected by the software architects exhibited both explorative as well as experimental traits and most were evolutionary. The architects found the distinction less interesting from a practical point of view as they failed to see the operational aspects. Some of the prototypes exhibited all three characteristics, like for instance in the DSE VERDI project in which several disjoint prototypes were crafted, each exploring a particular WPF rendering technique, and thus of an explorative nature, testing alternatives. However, they were all rejected as they did not match the performance requirements, thus being of an experimental nature. The present architectural prototype will now be part of an evolutionary prototyping process to explore database issues in the system.

Another observation where architectural prototype usage differs from the postulates in [1] is with respect to using architectural prototypes to explore alternatives. In several of the cases outlined by the industrial software architects, reasonably thorough but purely theoretical (in the sense outlined in Section 1) analyses where made first until a single candidate architecture was identified that stakeholders were sufficiently confident would match functional and architectural requirements. It was not until then prototyping was initiated. This is more in line with the concept of *architectural skeletal systems* as described by Bass et al. [3] or the usage of *executable architectural prototypes* in Rational Unified Process.

We speculate that there is a relation between these two observations: several of the prototypes are actually demonstrators *and* the same prototypes are also more akin skeletal systems than early explorations (Bang and Olufsen and Jyske Bank). The higher cost of making a demonstrator requires a stronger belief that this *is* the right architecture to reduce risks of wasted effort. Perhaps this experience even lessens the architect's tendency to architectural prototype purely architectural concerns.

6   Related Work

Few have written about the process of architectural prototyping [5,15,18]. Both Christensen [5] and Mårtensson et al. [18] base their exposition on their own experience with architectural prototyping and present a very simple framework and process that does not capture the rich use of architectural prototyping as outlined in this paper. The Rational Unified Process (as described in [15]) focus on one type of architectural prototype, viz. an evolutionary architectural prototype, and on a specific role of that prototype in the development process. In all cases, the analysis presented in this paper extends the work by showing how architectural prototyping is done in practice.

With respect to the qualitative and empirical research approach of the SA@Work project (observations, interviews, focus groups and, eventually, action research [22]) a sizable proportion of papers on software architecture argue their claims empirically. As noted in [6], we, e.g., found that of 16 papers from WICSA 2007 [20], 8 can be classified as having validated their results empirically. This is in contrasts to (much more thorough) investigations of the quantity of empirical validation in software engineering. One study, e.g., identified 12% validation through case studies (in 50 of 427 software engineering articles surveyed [13]). Few research projects use an action research approach, though. One exception is Farenhorst et al. [9] in which observations are followed by interventions in cycles.

7   Conclusion

The first important conclusion of the presented work is perhaps so obvious that it may be missed, namely that it documents that architectural prototyping *is* being used as an indispensable tool in the practicing software architects' tool box.

Architectural prototypes are used as an important tool to design and evaluate software architectures. The software architects, even experienced ones, trust the architectural answers demonstrated by executing code more than the output of brainstorming sessions, reviews meetings, and logical argumentation.

Next, we conclude that the five characteristics set forward as distinctive characteristics of architectural prototypes and setting them apart from general prototypes as defined by Floyd are generally observed in the set of architectural prototypes crafted by the participating companies. Indeed, the architectural prototypes are used to explore architectural designs, to learn about new architectural tactics, to assess limitations and benefits of emerging technologies, to reduce risks of taking the wrong decisions, to experiment with the balance of quality attributes in architectural proposals, and to transfer knowledge and ensure architectural conformance in the development teams. The only characteristic that is somewhat doubtful is the claim that architectural prototypes provide little functionality besides but rather is concerned with purely architectural issues. Several prototypes were effectively stakeholder demonstrators.

We speculate that architectural prototyping is not generally taken to its full potential by the software architects. The tendency to include demonstration quality functionality necessarily increases the cost of the prototypes, perhaps even substantially. This perceived "higher-than-necessary" cost may bias architects towards *not* building prototypes even in situations where they would provide more accurate answers to architectural dilemmas than theoretical techniques. If this is true, even more gains can come from architectural prototyping than reported in this work.

This speculation also hints at new directions in research. One aspect of action research [6] is intervention where researchers join teams of practitioners to introduce new techniques. Thus one may enter a project having architectural challenges and test ways of making "cheap" architectural prototypes. Another approach could be to analyze the prototype's code base to estimate the amount of "non-architectural" code to find the ratio.

Acknowledgements

The research presented in this paper has been partly funded by the ISIS Katrinebjerg competency centre, Aarhus, Denmark (`http://www.isis.alexandra.dk`). We thank the companies and software architects that participated in the project. Finally, we thank Kari Rye Schougaard who performed a main part of the field work.

References

1. Bardram, J.E., Christensen, H.B., Hansen, K.M.: Architectural Prototyping: An Approach for Grounding Architectural Design. In: Proceedings of Fourth Working IEEE/IFIP Conference on Software Architecture (WICSA4), Oslo, Norway, pp. 15–24 (June 2004)

2. Bardram, J.E., Christensen, H.B., Corry, A.V., Hansen, K.M., Ingstrup, M.: Exploring Quality Attributes Using Architectural Prototyping. In: Reussner, R., Mayer, J., Stafford, J.A., Overhage, S., Becker, S., Schroeder, P.J. (eds.) QoSA 2005 and SOQUA 2005. LNCS, vol. 3712, pp. 155–170. Springer, Heidelberg (2005)
3. Bass, L., Clements, P., Kazman, R.: Software Architecture in Practice, 2nd edn. Addison-Wesley, Reading (2003)
4. Buschmann, F., Meunier, R., Rohnert, H., Sommerlad, P., Stal, M.: Pattern-Oriented Software Architecture: A System of Patterns. Wiley, Chichester (1996)
5. Christensen, H.B.: Towards an Operational Framework for Architectural Prototyping. In: Proceedings of the 5th Working IEEE/IFIP Conference on Software Architecture (WICSA 2005), pp. 301–302 (2005)
6. Christensen, H.B., Hansen, K.M., Schougaard, K.R.: Ready! Set! Go! An Action Research Agenda for Software Architecture Research. In: Proceedings of Working IEEE/IFIP Conference on Software Architecture (WICSA) 2008 (2008)
7. Christensen, H.B., Hansen, K.M., Schougaard, K.R.: SA@Work - A Field Study of Software Architecture and Software Quality at Work (under submission, 2008)
8. Clements, P., Kazman, R., Klein, M.: Evaluating software architectures: methods and case studies. Addison-Wesley, Reading (2002)
9. Farenhorst, R., Izaks, R., Lago, P., van Vliet, H.: A Just-In-Time Architectural Knowledge Sharing Portal. In: Proceedings of the Seventh Working IEEE/IFIP Conference on Software Architecture (WICSA 2008), pp. 125–134 (2008)
10. Floyd, C.: A systematic look at prototyping. In: Budde, R., Kuhlenkamp, K., Mathiassen, L., Züllighoven, H. (eds.) Approaches to Prototyping, pp. 1–18. Springer, Heidelberg (1984)
11. Grønbæk, K., Kyng, M., Mogensen, P.: Toward a cooperative experimental system development approach. In: Kyng, M., Mathiassen, L. (eds.) Computers and Design in Context, pp. 201–238. MIT Press, Cambridge (1997)
12. Hammersley, M., Atkinson, P.: Ethnography Principles in Practice. London & New York, Routledge (1997)
13. Jørgensen, M., Sjøberg, D.: Generalization and Theory Building in Software Engineering Research. Empirical Assessment in Software Eng. Proc., 29–36 (2004)
14. Kazman, R., Klein, M., Clements, P.: ATAM: Method for Architecture Evaluation. Carnegie Mellon University, Software Engineering Institute (2000)
15. Kruchten, P.: The Rational Unified Process: An Introduction. Addison-Wesley Professional, Reading (2003)
16. Kruchten, P.: The 4+1 view model of architecture. IEEE Software 12(6), 42–50 (1995)
17. Larman, C., Basili, V.R.: Iterative and incremental development. A brief history. IEEE Computer 36(6), 47–56 (2003)
18. Mårtensson, F., Grahn, H., Mattsson, M.: An Approach for Performance Evaluation of Software Architectures using Prototyping. In: Proc. Int'l Conference on Software Engineering and Applications (SEA 2003), pp. 605–612 (2003)
19. Miluk, G.: Results of a field study of cmmi for small settings using rapid applied ethnography. Technical Report CMU/SEI-2006-SR-001, Software Engeneering Institute, Carnegie Mellon (2006)
20. Paulish, D., Gorton, I., Tyree, J., Soni, D. (eds.): Proceedings of Working IEEE/IFIP Conference on Software Architecture (WICSA) 2007. IEEE, Los Alamitos (2007)
21. Shaw, M., Garlan, D.: Software architecture: perspectives on an emerging discipline. Prentice-Hall, Upper Saddle River (1996)
22. Sjøberg, D., Dyba, T., Jørgensen, M.: The future of empirical methods in software engineering research. In: International Conference on Software Engineering, pp. 358–378 (2007)

An Iterative Framework for Software Architecture Recovery: An Experience Report

Banani Roy and T.C. Nicholas Graham

Queen's University, Kingston, Ontario, Canada K7L 3N6
{broy,graham}@cs.queensu.ca

Abstract. Both architecture recovery and architecture evaluation play an important role in the area of software reverse-engineering. In this paper, we propose and evaluate a framework for incremental and iterative application of automated architecture recovery (using SWAG Kit) and architecture analysis (using SAAM.) We conclude that SWAG Kit helps in generating a low-level architecture that forms the basis of analysis, while SAAM helps in deriving from this a deeply understood conceptual architecture. The process is iterative, where SAAM analysis helps refine the parameters fed to SWAG Kit, in turn leading to a superior architecture for further analysis. We have applied this process to the extraction of the architectures of three open source compression tools, and we report on the strengths and weaknesses of the approach that this case study exposed. Over all, we conclude that the framework allowed us to understand the software architectures more deeply than would have been possible with the software architecture recovery process alone.

Keywords: Software Architecture Recovery, SAAM, SWAG Kit, Iterative Framework, Evaluation.

1 Introduction

Legacy software systems often lack adequate architectural documentation. When present at all, architectural documentation is often inconsistent with the current state of the system [22,6]. Lack of architectural documentation can make it difficult to bring new developers into the project or to methodically analyze the effect of proposed architectural changes. To address this problem, numerous researchers have proposed the use of automated tools to recover the architecture of a system from its source code [6,19,14]. Architecture recovery tools such as Rigi [27], Shrimp [29], SWAG Kit [30] and Dali [17] automate parts of the process, requiring human guidance to create documentation of the architecture of software systems.

Despite decades of research and considerable progress in the development of such tools, they have yet to obtain wide-spread industrial adoption. In this paper, we argue that the quality of software architectural recovery can be improved by applying systematic analysis to the architectures generated by recovery tools. Architectural analysis helps identify the questions that we wish our description of

R. Morrison, D. Balasubramaniam, and K. Falkner (Eds.): ECSA 2008, LNCS 5292, pp. 210–224, 2008.

an architecture to answer, in terms of non-functional requirements such as modifiability, security, usability and availability [1,3,7]. In this paper, we present a framework for iteratively applying architectural recovery and architectural analysis. We present our experience in applying this method to the recovery of the architectures of three open-source compression toolkits. To our knowledge, this is the first experience report directly reporting on the benefits and limitations of combining these two techniques.

In our study, we examine whether value is added to the process of architectural recovery by using an architecture evaluation method in addition to a recovery tool. I.e., we address the question of wheher an architectural analysis helps provide a deeper understanding of the architecture in the recovery process, and whether it helps obtain a more accurate view of the architecture.

To help evaluate these questions, we have developed a framework that iteratively combines the SWAG Kit architecture recovery tool [30] with the SAAM architecture evaluation method SAAM [7,16]. In this framework, a recovery tool is first used to obtain a low-level architectural representation from the system's source. An architecture evaluation method is then applied to the extracted system representation. The automated recovery and analysis steps are iteratively applied until an acceptable architectural description is obtained.

We have applied this method to three open source compression applications/ libraries: *ZLib* [32], *ZDelta* [31] and *GZip* [15]. We applied SWAG Kit and SAAM to each application using the iterative framework. Through this, we are able to evaluate the benefits and weaknesses of the approach.

From the case study, we have learned several interesting lessons. We found that software architecture recovery is weak at identifying subsystem structures. In our experience, automatic decomposition of an architecture into subsystems did not contain the information a programmer needs to answer maintenance questions. E.g., the subsystem structure generated using SWAG Kit for *ZDelta* failed to identify its encryption/decryption units. SAAM helps in refining subsystem structure by helping to identify the questions that the architecture must answer. For example, maintenance scenarios quickly identified the importance of encryption/decryption in *ZDelta*, identifying the need to refactor the subsystem decomposition.

We found that SWAG Kit is limited to producing a static architectural view comprising components and connectors. SAAM evaluation requires a deeper understanding of how architectural components collaborate to accomplish a specific task suggested by SAAM's scenarios. Both of these approaches benefited from the iterative application of SWAG Kit and SAAM; as understanding of the architecture increased via analysis, it was possible to improve the architecture generated by SWAG Kit, which in turn resulted in improvements in the analysis.

Our experience shows that this iterative method is tractable for modestly sized systems. The three compression applications to which we applied the method were each approximately 10,000 lines of code in length. It took about one person-week per application to apply the method and extract an architecture. When scaling the approach to larger systems, we believe that the required time will vary based on the architecture recovery tool and its browsing facilities, the domain of the target application, the source code structure, the quality of comments in the source code and the availability of good documentation.

Our experience shows that the architecture recovery team and the architecture evaluation team should work closely together (or even be the same team), since there is a tight and iterative interaction between the architecture recovery tool and the evaluation process.

There are some limitations to this combined approach. For example, it was difficult to define a terminating point for the iterative process. Also, it was challenging to define appropriate scenarios for the evaluation process; if wrong scenarios are chosen, the final architecture may remain unsuitable for future analysis tasks. On balance, we conclude that despite these limitations, by iteratively applying architectural recovery and analysis, it is possible to gain a strong understanding of a software architecture with modest time investment.

The organization of the paper is as follows. In section 2, we review other techniques combining architectural recovery and evaluation. Section 3 explains how SWAG Kit and SAAM can be combined to extract a software architecture. In section 4, we illustrate the lessons that we learned from our case study, in which we applied our method to extract the architectures of *ZLib*, *ZDelta* and *GZip*. Section 5 concludes the paper.

2   Related Work

While there is significant literature on software architectural evaluation [16,10,8] (for a comprehensive summary of all architectural evaluation methods see our technical report [28]), little attention has been paid to its methodical application to architecture recovery. Some methods propose the combination of architecture recovery and architectural evaluation, but these approaches are purely sequential.

Lutz and Gannod [19], for example, have discussed the architectural analysis of a software product-line using a three-phase approach. The phases are software architecture recovery, scenario-based assessment of the extracted architecture and model checking of safety-critical behaviors. In contrast to our iterative approach, Lutz and Gannod use a purely forward approach. The software architecture is manually recovered from the available information and code base, and is compared to an existing software architecture using a scenario-based method. In this approach, the evaluation method plays no role in the recovery process.

A similar approach has been proposed by Bowman *et al.* [6]. This technique is based on dividing the software into subsystems based on its *ownership architecture*. The ownership architectures are then compared with existing conceptual architectures. Their study shows that ownership architecture is a good predictor of concrete architecture and is closely correlated to the conceptual architecture.

In addition to scenario-based approaches, some metrics-based evaluation methods have been applied to evaluating extracted software architectures. Again, in contrast to our iterative approach, these approaches are incremental. For example,

Medvidovic *et al.* [21] have quantitatively and qualitatively evaluated the Focus architectural recovery approach by extracting and validating the two middleware intensive systems: OODT [18] and the Globus Toolkit [12].

Guo *et al.* [14] have proposed a semi-automated architecture reconstruction method. This method uses patterns to guide users in achitectural recovery. This work is similar to ours in that it iteratively applies an architecture recovery tool (the Dali Workbench [17]) and an architecture evaluation technique. Little feedback is provided on the success of this iterative approach; the focus of Guo *et al.*'s approach is on evaluating the pattern matching approach.

We conclude, therefore, that there is room for study of the effectiveness of iterative application of automated architectural extraction and architecture analysis to the task of software architectural recovery.

3   Framework

In this section, we describe our framework for recovering the software architecture of legacy systems. We first explain how SWAG Kit supports automated extraction of software architectures from source code, and then describe how SAAM is used to evaluate the resulting software architecture. We then explain how these two can be applied together to recover meaningful architecture of legacy systems. In section 4, we report on our experience applying this framework to the recovery of the architectures of three open-source compression libraries.

3.1   Automated Software Architecture Extraction

Two types of software architectures are useful for understanding a complex software system: *conceptual* and *concrete*. A *conceptual architecture* provides an abstract view of the system by hiding its implementation details [3]. A *concrete architecture* shows the system as implemented. In this paper, we focus on recovering the conceptual architecture, as it serves our purpose of understanding the components and their relationships of the implemented system. In order to obtain a conceptual architecture, we use an architecture recovery tool to obtain a concrete architecture. This concrete architecture is then evaluated, abstracted and further refined into a conceptual architecture.

Architecture Recovery Steps: The general approach of recovering a software architecture consists of the following steps [26]:

1. Determine the low-level system representation (concrete architecture) by applying the architecture recovery tool on the source code of the target applications.
2. Identify the architectural elements/components by combining domain knowledge, design documents and the extracted low-level system representation.
3. Identify the relationships between the architectural elements to obtain a high level architectural representation of the system.

In the first step of the architectural recovery, we use *SWAG Kit* [30] to automatically extract the low-level system representation from the source code. We chose SWAG Kit because it is a mature toolkit which can be used for extracting, abstracting and exploring software architectures. This tool automatically extracts architectures from calls information in C or C++ source. SWAG Kit provides the *LSEdit* editor for visualizing and refining the architecture.

3.2   Software Architecture Analysis

The second major part of our framework is software architectural analysis. We use the *Software Architecture Analysis Method* (SAAM), as it is a widely-studied scenario-based method, and has been applied to numerous industrial problems.

Users of SAAM first identify the quality attributes of most importance to their application domain. They then elicit scenarios identifying plausible tasks involving the architecture (e.g., modification scenarios, or security attack scenarios.) After that, SAAM analysts determine the degree to which the software architecture has support for those scenarios. Analysts identify a list of changes that the scenarios require and provide necessary guidelines for addressing those changes in the software architecture.

3.3   The Combined Approach

Our combination of automated software architecture extraction and architectural analysis is incremental and iterative. The output of the architecture recovery tool is used as the input to the analysis method, and the analysis results are used to improve the extracted software architecture. Our combined framework is shown in Fig. 1. In the following, we discuss how SWAG Kit can be combined with SAAM using an incremental and iterative approach.

We automatically obtain a low-level system representation using SWAG Kit. The identification of architectural elements and derivation of a conceptual architecture is done manually. This manual analysis draws from domain knowledge, design documents, source code and source code comments; together, these form *architecturally significant concepts*. The overhead of this manual analysis can be significantly reduced if a reference architecture is readily available for the domain of interest [26,13,9].

Architecturally significant concepts, low-level system representation (from the recovery tool), and the reference architecture (if available) are then analyzed to obtain the subsystem structure and eventually, an initial version of the extracted architecture.

We use SAAM to identify shortcomings in the extracted architecture by examining the impact of scenarios on the architecture. SAAM helps find solutions to these shortcomings. This information is fed back to the recovery process. Concretely with SWAG Kit, this means manually modifying the inputs to the *LSEdit* tool that is used to view and refine archtictures.

Since the initial version of the software architecture is extracted using a tool, the architecture extraction team might focus too heavily on the tool output

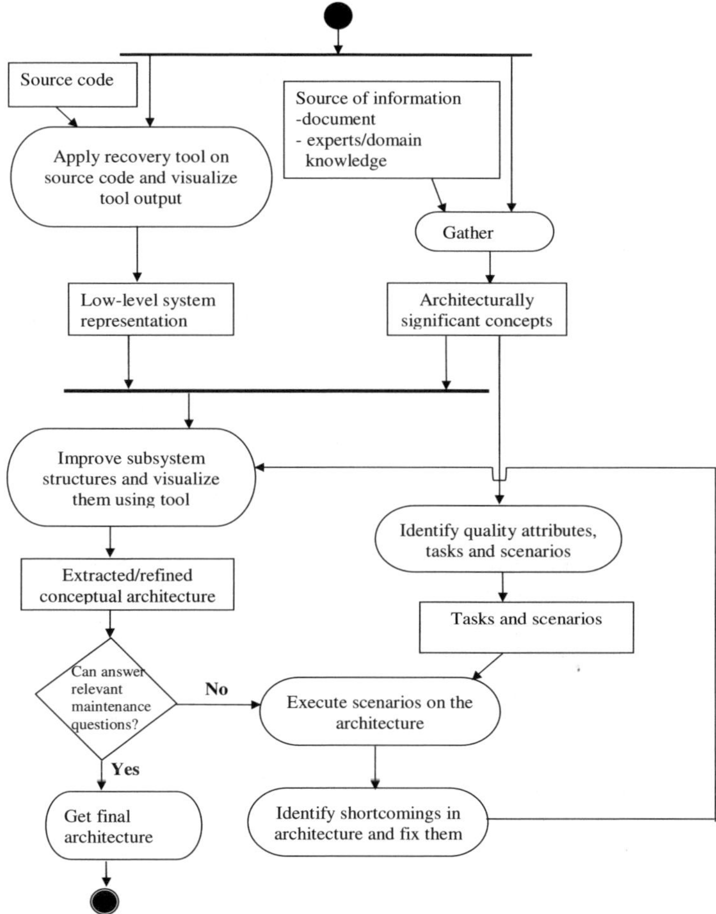

Fig. 1. The framework for combining architecture recovery tool and SAAM

when deriving a high level system representation. For example, the extraction team may fail to correctly identify the attributes that are most important to the application domain, the mechanisms by which these quality attributes are satisfied, and what protocols are used for the components' interaction. As a result, the initially extracted architecture might fail to capture important information required by maintenance programmers. SAAM can help improve this initial architecture by identifying scenarios that address relevant quality attributes.

On the other hand, the tool-supported analysis and visualization facilities of the recovery process can help SAAM analysts. SWAG Kit provides utilities to view the software architecture at a finer granularity, which SAAM can use to fine tune the analysis. For example, the *LSEdit* editor in SWAG Kit provides facilities for browsing internal elements of components/subsystems and their interfaces. These can help the evaluation team understand the functionality of abstract components.

Table 1. Some Relevant Information of *ZLib*, *ZDelta* and *GZip*

Application Name	Version	Number of lines	Number of files	Nature and language	Conceptual SA exists?
ZLib [32]	1.2.3	8.5KLOC	22	Library (C)	No
ZDelta [31]	2.0	7.0KLOC	27	Library(C)	No
GZip [15]	1.2.4	7.3KLOC	16	Application(C)	No

In this way, the architecture recovery process and evaluation method can be combined to enhance the correctness and suitability of an extracted software architecture.

4   Case Study and Lessons Learned

Our study had two aims. First, we wanted to investigate the practicality of using automatically recovered architectures as the basis for analysis of legacy systems for which no architectural documentation is available. Second, we wanted to examine whether architectural analysis plays a helpful role in the architecture recovery process. In particular, we wanted to see whether the use of an architectural analysis method (such as SAAM) can improve the quality of the architecture recovered by a tool (such as SWAG Kit).

In order to study these issues, we used our framework to recover the architectures of three open source compression/decompression systems: *ZLib*, *Zdleta* and *GZip*. *ZLib* is a general purpose lossless data-compression library. *ZDelta* is based on *ZLib*, but has been significantly modified; it provides new interfaces for streaming the target data and extensive runtime parameterizations. *GZip* is a compression utility that uses the same compression algorithm as *ZLib* and *ZDelta*. Information on these systems is listed in table 1.

With the case study we learned several interesting lessons as listed and explained below.

1. SWAG Kit is weak at identifying subsystem structure. On the other hand, architecture analysis is effective in identifying subsystem structure once the recovery process identifies low-level components and connectors.
2. The iterative application of SWAG Kit and SAAM helps to identify and resolve errors in the architecture, and leads to a deeper understanding of the architecture than that obtained with SWAG Kit alone.
3. SWAG Kit emphasizes architectural structure (components + connectors, and eventually subsystems). To get a dynamic view of a system (protocols used by components to collaborate; how specific tasks are carried out; data and control flow), the architecture analysis step is helpful.
4. Our approach can help evaluate which of a set of candidate libraries best suit a project's needs.
5. When applied to moderate applications ($\sim$10KLOC), only modest time investment (about one person week) was required to perform a complete analysis.

6. The iteration between architectural extraction and architecture analysis requires close collaboration between the people performing the tasks.

4.1 Improved Subsystem Structure

In order to aggregate low-level source code information into a higher level of abstraction, we were required to derive the subsystem structure. SWAG Kit is unable to provide subsystem structures automatically. Therefore, as a part of the recovery process, we manually analyzed the source code, the comments of the source code, and used domain knowledge to obtain an initial subsystem structure. However, we were unsure how well this substructure decomposition matched the system's true conceptual architecture. To verify the subsystem structures and to understand their dynamics, we evaluated them using SAAM.

First, we used SWAG Kit to derive a low-level architecture. Then, we derived the subsystem structures for each of the three applications; these are shown in Figs. 2(a), 2(b) and 2(c). A brief description of each subsystem or module follows:

- The **Input Module** is used to specify the compression/decompression algorithm and to specify compression levels. Runtime parametrization of the library is required to dynamically select between multiple compression/decompression algorithms and different files sizes. Separation of the *Input Module* from the *Main Module* localizes the changes that are necessary to adapt to a new compression algorithm.
- The **Main Module** coordinates the rest of the components. It consists of functions required to invoke and terminate the application, manage the session, specify the input file (to be compressed/ decompressed), output the result, and deal with errors.
- The **Compression Module** carries out the actual compression. The separation of the *Input Module* ensures that this module does not depend on any hard-coded compression or input algorithms.
- The **Decompression Module** provides the function of decompressing data streams.
- The **Utilities Module** provides useful functions to the rest of the application, such as memory management and graphical display.

However, this recovery process did not provide conceptual architecture adequate for answering maintenance questions. Therefore, we proceeded through the remaining steps of SAAM. At this stage, we first identified three quality attributes: *modifiability, integrability* and *security*. Scenarios illustrate the importance of these important quality attributes in the compression/decompression domain.

- Modifiability of compression libraries is important. Two examples of changes that might be required are: 1) *add a new compression algorithm to the toolkit* and 2) *modify the toolkit to run under a different operating system.*

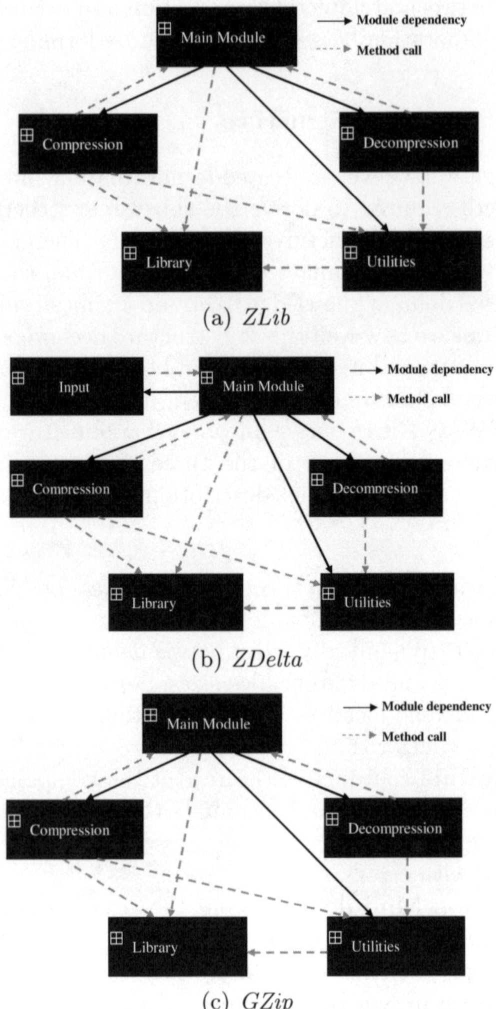

Fig. 2. Initial subsystem structures of *ZLib*, *ZDelta* and *GZip*

- Library applications such as *ZLib* and *ZDelta* should be easy to integrate with other applications. Two plausible scenarios are 1) *add compression functionality to a file transfer program* and 2) *provide a graphical user interface for a standalone file compression program.*
- Maintaining confidentiality in electronic documents is vitally important. Example scenarios might be 1) *encrypt a document before saving it on a USB key* and 2) *encrypt a document before emailing it.*

While analyzing the architectures with respect to the scenarios, we found that the subsystem structures obtained from SWAG Kit were insufficient to analyze how easily the scenarios could be enacted.

We successfully used SAAM to improve the subsystem structures. For example, we considered the following *integrability* scenario: *Rather than using the standard Bluetooth Device Discovery model to detect nearby mobile services, developers wish to implement a system that relies on machine-readable visual tags for out of band device and service selection. While implementing the visual tag application, the developers want to use an easily adaptable built-in compression library to store the image of the visual tag in order to save memory space.* The automatically extracted subsystem structures for *ZLib* and *ZDelta* lacked the information necessary to analyze how well their architectures could support this task. We were unable to find a component/subsystem specification that illustrated how to use the library application. Both architectures provide separate *Main* and *Utility* modules. This indicates that if a developer wants to adapt the entire compression/decompression library to another environment, changes can be localized to the *Main Module* only.

However, the separation between these two modules is far from sufficient to determine how easily this scenario could be enacted. We therefore further analyzed the architecture using the *LSEdit* visualization facilities. We browsed the tool output and searched for files and interfaces that might be related to this task. We found that both *ZDelta* and *ZLib* have files illustrating the use of the library applications. So we modified the subsystem structures of *ZLib* and *ZDelta* and displayed the improved structural views using *LSEdit*. These versions of the architectures are shown in Figs. 3(a) and 3(b).

In our experience, the automatically extracted architectures did not support analysis of the system with respect to our scenario. SAAM analysis can help identify and fix the shortcomings of the automatically extracted architecture, and can help improve the subsystem decomposition. However, the use of the recovery tool can significantly help in carrying out the SAAM analysis.

4.2 Better Understanding of the Architecture

In the remaining SAAM evaluation process, we again used the updated architectural views to execute the remaining scenarios. To analyze the architecture for the *security* quality attribute, we used the scenario: "*a developer wishes to incorporate encryption in the compression feature*". To map the scenario onto the architectures, we looked for the components in the architectures that support encryption/decryption. As we had not considered security issues during the recovery process, none of the extracted architectures contained the information that was required to address the security scenario.

To explore the scenario, we investigated the libraries' source code and comments and browsed the tool output to find interfaces that handle data streaming and security issues. Interestingly, we found that *ZDelta* handles data streaming in the target file and has a provision for incorporating data encryption in a modularized manner.

Therefore, we again refined the architectural view of *ZDelta* and introduced a new *Security Module* subsystem in *ZDelta*'s architecture (see Fig. 3(b)) in order to explicitly address the *security* quality attribute.

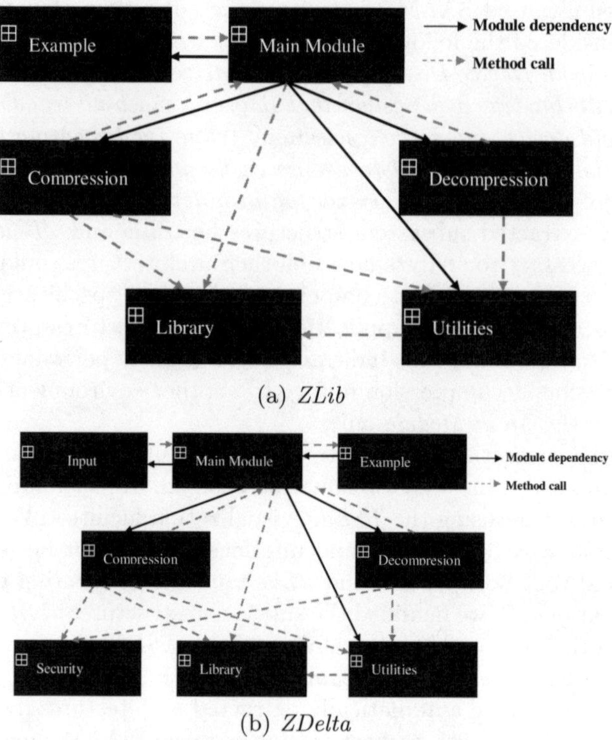

Fig. 3. Refined subsystem structures of *ZLib* and *ZDelta*

The investigation of the security scenario helped us learn more about what kinds of quality attributes a compression application can support and what kind of mechanisms it provides to address these quality attributes. Additionally, the repeated iterations of the *LSEdit* browser with further SAAM analysis guided our understanding in the compression area.

In summary, SAAM analysis using scenarios helped refine the conceptual architecture, while the SWAG *LSEdit* tool helped carry out this analysis on an imperfect view of the architecture. Incremental and iterative analysis helped move to a superior system decomposition.

4.3   Understanding the Dynamics of the Architecture

Architecture recovery using SWAG Kit helped us extract the applications' static architectures in terms of components and connectors. However, these static architectures did not help us understand the architectural dynamics, and did not support analysis of the strengths and weaknesses of the three software architectures. SAAM evaluation helped us in this regard by guiding us in understanding how components collaborate to perform a task. The browsing facility of SWAG Kit helped us find the appropriate component interfaces, which were used to accomplish the tasks quickly and easily.

As discussed in section 4.1, we determined two tasks to assess the *modifiability* quality attribute in this compression/decompression domain: *add a new compression algorithm to the toolkit* and *modify the toolkit to run under a different operating system*. A plausible scenario for the first task is: *A developer wants to add a new lossy compression algorithm for use with media files.*

When we analyzed how well the architectures support this scenario, we found that both *ZLib* and *GZip* use the *Deflating algorithm* along with *Huffman coding*, both directly encoded in the *Compression Module*. So, if the developers were to add a new compression algorithm, they would have to modify both the *Main* and *Compression* modules.

ZDelta provides better support for this task, as the *Input Module* is separated. The developers would only have to substitute the old algorithm with the new one, without making further modifications. The change is localized and does not affect other components.

For the second task, we found that as *ZLib*, *ZDelta* and *GZip* all have separate *Utility Modules*. They can be easily adapted to a new operating system, since the changes are localized to this one module only.

Scenario mapping helped us understand the interaction among components for executing the two tasks. By means of the interactions, we came to know that *ZDelta* has a more cohesive modular structure than that of *ZLib* and *GZip*. Thus, the combined approach helped us in understanding the dynamics of the extracted architectures.

4.4 Provision for Comparing Architectures

When architectural analysis is used during architecture recovery, developers can use the evaluation results to compare different candidate architectures. In our case, as all the applications/libraries are in the domain of compression/decompression, we used the result of the SAAM evaluation to compare them with respect to the identified quality attributes.

Based on the evaluation results of SAAM, we determined that they match up to different levels of conformance to the quality attributes, such as *modifiability*, *integrability* and *security*. The comparison results are summarized in Table 2.

Out of the three applications, *ZDelta* is the best in terms of *modifiability*, since the compression algorithm can be explicitly specified and the application can easily be adapted to a new operating system. The architectures of *ZLib* and *GZip* do not satisfy the modifiability requirement properly, since they do not have an explicitly defined *Input Module*. Both *ZLib* and *GZip* provide support for deploying the application on different platforms.

ZLib and *ZDelta* provide ease of adaptation, addressing the integrability quality attribute.

ZDelta provides better support for *Security* by separating the *Decompression* and *Security* modules. Both *ZLib* and *GZip* fail to handle data encryption in a modularized manner.

These examples show that combining architectural analysis with architectural extraction can help analyze which set of possible systems best meet a project's

Table 2. Comparison between Three Compression/ Decompression Applications

Application/ Quality Attribute	Modifiability		Integrability	Security
	Different Techniques	Different Platforms	Ease of Adaptation	
ZLib	X	√	√	X
ZDelta	√	√	√	√
GZip	X	√	X	X

√=**Supports the task or QA;**   X=**Does not support the task or QA**

needs. This ability is interesting, for example, for open source projects evaluating choices of what third party code to reuse.

4.5   Reasonable Tractability

Using our iterative approach, it took us about seven days to extract a conceptual architecture for each of the three applications (or a total of three staff weeks.) The applications were of modest size, each consisting of about 10KLOC.

This time benefited from SWAG Kit's detailed initial architecture and powerful browsing facilities. Extraction time also varies depending on the availability of the proper source code documentation, the quality of comments in the source code, and the structure of the source code. Further study is required to see how this time scales to large architectures. However, at least for a system of about 10KLOC, seven days seems a modest effort for the considerable payback in architectural knowledge.

4.6   Team Interactions

Our iterative approach requires considerable interaction between the architecture extractors and evaluators. In our case, the extractors and the evaluators were in the same group. While extracting the architectures using SWAG Kit and SAAM iteratively, we found that the close interaction between extractors and evaluators saved collaboration time and effort. We believe that this might be beneficial for larger systems.

4.7   Feedback

We contacted the authors of the three libraries to ask them how well the resulting architectures represented their system. Two of the three responded. The first respondent reported that the conceptual architecture seemed correct. The second reported that the architecture was incorrect, as it grouped the underlying source files differently from his understanding of the system. The latter result is interesting, as it shows that factoring the architecture around quality-driven scenarios can lead to different decompositions than intended by the original author. It is not clear whether the new decompositions are superior to the author's intuition of what belongs together for analysis and maintenance tasks. Considerable further research is required to address this question.

5   Conclusion

In this paper, we have detailed our experience applying a framework for extracting and evaluating architectures of legacy systems. Our case study applied SWAG Kit for architectural extraction and SAAM for architecture analysis. To our knowledge, no one has reported such a case study combining these approaches in an iterative and incremental manner.

In our case study, we extracted the architectures of three open source compression applications. We found that the combined approach was tractable (at least for modestly-sized applications). The use of SAAM can significantly improve the subsystem structures obtained using SWAG Kit. The combined approach helped us understand the dynamics of a software architecture in a better way than the architecture recovery process alone.

The primary limitation of our approach is that our data is largely subjective. A next step would be to perform a study in the combined approach with third party developers. Nonetheless, this study allowed us to demonstrate clear benefits and weaknesses of the incremental and iterative framework.

Acknowledgement

This work was supported in part by the Natural Science and Engineering Research Council of Canada. We thank Rob Fletcher for his help in an earlier version of this paper.

References

1. Abowd, G., Bass, L., Clements, P., Kazman, R., Northrop, L., Zaremski, A.: Recommended Best Industrial Practice for Software Architecture Evaluation (CMU/SEI-96-TR-025) (1996)
2. Babar, M.A., Zhu, L., Jefery, R.: A Framework for Classifying and Comparing Software Architecture Evaluation Methods. In: Australian Software engineering, pp. 309–318. IEEE CS, Washington (2004)
3. Bass, L., Clements, P., Kazman, R.: Software Architecture in Practice. SEI Series in Software Engineering. Addison-Wesley, Reading (1998)
4. Bergner, K., Rausch, A., Sihling, M., Ternité, T.: DoSAM - Domain-Specific Software Architecture Comparison Model. In: Reussner, R., Mayer, J., Stafford, J.A., Overhage, S., Becker, S., Schroeder, P.J. (eds.) QoSA 2005 and SOQUA 2005. LNCS, vol. 3712, pp. 4–20. Springer, Heidelberg (2005)
5. Bosch, J., Molin, P.: Software architecture design: Evaluation and transformation. In: Engineering of Computer Based Systems Symposium, pp. 4–10. IEEE CS, Los Alamitos (1999)
6. Ivan, T.B., Holt, R.C.: Software Architecture Recovery Using Conway's Law. In: Centre for Advanced Studies Conference, pp. 123–133. IBM Press, Toronto (1998)
7. Clements, P., Kazman, R., Klein, M.: Evaluating Software Architectures: Methods and Case Studies. Addison-Wesley Professional, Reading (2002)
8. Dobrica, L., Niemela, E.: A Survey on Software Architecture Analysis Methods. IEEE Transactions on Software Engineering 28, 638–653 (2002)

9. Eixelsberger, W.: Recovery of a Reference Architecture: A case study. In: 3rd International Software Architecture Workshop, pp. 105–108. ACM, New York (1998)
10. Graaf, B., Dijk, H.v.: Evaluating an Embedded Software Reference Architecture. In: 9th European Conference on Software Maintenance and Reengineering, pp. 354–363. IEEE CS, Washington (2005)
11. Garlan, D.: Software Architecture: A Roadmap. In: The Future of Software Engineering, pp. 93–101. ACM, New York (2000)
12. Globus, http://www.globus.org/
13. Gronbaek, K., Wiil, U.K.: Towards a Reference Architecture for Open Hypermedia, http://www.aue.aau.dk/~kock/OHS-HT97/Papers/gronbak.html
14. Guo, G.Y., Atlee, J.M., Kazman, R.: A Software Architecture Reconstruction Method. In: Working IFIP Conference on Software Architecture, pp. 15–34. Kluwer B.V., Deventer (1998)
15. GZip, http://www.gzip.org/
16. Kazman, R., Abowd, G., Webb, M.: SAAM: A Method for Analyzing the Properties of Software Architectures. In: 16th International Conference on Software Engineering, pp. 81–90. IEEE CS, Los Alamitos (1994)
17. Kazman, R., Carriére, S.J.: Playing Detective: Reconstructing Software Architecture from Available Evidence. Automated Software Engineering 6, 107–138 (1999)
18. OODT, http://oodt.jpl.nasa.gov/oodt-site/
19. Lutz, R., Gannod, G.C.: Analysis of a software product line architecture: an experience report. The Journal of Systems and Software 66, 253–267 (2003)
20. Matinlassi, M.: Evaluating the Portability and Maintainability of Software Product Family Architecture: Terminal Software Case Study. In: 4th Working IEEE/IFIP Conference on Software Architecture, pp. 295–298. IEEE CS, Wasington (2004)
21. Medvidovic, N., Jakobac, V.: Using Software Evolution to Focus Architectural Recovery. Automated Software Engineering 13, 225–256 (2006)
22. Mendonca, N.C., Kramer, J.: An Approach for Recovering Distributed System Architectures. Automated Software Engineering Journal 8, 311–354 (2001)
23. Monroe, R.T., Kompanek, A., Melton, R., Garlan, D.: Architectural Styles, Design Patterns, and Objects. IEEE Software 15, 43–52 (1997)
24. Murphy, G.C., Notkin, D., Griswold, W.G., Lan, E.S.: An empirical study of static call graph extractors. In: 18th International Conference on Software Engineering, pp. 158–191. ACM, New York (1996)
25. Perry, D.E., Wolf, A.L.: Foundations for the Study of Software Architecture. In: Software Engineering Notes. ACM Sigsoft, vol. 17, pp. 40–52. ACM, New York (1992)
26. Pinzger, M., Gall, H., Girard, J.F., Knodel, J., Riva, C., Pasman, W., Broerse, C., Wijnstra, J.G.: Architecture Recovery for Product Families. In: van der Linden, F.J. (ed.) PFE 2003. LNCS, vol. 3014, pp. 332–351. Springer, Heidelberg (2004)
27. Rigi, http://www.rigi.csc.uvic.ca/
28. Roy, B., Graham, T.C.N.: Methods for Evaluating Software Architecture: A Survey, p. 82, School of Computing TR 2008-545, Queen's University (2008), http://www.cs.queensu.ca/TechReports/reports2008.html
29. Shrimp, http://www.thechiselgroup.org/shrimp
30. SWAG Kit: Software Architecture Group, http://www.swag.uwaterloo.ca/SWAGKit/
31. ZDelta, http://cis.poly.edu/ZDelta/
32. ZLib, http://www.zlib.net/

Towards a Method for the Evaluation of Reference Architectures: Experiences from a Case

Samuil Angelov, Jos J.M. Trienekens, and Paul Grefen

Department of Technology Management,
Eindhoven University of Technology, The Netherlands
{s.angelov,j.j.m.trienekens,p.w.p.j.grefen}@tue.nl

Abstract. Reference architectures provide major guidelines for the structure of a class of information systems. Because of their fundamental role, reference architectures have to be of high quality. Before accepting a reference architecture, it has to go through a rigorous evaluation process. A number of methods exist for the evaluation of software architectures. In this paper, we analyze the main differences between concrete software architectures and reference architectures. We discuss the effects of these differences on the evaluation of reference architectures and show that existing methods cannot be directly applied for the evaluation of reference architectures. For the evaluation of a reference architecture for e-contracting systems, we used the Architecture Tradeoff Analysis Method with a number of adaptations and extensions. We present our approach and share our experiences from this evaluation process. Based on the analysis and our experiences gained, we present our vision for a method for the evaluation of reference architectures.

Keywords: software architecture, reference architecture, evaluation method.

1 Introduction

Every system has an architecture [20]. The software architecture of a program or computing system is "the structure or structures of the system, which comprise software elements, the externally visible properties of those elements, and the relationships among them" [6]. An architecture can be documented in an "architectural description". While an architectural description may be used after a system has been developed (e.g., for system maintenance purposes), its value is greater when it is defined and used prior to system development. It facilitates discussions on the system to be developed among its stakeholders [8]. By agreeing a priory on a software architecture, stakeholders can be certain that they have agreed on the functionalities and design choices that they would expect to be implemented in the system. In this paper, we use the term *concrete architecture* to refer to the architectural description of a concrete software system.

Architectural design choices have direct repercussions on the system to be designed. That is why it is important to evaluate the architecture of a system before system development starts. Architecture evaluation allows timely and cheap discovery

R. Morrison, D. Balasubramaniam, and K. Falkner (Eds.): ECSA 2008, LNCS 5292, pp. 225–240, 2008.
© Springer-Verlag Berlin Heidelberg 2008

and resolution of potential problems in the system to be developed. "Architecture evaluation is a cheap way to avoid disaster" [8]. An architecture that passes successfully through an evaluation process sets the fundaments for the development of a high-quality system. In recent years, a number of methods for the evaluation of software architectures have been proposed [5], [10], [16].

Reference architectures have emerged as a special type of architectures that provides major guidelines for the specification of concrete architectures of one class of systems. Depending on the context in which they are defined, we differentiate between two types of reference architectures: practice-driven and research-driven reference architectures. Practice-driven reference architectures are defined when sufficient knowledge has been accumulated in a domain to propose the "best of best-practices" architecture [19]. They are designed to provide a standardized view on a class of systems. Research-driven reference architectures provide a "futuristic" view on a class of systems that are expected to become important in the future, but by the time of the architecture definition are seen as hard to build (e.g., due to functional complexity). These architectures aim at facilitating the design of the first systems from a class of systems.

Nowadays, software is evolving rapidly regarding its size and complexity. Software components are often developed by different software providers and integrated at a later stage in a system. Systems have to communicate with other systems. The system complexity, and the need for integrability of system elements and for system interoperability have lead to a growing number of practice- and research-driven reference architectures (e.g., [4], [12], [13], [14], [15], [22], [23]).

Reference architectures influence the design of a set of concrete architectures and, thus, the design of a set of systems. That is why designers of a reference architecture have to present evidence for its qualities by evaluating it. However, existing methods for the evaluation of concrete architectures cannot be applied directly for the evaluation of reference architectures. The main reason for this is the generic nature of reference architectures. This characteristic of reference architectures leads to a number of differences between reference and concrete architectures. Existing methods for the evaluation of concrete architectures are not designed to deal with these specific characteristics of reference architectures. To the best of our knowledge, no method dedicated to the evaluation of reference architectures currently exists.

In this paper, we present our experiences with the evaluation of a reference architecture. We start with an analysis of the specific characteristics of reference architectures and their evaluation. This analysis allows us to motivate the need for attention to the evaluation of reference architectures and to provide the foundations for a dedicated method for the evaluation of reference architectures. Next, we present the case of the evaluation of a reference architecture for e-contracting systems and discuss our approach in this case. Based on our experiences in this case and the analysis of reference architectures, we present our vision for a method for the evaluation of reference architectures. We believe that the results presented in this paper will provide valuable pointers for the evaluation of reference architectures and will contribute to the design of a method for the evaluation of reference architectures.

The paper is organized as follows. In Section 2, we discuss concrete and reference architectures. We compare them and identify differences between them. In Section 3, we discuss the evaluation of concrete and reference architectures. We show that due to the differences between them, existing methods for the evaluation of concrete architectures cannot be applied directly for the evaluation of reference architectures. In Section 4, we present our experiences with the evaluation of a specific reference architecture. Based on this, we present our vision for a method for the evaluation of reference architectures. The paper ends with conclusions.

2   Concrete and Reference Architectures

In this section, we present concrete and reference software architectures and discuss the goals and outcomes of their design. We compare them and identify a number of differences between them.

2.1   Concrete Architectures

In the 1990's, complex and large software systems were becoming widely spread [8]. This has lead to an increased interest in the design and documentation of software architectures as a means to facilitate system development and maintenance.

An architecture description (or briefly "an architecture") defines a set of *functionalities* and addresses certain *system*, *business*, and *architectural qualities* that are required by the stakeholders [6]. System qualities (e.g. availability, modifiability) are qualities that stakeholders require in the system to be developed. Business qualities (e.g. cost, time-to-market) are business goals that affect the system architecture. Architectural qualities (e.g. conceptual integrity, buildability) are qualities of the architecture itself.

The design of high-quality concrete software architectures has been given significant attention in the literature [6], [20], [21].

2.2   Reference Architectures

According to [6] a reference model is *"a division of functionality together with data flow between the pieces"*, and a reference architecture is *"a reference model mapped onto software elements (that cooperatively implement the functionality defined in the reference model) and the data flows between them"*. A reference architecture is based on the functionalities and data flows defined in a reference model and applies architectural styles and patterns that help in addressing the main qualities expected from the architecture (see Fig.1). A "good" reference architecture can bring a number of benefits [19]. It may facilitate the design of high-quality concrete architectures; it may facilitate communications between domain professionals, etc.

A reference architecture can be defined before the existence of practical experiences with the design of concrete architectures. The design of such a reference architecture is inspired by existing research efforts. Thus, these reference architectures are research-driven. These architectures follow the "top-down" approach presented in Fig.1, i.e., a reference architecture is based mainly on a reference model and on existing architectural patterns. We call these reference architectures Futuristic Reference Architectures (FRAs), as their goal is to make an attempt to "look into the future" and to foresee the major design principles that will be of importance in the design of concrete architectures for a specific domain. Examples of a FRA are [4], [18], [22].

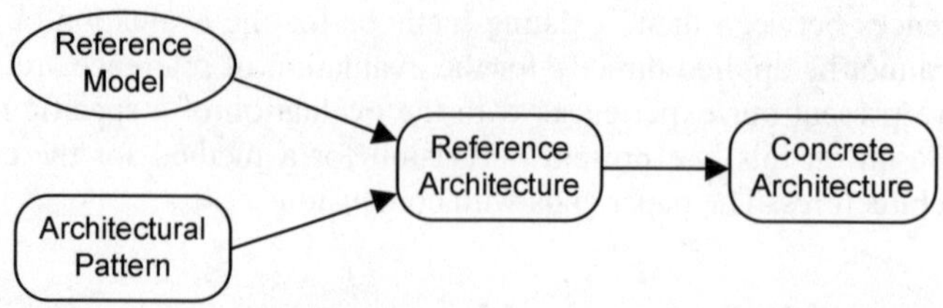

Fig. 1. The relationship between reference models, reference architectures and concrete architectures (adapted from [6])

Often, reference models and reference architectures are defined based on accumulated practical experience in domains, i.e., they are practice-driven. In this paper, we call practice-driven reference architectures Practice Reference Architectures (PRAs). As the design of PRAs is inspired from practice, the design process can be seen more as following a "bottom-up" approach in which concrete architectures play the major role for the design of a reference architecture (see Fig.2). Another consequence from the "practice" roots of PRAs is that they might address legacy issues in their design. PRAs are usually (but not necessarily) elaborated by recognized standardization bodies that facilitate developments within a domain, or by consortiums established by powerful companies within the domain which aim at establishing or even enforcing standards within the domain. Examples of a PRA are [13], [14], [23].

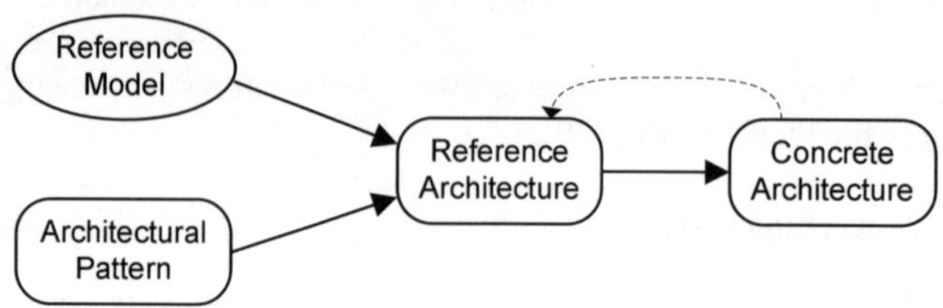

Fig. 2. The influence of concrete architectures in the case of PRAs

PRAs and FRAs have certain differences with respect to their origin and goals. In the case of PRAs, the functionalities that may be part of a system are known. PRAs are based on existing "best practices" often interwoven with existing legacy issues. Thus, we can view the origin of PRAs as *descriptive*. In the case of FRAs, only limited existing practices can be used (i.e., architectural patterns, architectures of prototypes). As there are not complete solutions that exist in practice, we can view the origin of FRAs as *prescriptive*.

Table 1. Origin and goals of PRAs and FRAs (P - prescriptive, D – descriptive)

	Origin	Goals
PRA	D	P
FRA	P	D

Generally, any architecture of a system-under-development has prescriptive goals with its design. However, an in-depth look into PRAs and FRAs reveals an interesting nuance. PRAs are designed to facilitate faster system design and development and to address standardization problems in a domain. Thus, their main goal is to serve as *prescriptive* tools. FRAs are designed to facilitate the design of architectures of *first* systems in a domain. FRAs provide detailed descriptions of their "novel" functionalities. These details are required to clarify the innovative elements in the architecture as well as to convince the domain users for the qualities of systems based on the FRA (e.g., their "buildability"). Due to their avant-guard features, FRAs will often never assert themselves as accepted reference architectures. Thus, FRAs are designed to serve as *descriptive* tools and have more limited goals as prescriptive tools. We represent the nuances in the origin and goals of PRA and FRA in Table 1.

2.3 Comparison of Concrete and Reference Architectures

There are a number of differences between reference architectures (PRAs and FRAs) and concrete architectures. Next, we present these differences. The results from this section provide the foundations for our discussion in Section 3.

Difference 1: Reference architectures are of a generic nature. A reference architecture is designed to address the functionalities and qualities desired by all stakeholders in their specific contexts (see Fig.3).

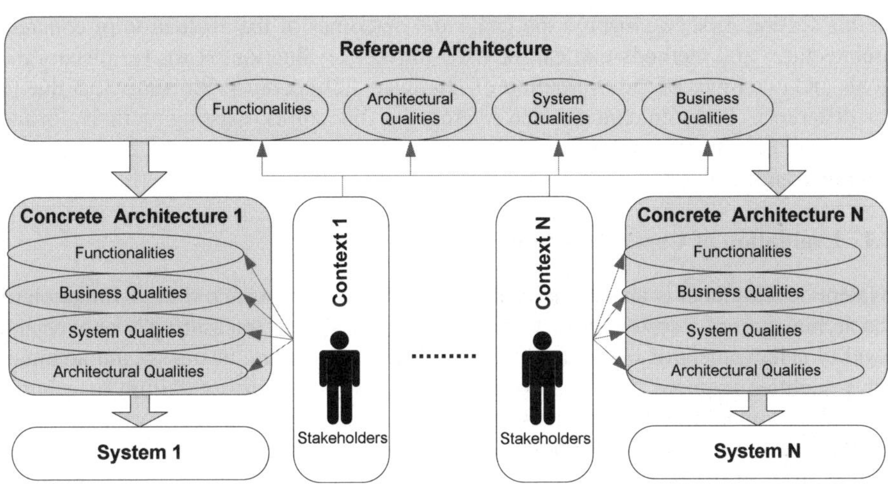

Fig. 3. The role of stakeholders and contexts for reference and concrete architectures

Difference 1 is a fundamental difference and is the basis of a number of specific differences:

Difference 2: *There is not a clear group of stakeholders of a reference architecture.* As stakeholders can be seen all companies from the domain, all companies developing software for the domain, etc. However, it is not possible to involve all these stakeholders in the definition of a reference architecture (due to logistic, political, etc. reasons).

Difference 3: *Due to their generic nature, reference architectures are defined on a high level of abstraction.* They may provide details only for specific elements. For example, as discussed in Section 2.2., in the case of FRAs, novel elements with complex structure may be paid a closer look. In the case of PRAs, elements critical for the standardization goals of the architecture may be defined in greater detail.

Difference 4: *A reference architecture has to address more architectural qualities than a concrete architecture.* These additional architectural qualities are due to the generic nature of reference architectures and their wider audience. For example, an "applicability" quality would be of importance for a reference architecture to indicate the level of applicability of the architecture to different contexts in the domain. This quality is superfluous for a concrete architecture as a concrete architecture is designed to be applicable for a specific context.

Because of these differences between concrete and reference architectures, reference architectures are considered by some authors as very distant from concrete architectures: "reference architectures are not architectures; they are useful concepts that capture elements of an architecture" [6].

3   Evaluation of Architectures

In this section, first, we discuss the goals and outcomes of the evaluation of concrete architectures and methods that can be used for their evaluation. Next, we discuss the goals and outcomes of the evaluation of reference architectures. We show that due to the differences between concrete and reference architectures, existing methods for the evaluation of concrete architectures cannot be directly applied for the evaluation of reference architectures.

3.1   Evaluation of Concrete Architectures

System development is an expensive process in terms of costs and time. Evaluation of the architecture of a system prior to its development allows "measuring" the expected level of achievement of the system functionalities and system, business, and architectural qualities required by the stakeholders. Timely discovery of failure to achieve desired functionalities and qualities means saved time and resources in the development process and avoids frustrations among stakeholders.

A number of methods exist for evaluation of software architectures. These methods differ in their evaluation techniques as well as in their goals. Most methods (e.g., SAAM, ALMA) rely on questioning techniques (asking the stakeholders qualitative questions) and use scenarios as their main tool [10]. Few methods (e.g., SAEM) rely on measuring techniques that support quantitative measurement and evaluation of architectures. Particular methods are designed to evaluate only specific architectural qualities. For example, SAAM and ALMA are suitable for the evaluation of the modifiability quality [16]. Other methods support the evaluation of multiple qualities (e.g., ATAM and SBAR). According to [10], some methods can be integrated easier in the design process than other methods (e.g., SBAR, ATAM). In [10], the authors conclude that ATAM (Architecture Trade-off Analysis Method) has as advantages its integration of questioning and measuring techniques, the wide set of qualities that can be evaluated through it, and the possibility of integrating the method easily in the design process. An overview and comparison of existing methods can be found in [5], [10], [16].

It must be noted that existing evaluation methods provide techniques mainly for the evaluation of system qualities. The definition and evaluation of business and architectural qualities has received little attention in the literature. CBAM [6] can be distinguished as a method for the evaluation of costs, benefits, and risk business qualities. ATAM [8] addresses explicitly the evaluation of the "conceptual integrity" architectural quality. Though it is not explicitly stated in the method, the generation of scenarios in ATAM can be used for the evaluation of the "completeness" architectural quality as well.

3.2 Evaluation of Reference Architectures

In order to establish an effective reference architecture with respect to many concrete architectures, a reference architecture should have a high degree of excellence. To identify the aspects that may require additional attention before its release and to prove its final value, a reference architecture requires evaluation. In Section 2.2, we discussed that a reference architecture contains a description of functionalities and addresses certain system, business and architectural qualities. Thus, concrete and reference architectures have to be evaluated for the same aspects. However, as discussed in Section 2.3, concrete and reference architectures have certain differences. These differences lead to a number of problems that do not allow the direct application of methods for the evaluation of concrete architectures in the case of reference architectures. Next, we explain our motivation for this statement.

Problem 1: One of the problems for applying an existing method for the evaluation of reference architectures is caused by the lack of a clearly defined group of stakeholders (see Difference 2). ATAM and most other methods heavily rely on the participation of all stakeholders in its evaluation. However, reaching all stakeholders of reference architectures and convincing them to participate in an evaluation is problematic. In both cases (PRAs and FRAs), the big number of stakeholders makes it impossible to address all of them. Furthermore, in the case of PRAs, often, stakeholders will not unite around a common reference architecture due to political and contextual differences (rivalry, different legacies, etc.). In the case of FRAs, most stakeholders will have limited incentives (as there are no direct benefits for them) and capabilities (due to lack of visionary thinking and knowledge) to contribute to the architecture evaluation.

Problem 2: As discussed in Section 3.1 most evaluation methods make use of scenarios. However, the generic nature of reference architectures (see Difference 1) and their high level of abstraction (see Difference 3) make the generation of a usable set of scenarios difficult. Due to the generic nature of reference architectures, evaluators have the choice to either define a large set of "concrete" scenarios for the possible contexts in which the reference architecture can be applied or define highly general scenarios which cover all these contexts. In the first approach, the huge number of possible contexts results in a huge number of scenarios. This makes defining and prioritizing them a problematic task. In the second approach, the generality of scenarios makes it hard to evaluate their adequate support in the architecture. This problem has already been observed even in the evaluation of concrete architectures of information systems, whose complexity leads to the definition of highly general scenarios [7]. The abstract nature of (parts of the) reference architectures further aggravates the problem of generating concrete scenarios. In the case of FRAs, the lack of practical knowledge for the contexts in which concrete architectures will be defined makes generation of scenarios a "guessing game".

Problem 3: In Section 3.1, we mentioned that from the existing methods for the evaluation of concrete architectures only ATAM addresses explicitly the evaluation of the "conceptual integrity" architectural quality and implicitly of the "completeness" architectural quality. However, reference architectures have to address more architectural qualities than concrete architectures (see Difference 4). Consequently, existing methods fall short in providing techniques for the evaluation of the architecture qualities of PRAs and FRAs.

This brief discussion shows that existing methods on the evaluation of concrete architectures are not directly applicable for an evaluation of reference architectures. In the recent years, software product lines gained the attention of research and industry [6], [9]. Software product line architectures (also called family architectures) are abstractions of concrete architectures that allow architecture reuse for a number of software products that share a common foundation. In [11], software product line architectures are positioned between reference architectures and concrete architectures and a dedicated method for their evaluation called FAAM is proposed. The more generic nature of software product line architectures suggests that FAAM may be more suitable for the evaluation of reference architectures than methods for the evaluation of concrete architectures. However, similar to methods for the evaluation of concrete architectures, FAAM does not deal with the evaluation of architectural qualities. Furthermore, in FAAM, the stakeholders are expected to be involved actively in the evaluation process. Thus, FAAM does not resolve the problems identified in this section and cannot be applied for an evaluation of reference architectures.

4   An Approach to the Evaluation of Reference Architectures

In our previous work, we have faced the problem of evaluating an E-contracting Reference Architecture (ERA) [4]. This section starts with a brief presentation of the context of ERA. For the evaluation of ERA, we used the Architecture Tradeoff Analysis Method (ATAM). As ATAM is designed for the evaluation of concrete architectures, we had to apply a number of adaptations and extensions on it. We present our evaluation approach and share our experiences from it. Based on our experiences and the discussion in Section 3, we present our vision for a method for the evaluation of reference architectures.

4.1 The E-contracting Reference Architecture (ERA)

Business-to-business e-contracting uses information technology for improving the efficiency and effectiveness of contracting processes of companies. A reference architecture that provides guidelines for the design of concrete architectures of highly automated e-contracting systems will significantly facilitate the software development process and will introduce a standardized view on e-contracting systems. So far, the domain of highly automated e-contracting has been addressed mainly by the research community. Over many years, industry considered it to be too complex and rigid and hardly applicable in practice. However, there is currently an increasing interest in the industry in the development of more advanced contracting systems with a higher level of automation.

In [1], we presented our initial design of ERA. According to the discussion in Section 2.2, ERA can be classified as a FRA. In the next section, we explain the approach that we took for the evaluation of ERA and the results from it. A detailed description of the evaluation process and of the final version of ERA can be found respectively in [3] and [4].

4.2 The Evaluation of ERA

Our initial approach was to evaluate ERA by means of an existing method for the evaluation of concrete architectures. We chose to use ATAM as a method for the evaluation of ERA because of its advantages in a number of aspects over other methods (see Section 3.1), and because of its successful application in many projects [5]. Our team had no previous experiences with ATAM. After introducing ourselves to ATAM, we foresaw a number of problems (presented in Section 3.3). Realizing the lack of a dedicated method for the evaluation of reference architectures, we decided to attempt the evaluation of ERA with ATAM and to make adaptations and extensions on ATAM where the "reference architecture" context required it. Next, we describe the phases in the evaluation of ERA (based on ATAM) and the adaptations and extensions that we made on ATAM.

Phase 1: Identification of the stakeholders of ERA that will be involved in its evaluation; preparation of the evaluation process.

Activities: We invited 3 researchers with experience in e-contracting and software architectures in the role of software architects/designers with whom we performed Phases 2a and 2b of ATAM. For Phase 3 of ATAM, we involved a group of 25 contract business professionals.

Adaptations of ATAM: ATAM assumes the identification of stakeholders and their participation in the evaluation process to be a rather straightforward process. As discussed in Problem 1 (see Section 3.2), this is not the case in reference architectures. To solve this problem, we identified first the roles for the different stakeholders, i.e., contract (procurement) managers, software architects/designers/managers, contract engineers, legal officers, and CEOs. We estimated that people acting in these roles in a company might be affected by the development and introduction of an e-contracting system. Next, we searched for people representative for these roles. As ERA is a FRA, we were looking for people with visionary thinking who had (or can build) understanding for the advanced elements in ERA. We managed to approach people with such qualities for Phases 2a and 2b. However, approaching business professionals for the evaluation of ERA was difficult. As discussed, a FRA may never be accepted as a reference architecture. Thus, there was no direct incentive for business professionals to participate in the evaluation of ERA. To offer an incentive for the business professionals to spend time on the evaluation of ERA, we organized a five-hour tutorial on electronic contracting within the scope of the "4th Annual Contract Management Conference" [2]. The main goal of the tutorial was to present the basic aspects of e-contracting. A discussion on the architecture of advanced e-contracting systems was announced as secondary element of the tutorial. The educational goal of the tutorial appeared to be a sufficient incentive for attracting 25 attendees. The attendees had the following role distribution: 8 contract managers (2 of the contract managers had also a function as IT experts in their departments); 4 procurement managers, 2 contract engineers, 3 CEOs; 2 legal officers; 2 government representatives; 4 professionals with other business functions.

Phase 2a: Elicitation of the architecture and required qualities; identification of architectural approaches.

Activities: We evaluated the set of required qualities in ERA. At the end of this step, we had a list of system and architectural qualities (system qualities: security, flexibility, modifiability, integrability, high automation, interoperability; architectural qualities: conceptual integrity, completeness, buildability, applicability, usability, acceptability). After this phase, the amount of quality attributes required in ERA has increased compared to our initial list of required qualities. Furthermore, our understanding for the required qualities in ERA has improved. Next, we defined scenarios for the qualities that we identified. Finally, we identified the architectural approaches that we used in ERA.

Adaptations of ATAM: Initially, the lack of concrete context resulted in the definition of highly-general and (mostly) equally important scenarios (related to Problem 2). ATAM does not provide any guidelines on the definition and prioritization of scenarios in such general settings. Our approach to resolve this problem was to select a number of contexts in which ERA can be applied and define concrete scenarios relevant for them. We selected three trading domains (i.e., the advertising, the logistics, and the insurance domains) for the e-contracting aspects of which we had knowledge from previous research. As contracting practices differ mainly per domain, selection of different domains was a sufficient concretization in our case. However, the domains that we selected were by no means representative for the large set of domains where e-contracting can take place. So, the selection was a pragmatic choice. Having in mind the generic nature of reference architectures, we looked only for scenarios that were applicable for all three selected domains.

Phase 2b: Analysis of the architectural approaches and their effect on the selected qualities.

Activities: We analyzed the suitability of the architectural approaches used in ERA for achieving the security, flexibility, automation, modifiability, integrability, and interoperability qualities. We discussed the risks, non-risks, sensitivity points and tradeoffs of ERA. These activities led to a number of improvements of ERA. Lack of a consistent strategy for the exchange of data among components and invocation of components was discovered. The requirements for modifiability and integrability were not addressed consistently throughout the architecture as well. To address these problems, a number of additional architectural styles and patterns were introduced in ERA. We discovered also that a new component had to be added to the architecture to satisfy the interoperability requirement. Thus, the evaluation of desired qualities of ERA through ATAM led to substantial improvements in the architecture. After improving ERA, we re-evaluated it and elaborated a final list of risks, non-risks, sensitivity points and tradeoffs in ERA. This list contained issues that were all within our scope of expectations.

Adaptations of ATAM: As discussed in Problem 3, ATAM is designed to address mainly system qualities and the conceptual integrity architectural quality. That is why, at this stage, we selected and evaluated only the qualities of ERA that can be evaluated through this step in ATAM, and we skipped the remaining qualities.

Phase 3: Verification of the results from Phase 2 by involving "business" stakeholders.

Activities: As already mentioned, in this phase, we organized a tutorial on e-contracting [2]. In this tutorial, first, we presented the main aspects of e-contracting to the audience (time used: 2 hours). As a next step, we presented ERA (time used: 1 hour). In the remaining time of the tutorial (2 hours), we organized a discussion session on the qualities which the participants would expect from an e-contracting system. We asked the participants to generate scenarios which they think would be relevant for such a system and to rank them. Each participant was given the right to cast 3 votes in total. The results from the workshop helped us to make final adaptations to ERA. The qualities that the tutorial participants identified overlapped with the qualities already identified in Phase 2a. We used the scenarios generated in Phases 2a and 3 to evaluate the functional completeness quality of ERA. For our surprise, the scenario that was ranked highest by the participants was not addressed properly in ERA. As a consequence, we introduced a new component in ERA to address the scenario identified by the participants.

Adaptations of ATAM: The results from this phase proved that this phase was a useful element of the evaluation process. However, in this phase, we faced a number of problems for the resolution of which we had to make adaptations to ATAM.

ERA is defined for the design of highly-automated contracting systems. The idea of such advanced systems is currently addressed only in the research world. Though we spent a significant amount of time in presenting the essential aspects of e-contracting and the goals of ERA, the participants did not accept this idea and discussed a system with a low-level of automation. This can be explained by the lack of visionary thinking by some of the participants and by the conflict of interests between the goals of the participants and our goals. The participants had to suggest scenarios for a futuristic system which was beyond the imagination of many of the participants. Furthermore, the participants were interested in practical solutions that can be implemented straightforwardly. Thus, they were interested in discussing a less advanced system that could be developed on the basis of existing technology. As a consequence, we had to re-formulate the scenarios defined by the participants for the situation of a highly automated e-contracting system. Some scenarios made no sense in the case of highly-automated system and had to be removed from the list. From the 22 scenarios that were generated, finally we considered 16 to be relevant.

We gave all participants 3 votes that they could use for the prioritization of the scenarios. In ATAM participants are given votes equal to around 30% of the number of scenarios defined (this would mean 4-5 votes in our case). The reason to decrease the number of votes was the lack of time combined with the inability of some participants to easily rank the scenarios. Some participants could not prioritize the scenarios as they did not have a good base for reasoning. In the voting process, we did not take into consideration the different roles of the participants. As not all people had the visionary thinking required for this evaluation, any attempt to influence the voting process based on the different roles might have had a negative rather than a positive effect on the process (e.g., people with more visionary ideas might get less votes in case they are representing the same role).

We had to omit a number of steps advocated in ATAM. We did not present to the participants ATAM in detail and the results from the previous steps of ATAM. We estimated that presenting explicitly ATAM and our previous results from the evaluation process would consume too much time (which we did not have) and would demotivate people to present their own views on e-contracting systems. Due to the lack of time, we did not perform an in-depth discussion on the ranking of the scenarios. ATAM advocates analysis of the architectural approaches in this phase. However, we decided to skip this step in our evaluation as the knowledge of all participants was insufficient for such analysis. These adaptations are related to Problems 1 and 2.

Additional uses and extensions of ATAM: To evaluate some of the qualities not evaluated in Phase 2b, we made use of certain steps in ATAM and extended these steps with techniques for the evaluation of the qualities. For the evaluation of the remaining qualities, we had to add additional steps and techniques to ATAM.

We *used* Phase 2a and Phase 3 of ATAM to evaluate the usability and acceptability architectural qualities of ERA. We considered the time required to introduce ERA to the stakeholders and the level of their understanding of the architecture as metrics for the achievement of this quality.

As it was not possible to address all domain stakeholders and obtain their agreement on the scope of ERA (see Problem 1), we concluded that completeness of ERA has to be evaluated beyond the scenario-based technique provided in ATAM. We *extended* ATAM with two additional techniques for the evaluation of the completeness of ERA. First, we used a reference model on e-contracting and reasoned whether the concepts in it were addressed in ERA. Second, we compared ERA to existing concrete e-contracting architectures and showed that ERA addresses the functionalities defined in these architectures. We could not evaluate the applicability and buildability qualities in any step in ATAM and had to *extend* it with additional techniques. To demonstrate the applicability of ERA to different contexts, we applied it for the analysis of existing concrete e-contracting architectures and for the design of hypothetical architectures in the sample domains that we selected in Phase 2a. In [6], the evaluation of the buildability quality is done through ATAM. However, in the case of ERA, many components support functionalities that are addressed only in recent research developments from different research domains and that implement complex, little tested (or even not defined) algorithms. We realized that a component might be easily buildable in one business context and very complex to build for another context. Certain domains make use of simple trading scenarios, while others involve complex interactions among companies for the establishment and enactment of a contract. A brainstorming session during Phase 2a of ATAM on the buildability quality of ERA could not be carried out, as none of the participants had detailed and up-to-date knowledge on the status quo of the research results for the components supporting complex functionalities. In order to present convincing evidence for the buildability of ERA, we performed a literature survey on the existing research results. This step required a substantial amount of time. The results from this step were a list of existing research and industry results that can be used as a basis for building some of the components and a list of "buildability risks" that exist due to the impossibility to estimate the buildability quality of some components for all business contexts.

Discussion on the evaluation process: ERA evolved substantially after its evaluation. Its structure, conceptual integrity, and functional completeness improved. The adaptations and extensions to ATAM that we used in our case allowed us to better evaluate our reference architecture for the identified required qualities. In contrast to the original ATAM process that has relatively fixed time duration, these additional activities required substantial time and resulted in a long-running evaluation process (around 3 months).

We concluded that the heterogeneity in knowledge and background of the participants in Phase 3 led to the inability of some of them to contribute to the evaluation process. Particular steps in ATAM were beyond the skills of all participants in this phase. We failed in involving a sufficient number of highly motivated, experienced, information technology knowledgeable, and visionary practitioners for Phase 3.

ERA has not been applied for the design of e-contracting systems yet. We are currently disseminating it to parties that may be interested in it. Its application for the design of concrete e-contracting architectures will give an indication for the quality of the architecture and thus for the quality of the evaluation process.

4.3 Generalization of the Approach

In this section, we generalize our findings from the evaluation of ERA. Our experience with the evaluation of ERA showed that though ATAM is not designed explicitly for the evaluation of reference architectures, its application may bring substantial improvements to a reference architecture. However, direct application of ATAM is not possible. A number of adaptations and extensions on ATAM are required for its successful application for the evaluation of reference architectures. That is why we think that a method for the evaluation of reference architectures may use ATAM with certain adaptations as a foundation and extend ATAM with a number of steps and techniques. Our discussion in Section 2 shows that due to the differences between PRAs and FRAs, the adaptations and extensions of ATAM will vary for the evaluation of PRAs and FRAs.

Usage of ATAM: ATAM is applied for the evaluation of system qualities like interoperability, modifiability, performance, conceptual integrity, etc. Scenarios are used for evaluation (partially) of the completeness quality. Furthermore, we suggest using the discussion meetings in ATAM to evaluate the level of understanding and acceptance of the architecture by the stakeholders (i.e., usability and acceptance qualities).

Adaptations of ATAM: For an evaluation of reference architectures, ATAM has to be adapted at two points, i.e., identification of stakeholders and scenario definition and prioritization. We suggest that evaluators adapt ATAM in the following ways:

- Define roles for the stakeholders from the domain and invite representatives for these roles that will participate in the evaluation process. In the case of PRAs, representatives from leading industry solutions are recommended for the evaluation sessions. Selection of a "good" set of representatives is the main challenge in this situation (i.e., stakeholders that are willing to collaborate and have common goals). In the case of FRAs, leading researchers should play a main role in Phase 2 of ATAM and experienced and interested in future developments business stakeholders in Phase 3. The identification and involvement of stakeholders who have the knowledge and the motivation to contribute to the evaluation of the FRA is a challenge in this situation.
- Select a number of contexts and define scenarios for these contexts. Prioritize scenarios within a concrete context, and merge the prioritized scenarios in a general set of scenarios.

Extensions of ATAM: ATAM needs complementary activities and techniques for evaluation of certain architecture qualities. In our experience, we have faced the need to extend ATAM for the evaluation of three architecture qualities, i.e., completeness (besides scenario-based evaluation), applicability, and buildability. As for many PRAs and FRAs these qualities will be of importance, next, we present the activities and techniques that we propose as extensions of ATAM.

- To thoroughly evaluate completeness, we suggest the usage of existing, "best-practice", concrete architectures and comparing their functionalities to the functionalities of the reference architecture. However, in the case of FRAs, there might be too few (or none at all) relevant concrete architectures. That is why, for FRAs, we suggest also the usage of a recognized reference model and analysis of the architecture for its support. This reference model has to be different from any reference model used in the design of the reference architecture.
- To evaluate the applicability of FRAs and PRAs, we propose the definition of a number of concrete architectures for specific contexts based on the reference architecture and an evaluation of the applicability of the reference architecture in these contexts. For PRAs (and when possible for FRAs), existing concrete architectures in specific contexts can be analyzed directly from the perspective of the reference architecture.
- To evaluate the buildability quality, a number of concrete contexts have to be selected in which the buildability of components is discussed. The contexts should be selected on the basis of the complexity of the required system functionalities. In the case of FRAs, evaluators should address not only existing technology but also existing research results (prototypes and theoretical developments) and provide examples about how these can be used or adapted to support the functionalities defined in the reference architecture.

5 Conclusions

In this paper, we distinguish between two types of reference architectures, i.e., Practice Reference Architectures (PRAs) and Futuristic Reference Architectures (FRAs). We compare reference architectures to concrete architectures and show that the specific characteristics of reference architectures do not allow existing methods for the evaluation of concrete architectures to be used straightforwardly for the evaluation of reference architectures. We share our experiences and conclusions from a case on the evaluation of a FRA. Based on our experiences from this case, we outline a number of adaptations and extensions that in our opinion must be applied on the existing evaluation method ATAM for the evaluation of reference architectures.

Currently, we are involved in the evaluation of another FRA called e-Sourcing Reference Architecture (eSRA) [18]. The first results from its evaluation confirmed our findings regarding the differences between concrete and reference architectures. We also faced the problems discussed in this paper in using ATAM. We currently use the case of the evaluation of eSRA to further elaborate our approach for the evaluation of reference architectures.

As future work, we aim at defining a detailed method for the evaluation of reference architectures. To reach this goal, a number of points in our approach require further attention. Guidelines for the identification and involvement of stakeholders in the cases of PRAs and FRAs must be elaborated. We shall base our future work in this direction on existing literature on stakeholder analysis, e.g., [17]. Definition and prioritization of scenarios is paramount for the approach but is currently not a precisely defined process. Guidelines for the selection of contexts are required. Our experiences showed that different criteria for the selection of contexts can be applied in the different evaluation steps. This indicates that different guidelines for the selection of contexts in the different evaluation steps should be defined. Metrics for the evaluation techniques suggested by us must be defined as well. The specific characteristics of PRAs and FRAs indicate that a method for the evaluation of reference architectures has to recognize the differences between them and has to address these differences in separate ways at certain points. Our current conclusions are based on the evaluation of FRAs. In our future work, we plan to test our findings for the evaluation of PRAs as well.

References

1. Angelov, S.: Foundations of B2B Electronic Contracting, PhD Thesis. Eindhoven University of Technology, Eindhoven (2006)
2. Angelov, S.: Defining E-Contracting and Measuring its Significance. In: Post-Conference Workshop at the 4th Annual Contract Management Conference, Dubai. Institute for International Research (2007)
3. Angelov, S.: Evaluation of the E-Contracting Reference Architecture. Technical report, Beta Working Paper, WP 225, Eindhoven University of Technology (2007)
4. Angelov, S., Grefen, P.: An E-contracting Reference Architecture. Journal of Systems and Software (to appear) (February 26, 2008)

 5. Babar, M., Gorton, I.: Comparison of Scenario-Based Software Architecture Evaluation Methods. In: 11th Asia-Pacific Software Engineering Conference (APSEC 2004), pp. 600–607. IEEE Computer Society, Washington (2004)
 6. Bass, L., Clements, P., Kazman, R.: Software Architecture in Practice, 2nd edn. Addison-Wesley Professional, Reading (2003)
 7. Bengtsson, P., Bosch, J.: Scenario-Based Software Architecture Reengineering. In: Fifth International Conference on Software Reuse, 1998, Victoria, Canada, pp. 308–317 (1998)
 8. Clements, P., Kazman, R., Klein, M.: Evaluating Software Architectures: Methods and Case Studies. Addison-Wesley Professional, Reading (2002)
 9. Clements, P., Northrop, L.: Software Product Lines: Practices and Patterns. Addison-Wesley Professional, Reading (2001)
10. Dobrica, L., Niemelä, E.: A Survey on Software Architecture Analysis Methods. IEEE Transactions on Software Engineering 28(7), 638–653 (2002)
11. Dolan, T.: Architecture Assessment of Information-System Families - A Practical Perspective, PhD Thesis. Eindhoven University of Technology, Eindhoven (2001)
12. Ferrara, F.: The Standard Healthcare Information Systems Architecture and the DHE middleware. International Journal of Medical Informatics 52(1), 39–51 (1998)
13. Grefen, P., Remmerts de Vries, R.: A Reference Architecture for Workflow Management Systems. Data & Knowledge Engineering 27(1), 31–57 (1998)
14. Hollingsworth, D.: The Workflow Reference Model. Technical report, Workflow Management Coalition Documents, TC00-1003, Workflow Management Coalition (1995)
15. Bontempo, C., Zagelow, G.: The IBM Data Warehouse Architecture. Communications of the ACM 41(9), 38–48 (1998)
16. Ionita, M., Hammer, D., Obbink, H.: Scenario-Based Software Architecture Evaluation Methods: An Overview. In: Workshop on Methods and Techniques for Software Architecture Review and Assessment at the International Conference on Software Engineering, Orlando, Florida, USA (2002)
17. Kusters, R., Solingen, R., Trienekens, J.: Identifying Embedded Software Quality: Two Approaches. Quality and Reliability Engineering International 15(6), 485–492 (1999)
18. Norta, A.: Exploring Dynamic Inter-Organizational Business Process Collaboration, PhD Thesis. Eindhoven University of Technology, Eindhoven (2007)
19. Reed, P.: Reference Architecture: The Best of Best Practices (2002),
    http://www.ibm.com/developerworks/rational/library/2774.html
20. Rozanski, N., Woods, E.: Software Systems Architecture: Working With Stakeholders Using Viewpoints and Perspectives. Addison-Wesley Professional, Reading (2005)
21. Shaw, M., Garlan, D.: Software Architecture: Perspectives on an Emerging Discipline. Prentice-Hall, Englewood Cliffs (1996)
22. Wu, H.: A Reference Architecture for Adaptive Hypermedia Applications, PhD Thesis. Eindhoven University of Technology, Eindhoven (2002)
23. Zimmermann, H.: OSI Reference Model - the ISO Model of Architecture for Open Systems Interconnection. IEEE Transactions on Communications 28(4), 425–432 (1980)

On the Role of Architectural Design Decisions in Software Product Line Engineering

Rafael Capilla[1] and Muhammad Ali Babar[2]

[1] Universidad Rey Juan Carlos, Spain
rafael.capilla@urjc.es
[2] LERO, UL, Ireland
malibaba@lero.ie

Abstract. An increased attention to documenting architectural design decisions and their rationale has resulted in several approaches and prototype tools for capturing and managing architectural knowledge. However, most of them are focused on architecting single products and little attention has been paid to include design decisions in the context of product line architectures. This paper reports our work on analyzing the existing work on architectural design decisions for the specific needs of software product line engineering. We have studied two existing tools for managing design decisions to identify the changes required in these tools for supporting product line specific requirements. Based on this study, we report the extensions required in the data models of the tools and propose a unified data model to guide the tool development research for supporting explicitly the relationships between design decisions and variability models for software product line engineering.

1 Introduction

Early in the nineties, Perry and Wolf emphasized the importance of Design Rationale (DR) in Software Architecture (SA) [23]. To date, the traditional approaches to documenting software architectures have been mainly based on the description of architecture views that reflect the interest of different stakeholders [11] [19] [24], but little attention has been paid to capturing and managing the rationale for key design decisions. The need to reduce the maintenance effort and to avoid architecture erosion because decisions are never recorded requires them to be captured.

Many claims have been made about the problems caused when design decisions are not explicitly documented [28], as they constitute a clear way to mitigate the effort required in understanding the architecture of a system when the experts or the creators of the architecture are no longer available. Bosch pinpoints [7] that *we do not view a software architecture as a set of components and connectors, but rather as the composition of a set of architectural design decisions*". This idea, also stated in [11], claims for methods and techniques to enable the representation and capture of architectural design decisions in parallel with their architectures. In order to bridge the traditional gap between requirements and designs, a "new" architecture view so-called the "decision view", is proposed in [12], which considers design decisions as a crosscutting information with respect to the other traditional architecture views that have to be documented explicitly.

R. Morrison, D. Balasubramaniam, and K. Falkner (Eds.): ECSA 2008, LNCS 5292, pp. 241–255, 2008.
© Springer-Verlag Berlin Heidelberg 2008

Other research works rely on the definition of specific templates for capturing and representing the knowledge that should be part of the description of a design decision. Some research efforts (such as reported in [20] [31]) have proposed extensive list of attributes for characterizing the design decisions while others [9] advocate the use of more flexible approaches based on a list of mandatory and optional attributes that can be tailored for different organizations and user's needs in order to reduce the effort spent during the knowledge capturing activity. Kruchten et al. [20] consider that Architectural Knowledge (AK) = Design Decisions + Design, and they use ontologies to describe both the decisions and the relationships between them. Since design decisions can bridge the gap between requirements and architectures and code, recording these relationships [32] can benefit maintenance and evolution processes, and help to understand the root causes of changes or to estimate change impact analysis. To date, only a few researchers have partially addressed using design decisions in the context of software product line engineering. We assert that more work is required to providing methodological and tooling support for capturing and managing architectural design decisions in the context of product line engineering. In this paper, we propose a model for characterizing architectural design decisions in software product lines and compare two existing tools for possible extension to explicitly link architectural design decisions with product line variability models.

The rest of the paper is structured as follows. Section 2 identifies product line specific features of design decisions and some approaches that explicitly consider design decisions in product line practices. Section 3 discusses our approach to relate architectural design decisions to product line features. Section 4 discusses how existing tools for managing design decisions can support the specific needs of product lines. Section 5 describes a unified data model to guide the research on tooling support for design decisions for product line architectures. Section 6 discusses the related work and Section 7 describes our future direction for this line of research.

2 Product Line Engineering Features

Software Product Line Engineering (SPLE) has emerged as a successful mode of developing software. SPLE aims to create a family of related products based on a single architecture that can be tailored to meet the requirements of different products. This is achieved through the identification of commonalities and variations among the different systems of a given family which are represented in a product line architecture (PLA). The required variability can be realized using different variability realization techniques such as reported in [27]. A PLA has several unique features that allow the creation of multiple products by means of derivation techniques [6]. Here we discuss some of the key characteristics of PLA practices. Our discussion is focused only on those issues of SPLE that are closely related to the architecture development practices.

- **Variability modelling:** Product lines rely on the description of a set of common and variable characteristics of systems, and variability modelling deals with the representation of the common and variable aspects through a set of interrelated variation points and variants. Variability modelling is a challenging activity that needs suitable tooling support for managing the hundreds of variation points in complex systems. A major weaknesses of one of the most widely used modelling languages like UML, is that all variability concerns are difficult to be represented in a UML model. For instance, the relationships and constraints between variation points and variants that can be represented in a FODA tree [18] are hardly to be described in a UML diagram. Only the OCL (Object Constraint Language) combined with UML provides better support. A variability model is a decision model in which variation points and their variants have to be selected and instantiated for configuring a particular product.

- **Binding time:** This mechanism is used to delay design decisions as late as possible. The realization of variability can also be achieved through different binding times, such as; compilation, integration, deployment, or runtime. Different techniques can be used to resolve the binding time [15] of a particular software product. In general, binding times are not described in UML architecture models and they are documented separately from architectural designs.

- **Variability dependencies and product constraints:** Variation points and variants may depend on other variation points. Therefore, the selection of a certain variation point or variant may depend on a previous selection. These dependencies are usually represented in the variability model [17] [22]. Dependency models have a great impact on traceability as they provide viable paths to traverse from feature models to products and vice-versa. Frequently, dependencies are used to delimit the scope and the number of products during product configuration and mostly driven by economic and business factors. For instance, more complex rules like *if-then-else* conditions can be defined using a logic formula to specify product constraints. Such rules often crosscut variability models. Because product lines are market-driven, the domain scoping activity aims to define the number and types of products to be delivered with specific constraints. Hence, when making design decisions to produce a particular product, all the constraints should be resolved to avoid the selection of incompatible variation points that may lead to incompatible products.

- **Common and specific requirements:** Traditional software development use different types of requirements to motivate the design decisions made in the design phase. In product lines, only a subset of these requirements are common, whilst product specific requirements motivate the decisions to characterize each product by means of variation points defined in the modelling phase.

2.1 Reasoning Models in Product Lines Approaches

The majority of the approaches that try to capture design decisions alongside architectures do not consider the specificities of product lines. Only some proposals attempt to do this and they try to introducing reasoning in variability models. For instance, in [5] the authors describe a tool for supporting the analysis of feature models using an automatic reasoning mechanism to deal with extra functional features, like for instance quality aspects. This reasoning mechanism can be used to ask questions, such as: which is the number of potential products in a given feature model? Dhungana et al. [13] state the difficulty to transfer general architectural knowledge from tacit to an explicit form understandable by the users, and map this concept to product line variability models in which features have to be linked to architectural artifacts. More specifically, Dhungana et al. [14] perceive decisions as variation points for asset composition. These decisions are organized hierarchically and they become relevant if they are made in a certain order. The consequences of a decisions are expressed a logical dependencies. Decisions are represented in a decision model which only describes the need, the scope, and the constraints, but the same as in [5] no additional information about the rationale or the impact of the decision is supported. In [30], the authors address how to represent and document design decisions in product lines that follow a compositional approach to derive the final products. This composition is supported by the AHEAD tool suite [4], where product line features are used as building blocks of systems. In [30], decisions are documented as XML artifacts during the synthesis of the architecture. In their approach, text descriptions for understanding the decisions are included with product line assets. Finally, none of the tools analyzed in [10] for modeling and managing product line variability models considers the description of architectural design decisions as first class entities. In most cases, the tools only focus on how to deal with feature models or in product derivation tasks.

3   Design Decisions for Product Line Architectures

Because almost all the approaches described in section 2 suffer from the lack of support from explicit description of the decisions and their underlying reasons that accomplish the selection of variation points and variants in a product line, this section presents our attempt to link both concepts as a way to include the rationale used in architectural decisions with the definition and selection of variation points in the PLA. Hence, we propose to associate the concept of design decision with variability models in order to enrich the reasoning activity that takes place during product line modeling and derivation phases. We have also designed a general model that can be instantiated for building tool to support the proposed approach to incorporating the design decisions into variability models. Following are the elements of the proposed model.

- **Design decisions and variability modeling:** A variability model constitutes a decision model in which variation points and variants have to be resolved in order to achieve a specific product configuration. From our view, the definition of these variations should be considered fine grained decisions (as opposed to coarse grained decisions based on design patterns and architectural styles). Different levels of granularity in the decisions can be considered, but from an architecture point of view, the main decisions are precisely made in the early stages of the design phase for the core architecture whereas variation points are introduced later to refine the classes of a product line architecture. In our approach we propose a mapping between the design decisions that affect the definition or the selection of a variation point and variant in order to explain the reasons by which we arrived at a particular feature model.
- **Binding time:** The binding time should be understood in the traditional use of product lines, but the selection of a particular binding time should also be explained as a design decision. Hence, we believe that the binding time of a particular variation point should have a decision associated with it that explains

the realization of such variation point in the architecture. This binding time should not be confused with the time in which the decision is made, as all of them are defined at design time. We assume that the binding time of a set of related variation point should happen at the same moment. Otherwise, the realization of the variability will not be feasible.

- **Product constraints:** In the same way as we connect different decisions with specific relationships, we need to specify the links between variation points. Such links are usually defined by means of logical operators such as AND, OR, XOR, and NONE. More complex formulas can also be defined to support crosscutting relationships in the feature model or to include functional dependencies between features that usually happen during the execution of a system. These constraints delimit the scope of the products and may affect to previous decisions. From our viewpoint, a new design decision should document each product constraint to explain the rationale and the impact for such relationship in the variability model. Additionally, because one constraint may depend on a previous constraint in the variability model, the dependencies between design decisions could be also used to define the links between different product constraints and to avoid duplicate networks of dependencies.

- **Common and specific requirements:** In order to discriminate between requirements for a PLA and for a single product, we introduce a new attribute, to discriminate between common and specific requirements.

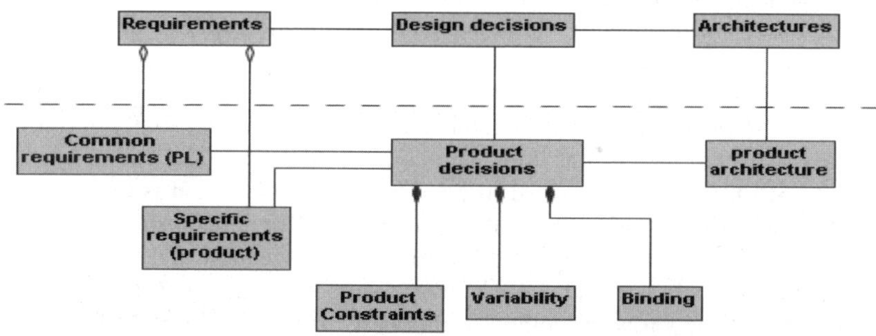

Fig. 1. A general model that maps the decisions to requirements and architectures and its corresponding relationships for product line architectures

The upper part of Figure 1 shows that design decisions are used to bridge the gap between requirements and architectures as requirements motivate the decisions that produce a particular architecture description. The lower part of the figure adds the additional entities that belong to SPLE. Common and specific product requirements motivate the decisions that lead to a concrete product architecture. These decisions are also design decisions but enhanced with some distinct features like decisions associates to: *product constraints, variability models, and binding time.* Similar traces between both parts of the figure provide a complete traceability among the entities. Our improvement in this general model is to map significant decisions to the product line variability model which need to be documented explicitly. We assert that this general model can be instantiated for building specific tool support.

4 Tool Support for Capturing Architectural Design Decisions

Having reviewed the existing variability management tools, we assert that none of them provide sufficient support for capturing and managing design decisions and the rationale that lead to the selection of any particular product line architecture or to a concrete variability model. Additionally, the research tools developed for managing architectural knowledge (such as Archium [16], AREL [29], ADDSS [8], and PAKME [3]) do not support product line features; neither do these tool support variability management. However, we believe that existing architectural knowledge management tools can easily be extended to support architectural decisions and their rationale in SPLE. In order to determine the requirements for extending the tools, we decided to analyze the data models of two architectural knowledge management tools (i.e., ADDSS and PAKME) we have developed. This Section provides brief descriptions of both tools and the level of support provided by them for SPLE.

4.1 Product-Line Support in ADDSS

ADDSS (Architecture Design Decision Support System [8] is a web-based tool for managing architectural design decisions (http://triana.escet.urjc.es/ADDSS). The tool supports an iterative process in which design decisions are captured along with their rationale and models. ADDSS supports basic dependencies between decisions and traceability between requirements, design decisions, and architectures. The chain of dependencies between decisions is documented explicitly for traceability purposes.

We have analyzed the current implementation of ADDSS to determine how it can support the SPLE features described in Section 3. Our conclusion is that in order to support the inclusion of variation points, variants and their relationships, the ADDSS data model can be easily extended to store such information and relate this with logical operators (such as AND, OR, XOR) to support product constraints and relationships between the variation points. Additionally, it is possible in ADDSS to associate each design decision to its respective variation points and variants, as a way to motivate and explain the definition or the selection of a particular variation point. However, relating parts of the variability model to a subset of the architecture is not possible because the current version of ADDSS cannot relate a set of design decisions to individual architectural parts. A complementary issue that needs to be addressed is to check the inconsistencies in the variability model to avoid incompatible product configurations. This should be implemented separately in order to ensure the integrity of the decision model for detecting unnecessary violations in the decisions when these are added, changed, or removed, but at present this feature is not supported yet. Also, including the binding time as an entity or attribute into the ADDSS data model should not be a problem, and the same stands for discriminating between common and specific requirements that are selected during the reasoning activity in the architecting process. We can also improve the documentation generated by the tool if we include the information belonging to the variability model of all product architectures.

4.2 Product-Line Support in PAKME

Process-centric Architecture Knowledge Management Environment, PAKME, is a web-based tool to support software architecture design, documentation and evaluation activities [3]. PAKME provides a knowledge repository, templates and features to capture, manage, and present architectural knowledge and design rationale. PAKME's knowledge repository is logically divided into two types of knowledge:

- **Generic:** such as general scenarios, quality attributes, design options; and
- **Project specific:** such as concrete scenarios, contextualized patterns, quality factors, architecture design decisions and rationale underpinning them.

Project-specific AK consists of the artefacts either instantiated from the generic knowledge or newly created during the software architecture process. Access to a repository of generic AK enables designers to use accumulated "wisdom" from different projects when devising or evaluating architecture decisions for projects in the same or similar domains. The project specific part of the repository captures and consolidates other AK artefacts and rationale such as concrete scenarios, design history, and findings of architecture evaluation. A project specific AK repository is also populated with knowledge drawn from an organisational repository, standard work products of the design process, logs of the deliberations and histories of documentation to build organisation's architecture design memory.

Though, PAKME has initially been developed to support the architecting activities for a single product, many of its artifacts (such as general scenarios, design options, and analysis models) can be used to support the activities for designing and evaluating PLAs. However, there needs to be certain changes required in the data model and interface for establishing and maintaining explicit relationships between different artifacts of a product specific architecture and PLAs. PAKME's data model also needs to be modified to accommodate the requirements of the solution proposed in Figure 1. Such changes can easily be accommodated as PAKME has successfully tailored to a specific domain and the experience showed such modifications are easy [1].

5 Design Rationale Support for Product Line Architectures

In order to assess the data models of PAKME and ADDSS for potential extension, we have used an illustrated example from the Intrada Product Family [25]. The objective of this assessment was to determine how variability, product constraints, and common and specific product requirements can be supported by both tools. We have identified the entities in both data models that support similar or completely different features in their respective tools. We have identified those entities that do not exist in either of the studied tools but required to support the architectural decisions in SPLE. Table 1 (i.e., Appendix 1) shows the entities associated concepts that are similar or equal in the studied tools as well as those which are not supported by either of the tool. The blue rows in Table 1 show the entities of PAKME not supported by ADDSS and light brown row identifies one feature of ADDSS not supported by PAKME).

5.1 A Unified Data Model for Architectural Design Decisions

Based on our analysis of the data models of ADDSS and PAKME, we have identified the minimum number of entities required to support architectural knowledge management by ADDSS and PAKME and left out other complementary entities that characterize concepts like quality attributes, quality factors, and findings included in PAKME's data model to support the software architecture evaluation activities. Table 2 (in Appendix 2) show the entities that comprise the proposed core data model to integrate the two tools for supporting architectural design decisions in SPLE. Figure 2 depicts the core data model using the UML class diagram notation.

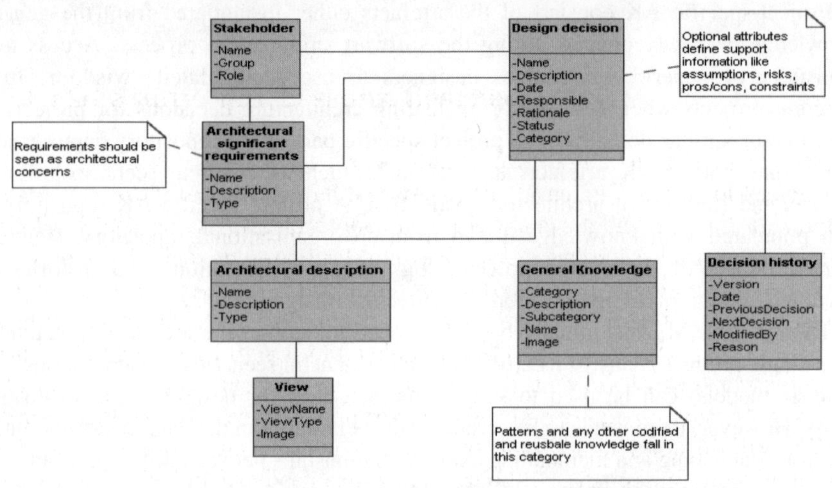

Fig. 2. Unified data model comprising the core entities that support architectural knowledge

Figure 2 shows that design decisions are related to architectures, requirements, and to the stakeholders that make the decision. Architecture descriptions are represented in terms of views, while design decisions comprise reusable chunks of knowledge like patterns and style. It should be noted that "rationale" of a decision is defined as an attribute in the proposed model, but from a higher level perspective, rationale is considered an entity in the ANSI/IEEE 1471-2000, currently under review. The data model support decision evolution by a specific entity, which records all the modifications and changes made to a particular decision. We have kept the data model simple and attributes of its entities as less as possible. However, the data model can easily be extended to support new features required for SPLE. In the next Section, we demonstrate how to extend the core model in Figure 2 to support the features of software product lines.

5.2 Extended Data Model to Support Product Line Features

We have extended the core data model characterizing architecture knowledge shown in Figure 2 to incorporate the features of SPLE mentioned in Section 3. We have refined the description given in Figure 1 to add the entities and attributes perceived necessary to link architectural design decisions to the product line variability model. The result of this customization is presented in Figure 3, which shows that we have added three different entities as well as some attributes to cater the new needs. One new entity captures the information representing the variations points, including a constraint rule that defines the logical relationship between the variants. In addition, a *category* attribute is used to perform a classification of different variation points that can be filtered for visualization purposes. This *variation point* decision is attached to the architectural design decision which explains and motivates the definition of a particular variation point.

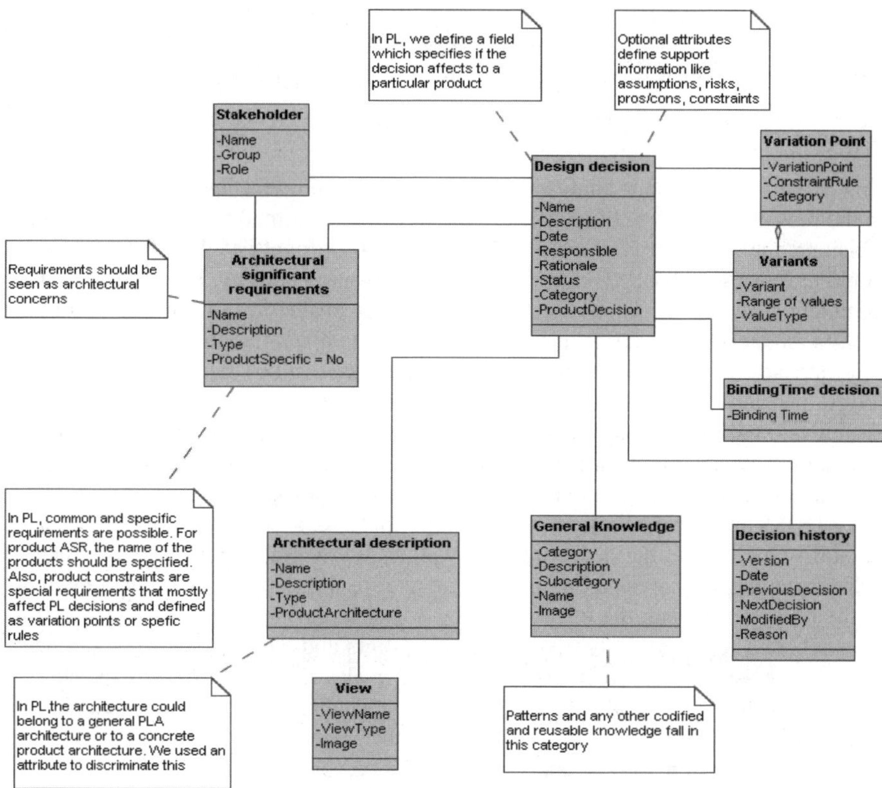

Fig. 3. Extended data model to incorporate product line feature in design decisions model

We took similar steps for incorporating the variants defined in the variability model. This fine-grained decision has also its corresponding architectural design decision which justifies the selection of particular variant in the architecture. A new *binding time decision* class was added to indicate the binding time of a particular variation point or variant, which is related to the architectural design decision that indicates why a binding time has been chosen, but also to the variant or variation point affected by such binding time. Therefore, we can achieve a fine-granularity to define different binding times for different variants and variation points. The *design decision* class has also a new attribute, *ProductDecision*, which defines if a design decision concerns to a product line decisions ("yes") or to a single architecture ("no"). Other two entities provide attributes for supporting additional product line features. The *architectural significant requirement* class uses an attribute ("ProductSpecific") to distinguish between common requirements for the entire line or for a single product, or a product specific requirement. Finally, the *architectural description* entity uses a new attribute to indicate if the description belongs to a PLA (this will imply that the variability model has been resolved and the decisions are made). The data model shown in Figure 3 does not consider multi-product lines (a product line composed of product lines). Neither does it represent the dependencies between design decisions as these are supported by PAKME and ADDSS as intermediate classes that relate one decision to others decisions. The same also applies to defining relationships between different variation points. These aspects have been left out to avoid cluttering.

5.3 Impact of Product Line Features in the Reasoning Activity

This Section presents our analysis of the impact that product line features may have on the reasoning process. In addition to the information aimed to support product line decisions, the process by which a variation point or variant is selected or configured would have some influence on the steps of the reasoning activity. For instance, typical architectural design decisions are selected after an evaluation of the best or optimal choices among several design options. However, the instantiation of a variation point only depends of the selection of their variants and values. Hence, no alternative design decisions are evaluated or stored for this case. Otherwise, the selection of a particular binding time may imply to consider and evaluate different binding time alternatives, which might not be the same for different architectures of subsystems. Additionally, the existing architectural knowledge management tools like PAKME and ADDSS must capture new relationships that are now established between the variability model and the decisions that explain such variability model. To make the decision capturing process more agile, these relationships should be defined internally by the tools to alleviate the effort spent by a user to define new links. Only in those cases where a relationship between variation points and variants has to be defined, a user must reason about such dependency and make it explicit when capturing the decision. Such effort can also be reduced if the dependency that models a relationship in the variability model also serves to model the dependency between the decisions attached to variation points and variants. Hence, product lines slightly modified the way in which dependencies are modeled with respect to single architecture, as the architect would define the relationship in the variability model and the tool implicitly uses that relationship to internally establish the relationships with its associated decisions.

6 Related Work

Recently, many researchers have emphasized the importance of treating architectural design decisions as first class entity, however, only a few have mentioned the use of design decisions in SPLE. In [2], the authors present a framework for representing design decisions in a SPL, which is structured as a design decision tree (DDT) where nodes represent design decisions and branches relate nodes to each other. Some of these nodes represent the variations in a product family. Lago and Vliet [21] show how to introduce assumptions in UML models representing architectures and variability concerns in SPLE. They present assumptions with feature models to show the influence of the assumptions on the features used to model variability. The work reported in [30] focuses on the reuse of design decisions in order to customize product line using composition techniques as a step-wise refinement for product derivation. Design decisions are captured in XML files that can be reused during the transformations needed to obtain a final product. Extensions to products and their design decisions can easily be traced by viewing the ways decisions extend architectures through successive refinements. The COVAMOF model for managing variability described in [26] is used to support the notion of architectural design decisions in a SPL. The authors map architectural concepts (including decisions) to COVAMOF concepts to demonstrate the feasibility of capturing architectural knowledge and link this to variability models by mapping similar concepts. All these approaches attempt to map conceptual entities related to architectural design decisions to product line variability models and even introduce some basic notation to explain the selection of the variation points, but all of them lack detailed guidance on how to model and explicitly represent the relationships between design decisions and a product line variability model. Though, some of these approaches use existing PL infrastructure to add information about design rationale, they do not provide explicit data model and conceptual guidance about extending tools to relate the product line features with decision models. These are some of the shortcoming of the existing approaches to describing architectural decisions and variability modeling in SPLE that has been addressed by the work reported in this paper. We believe that the presented data model can provide sufficient guidance to extend the current tools or develop new ones to support explicit relationships between architectural design decisions and variability models along with rationale for those decisions.

7 Conclusions

This paper presents the continuation of our efforts in integrating two similar tools for capturing and documenting architectural design decisions. Because there is a lack of specific support for product line architecture decisions, we have merged the data models of both tools in order to distill a common data model. The proposed unified model supports the decisions made in a product line context in order to explain the decisions made in variability models. Thus, thriving research area provides the necessary infrastructure for systematically and rigorously incorporating the notion of design decisions and their rationale in designing and maintaining PLAs. Our work identifies the characteristics of architecture design decisions in the context of SPLE. From the common model based on the data models of two architectural knowledge management tools, we have observed that it is not very difficult to incorporate the decisions made in a variability model to support the specificities of product lines. However, accommodating this new information may result in a large number of medium-size or fine grained decisions. Based on our research on the role of architectural design decisions in SPLE and providing appropriate tool support, we believe that the same dependencies defined for the architectural design decisions can be used to define the relationships in the variability model in order avoid introducing duplicate dependency links. Additionally, supporting common and specific requirements is also necessary to distinguish those decisions that are specific to a single product. For future work in this line of research, we intend to build a web-based tool by integrating ADDSS and PAKME's features and extending them in order to support new ones based on the proposed unified data model and test the new capabilities in a product line environment.

Acknowledgements

Ali Babar's work is supported by Science Foundation Ireland under grant number 03/CE2/I303-1. The work of Rafael Capilla is partially funded by the PILOH project of the Spanish Ministry of Education and Research programme under grant number URJC-CM-2006-CET-0603.

References

1. Ali-Babar, M., Northway, A., Gorton, I., Heurer, P., Nguyen, T.: Introducing Tool Support for Managing Architectural Knowledge: An Experience Report. In: Proceedings of the 15th IEEE International Conference on Engineering Computer-Based Systems, Belfast, Northern Ireland (2008)
2. Alonso, A., León, G., Dueñas, J.C.: Framework for Documenting Design Decisions in product Families Development. In: ICECSS, pp. 206–211. IEEE CS, Los Alamitos (1997)
3. Babar, M.A., Gorton, I.: A Tool for Managing Software Architecture Knowledge. In: Proceedings of the 2nd Workshop on Sharing and Reusing Architectural Knowledge, ICSE Workshops (2007)
4. Batory, D.S., Sarvela, J.N., Rauschmayer, A.: Scaling Step-Wise Refinement. IEEE Transanctions on Software Engineering 30(6), 355–371 (2004)
5. Benavides, D., Trinidad, P., Ruiz Cortés, A.: Automated Reasoning on Feature Models. In: Pastor, Ó., Falcão e Cunha, J. (eds.) CAiSE 2005. LNCS, vol. 3520, pp. 491–503. Springer, Heidelberg (2005)
6. Bosch, J.: Design and Use of Software Architectures. Addison-Wesley, Reading (2000)
7. Bosch, J.: Software Architecture: The Next Step. In: Oquendo, F., Warboys, B.C., Morrison, R. (eds.) EWSA 2004. LNCS, vol. 3047, pp. 194–199. Springer, Heidelberg (2004)
8. Capilla, R., Nava, F., Pérez, S., Dueñas, J.C.: A Web-based Tool for Managing Architectural Design Decisions. In: Proceedings of the Workshop on Sharing and Reusing Architectural Knowledge. ACM Digital Library, Software Engineering Notes, vol. 31(5)
9. Capilla, R., Nava, F., Dueñas, J.C.: Modeling and Documenting the Evolution of Architectural Design Decisions. In: Proceedings of the 2nd Workshop on Sharing and Reusing Architectural Knowledge, ICSE Workshops (2007)
10. Capilla, R., Sánchez, A., Dueñas, J.C.: An Analysis of Variability Modelling and Management Tools for Product Line Development. In: Proceedings of the Software and Services Variability Management Workshop – Concept Models and Tools. Helsinki University of Technology Software Business and Engineering Institut, Helsinki, Finland, HUT-SoberIT-A3, pp. 32–47 (2007) ISBN: 978-951-22-8747-5

11. Clements, P., Bachman, F., Bass, L., Garlan, D., Ivers, J., Little, R., Nord, R., Stafford, J.: Documenting Software Architectures. Views and Beyond. Addison-Wesley, Reading (2003)
12. Dueñas, J.C., Capilla, R.: The Decision View of Software Architecture. In: Oquendo, F., Warboys, B.C., Morrison, R. (eds.) EWSA 2004. LNCS, vol. 3047, pp. 222–230. Springer, Heidelberg (2004)
13. Dhungana, R.R.D., Grünbacher, P., Prähofer, H., Federspiel, C., Lehner, K.: Architectural Knowledge in Product Line Engineering: An Industrial Case Study. In: Euromicro Conference on Software Engineering and Advanced Applications, pp. 186–197 (2006)
14. Dhungana, D., Grünbacher, P., Rabiser, R.: DecisionKing: A Flexible and Extensible Tool for Integrated Variability Model. In: Proceedings of the 1st Workshop on Variability Modelling of Software-intensive Systems (VAMOS), LERO, UL, Ireland (2007)
15. Fritsch, C., Lehn, A., Strohm, T.: Evaluating Variability Implementation Mechanisms. In: Procs. of International Workshop on Product Line Engineering (PLEES 2002), Technical Report at Fraunhofer IESE (No. 056.02/E), pp. 59-64 (2002)
16. Jansen, A., Bosch, J.: Software Architecture as a Set of Architectural Design Decisions. In: 5th IEEE/IFIP Working Conference on Software Architecture, pp. 109–118 (2005)
17. Jaring, M., Bosch, J.: Variability Dependencies in Product Family Engineering. In: van der Linden, F.J. (ed.) PFE 2003. LNCS, vol. 3014, pp. 81–97. Springer, Heidelberg (2004)
18. Kang, K.C., Cohen, S., Hess, J.A., Novak, W.E., Peterson, A.S.: Featured-Oriented Domain Analysis (FODA) Feasibility Study. Technical Report, CMU/SEI-90-TR-21 ESD-90-TR-22, Software Engineering Institute, Carnegie Mellon University, Pittsburgh (1990)
19. Kruchten, P.: Architectural Blueprints. The "4+1" View Model of Software Architecture. IEEE Software 12(6), 42–50 (1995)
20. Kruchten, P., Lago, P., van Vliet, H.: Building up and Reasoning About Architectural Knowledge. In: Hofmeister, C., Crnković, I., Reussner, R. (eds.) QoSA 2006. LNCS, vol. 4214, pp. 43–58. Springer, Heidelberg (2006)
21. Lago, P., van Vliet, H.: Explicit Assumptions Enrich Architectural Models. In: Inverardi, P., Jazayeri, M. (eds.) ICSE 2005. LNCS, vol. 4309, pp. 206–214. Springer, Heidelberg (2006)
22. Lee, K., Kang, K.C.: Feature Dependency Analysis for Product Line Component Design. In: Bosch, J., Krueger, C. (eds.) ICOIN 2004 and ICSR 2004. LNCS, vol. 3107, pp. 69–85. Springer, Heidelberg (2004)
23. Perry, D.E., Wolf, A.L.: Foundations for the Study of Software Architecture. Software Engineering Notes, ACM SIGSOFT, pp. 40–52 (October 1992)
24. Rozanski, N., Woods, E.: Software Systems Architecture: Working with Stakeholders Using viewpoints and Perspectives. Addison-Wesley, Reading (2005)
25. Sinemma, M., Deelstra, S., Nijhuis, J., Bosch, J.: COVAMOF: A Framework for Modeling Variability in Software Product Families. In: Nord, R.L. (ed.) SPLC 2004. LNCS, vol. 3154, pp. 197–213. Springer, Heidelberg (2004)
26. Sinemma, M., van der Ven, J.S., Deelstra, S.: Using Variability Modeling Principles to Capture Architectural Knowledge. In: 1st SHARK Workshop (2006)
27. Svahnberg, M., van Gurp, J., Bosch, J.: A Taxonomy of Variability Realization Techniques. Software Practice & Experience 35(8), 705–754 (2005)
28. Tang, A., Babar, M.A., Gorton, I., Han, J.A.: A Survey of the Use and Documentation of Architecture Design Rationale. In: 5th IEEE/IFIP Working Conference on Software Architecture (2005)
29. Tang, A., Jin, Y., Han, J.: A rationale-based architecture model for design traceability and reasoning. Journal of Systems and Software 80(6), 918–934
30. Trujillo, S., Azanza, M., Diaz, O., Capilla, R.: Exploring Extensibility of Architectural Design Decisions. In: Proceedings of the Workshop on Sharing and Reusing Architectural Knowledge and Design Intent (SHARK/ADI 2007), ICSE Workshops, Minneapolis, USA, May 2007. IEEE CS, Los Alamitos (2007)

31. Tyree, J., Akerman, A.: Architecture Decisions: Demystifying Architecture. IEEE Software 22(2), 19–27 (2005)
32. Wang, A., Sherdil, K., Madhavji, N.H.: ACCA: An Architecture-centric Concern Analysis Method. In: 5th IEEE/IFIP Working Conference on Software Architecture (2005)

Appendix 1: PAKME-ADDSS Data-Model Comparison

Table 1. Comparison of the entities supported in both PAKME and ADDSS data models

PAKME	PAKME description	ADDSS	ADDSS description	Matched
Stakeholder	People interested in the architecture process or product	Users	Stakeholders with different roles interested in architectures	Yes
Stakeholder Group	Define the project access rights	Permissions	Rights for each user type	Yes
Architectural significant requirements (ASR)	Are NFR (QA) Quality goals can be derived. An ASR must be satisfied by one or several design decisions	Requirements	Functional and non-functional requirements. Only the type, the number, and a text description is provided	Yes
Scenario	Is a refinement of ASR and are QA	NFR	A non-functional requirement	Partially through requirements
Quality factors	Are the factors a QA should match			Only quality attributes are supported
Findings	A description for the QA that meet a particular scenario			Not supported in ADDSS
Analysis Model	Is a reasoning framework that reasons about the effect of different tactics on QA scenarios			Not supported in ADDSS
Design Tactic	Is a design mechanism for achieving the desired level			Not supported in ADDSS
Pattern	Characterizes a design solution in a given context	Pattern	Describes a design solution. Patterns are classified by its type, description and an usage example	Yes
Effect of pattern	Defines the effect of the pattern on a particular QA			Not supported in ADDSS
Support Information	Captures the background information required to justify the choice of a decision for a particular scenario	Optional attributes	Optional attributes capture extra information	Partially supported
Architecture Decision	Is a high level decision that satisfies FR and NFR. There are	Design Decision	Captures the design decision and its rationale through a set	Yes

Table 1. (*continued*)

	dependencies between decisions.		of attributes. Basic dependencies can be defined but not the of the dependency	
Architecture Decision Rationale	Is the reason behind the architecture	Rationale	Is the reason behind the architecture	Yes
Design history	A history of decisions is supported	Version and responsible	Some attributes in ADDSS are used for the same goal	Partially supported
Alternative	Design decisions may be related to other design alternatives	Status and category attributes	ADDSS offers a category attribute to indicate if a decision is alternative design choice but also an status to know if the decisions has been approved or rejected	Yes
Architecture Description	Prescribes the architecture to be realized	Architecture	Provides the information about a particular architecture and a link to the views supported	Yes
Architectural View	Provides a description for architectural views with the images	View attribute	Describes the view of the architecture and provides a link to it	Yes
		Translation	Provides multilingual support	Not supported in PAKME

Appendix 2: Core Common Entities between PAKME and ADDSS

Table 2. Main common entities distilled from PAKME and ADDSS data models

Common entity	Entity description
Stakeholder	Are those persons interested in the architecture process or product
Architectural significant requirements	Functional and non functional architectural significant requirements drive the selected design decisions
General Knowledge	Characterizes a design solution in a given context, like patterns or styles
Design Decision	Is a high level design decision that explains the decisions and its underpinning rationale
Decision history	A history of decisions is supported
Architectural Description	Prescribes the architecture to be realized
View	Provides a description for architectural views with the images

Towards a Dependency Constraint Language to Manage Software Architectures

Ricardo Terra and Marco Tulio de Oliveira Valente

Institute of Informatics, PUC Minas, Brazil
`rterrabh@gmail.com,mtov@pucminas.br`

Abstract. This paper presents a dependency constraint language that allows software architects to restrict the spectrum of dependencies that can be presented in a given software system. The ultimate goal is to provide designers with means to define acceptable and unacceptable dependencies according to the planned system architecture. Once defined, such restrictions will be automatically enforced by a tool, thus avoiding silent erosions in the architecture. The paper also presents first results of applying the language in a Web-based system.

1 Introduction

Software architecture is usually defined as the set of design decisions that have impact on each aspect of the construction and evolution of large software systems. This includes how systems are structured into components and constraints on how components should interact [3,2]. Despite its unquestionable importance, the documented architecture of a system – if available at all – usually does not reflect its actual implementation. In practice, deviations from the planned architecture are usually common, due to unawareness by the developers part, conflicting requirements, technical difficulties etc [6]. More important, such deviations are usually not captured and resolved, leading to the phenomena known as architecture erosion and architectural drift [10].

This paper is centered on the observation that improper inter-module dependencies are one of the principal sources of architectural violations. For instance, suppose a strictly layered system $M_p, M_{p-1}, \ldots, M_0$ (where M_0 represents the module in the lowest level of the hierarchy). Therefore, in this system, M_i can only use services provided by module M_{i-1}, $i > 0$. Any system change that violates this rule is, in fact, undermining its planned architecture. As another example, suppose a web-system that includes a controller module C and a module P that encapsulates persistence services. Clearly in this system, C is the only module that can handle HTTP requests and responses (using servlets or another similar technology). In the same way, P is the only module that can rely on the services provided by a persistence framework (such as Hibernate, for example).

Current mainstream programming languages support information hiding by the means of interfaces and visibility modifiers (such as `public`, `private`, and `protected`). However, they do not provide means to restrict inter-module dependencies. In practice, any public service provided by a module (or class) M

R. Morrison, D. Balasubramaniam, and K. Falkner (Eds.): ECSA 2008, LNCS 5292, pp. 256–263, 2008.

can be used by any other system module. In order to tackle this problem, we are working on a dependency constraint language that allows software architects to restrict the spectrum of dependencies that can be presented in a given software system. This language should provide designers with means to define acceptable and unacceptable dependencies according to the planned system architecture. Once defined, such restrictions can be automatically enforced by a tool integrated to common programming environments (such as Eclipse). Thus, our ultimate goal is to provide architectural conformance by construction, using a static, declarative dependency constraint language.

The remainder of this paper is organized as follows. Section 2 provides a preliminary description of the dependency language that we are designing. Section 3 illustrates the application of the proposed language in a simple case study. Section 4 discusses related work and Section 5 concludes.

2   Dependency Constraint Language

The main purpose of the proposed language is to support the definition of constraints between modules. In our notation, a module is just a set of classes. Suppose, for example, the following module definitions:

```
module A: org.foo.persistence.*
module B: org.foo.view.*, org.foo.model.Ticket, org.foo.model.Driver
```

Module A includes all public classes from the package `org.foo.persistence`. Module B includes all public classes from the package `org.foo.view` and classes `Ticket` and `Driver` from the package `org.foo.model`.

The language supports the definition of the following constraints:

- *Only classes from module A can depend on types defined in module B*, where the possible dependencies are as follows:

    - only A `can-access` B: only classes declared in module A can access non-private members of classes declared in module B. Access in this case means calling methods, reading or writing to fields.
    - only A `can-declare` B: only classes declared in module A can declare variables of types declared in module B.
    - only A `can-handle` B: only classes declared in module A can access and declare variables of types declared in module B. In other words, this is an abbreviation for only A `can-access, can-declare` B.
    - only A `can-create` B: only classes declared in module A can create objects of classes declared in module B.
    - only A `can-extend` B: only classes declared in module A can extend classes declared in module B.
    - only A `can-implement` B: only classes declared in module A can implement interfaces declared in module B.
    - only A `can-throw` B: only methods from classes declared in module A can throw exceptions declared in module B.

- *Classes declared in module A cannot depend on types defined in module B*, where the dependencies that can be forbidden are as follows:
  - A `cannot-access` B: no classes declared in module A can access non-private methods or fields of classes declared in module B.
  - A `cannot-declare` B: no classes declared in module A can declare variables of types declared in module B.
  - A `cannot-handle` B: no classes declared in module A can access or declare variables of types declared in module B.
  - A `cannot-create` B: no classes declared in module A can create objects of classes declared in module B.
  - A `cannot-extend` B: no classes declared in module A can extend classes declared in module B.
  - A `cannot-implement` B: no classes declared in module A can implement interfaces declared in module B.
  - A `cannot-throw` B: no methods from classes declared in module A can throw exceptions declared in module B.
- *Classes declared in module A must depend on types defined in module B*, where the dependencies that can be required are as follows:
  - A `must-extend` B: all classes declared in module A must extend a class declared in module B.
  - A `must-implement` B: all classes declared in module A must implement at least an interface declared in module B.

3   Case Study

In order to illustrate and motivate the need of a dependency language we have devised and implemented the main modules of an electronic government information system used by state's department of motor vehicles to handle traffic law violations, such as exceeding the speed limit, parking in an unauthorized area, driving without license etc. The devised system, called Traffic Ticket Online, has a web-based user interface that drivers can use to search for detailed information about their tickets and also paying tickets online. On the other hand, traffic authorities use the system to register tickets and perform associated operations.

Architecture: As described in Figure 1, the architecture of the system follows the Model-View-Controller (MVC) architectural pattern [2]. The Model layer contains Business Objects (BO), Data Transfer Objects (DTO), and Data Access Objects (DAO). Business Objects represent objects that encapsulate business rules and behavior. Data Transfer Objects represent domain entities such as drivers, tickets, law violations etc. Data Access Objects provide an abstract interface to the underlying persistence framework. Particularly, in the current system implementation we are using Hibernate for object/relational persistence. The Controller layer contains components that monitor user inputs, manipulate the Model, and update the View accordingly. The Traffic Ticket Online architecture prescribes that the Struts framework should be used by the Controller to handle HTTP requests. Such requests are then forwarded to a facade component, which provides a unique point

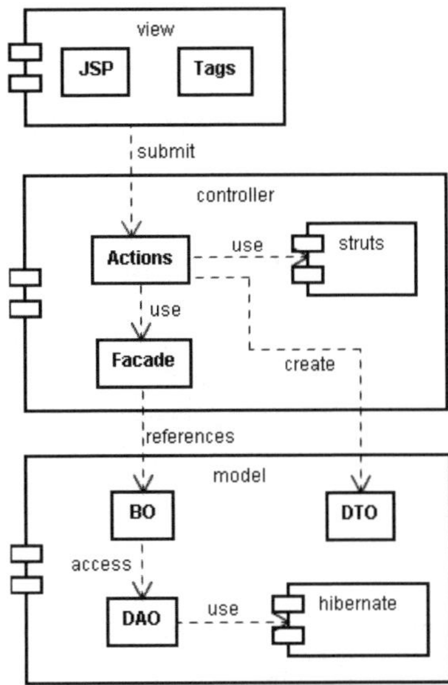

Fig. 1. Traffic Ticket Online Architecture

of access to the model. Finally, the View layer is composed by Java Server Pages (JSP). In summary, the architecture of the system relies on patterns (MVC, Factory, Facade, Business and Data-Access Objects etc) and frameworks and technologies (Hibernate, Struts, JSP etc) that are widely used nowadays when architecting web-based systems.

Constraints: Figure 2 illustrates how the proposed language can be used to regulate acceptable and unacceptable dependencies in the Traffic Ticket Online system. Initially, a sequence of `modules` definitions are used to group related classes (lines 1-12). It can be observed that the defined modules closely resemble the modules presented in the architectural view of the system depicted in Figure 1. This provides evidence that the proposed language can regulate dependencies between entities normally used by software architectures to describe their systems.

In lines 13-23, sequences of *only* constraints are defined. Essentially, such constraints are fundamental to guarantee that the original MVC architecture is preserved during the evolution of the system. For example, some of the constraints define that only classes from the Controller layer can handle (i.e. access and declare) types from the `Facade` module and from the Struts framework (line 16). This avoid for example the View layer to bypass the Controller and access directly the Model. Moreover, a specific constraint specifies that the `Facade` is the only module in the Controller layer that can handle types associated to business objects (line 18). In summary, the constraints express a key property about the dependencies directions in the MVC pattern: the Controller should depend on the Model, but the Model does not depend on the Controller. Instead, the Model only depends on the Hibernate persistence framework (line 20).

```
 1: %Modules
 2: module Tags:              com.tto.view.taglib.*
 3: module Controller:        com.tto.controller.action.*
 4: module ControllerExcp:    com.tto.controller.exception.*
 5: module Facade:            com.tto.controller.facade.*
 6: module BO:                com.tto.model.bo.*
 7: module DAO:               com.tto.model.dao.*
 8: module HibernateDAO:      com.tto.model.dao.hibernate.*
 9: module DTO:               com.tto.model.dto.*
10: module ModelExcp:         com.tto.model.exception.*
11: module Hibernate:         org.hibernate.*
12: module Struts:            com.opensymphony.xwork2.*

13: %Can constraints
14: only Controller can-create, can-declare DTO
15: only Controller can-access com.tto.service.FacadeService
16: only Controller can-handle Facade, Struts
17: only Controller, Facade can-throw ControllerExcp
18: only Facade, BO can-handle BO
19: only BO can-handle DAO
20: only HibernateDAO can-handle Hibernate
21: only com.tto.model.BOFactory can-create BO
22: only com.tto.model.DAOFactory can-create DAO
23: only BO, DAO can-throw ModelExcp

24: %Cannot constraints
25: Facade cannot-access DTO

26: %Must constraints
27: BO must-extend com.tto.model.bo.DefaultBO
28: Controller must-extend com.opensymphony.xwork2.ActionSupport
29: DAO must-implement com.tto.model.IDefaultDAO
30: DTO must-extend com.tto.dto.Persistent
31: com.tto.dto.Persistent must-implement java.io.Serializable
32: Facade must-implement com.tto.facade.IFacade
33: HibernateDAO must-extend
        com.tto.model.dao.hibernate.DefaultHibernateDAO
34: HibernateDAO must-implement DAO
35: Tags must-implement javax.servlet.jsp.tagext.JspTag
```

Fig. 2. Dependency Constraints Rules for the Traffic Ticket Online system

It is also important to mention the role of the different *can* relations types in the constraints of lines 13-25. For example, using the proposed constraint language, it was also possible to make explicit the difference between factories and clients of a given type. For example, there is a constraint that requires that BOs can only be created in the BOFactory class (line 21). Moreover, another constraint expresses that only the Facade can rely on BO's services, (but it cannot create such objects, as described). As another example, exceptions defined in the module `ControllerExcp` can only be throwed by methods in the `Controller` and `Facade` modules (line 17).

In lines 26-35, sequences of *must* constraints are defined. Such constraints are used to guarantee that all classes that integrate a given module implement or extend a given type. Usually, this type can be defined in another system module or can be provided by an external framework. As an example of the first case, each `BO` must extend an internal class named `DefaultBO` (line 27). As an example of the second case, each class in the `Tags` module must implement the `javax.servlet.jsp.tagext.JspTag` interface (line 35). Such constraints are important to guarantee that the system correctly reuses services provided by other classes and frameworks. In some way, they contribute to guide developers to use external frameworks correctly, as prescribed by the system architecture.

4   Related Work

Over the past decade, at least the following techniques have been proposed to deal with the architecture erosion and drift problems.

Constraint Languages: Sangal et al. have proposed the use of Dependency Structure Matrixes (DSM) to reveal existing dependencies and the underlying architectural pattern of complex software systems [11]. They also propose the use of design rules in order to highlight DSMs entries that violate the planned architecture. The dependency constraint language proposed in this paper is inspired in the design rules language. However, Sangal's language supports the definition of only two forms of relations between modules: `can-use` and `cannot-use`. On the other hand, our language allows the definition of a richer set of relations.

Architectural Recovery and Conformance Tools: Architectural recovering frameworks rely on reengineering technologies to extract high-level architectural models from existing systems [13,4,8]. The main challenge of such frameworks is recovering models that are similar to the ones sketched by developers, in terms of conciseness, abstraction level and architectural elements. Reflexion models (RM) aim to handle such problem by requiring developers to provide a high-level model of the planned system architecture and a declarative mapping between such model and the source code [9]. A RM-based tool (such as the SAVE Eclipse plug-in [5,6]) highlights convergence, divergence and absence relations between the high-level model and the source code. However, we believe that our approach supports a richer set of relations between modules than the language used in RMs. Moreover, our language is designed to foster architecture conformance by construction, i.e. using our language modifications that violate the planned architecture are detected soon after they are implemented in the source code.

Architectural Description Languages (ADL): ADLs represent another alternative to enforce architectural conformance by construction [7]. Such languages allow developers to express the architectural behavior and software systems structure in an abstract, declarative language. Code generation tools can then be used to map architectural descriptions to source code in a given programming language. However, such approaches normally require the use of specific architecture-based development tools and compilers, in order to keep the generated code synchronized with the architectural specification. A variant of this approach advocates the extension of current programming languages with architectural modeling constructs, which in practice demand developers to dominate a completely new programming language [1]. Our approach tackles this problem proposing a simple and declarative language to define dependencies constraints between modules. Stafford and Wolf have proposed a dependence analysis technique for use with ADLs [12]. Therefore, their main objective is to support architectural conformance at the ADL-level, i.e. the proposed technique does not require the availability of the system source code.

5   Conclusions and Future Work

Our research is centered on three hypotheses: (i) that improper inter-module dependencies are an important source of architectural violations; (ii) that a small, declarative dependency constraint language as the one presented in the paper can be employed to detect many of such violations; (iii) that such language can be integrated with a small overhead to the common edit/compile/run cycle performed by developers when building software systems with modern IDEs, thus enforcing architecture conformance by construction.

The Traffic Ticket Online system presented in Section 3 has provided us with encouraging feedback about the application of our dependency language. However, in order to provide more robust arguments that can support the first two hypotheses mentioned above we are starting to apply the proposed language to a human resource management system, used by the Brazilian Federal Government to handle information about public employees. Previous versions of this system are accessible from a CVS repository, which will allow us to apply our dependency language to several of such versions. The ultimate goal is to demonstrate that the proposed language could have been used to prevent important violations perpetrated to the original system architecture.

Our initial plan is starting the second case study by first defining the dependency constraints of the evaluated system. Next, we will check such constraints manually, i.e. our plan is starting the implementation of a tool that can check the proposed constraint language only after finishing this second case study. The reason is that we believe that the study will help us to improve the language, possibly suggesting new kinds of dependencies not supported by its initial version.

References

1. Aldrich, J., Chambers, C., Notkin, D.: ArchJava: connecting software architecture to implementation. In: 22nd International Conference on Software Engineering, pp. 187–197 (2002)
2. Fowler, M.: Patterns of Enterprise Application Architecture. Addison-Wesley, Reading (2002)

3. Garlan, D., Shaw, M.: Software Architecture Perspectives on an Emerging Discipline. Prentice-Hall, Englewood Cliffs (1996)
4. Kazman, R., Carrière, S.J.: Playing detective: Reconstructing software architecture from available evidence. Automated Software Engineering 6(2), 107–138 (1999)
5. Knodel, J., Muthig, D., Naab, M., Lindvall, M.: Static evaluation of software architectures. In: 10th European Conference on Software Maintenance and Reengineering, pp. 279–294 (2006)
6. Knodel, J., Popescu, D.: A comparison of static architecture compliance checking approaches. In: IEEE/IFIP Working Conference on Software Architecture, p. 12 (2007)
7. Medvidovic, N., Taylor, R.N.: A classification and comparison framework for software architecture description languages. IEEE Transactions on Software Engineering 26(1), 70–93 (2000)
8. Muller, H.A., Klashinsky, K.: Rigi a system for programming-in-the-large. In: International Conference on Software Engineering, pp. 80–87 (1988)
9. Murphy, G.C., Notkin, D., Sullivan, K.J.: Software reflexion models: Bridging the gap between source and high-level models. In: SIGSOFT Symposium on Foundations of Software Engineering, pp. 18–28 (1995)
10. Perry, D.E., Wolf, A.L.: Foundations for the study of software architecture. Software Engineering Notes 17(4), 40–52 (1992)
11. Sangal, N., Jordan, E., Sinha, V., Jackson, D.: Using dependency models to manage complex software architecture. In: 20th Conference on Object-Oriented Programming, Systems, Languages, and Applications, pp. 167–176 (2005)
12. Stafford, J.A., Wolf, A.L.: Architecture-level dependence analysis for software systems. International Journal of Software Engineering and Knowledge Engineering 11(4), 431–451 (2001)
13. Yan, H., Garlan, D., Schmerl, B.R., Aldrich, J., Kazman, R.: DiscoTect: A system for discovering architectures from running systems. In: 26th International Conference on Software Engineering, pp. 470–479 (2004)

Automating Architecture Trade-Off Decision Making through a Complex Multi-attribute Decision Process

Majid Makki, Ebrahim Bagheri, and Ali A. Ghorbani

Faculty of Computer Science,
University of New Brunswick, Fredericton, Canada
{majid.makki,e.bagheri,ghorbani}@unb.ca

Abstract. A typical software architecture design process requires the architects to make various trade-off architecture decisions. The architects need to consider different possibilities and combinations of tactics and patterns to satisfy the elicited quality scenarios of the intended software system, some of which may be conflicting or inconsistent in nature. The formation of the correct composition of these elements of architecture decisions for the satisfaction of the quality scenarios can be considered an important art of the architect; however, in cases where the architect is dealing with multiple stakeholders with inconsistent preferences, this can be an awkward task. In this paper, we formalize this process as a complex multi-attribute decision making procedure within the Attribute Driven Design methodology. In such a context, we are able to incrementally elicit the communal preferences of the stakeholders with regards to the available quality scenarios and hence assist the software architect in methodically making the architecture decisions with the highest expected utility for the stakeholders. We will also introduce our implementation of a decision support system, which embodies the methods proposed in this paper, along with a case study.

1 Introduction

It is commonly accepted that quality and functional requirements are orthogonal in nature. The functional requirements of a software system could be achieved even without considering the notion of software architecture; therefore, the main focus of software architecture is on the satisfaction of quality requirements such as modifiability, availability, and performance. In addition, quality attributes of a software system need to be considered collectively and an isolated analysis of those attributes may not result in a comprehensive solution. For instance, Bass et al point out that the full satisfaction of security and availability measures is not simultaneously achievable. Better stated, active redundancy is a reasonable architecture tactic for elevating the level of availability of a software system; however, this may increase the vulnerability of the system [2].

The Attribute Driven Design (ADD) method is a recursive decomposition process aiming to address the aforementioned issue where at each stage a subset

R. Morrison, D. Balasubramaniam, and K. Falkner (Eds.): ECSA 2008, LNCS 5292, pp. 264–272, 2008.

of the quality scenarios that need to be satisfied are chosen and some architecture decisions, in terms of applying appropriate tactics or patterns, are made [3]. On the other hand, the importance of acquisition processes and management of uncertainties associated with the requirements and technical solutions have been previously mentioned in [4]. Even though, the formality of the ADD method assists the architects in effectively designing the architecture, the success of the decision making process involved in each iteration of ADD is highly dependent on the ability of the architect to interact with and elicit stakeholders' preferences over the quality scenarios.

In their recent critical analysis of the software architecture domain, Shaw and Clements have put forth several intriguing ideas that need to be addressed [10]. There, the development of practical and sophisticated automated architecture design assistants that can aid the architects in exploring the relationship between architectural design decisions and quality attributes is considered to be important. In an early attempt, a rule-based expert system called ArchE has been developed at SEI-CMU that serves as a software architecture design assistant by incorporating a body of knowledge about how quality requirements can be achieved using different architecture patterns and tactics [1]. The required input of this tool is a set of quality requirements (limited to performance and modifiability at this stage) and the output is the architecture design for the given requirements.

Experience shows that different stakeholders may prefer dissimilar quality requirements [2], which will impose various design constraints that can be inconsistent or conflicting in practice. In this paper, we take a more stakeholder-centric approach to architecture trade-off decision making in which the conflicting stakeholders' preferences over the quality requirements are incrementally elicited through a utility elicitation procedure. The architecture decision with the highest expected utility (based on the elicited utilities of the outcome of each architecture decision for the stakeholders) would be suggested as an optimal architecture decision in each round.

2 ADD+: An Extension to ADD

In the ADD method, it is assumed that all of the quality requirements of the system have been elicited and in each round, the architect is responsible for choosing a subset of the concrete quality scenarios that need to be satisfied at that stage. An architect may struggle with two main issues in this approach:

1. Stakeholders may have dissimilar preferences over quality scenarios. For example, the maintenance organization stakeholder usually prefers modifiability quality scenarios over performance, whereas the end user stakeholder prefers the vice-versa. One simplistic solution is to elicit the stakeholders' ordinal preferences with regards to the quality scenarios where quality scenarios of higher order are preferred over the others. In this approach, one may infer that quality scenarios of lower order should be sacrificed for the satisfaction of higher order quality scenarios when conflicts arise. However

while in most cases, a decision considering a trade-off between the conflicting quality scenarios results in a better outcome, the decision about the optimal trade-off is dependent upon the architect's expertise.

2. Although software architecture plays the most important role in achieving the quality requirements, architecture decisions do not always guarantee the promised level of quality for the software with regards to the quality scenarios of that iteration. This is due to various factors such as later decisions made in detailed design, implementation and deployment issues, and probable runtime uncertainties [2,5,9]. Such kind of uncertainty does not allow the architect to be fully confident of the outcomes of his/her decisions while interacting with the stakeholders in the preference elicitation process.

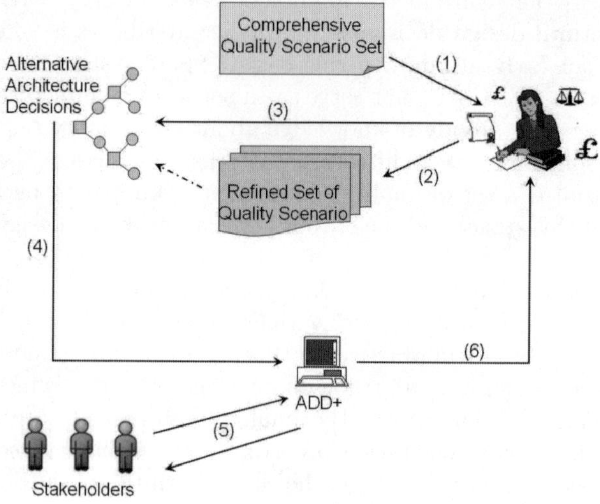

Fig. 1. The Workflow of ADD+

In this paper, we propose an extension to the ADD method (ADD+) by incorporating the role of system stakeholders in making architecture trade-off decisions. At each stage of ADD+, the architect chooses a subset of concrete quality scenarios, and specifies those quality scenarios within this subset that are conflicting. Based on the conflicting scenarios, the architect is required to propose various alternative architecture decisions along with the degree of quality scenario satisfaction obtained as a result of that architecture decision. A realistic approach should not make oversimplifying assumptions with regards to the degree of satisfaction of each quality scenario due to the uncertainties imposed by the before-mentioned factors. Once the set of alternative architecture decisions and their probable outcomes are specified by the architect, the preference elicitation process of the ADD+ commences: in each round of preference elicitation, system stakeholders are asked to answer a standard gamble query. Based on the stakeholders' responses, the utility of the outcomes of each architecture decision can be deduced. The architect can iterate over the steps of preference elicitation until he/she is satisfied with the gained knowledge about the stakeholders' preferences. This information would allow the architect to make the optimal choice with regards to the most suitable architecture decision. Figure 1 summarizes this process.

3   Formalizing the Decision Problem

It is possible to model the process of stakeholders' preference elicitation and architecture decision making as a multi-attribute decision problem [6,7]. Here, the multi-attribute decision problem consists of attributes which represent the degree of satisfaction of the conflicting quality scenarios and the outcome is the quality of the resulting software system marginalized to those quality scenarios.

Let $CQS^i = \{cqs_1^i, ..., cqs_n^i\}$ be the set of conflicting quality scenarios at the ith iteration of ADD+, $R^i = \{r_1^i, ..., r_n^i\}$ be their corresponding response measures and $AD^i = \{ad_1^i, ..., ad_k^i\}$ be the set of alternative architecture decisions at that iteration. Furthermore, suppose r_j^i is a random variable, and $\forall ad_l^i \in AD^i$, ad_l^i satisfies cqs_j^i to the degree of r_j^i according to a Gaussian probability distribution $P_{l,j}^i \sim N(\mu_{l,j}^i, \sigma_{l,j}^i)^1$.

Since the utility elicitation and decision making methods adopted here [6,7] assume that the set of outcomes is finite and countable, a discrete approximation of the Gaussian probability distribution is needed. The Pearson-Tukey approximation provides a three point representation of the Gaussian distribution. The representative points are the 5%, 50%, and 95% points and the probability of each point is 0.185, 0.63, and 0.185, respectively [8]. For a response measure r_j^i and an architecture decision ad_l^i, these three points are $r_{l,j_1}^i = -0.645 \times \sigma_{l,j}^i + \mu_{l,j}^i$, $r_{l,j_2}^i = \mu_{l,j}^i$, and $r_{l,j_3}^i = 0.645 \times \sigma_{l,j}^i + \mu_{l,j}^i$.

Suppose that we define a snapshot of the software system as a n-tuple s, which represents the state of the system at a certain time with regards to R^i. The set of all snapshots of the system, denoted S^i, consists of all possible combinations of configurations of R^i according to AD^i. S^i contains $k \times 3^n$ snapshots. The aim of the decision making problem is to choose the architecture decision whose corresponding snapshots (along with the probabilities of occurrence of those snapshots) satisfy the stakeholders' preferences and interests the most. So the set of attributes in this problem is R^i, the set of alternative decisions is AD^i, and the set of feasible outcomes is S^i.

4   Stakeholders' Preference Elicitation

The aim of preference elicitation is to elicit the utility of the snapshots for the stakeholders so that decision making can be done more confidently. The domain of a utility function u is S^i and its range is the real interval $[0,1]$. We do not need to know the complete utility function in order to make the optimal decision.

---

[1] Any other probability distribution could alternatively be used if a discrete approximation of it exists.

Instead we represent the utility of each snapshot by its lower and upper bounds. An elicitation query asks the stakeholders whether the utility of a snapshot is greater or less than a given value. This type of question can be easily translated into a standard gamble query. The query reduces the uncertainty in the calculation of the expected utility of each decision and thus helps the architect in confidently making the optimal decision.

According to [6], the number of possible elicitation queries, in each round of elicitation, is equal to the number of intersection points. An intersection point for an outcome (here, the outcomes of a decision are snapshots associated with it) is a point in its utility interval that is decisive for optimal decision making i.e. the true utility of the outcome being greater or less than the intersection point changes the optimal decision. The main difference between the original version of utility elicitation method and the one adopted here is that we are dealing with more than one stakeholder. We skip the details of calculating intersection points since it is independent of the number of stakeholders. For a more detailed discussion on how to calculate intersection points see [6] .

The optimal utility elicitation strategy is the one which asks a query with the highest expected value. The expected value of a query is the expected amount of increase in the expected utility of the optimal decision after asking that query.

The expected utility of the optimal decision at the current stage (before asking the query) can be calculated using the following equation:

$$EUOCD = \sum_{s_i} p_{s_i} \times \frac{u_{s_i}^{\uparrow} + u_{s_i}^{\downarrow}}{2} \tag{1}$$

where s_i is an obtained snapshot after making the optimal decision, p_{s_i} is the probability associated with it, $u_{s_i}^{\uparrow}$ and $u_{s_i}^{\downarrow}$ are the upper and lower bounds of its utility, respectively.

In order to calculate the expected utility after asking the query, all possible stakeholders' responses to that query need to be considered. Note that each individual stakeholder has two possible responses to a specific query, thus the number of possible communal responses to a query is equal to the number of all stakeholders plus one. The probability of a communal response can be calculated using the following equation:

$$p_{cr} = \binom{\eta}{\eta_>} \times \Pi_{i=1}^{\eta} p_i \tag{2}$$

where η is the number of stakeholders, $\eta_>$ is the number of stakeholders who stated that utility of the corresponding snapshot is greater than the intersection point, and p_i is the probability of an individual response. The probability of an individual response is either $\frac{u_{s_i}^{\uparrow} - ip}{u_{s_i}^{\uparrow} - u_{s_i}^{\downarrow}}$ or $\frac{ip - u_{s_i}^{\downarrow}}{u_{s_i}^{\uparrow} - u_{s_i}^{\downarrow}}$ where ip is the intersection point at which the query is being asked.

After receiving the stakeholders' responses, the utility of the snapshot for which the query had been asked can be updated by two alternative approaches.

One approach is to perform a voting process and update the utility interval of the snapshot based on the majority vote (e.g. if most of the stakeholders stated that the utility of the snapshot is greater than the intersection point, lower bound of the utility interval would be updated to the intersection point). However, this approach ignores the minority vote. A more sound approach is to alter both boundaries of the utility interval based on the number of votes given to each response. In this approach, we update the utility boundaries according to the following equations:

$$u_{s_i}^{\downarrow} \longleftarrow ip - \frac{\eta_< \times (ip - u_{s_i}^{\downarrow})}{\eta} \tag{3}$$

$$u_{s_i}^{\uparrow} \longleftarrow ip + \frac{\eta_> \times (ip - u_{s_i}^{\uparrow})}{\eta} \tag{4}$$

Note that introducing weights to represent stakeholder importance is a trivial task e.g. in our implementation one can define three End User stakeholders and only one Marketing stakeholder to show that the End User stakeholder is three time more important than the Marketing stakeholder. As mentioned above, the expected value of a query is equal to the difference between the expected utility of the optimal decision after the query and the expected utility before asking the query (see Equation 1). The expected utility after a query, can be calculated by the multiplication of the probability of each communal response (Equation 2) with the expected utility after receiving the specific response. In order to calculate the expected utility after receiving the responses, we can update the boundaries according to Equations 3, 4 and the expected utility of the optimal decision is recalculated. Therefore, after calculating the expected value of each query, we can choose the query with the highest expected value. The round of elicitation would be stopped either when there is no more query with expected value greater than zero or when the expected value of the best query does not satisfy the architect.

5   Case Study

Based on these theoretical foundations, a decision support system has been implemented, which assists the architect in eliciting the stakeholders' preferences and making the optimal decision with the highest expected utility. In this section, we will go through a case study using the implemented system.

We customize the case of the Garage Door example from [2] where three different stakeholders are involved: the End User Stakeholder, the Marketing Stakeholder and the Maintenance Organization Stakeholder. Two high prioritized quality scenarios are defined: a modifiability quality scenario called Low Recovery Time After Failure and a business quality scenario called Low Price. Obviously, the Marketing Stakeholder prefers the latter and the Maintenance Organization Stakeholder prefers the former. However, the End User Stakeholder prefers a low price system that can be fixed in a reasonable amount of time in case of failure.

Table 1. Response Measures of the Case Study

	Low Price ($200)	Low Recovery Time(20 minutes)
Monolithic Design	N(90,2)	N(60,10)
Structured Design	N(75,5)	N(85,4)

At the first stage, the architect needs to know whether he should design a monolithic system or a well-structured system. Assume that performance quality scenarios of this project would not be affected by applying modifiability tactics such as *maintaining semantic coherence, generalizing the module, information hiding, maintaining existing interfaces* and *using an intermediary*. However, these tactics may have a significant effect on the price of the system i.e. one of the business quality scenarios. This is due to the time required to implement these tactics and moreover the experienced programmers needed to implement them. The most important issue the architect has to deal with is which architecture decision would satisfy the community of stakeholders the most. We will see how the decision support system implemented for ADD+ can assist the architect in this case.

In the system, the architect may define the set of quality scenarios. The response measures of Low Price and Low Recovery Time are defined as *$200* and *20 minutes*, respectively by the system requirement specifications. After starting the first iteration, the architect would choose these two quality scenarios as the set of conflicting scenarios for this iteration. Afterwards, alternative decisions could be defined in the manner shown in Figure 2. Table 1 shows the normal distributions over response measures of conflicting scenarios in this case. One of the decisions, which is called Monolithic Design, satisfies the Low Price quality scenario to a higher degree ($\mu = 90$) more confidently ($\sigma = 2$) and the Low Recovery Time scenario to a lower degree ($\mu = 60$) with more uncertainty ($\sigma = 10$).

After starting the rounds of elicitation, one of the influential queries posed to the stakeholders could be interpreted as the following:

Which option would you prefer?

1. *A system which costs $220 and can be fixed in 28 minutes after a failure.*
2. *A system which costs the lowest possible amount and can be fixed in the lowest possible amount of time with 90% chance or a system which costs the highest amount and can be fixed in the highest amount of time with 10% chance.*

Note that the first choice in the above query is the interpretation of one of the snapshots generated by the support system automatically.

After some rounds of elicitation, the expected value of the next query was 0.09 and the expected utility of the Monolithic Design was 0.68 and the expected utility of the Structured Design was 0.71. We stopped the elicitation process due to the low expected value of the next query. Note that the expected utility

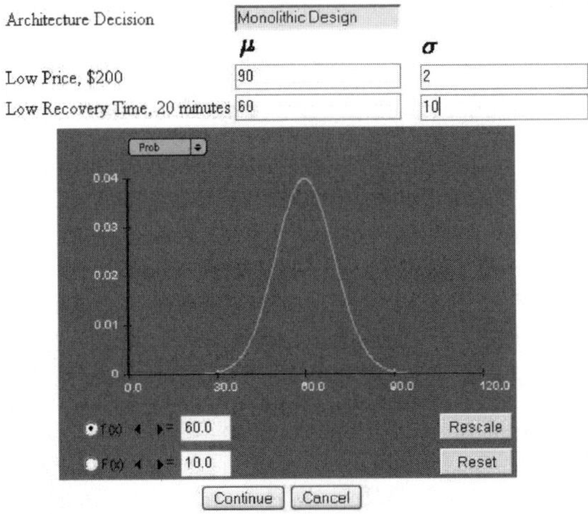

Fig. 2. Defining an Architecture Decision in the Decision Support System for ADD+

of alternative decisions are not accurate, but a rational decision could be made because the increase in the expected utility would not be greater than 0.09.

Since the end users are not satisfied either with a low price system with an extremely high recovery time or with an expensive system, which is recoverable in a reasonable amount of time, even the Marketing Stakeholder is not in favor of sacrificing the modifiability quality scenario for the sake of a lower price. As a result, the suggestion of the system, being the selection of the Structured Design alternative, makes sense.

6   Concluding Remarks

In this paper, we have reported a preliminary investigation of the applicability of decision theory and utility elicitation techniques for addressing the issue of stakeholders' preference elicitation by introducing an extension to the ADD method. Even though, we are at the early stages of our investigation, we believe that techniques employed here and some other similar techniques would be beneficial to the domain of software architecture. Many sources of uncertainty reported to be associated with software architecture decisions can be managed by theoretical foundations provided by decision theory and be automated using AI techniques based on those theories.

As future work, we are interested in both theoretical and empirical exploration of the relationship between the complexity of the conflicting quality scenarios and the number of elicitation queries posed to the stakeholders. We are also considering the evaluation of the proposed ADD+ method and its supporting toolset through various real-world case studies.

Acknowledgements

The authors graciously acknowledge the funding through grant RGPN 227441 from the National Science and Engineering Research Council of Canada (NSERC) to Dr. Ghorbani.

References

1. Bachmann, F., Bass, L., Klein, M.: Preliminary design of arche: A software architecture design assistant. Tech. rep., Software Engineering Institute Carnegie Mellon (2003)
2. Bass, L., Clements, P., Kazman, R.: Software architecture in practice. Addison-Wesley Longman Publishing Co., Boston (1998)
3. Bass, L.J., Klein, M., Bachmann, F.: Quality attribute design primitives and the attribute driven design method. In: van der Linden, F.J. (ed.) PFE 2002. LNCS, vol. 2290, pp. 169–186. Springer, Heidelberg (2002)
4. Brown, A.W., McDermid, J.A.: The Art and Science of Software Architecture. In: Oquendo, F. (ed.) ECSA 2007. LNCS, vol. 4758, pp. 237–256. Springer, Heidelberg (2007)
5. Celiku, O., Garlan, D., Schmerl, B.: Augmenting architectural modeling to cope with uncertainty. In: Proceedings of the International Workshop on Living with Uncertainties (IWLU 2007), co-located with the 22nd International Conference on Automated Software Engineering (ASE 2007), Atlanta, GA, USA, November 5 (2007), http://godzilla.cs.toronto.edu/IWLU/program.html
6. Chajewska, U., Koller, D., Parr, R.: Making rational decisions using adaptive utility elicitation. In: Proceedings of the Seventeenth National Conference on Artificial Intelligence and Twelfth Conference on Innovative Applications of Artificial Intelligence, pp. 363–369. AAAI Press / The MIT Press (2000)
7. Fishburn, P.C.: Utility theory for decision-making. Wiley, New York (1970)
8. Pearson, E.S., Tukey, J.W.: Approximate means and standard deviations based on distances between percentage points of frequency curves. Biometrika 52(3-4), 533–546 (1965)
9. Poladian, V., Shaw, M., Garlan, D.: Modeling uncertainty of predictive inputs in anticipatory dynamic configuration. In: Proceedings of the International Workshop on Living with Uncertainties (IWLU 2007), co-located with the 22nd International Conference on Automated Software Engineering (ASE 2007), Atlanta, GA, USA, November 5 (2007), http://godzilla.cs.toronto.edu/IWLU/program.html
10. Shaw, M., Clements, P.C.: The golden age of software architecture. IEEE Software 23(2), 31–39 (2006)

Representing Service-Oriented Architectural Models Using π-ADL

Marcos López-Sanz[1], Zawar Qayyum[2], Carlos E. Cuesta[1], Esperanza Marcos[1], and Flavio Oquendo[2]

[1] Kybele Research Group
Rey Juan Carlos University
Mostoles – 28933 Madrid Spain
marcos.lopez@urjc.es, carlos.cuesta@urjc.es,
esperanza.marcos@urjc.es
[2] VALORIA Laboratory
University of South Brittany
Tohannic Campus, Vannes 56017 France
zawar.qayyum@univ-ubs.fr, flavio.oquendo@univ-ubs.fr

Abstract. Despite the well-known advantages of applying the MDA proposal to SOA developments, there are still some gaps that need to be filled. At PIM-level, for example, there is no possibility of having an executable version of the system as it solely comprises technologically independent models. In order to solve this we propose to formalize the architectural model at this level with π-ADL, an ADL supporting the description of dynamic and evolvable architectures like SOA itself is. Since π-ADL allows the definition of executable versions of the architecture, the specification written embodies a prototype of the system at the PIM-level. We illustrate this by describing a real case study based on the SMPP standard for sending SMS messages.

Keywords: Service-Oriented Architecture, Model-Driven Architecture, PIM-level modelling, π-ADL.

1 Introduction

Service orientation has emerged as a leading technological trend due to its advantages for cross-organization integration, flexibility and scalability. As the Service-Oriented Computing (SOC) paradigm [2] is largely established as the de-facto solution for emerging information society challenges, many Software Engineering areas are taking advantage of services, ranging from the field of Software Architecture to the definition of software development processes [3].

Taking a deeper look at the methodological field we found strategies that benefit from and contribute to the SOC paradigm. The model-driven approach and the Model-Driven Architecture (MDA) proposal in particular [8], are amongst the best examples [1]. However, and despite the well-known advantages of MDA, this approach lacks in the ability to define early executable versions of the system. Taking into account the separation in abstraction levels stated by that proposal, it is not until

R. Morrison, D. Balasubramaniam, and K. Falkner (Eds.): ECSA 2008, LNCS 5292, pp. 273–280, 2008.

the lower level (PSM) when the characteristics of a specific technology are reflected in the developed models and therefore when it is possible to get a working prototype. In this paper we study that problem applied to SOA development, focusing on a possible solution by means of using an executable Architecture Description Language (ADL) for the definition of the system architecture. This study is accomplished within a MDA-based methodological framework called MIDAS [2].

In previous work [4] we defined the architectural metamodel at the PIM level supporting all the principles of SOA. Providing the role of the architecture in MIDAS [6] and the necessity of an early executable version of the system, we have found that using an ADL is the best option for achieving that goal. We have chosen π-ADL [9] for the representation of the service architecture. π-ADL is suitable for that purpose mainly because, first, it allows the representation of the features and constraints of services reasonably and consistently and, second, it allows the representation of dynamic architectures such as SOA.

The structure of the paper is as follows: Section 2 gives an overall view of the three main concepts considered in this paper: π-ADL, MDA and SOA. Section 3 presents a case study used to illustrate the benefits of using π-ADL for describing SOA when architectural models. Finally, Section 4 discusses the main contributions of this article and some of the future works.

2   Previous Concepts

In this section we present the foundations of MDA and the MIDAS methodological framework, in which the architectural model is framed and used; SOA and the concepts involved in the definition of the architectural model; and π-ADL for the formalization of dynamic service architectures.

2.1   MDA and the MIDAS Methodological Framework

The main contribution of this article (i.e. to achieve an executable representation of the PIM-level system architecture using π-ADL) is part of a much broader research effort: the refinement of MIDAS [2], a complete development framework based on the MDA principles.

MIDAS follows an ACMDA (Architecture-Centric Model-Driven Architecture) approach [6]: it defines a method for the development of information systems based on models and guided by the architecture. The architecture is considered to be the driving aspect of the development process as it allows specifying which models, elements inside models or relationships within models should be created during the entire software development process.

With an architectural view of the system at PIM level, we ensure that there are no technology or implementation constraints in the model. Moreover, it facilitates the establishment of different PSM-level models according to the specific target platform from a unique PIM model. However, as stated in the introduction, this has as main drawback the impossibility of having a precise executable version of the system.

2.2 Service-Oriented Architectural Metamodel

This subsection explains briefly the elements contained in the metamodel used to define service-based architectural models at PIM level in MIDAS. For a deeper explanation, please refer to [4].

Services are computational entities in charge of a resource and which offer functionalities associated to that resource in the form of operations. Those service operations are considered as atomic functionalities that collaborate to build a joint description of the service. The distinction between operation types is made depending on its synchronicity. In asynchronous operations the requester of the operation does not wait for the answer or return value (if any). In turn, in synchronous operations the requester will wait for the answer or return value (that always exists).

Services relate, communicate and interact with each other through contracts. The main property of a contract is the message exchange pattern describing the message flow between the contracted services. We reduce the pattern types for message exchange to three alternatives. *'One-way'*, in which no response is expected; *'Query/Response'*, in which there is an explicit answer to the operation requested; and, finally, *'Dialogue'*, in which the concrete protocol can be complex and, therefore, it must be represented by means of a state machine.

Services can be classified depending on different criteria: the kind of interaction (interaction services or 'pure' services), their atomicity (simple or composite services) or the role played within the architecture (basic services or supporting services).

According to the kind of interaction. Services capable to perform synchronous operations are clearly identified as interaction services. Services not offering any synchronous operation need not to be particularly marked as they are considered 'pure' or 'traditional' services.

According to the atomicity of the service. Simple services represent behaviours of the system that do not entail the invocation of any other service defined within the system. Their functionality is satisfied entirely by means of the operations they define. On the contrary, composite services are identified as services in which service coordination is needed. This coordination can be achieved by means of choreographies or by using orchestration. The latter refers to the existence of a 'special' service in charge of carrying out a workflow defined as a complex operation involving the invocation of external service operations. The former, on the other hand, represents a coordination environment in which each service remain autonomous and in which no party member is master over any other.

According to the role played in the architecture. Basic services offer operations related to the functionalities defined in the business process of the system. Services with no direct relation to the modelled system functionality but with the performance of several other operations necessary for the rest of services to operate correctly are known as 'supporting services'. Among them we specifically identify two: orchestration services; and discovery services, understood as architectural entities that act as dynamicity enactors by providing the four common operations that set up a dynamic environment (link, unlink, create and destroy) [5].

2.3 Foundations of π-ADL

π-ADL [9] is a language designed for defining software architectures and is formally founded on the higher-order typed π-calculus described in [7].

In a π-ADL program, the top level constructs are behaviours and abstractions. Each behaviour definition results in a separate execution entry point, meaning that the program will have as many top level concurrent threads of execution as the number of behaviours it defines. Abstractions are reusable behaviour templates and their functionality can be invoked from behaviours as well as other abstractions. An abstraction is capable of receiving a single argument when invoked.

The body of a behaviour or an abstraction can contain variable and connection declarations. Connections provide functionality analogous to channels in π-calculus: code in different parts of behaviours or abstractions can communicate synchronously via connections, and connections can also connect behaviours with abstractions or abstractions with abstractions. Connections are typed, and can send and receive any of the existing variable types, as well as connections themselves.

3 Architecture Model of a Case Study with UML and π-ADL

The aim of the selected case study is to emulate the functionality of a SMPP [11] gateway system by means of services. SMPP stands for Short Message Peer-to-Peer Protocol and is a telecommunications industry protocol for exchanging SMS messages between peer entities (*Short Message Service Centres*). Through a service interface a user is able to send SMS text messages to multiple addressees. Although the system is made up by many other elements, here we focus only on the building blocks and functionalities depicted in Figure 2.

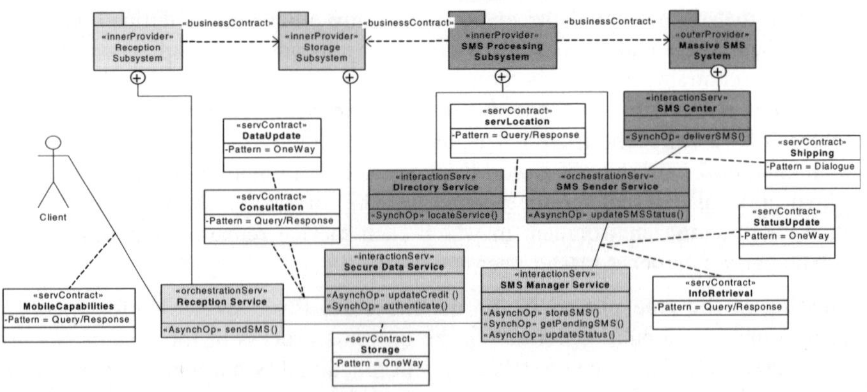

Fig. 1. UML model of the architecture of the case study

Next, we present part of the architectural model specification emphasizing the aspects of π-ADL that provide an adequate solution for our system as well as explaining how the structures and principles of π-ADL are adapted to our vision of PIM-level service architecture:

Representation of a service and its operations. Services represent computating entities performing a specific behaviour within the system architecture and thus they are specified by means of π-ADL abstractions (see Listing 3.1 for the specification of the *ReceptionService*).

```
value ReceptionService is abstraction () {
    outConn, inConn:Connection[view [operation: String, data: any]];
    output, input:view [operation: String, data: any];
    if (input::operation == "sendSMS") do {
        via SendSMS send input::data
            where {resultConn renames resultConn};
        via resultConn receive result;
        compose {
            via outConn send result;
        and   done;      }}}
```

Listing 3.1. Specification of the ReceptionService

Every service abstraction defines its own communication channels through input and output connections. The data acquired and sent by these connections comprises a description of the operation and the data associated to that message. Depending on the operation requested, the service abstraction will transfer the control of the execution to the corresponding operation. Operations are also specified by means of abstractions as they encapsulate part of the functionality offered by services. Like any other abstraction used in the description of the service architecture, operation abstractions will receive the information tokens through connections, sending back an answer when applicable.

In π-ADL, communication through the connections is performed synchronously. This means that communication with operations is synchronous. Therefore, the semantics associated with the asynchronous operations are lost since the abstraction will be blocked in a send operation until any other abstraction in the architecture perform a receive operation over that channel. In order to model asynchronous operations, the specification can be placed in one of the sub-blocks of a compose block, with the second sub-block returning immediately with the done keyword.

Representation of contracts. As stated previously, services relate and communicate through contracts. Within the architecture these contracts are active connectors in charge of enabling the message exchange between services according to a specific pattern, represented by means of the programmatic specification of a state machine. Similarly, connectors in π-ADL are represented by means of abstractions.

In a static service environment, in which contracts between services are established at design time, all the information needed by a contract to correctly fulfil its behaviour (message exchange pattern and contractors) is defined and initialized internally within the contract abstraction when the system starts. In dynamic environments, however, this is normally accomplished by transferring all the information through the channel opened simultaneously when the abstraction is executed.

Listing 3.2 depicts part of the analysis of a state of the message pattern execution. In it, it is shown how, in order to send anything to one of the services connected through the Shipping contract, a compose structure should be used: first to send the data through the connection and second to execute the abstraction and unify the connections.

Because of the dynamic nature of service architectures, contract abstractions can be reused as the instances of the services they communicate can vary during the lifecycle of the system. In order to achieve this behaviour, contracts (or more appropriately abstractions performing the contract role) must be able to dynamically instantiate the channel that they have to use to send or receive the data transferred in each moment. To deal with this issue π-ADL defines the `dynamic(<connection_name>)` operator. This operator represents one of the main advantages for dynamic architecture specification since π-ADL allows the transference of connections through connections.

```
...
if (state::via_SERVID == "S") do{
 compose        {
   via outConnectionS send inData;
 and
   via dynamic(input::ServConnGroup(0)::SERVID) send Void
   where {outConnectionS renames inConn,inConnectionS renames outConn};
 }
}else do{
   via outConnectionC send inData;}
...
```

Listing 3.2. Fragment extracted from the Shipping contract

Representation of dynamism. In our case study, In order to send the SMS messages stored on the database, it is necessary to know which specific service should be used. To achieve that behaviour it is essential to be aware of the existence of a specialized service attending to requests from services asking for other services to perform tasks with specific requirements. This represents a dynamic environment since it is necessary to create a communication channel that did not exist at design time but is discovered when the system is in execution (i.e. when the *SMSManagerService* must send the SMS texts to a concrete *SMSCenterService*).

In a service-oriented environment the dynamicity may occur in several scenarios: when it is necessary to create a new contract between services or when the new element to add is another service (or service type). In those cases it is mandatory to have a special service in charge of performing the usual operations that occur in dynamic environments, i.e. link, unlink, create and destroy of contract abstractions (inclusion of new services is a topic left for ongoing research). This service will be the *DirectoryService* shown in Figure 2.

Provided that the *DirectoryService* already knows the *SERVID* of any *SMSCenterService* requested, the tasks it performs when queried for a specific service include: the creation of the contract needed to communicate with the *SMSCenterService* and the connection that will be used by both the *SMSSenderService* and the contract. The information provided by this service for the *SMSSenderService* comprises a connection to the contract allowing the communication with the *SMSCenterService*. The new contract created will receive as initial information, the *SERVID* of the *SMSCenterService* that it will connect with and the connection channel that should be used to communicate with it.

Representation of service composition. Coordination among services can be achieved by defining choreographies or orchestrations. Choreographies can be formalized with π-ADL by means of shared connections. Orchestrations, in turn, depend mostly on the code specified inside a unique abstraction belonging to a service playing the role of co-ordinator of the composition.

In our case study the only service taking the orchestrator role is the SMS Sender Service which coordinates the access to the storage subsystem (using the SMS Manager service), the retrieval of the information of the concrete *SMSCenterService* to be used to send the SMS texts by invoking the Directory Service and finally the *SMSCenterService* to complete the desired functionality.

4 Conclusions and Future Works

MDA is one of the current leading trends in the definition of software development methodologies. Its basis lies in the definition of model sets divided in several abstraction levels together with model transformation rules. This separation in abstraction levels allows the reutilization of models at different stages of the development and favours the migration from one platform to another. This aspect is crucial when taking into account some technological approaches that have come up in the last years. The principles of the SOC paradigm and its inherent features for system integration and interoperability make MDA a suitable approach for the development of SOA solutions. In that sense, several research efforts have been carried out to cope with the complexity of defining methodological frameworks for and based on the SOC principles. One of those methodologies is MIDAS, in which we frame our research work.

While defining MDA-based frameworks, the architecture has been demonstrated to be the ideal source of guidance of the development process since it reflects the structure of the systems embedded in its components, the relations among them and their evolution during the lifecycle of the software being developed. In the case of MIDAS, we have defined UML metamodels for the PIM-level view of the architecture.

In this work, and in order to solve the initial lack of early prototypes in MDA-based developments, we have proposed to give a formal definition of the system architecture by means of an ADL. Specifically we have chosen π-ADL because of its support for representing dynamic and evolvable architectures as well as the largely faithful compiler tool available for this language. Moreover, by using a formal representation of the system we can use mathematical formalisms to validate the UML models created for each of the abstraction levels defined within MIDAS.

There are many research lines that arise from the work presented in this paper. One research direction is, given the already defined UML notation and metamodel for the π-ADL language, the definition of transformation rules between the UML metamodel of the architecture at PIM-level and that of the π-ADL language. Another open research line is the definition of the PSM-level architectural model as well as the influence of the election of π-ADL as the ADL of choice when defining technologically dependent architectural models.

Acknowledgements

This research is partially granted by project GOLD (TIN2005-00010) financed by the Ministry of Science and Technology of Spain, the IASOMM project (URJC-CM-2007-CET-1555) co-financed by the Rey Juan Carlos University and the

Regional Government of Madrid, and the Spanish project 'Agreement Technologies' (CONSOLIDER CSD2007-0022, INGENIO 2010).

Bibliography

[1] Broy, M.: Model Driven, Architecture-Centric Modelling in Software Development. In: Proceedings of 9th Intl. Conf. in Engineering Complex Computer Systems (ICECCS 2004), pp. 3–12. IEEE Computer Society, Los Alamitos (2004)

[2] Cáceres, P., Marcos, E., Vela, B.: A MDA-Based Approach for Web Information System Development. In: Workshop in Software Model Engineering (retrieved March 2007), `http://www.metamodel.com/wisme-2003/`

[3] De Castro, V., Marcos, E., López-Sanz, M.: A Model Driven Method for Service Composition Modeling: A Case Study. Intl. Journal of Web Engineering and Technology 2(4), 335–353 (2006)

[4] López-Sanz, M., Acuña, C.J., Cuesta, C.E., Marcos, E.: Modelling of Service-Oriented Architectures with UML. In: Proc. of FOCLASA 2007, pp. 21–36 (2007)

[5] Magee, J., Kramer, J., Sloman, M.: Constructing Distributed Systems in Conic. IEEE Transactions on Software Engineering 15(6), 663–675 (1989)

[6] Marcos, E., Acuña, C.J., Cuesta, C.E.: Integrating Software Architecture into a MDA Framework. In: Gruhn, V., Oquendo, F. (eds.) EWSA 2006. LNCS, vol. 4344, pp. 127–143. Springer, Heidelberg (2006)

[7] Milner, R.: The Polyadic π-Calculus: A Tutorial. Logic and Algebra of Specification. Springer, Heidelberg (1993)

[8] OMG. Model Driven Architecture. Miller, J., Mukerji, J. (eds.), Document No. ormsc/2001-07-01 (retrieved May 2006), `http://www.omg.com/mda`

[9] Oquendo, F.: π-ADL: An Architecture Description Language based on the Higher Order Typed π-Calculus for Specifying Dynamic and Mobile Software Architectures. ACM Software Engineering Notes 3 (May 2004)

[10] Papazoglou, M.P.: Service-Oriented Computing: Concepts, Characteristics and Directions. In: Proc. of WISE 2003, Roma, Italy, December 10-12, pp. 3–12 (2003)

[11] SMPP Forum. SMPP v5.0 Specification (retrieved September 2007), `http://www.smsforum.net/`

Managing Dynamic Evolution of Architectural Types

Cristóbal Costa-Soria[1], Jennifer Pérez[2], and José Angel Carsí[1]

[1] ISSI, Dept. of Information Systems and Computation,
Universidad Politécnica de Valencia, Camino de Vera s/n, 46022 Valencia, Spain
[2] Escuela Universitaria de Informática,
Technical University of Madrid (UPM), Ctra. Valencia km. 7, 28051 Madrid, Spain
ccosta@dsic.upv.es, jenifer.perez@eui.upm.es, pcarsi@dsic.upv.es

Abstract. Software systems evolvability is more and more required in current software developments, in order to provide systems with enough flexibility to adapt to future requirements. The evolvability in the field of Software Architecture can be classified into two kinds: dynamic reconfiguration or dynamic architectural type evolution. The former enables an architecture to change its configuration at run-time, by creating or destroying architectural element instances and their links dynamically. The latter enables an architecture to change entirely its specification at run-time, by introducing new architectural element types and connections or by modifying the type and the running instances of its architectural elements. This paper presents an approach to address how to dynamically evolve the architectural types of a system from a platform-independent view. This approach identifies the different concerns involved in the adaptation process by encapsulating them into aspects, and makes use of reflection mechanisms to perform the type updating process.

Keywords: dynamic evolution, run-time adaptation, architectural types, reflection, software architectures, AOSD.

1   Introduction

The development of current software systems is a difficult task due to their complexity, heterogeneity, and the need of supporting a wide variety of non-functional requirements. Since it is very difficult to predict all the future situations these complex software systems are going to face along its lifetime, to provide evolution capabilities is a mandatory requirement. But it is also necessary to take into account that it is very common that such complex systems are going to be continuously and uninterruptedly executed in very demanding environments. So, not only evolution capabilities are required, but also dynamic evolution capabilities, which allow us to introduce changes without stopping the system, are required.

Software Architecture is the branch within Software Engineering which provides techniques for describing complex software systems, by hiding low level details and highlighting their structure. The dynamic evolution of software architectures can be classified into two kinds, depending on whether the configuration or the types of the architecture are modified at run-time. The former, called *dynamic reconfiguration* (also called structural dynamism [8]), enables a software architecture to change its

R. Morrison, D. Balasubramaniam, and K. Falkner (Eds.): ECSA 2008, LNCS 5292, pp. 281–289, 2008.
© Springer-Verlag Berlin Heidelberg 2008

configuration at run-time, that is, to create or destroy architectural element instances (i.e. component and connector instances) and their links dynamically. The latter, called *dynamic evolution of architectural types* (also called architectural dynamism [8]), enables a software architecture to change its type (that is, its specification), by introducing new architectural element types (i.e. component and connector types), by removing existing types, or by changing the way the types of the architecture interact, thus changing the entire composition and behaviour of the architecture.

Dynamic reconfiguration of software architectures has been addressed in other works [2, 6]. However, a set of uncontrolled architecture reconfigurations can lead the software system to a configuration where the system is no more operational. Hnetynka defined this as the *evolution gap problem* [11], although we would prefer the term *configuration erosion* because of being more descriptive. In contrast to the term *architecture erosion*, which refers to the situation in which code changes but the architecture of that code is not updated, by *configuration erosion* we refer to the situation where, as a consequence of several dynamic reconfigurations, the architecture has lost its initial purpose. In order to deal with the configuration erosion problem, we have used software architecture patterns to limit the set of dynamic reconfigurations that can be performed on an architecture. Architecture patterns, which are based on the notion of architectural patterns and on the PRISMA model [16], define: (i) the set of types that can be used on a software architecture, (ii) the set of correct connections that can be established among these types, and (iii) the constraints over the number of instances that can be created from these connections and types. In this way, an architecture pattern will only allow those reconfigurations that make sense in the architecture, thereby reducing the configuration erosion.

However, dynamic reconfiguration is not enough when also the architecture pattern, i.e. the type of the architecture, needs to be evolved at run-time. For instance, a new component type can only be introduced in a running system by modifying the architecture pattern to allow instances of the new type to be executed. In order to change an architecture pattern, the dynamic evolution of types is needed. The contribution of this paper is to present an infrastructure to support the dynamic evolution of architectural types, by using as a case study how to evolve architectural patterns. This work continues a previous work about the dynamic evolution of simple architectural element types (i.e. components and connectors) [7], and extends it to support the evolution of complex architectural element types (i.e. components composed of other architectural elements and connections). This dynamic evolution of types allows introducing new architectural element types, modifying the existing types, modifying the connections among architectural element types, creating new connections among types, etc. It is also important to take into account that this dynamic evolution of types not only updates the specification of the architectural element types, but also propagates the changes to their running instances. The different concerns involved in the evolution process have been identified and encapsulated into aspects [5], in order to allow the reuse of the same aspects in different entities of the system and its easy maintenance.

This work is based on PRISMA [16], an approach which combines software architectures with aspect-oriented software development. This provides the following benefits: (1) architectural elements are used to model functional decomposition and aspects are used to model crosscutting-concerns (functionality, coordination, evolution, etc.). Thus, components and aspects encapsulate properties thereby avoiding tangled code, and they provide good maintenance properties for supporting dynamic evolution; (2) the Architecture Description Language of PRISMA is a formal language, so the evolution requirements of our proposal can be easily formalized and executed without ambiguity; (3) PRISMA software architectures can be automatically compiled for a specific technological platform using code generation techniques, so a technology-independent evolution approach can be defined; and (4) the PRISMA tool supports the development of aspect-oriented software architectures following the Model-Driven Development (MDD) paradigm [14].

This paper is structured as follows. The PRISMA approach is introduced in section 2. In section 3, our proposal to support dynamic evolution of architectural types is presented. Related works that address dynamic evolution of software architectures are discussed in section 4. Finally, conclusions and further works are presented.

2 PRISMA

PRISMA is an approach to develop technology-independent, aspect-oriented software architectures [16]. The PRISMA approach consists of a model [18] and a formal Aspect-Oriented Architecture Description Language (AOADL) [17].

In PRISMA, a crosscutting-concern can be specified by several **aspects** of a software architecture, whereas an aspect represents a concern that crosscuts the software architecture. This crosscutting is due to the fact that the same aspect can be imported by more than one architectural element of a software architecture.

The PRISMA encapsulation of crosscutting concerns facilitates the evolution of the system due to the fact that the change of a property only requires the change of the aspect that defines it, and then, each architectural element that imports the changed aspect is also updated. A PRISMA **architectural element** can be seen from two different views: internal and external. In the external view, architectural elements encapsulate their functionality as black boxes and publish a set of services that they offer to other architectural elements through their ports.

PRISMA has three kinds of architectural elements: components, connectors, and systems. Components and connectors are simple, but systems are complex components. The internal view of a **simple** architectural element shows the set of aspects that it imports (white box view). Aspects are synchronized inside the architectural element by means of weavings relationships. A weaving indicates that the execution of an aspect service can trigger the execution of services in other aspects. As a result, a simple architectural element in PRISMA is formed by a set of aspects, their weaving relationships, and one or more ports.

The internal view of a **complex** architectural element (system) includes a set of architectural elements (components, connectors and other systems) and the connections among them. A system is specified as a **pattern**, so that it can be reused in any software architecture where necessary. This permits not only defining how its architectural elements are connected, but also constrains the number of instances that can be created for each one of its architectural elements, and the number of connections allowed between the architectural element types. These constraints concern the minimum and maximum cardinalities, whose default values are one and infinite, respectively. For example, the pattern of a PRISMA system type allows to constrain the maximum and minimum number of connection instances the architectural elements of the system can have through their respective. When a PRISMA system type is instantiated, it gets an initial configuration which satisfies the architectural pattern of the system type. This initial configuration can be modified by several reconfigurations, but only while satisfying the system architectural pattern.

Figure 1 shows an example of how the maximum cardinality of a connection can vary the configuration of an architecture at the instance level. The attachment defined between the Joint component type and the CnctMUC connector type of the Teach-Mover architecture is used to exemplify this variation (see the four possible allowed configurations in Figure 1). In this way, architectural patterns can help to address the configuration erosion problem, by allowing only to reconfigure architecture instances in a suitable way.

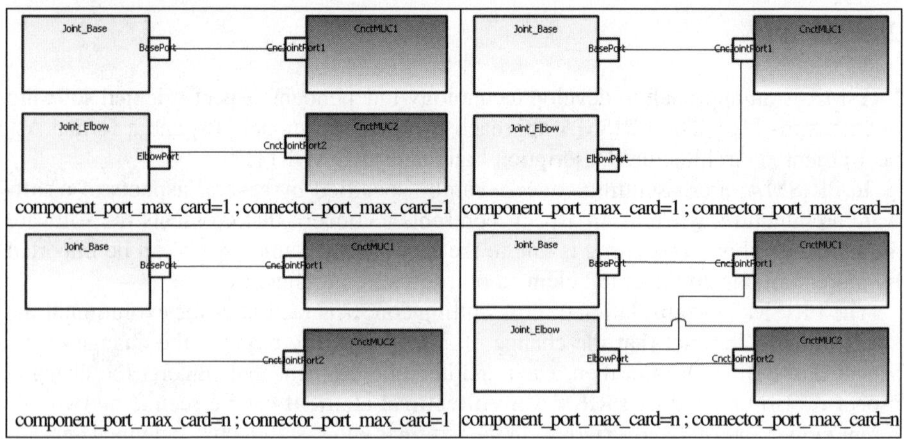

Fig. 1. Different configurations of an architecture depending on the maximum cardinality of a connection between the Joint component type and the CnctMUC connector type

3   Dynamic Evolution of PRISMA Systems

As it has been mentioned in the introduction, the contribution of this work is to present how the dynamic evolution of types is supported in PRISMA. There is not enough space here to describe all the details. There are however previous works about the set of evolution services the PRISMA model [18] requires, and about the infrastructure for the dynamic evolution of simple architectural types [7].

PRISMA systems and its configurations are changed by means of evolution services. If a system needs to be dynamically evolved, (i.e., to change its architectural pattern), the different instances (i.e. configurations) of the system will also need to be evolved in order to be compliant with the new architectural pattern. This type evolution is possible at run-time due to the fact that not only instances are executed, but also the system types that describe them. A system type at runtime is a special component that manages both the creation and destruction of its instances, and the evolution of the type (the specification) it represents. Figure 2 shows a system S that is being executed and two different instances of it, S1 and S2. The figure is divided into two levels: types and instances. This is due to the fact that the dynamic evolution is performed in two steps: first the type is evolved (the old architectural pattern is replaced by the new one), and then the change is propagated to each one of its instances. Next, the dynamic evolution of systems is presented in detail at this two levels.

3.1 Type Level

On the one hand, the type (S_T) provides the architectural element types that can be instantiated in the architecture and how they can be connected among them: this is the architectural pattern that instances must conform to. In addition, the type can be seen like a factory of instances due to the fact that it is in charge of creating and destroying its instances. On the other hand, an instance defines a particular configuration: it has several instances of the architectural elements described in the architecture pattern and several connections among these instances. For example, the S1 system instance is configured with three component instances: A1, B1 and S1_Evolver (see Figure 2).

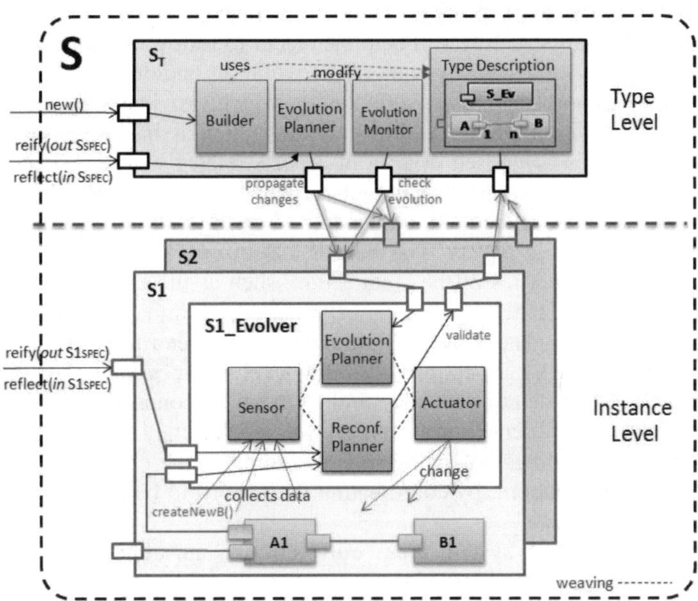

Fig. 2. Architectural types at runtime and its dynamic evolution mechanisms

From our experience in AOSD, we have been able to identify four different common concerns for evolving dynamically a type, in order to take advantage of the encapsulation, reusability and maintenance properties that AOSD provides. These different concerns have been encapsulated in four aspects that a dynamic system imports: the TypeDescription, the Builder, the EvolutionPlanner, and the EvolutionMonitor (see Type Level, Figure 2). The TypeDescription aspect encapsulates the architectural type specification. In the case of PRISMA Systems, it describes the architectural pattern to which instances must conform to. The Builder aspect is the instance factory: it creates and destroys instances and manages them. It creates instances using the information provided by the TypeDescription aspect.

The EvolutionPlanner aspect provides the dynamic evolution mechanisms at the type-level. It provides the Reify and Reflect services. Reify allows to obtain a reification of the architectural type (i.e. a type specification, S_{SPEC}), modify this reification and, by reflecting this reification (Reflect service), the type evolution process is started. First, the EvolutionPlanner aspect uses services of the TypeDescription aspect to update the architectural type specification. Next, the new specification is propagated to each system instance. Finally, the EvolutionMonitor aspect supervise if changes have been applied or not on each running instance, in order to guarantee that in a certain amount of time all the running instances have been evolved to the new type specification, or at least, are compliant with.

3.2 Instance Level

Each instance is provided with mechanisms to evolve themselves, in order to enable its autonomous evolution. Both types (S_T) and instances (S_1, S_2) are executed in the same platform, but this structure will help the reader to follow our approach.

Each PRISMA system with dynamic type evolution and/or dynamic reconfiguration needs must import an Evolver component, which provides the mechanisms for supporting the evolution of the architecture on which it has been imported. The Evolver component is composed of a set of aspects related with the Dynamic Evolution concern: the Sensor aspect, the EvolutionPlanner aspect and the Actuator aspect (there are other aspects, related to the Dynamic Reconfiguration concern, but they are outside the scope of this paper). The Sensor aspect provides low-level services to *monitorize* several properties of the architecture, such as the current configuration of the architecture or the status of the architecture, that determine whether an evolution can be performed safely (i.e. running transactions have been finished in a consistent way) or not. The *Actuator* aspect provides low-level services to *change* the architecture, by introducing or deleting architectural elements or connections. The *Evolution-Planner* aspect (it is different from the type-level one, but they are directly connected) is responsible for updating the architecture according to the changes reflected in the software architecture pattern, by coordinating the actions to be performed by the Actuator and Sensor aspects.

However, as PRISMA system types only describe an architecture pattern, each configuration (S_1, S_2) of the PRISMA system (S) will only be evolved in a conservative way. For instance, in the architectural pattern of S, it is described that a component A can be connected to n instances of B. If the pattern is changed to allow only a connection of A components to 1 instance of B components, how can be determined which of the B instances should remain and which should be deleted? This is addressed in a conservative way: the old configuration is preserved, but new reconfigurations will only be made to conform with the new architectural pattern. In this way, the set of available reconfiguration services are those that allow to add new instances or connections described in the architectural pattern, and those that allow to remove old instances and connections which are not already permitted in the pattern.

4 Related Works

Several works have addressed dynamic evolution of software systems [3, 8, 12]. SOFA [4] and Plastik [1] component models both provide support for dynamic reconfiguration of software architectures. However, these works do not model how the evolution mechanisms are provided to software architectures. Several architecture-based approaches that provide self-adaptation capabilities [15] have emerged. Dashofy [9] and the Rainbow framework [10] describe an architecture-based approach to provide the self-healing and the self-adaptation of running systems, respectively. However, both approaches use external and centralized reconfiguration mechanisms instead of using localised mechanisms to each system instance. Ramdane-Cherif [20] uses an agent-based approach to dynamically adapt software architectures. Compared to our approach, it also provides a software artifact (an agent) responsible for the dynamic evolution of a complex component. However, it does not address how the mechanisms for dynamic evolution are made accessible for the agent, which is a kind of external entity of the system.

Morrison et al. [13] describes evolvable systems as structured in two functional processes: a Producer, which provides the system behaviour (i.e. an architecture), and an Evolver, which is able to evolve this behaviour (i.e. to change the architecture). The Evolver process decides when to evolve the Producer process taking into account the feedback received both from the Producer or the environment. This approach is closely related to ours, as it provides localised change to each complex component instance and it separates specifically functionality from evolution. In contrast, we have separated the evolution concern by using aspects, in order to benefit the reuse and easy maintenance they provide.

5 Conclusions and Further Work

This paper has described an approach to manage the dynamic evolution of architectural element types from a platform-independent view. The infrastructure described supports the dynamic evolution of types as well as its instances, in a consistent way and without erode the system architecture. For that, the approach is based on the ideas of architectural patterns and aspect-oriented development. On the one hand, architectural patterns of PRISMA systems are used as a way for describing (and limiting) the set of possible configurations on which a complex component can be dynamically reconfigured. On the other hand, aspects are used to encapsulate the different concerns involved in the dynamic evolution process. In this way, another contribution of this work is the categorization of the main concerns to take into account when evolving software architectures at run-time. Furthermore, evolution does not depend on external or system centralized entities. The main advantage of providing local evolution is that the encapsulation principle is preserved: an architectural type is a black box and its evolution can only be performed by the internal mechanisms of the type, which are aware of the internal type structure and how to change it. We are currently working in mapping the concepts described in this paper to the PRISMANET middleware [19], which supports the execution of PRISMA architectures and its dynamic reconfiguration. We also plan to study and compare the run-time overhead added to the execution of PRISMA systems by the dynamic evolution mechanisms introduced in this work.

Acknowledgements. This work is funded by the Spanish Dept. of Sci. and Tech. under the National Program for R+I+D, META project TIN2006-15175-C05-01 and cofunded by the Comunidad de Madrid and the Rey Juan Carlos Univ. under the IASOMM project URJC-CM-2007-CET-1555. This work is also supported by a FPI grant from Conselleria d'Educació i Ciència (Generalitat Valenciana) to C. Costa.

References

1. Batista, T., Joolia, A., Coulson, G.: Managing Dynamic Reconfiguration in Component-Based Systems. In: Morrison, R., Oquendo, F. (eds.) EWSA 2005. LNCS, vol. 3527, pp. 1–17. Springer, Heidelberg (2005)
2. Bradbury, J.S., Cordy, J.R., Dingel, J., Wermelinger, M.: A Survey of Self-Management in Dynamic Software Architecture Specifications. In: Proc. of 1st ACM SIGSOFT Workshop on Self-Managed Systems (WOSS 2004), Newport Beach, California, pp. 28–33 (2004)
3. Buckley, J., Mens, T., Zenger, M., Rashid, A., Kniesel, G.: Towards a taxonomy of software change. Journal on Software Maintenance and Evolution 17(5) (2005)
4. Bures, T., Hnetynka, P., Plasil, F.: SOFA 2.0: Balancing Advanced Features in a Hierarchical Component Model. In: 4th Int. Conference on Software Engineering Research, Management and Applications (SERA 2006), Seattle, Washington, USA, pp. 40–48 (2006)
5. Chitchyan, R., Rashid, A., Sawyer, P., et al.: Report Synthesizing State-of-the-Art in Aspect-Oriented Requirements Engineering, Architectures and Design. Technical Report AOSD-Europe Deliverable D11, AOSD-Europe-ULANC-9. Lancaster Univ., UK (2005)
6. Costa, C., Ali, N., Pérez, J., Carsí, J.A., Ramos, I.: Dynamic Reconfiguration of Software Architectures through Aspects. In: Oquendo, F. (ed.) ECSA 2007. LNCS, vol. 4758, pp. 279–283. Springer, Heidelberg (2007)
7. Costa, C., Pérez, J., Carsí, J.A.: Dynamic Adaptation of Aspect-Oriented Components. In: Schmidt, H.W., Crnković, I., Heineman, G.T., Stafford, J.A. (eds.) CBSE 2007. LNCS, vol. 4608, pp. 49–65. Springer, Heidelberg (2007)
8. Cuesta, C.E., Fuente, P.d.l., Barrio-Solárzano, M.: Dynamic Coordination Architecture through the use of Reflection. In: Proc. of 2001 ACM Symposium on Applied Computing, Las Vegas, Nevada, United States, pp. 134–140 (2001)
9. Dashofy, E.M., van der Hoek, A., Taylor, R.N.: Towards Architecture-Based Self-Healing Systems. In: Proc. of 1st Workshop on Self-Healing Systems (WOSS 2002), Carolina (2002)
10. Garlan, D., Cheng, S., Huang, S., Schmerl, B., Steenkiste, P.: Rainbow: Architecture-Based Self-Adaptation with Reusable Infrastructure. Computer 37, 46–54 (2004)
11. Hnetynka, P., Plásil, F.: Dynamic Reconfiguration and Access to Services in Hierarchical Component Models. In: Gorton, I., Heineman, G.T., Crnković, I., Schmidt, H.W., Stafford, J.A., Szyperski, C.A., Wallnau, K. (eds.) CBSE 2006. LNCS, vol. 4063, pp. 352–359. Springer, Heidelberg (2006)
12. McKinley, P.K., Sadjadi, S.M., Kasten, E.P., Cheng, B.H.C.: Composing Adaptive Software. Computer 37(7), 56–64 (2004)
13. Morrison, R., Balasubramaniam, D., Kirby, G., et al.: A Framework for Supporting Dynamic Systems Co-Evolution. Autom. Software. Eng. 14(3), 261–292 (2007)

14. OMG: Model Driven Architecture Guide,
    `http://www.omg.org/docs/omg/03-06-01.pdf`
15. Oreizy, P., Gorlick, M., Taylor, R.N., Heimbigner, D., Johnson, G., et al.: An Architecture-Based Approach to Self-Adaptive Software. IEEE Intelligent Systems 14, 54–62 (1999)
16. Pérez, J.: PRISMA: Aspect-Oriented Software Architectures. PhD Thesis, Department of Information Systems and Computation, Polytechnic University of Valencia (2006)
17. Pérez, J., Ali, N., Carsí, J.A., Ramos, I.: Designing Software Architectures with an Aspect-Oriented Architecture Description Language. In: Gorton, I., Heineman, G.T., Crnković, I., Schmidt, H.W., Stafford, J.A., Szyperski, C.A., Wallnau, K. (eds.) CBSE 2006. LNCS, vol. 4063, pp. 123–138. Springer, Heidelberg (2006)
18. Pérez, J., Ali, N., Carsí, J.A., Ramos, I.: Dynamic Evolution in Aspect-Oriented Architectural Models. In: Morrison, R., Oquendo, F. (eds.) EWSA 2005. LNCS, vol. 3527, pp. 59–76. Springer, Heidelberg (2005)
19. Pérez, J., Ali, N., Costa, C., Carsí, J.A., Ramos, I.: Executing Aspect-Oriented Component-Based Software Architectures on .NET Technology. In: Proc. of 3rd International Conference on .NET Technologies, Pilsen, Czech Republic, pp. 97–108 (2005)
20. Ramdane-Cherif, A., Lévy, N., Losavio, F.: Agent Paradigm for Adaptable Architecture. Journal of Object Technology 3(8), 169–182 (2004)

TADL - An Architecture Description Language for Trustworthy Component-Based Systems[*]

Mubarak Mohammad[1] and Vasu Alagar[1,2]

[1] Concordia University, Montreal, Canada
[2] X'ian Jiaotong-Liverpool University, Suzhou, PRC
`{ms_moham,alagar}@cse.concordia.ca`

Abstract. Existing architecture description languages mainly support the specification of the structural elements of the system under design with either only a limited support or no support to specify non-functional requirements. In a component-based development of trustworthy systems, the trustworthiness properties must be specified at the architectural level. Analysis techniques should be available to verify the trustworthiness properties early at design time. Towards this goal we present in this paper a meta-architecture and TADL, a new architecture description language suited for describing the architecture of trustworthy component-based systems. The TADL is a uniform language for specifying the structural, functional, and nonfunctional requirements of component-based systems. It also provides a uniform source for analyzing the different trustworthiness properties.

1 Introduction

This paper presents a meta-architecture model that serves as a type for defining the basic elements for building a trustworthy component-based system. These elements can be divided into (1) the essential structural elements of component-based development, such as components, interfaces, and connectors, and (2) trustworthiness features including a safety contract and a security mechanism defined as first class architectural elements. A system definition, when instantiated from the meta-architecture, includes hardware and software components along with deployment configuration. Also, the paper introduces TADL, a new architecture description language suited for describing the architecture of trustworthy component-based systems. The meta-architecture is based on formal foundation presented in our earlier work [1]. The formalism provides a formal notation for specifying trustworthy components and a method for composing components. The composition preserves trustworthiness properties. The formalism is supported by a verification oriented formal methodology [2] for the automatic generation of component behavior and a model checking method for verifying the trustworthiness properties.

2 Meta Architecture

In the literature [3,5], there is a consensus that trustworthiness involves achieving *availability*, *reliability*, *safety*, and *security*. System *availability*, and *reliability* are run-time

---

[*] This research is supported by a Research Grant from Natural Sciences and Engineering Research Council of Canada.(NSERC).

R. Morrison, D. Balasubramaniam, and K. Falkner (Eds.): ECSA 2008, LNCS 5292, pp. 290–297, 2008.

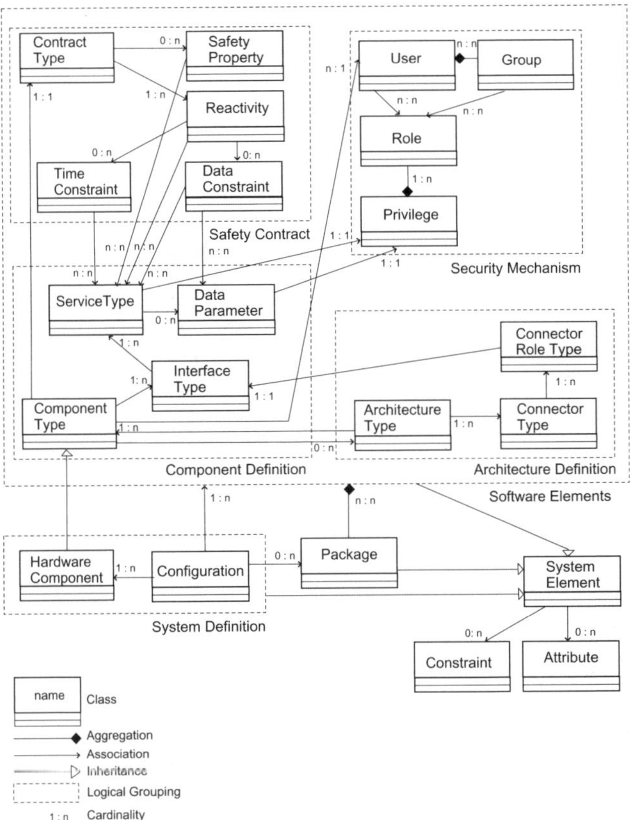

Fig. 1. Meta-Architecture

quality of service requirements, where as *safety* and *security* are specifiable at design time. Hence we define them as the credentials of trustworthiness at architectural level. We address methods for achieving availability and reliability as part of our rigorous development process, which is under development now.

Figure 1 depicts the meta-architecture. The meta architecture that we define is a type from which different system architectures can be created. The main building blocks of the meta-architecture are *component definition, component architecture definition, safety contract, security mechanism, system definition, package, constraint*, and *attribute*. All the elements in the model inherit from the *System Element* which contains basic class definition along with attributes and constraints. A component definition includes an architecture definition, the internal structure of the component implementation, and a safety contract specification, a description of the associations between requests for services and their responses together with restrictions that constrain the behavior of interactions. In addition, a component definition uses a security mechanism to control the requests of services at its interfaces and the information communicated through interfaces. The system definition contains *hardware components* description

```
ElementType < name > {                 ServiceType < name > {
      (Attribute < name >)*;                 (Attribute < name >)*;
}                                             (Constraint < FOPL >)*;
                                              (ParameterType < name >)*;}
ParameterType < name > {
      < DataType >< name >;           Attribute< name > {
      Default < value >;}                     < DataType >< name >;
                                              Default < value >;}
```

Fig. 2. The TADL syntax of Element Type, Parameter Type, Service Type, and Attribute

and system *configuration* specification. A package contains a collection of definitions of related elements. Detailed descriptions and further discussion of the elements of the meta-architecture are provided while discussing TADL features in the next section.

3 TADL

This section introduces an architecture description language for trustworthy systems (TADL). The TADL introduces new concepts such as safety contract and security mechanism. Also, it provides a detailed specification of components by introducing the new concepts *service*, *data parameter*, *contract* and *architecture* at the interface level.

In TADL, every element of the meta-architecture is described separately. The rationale behind this is to increase reuse and allow reconfiguration without affecting other definitions. The description of an element contains: (1) element type, (2) element name, and (3) specification of the contents of the element. Figure 2 gives an example of an element specification. Note that $(Attribute < name >)*$ means that 0 or more attributes can be defined as part of the element. The following sections describe the elements of the meta architecture shown in Figure 1.

Service and data parameter: Components provide/request parameterized services via interfaces. A *data parameter* is a variable value passed to the component within a request for service or passed from the service within a provided service (similar to a function parameter in C++). The definition of a data parameter includes name, data type, and possible default value. Data types can be simple (e.g., integer, float, char, etc) or complex data structures (e.g., queue, stack, structure, object, etc). The ADL description of a data parameter type is given in Figure 2. Modeling data parameters as first class architectural elements has three important implications. These are:

- It allows modeling different types of simple and complex data communicated at the interfaces of a component, which results in a rich communication specification.
- It provides a mechanism for securing the information passed through the interfaces of a component. Security is essential for both the services and the data communicated at the interfaces. Therefore, explicit modeling of data parameters enables designing information security at architectural level.

– It enables rich specification of safety contracts by regulating reactions of the component based on values of data parameters.

Services model the functionalities provided or required by a component. A service is provided at an interface. It can have an arbitrary number of data parameters. There is no other ADL, that we are aware of, which explicitly defines services as architectural elements. The service definition may include *attributes* in addition to data parameters. Attributes are semantic information associated with any meta-architecture element. The data type of an attribute can be simple or complex data structure. As an example, attributes can be used to define real-time information, such as priority and worst-case execution time, that is necessary for performing real-time schedulability analysis. Also, the service definition can include *constraints*, which are invariants defined as part of the specification of meta-architecture elements. We use a first-order predicate logic (FOPL) for defining constraints. The syntax of the service type and attribute definitions are described in Figure 2.

Safety contract: The explicit specification of services as first class architectural elements enriches the trustworthiness specification by providing a mechanism to regulate, restrict, and filter services at the interfaces of a component. Regulating services enables real-time schedulability analysis. Restricting services promotes safety. Filtering services enforces security at the interfaces of a component.

Regulating services: The responses of a component are regulated by defining *time constraints*. A time constraint specifies the maximum amount of time allowed to elapse between the time of receiving a request and the time of sending the response. This is an essential requirement for safety critical systems where timeliness is a critical factor in defining safety. Figure 3 shows the syntax of a time constraint. It comprises a set of attributes and constraints, two service types defining the request and response services, two predicates specifying which one is the request ($RequestService$) and which one is the response ($ResponseService$), and the *maximum safe time*. The maximum safe time is the time interval between the occurrence of a request and the corresponding response.

Restricting services: The responses of a component are restricted using *data constraints*, a special type of constraint that is used to decide whether or not a specific response for a requested service should be sent. The decision is based on the values of the data parameters associated with the service and the attributes of the requested service, the interface through which the response is to be provided, and the component that provides the service. The response is given only if the constraint evaluates to true. Figure 3 includes the syntax of the data constraint.

Filtering services: The responses of a component are filtered according to the security specification. A service request will be accepted only from a component which is executing on behalf of a user who has a privilege to request it, and a service response will be sent only if the user, on whose behalf the receiving component is executing, has a privilege to receive it. Moreover, the data parameters associated with the service (requested or provided) are subject to security inspection. These data information will be filtered unless the user who sent the request or waiting for response has proper privilege to view it. Further discussion of security mechanism is provided later on.

TimeConstraint $< name > \{$
    (Attribute $< name >$)*;
    (Constraint $< FOPL >$)*;
    ServiceType $< request - name >$;
    $RequestService$
    $(< request - name >)$;
    ServiceType $< response - name >$;
    $ResponseService$
    $(< response - name >)$;
    $float\ MaxSafeTime;\}$

DataConstraint $< name > \{$
    (Attribute $< name >$)*;
    ServiceType $< request - name >$;
    $RequestService$
    $(< request - name >)$;
    ServiceType $< response - name >$;
    $ResponseService$
    $(< response - name >)$;
    Constraint $< FOPL >;\}$

Reactivity $< name > \{$
    ServiceType $< request - name >$;
    $RequestService$
    $(< request - name >)$;
    ServiceType $< response - name >$;
    $ResponseService$
    $(< response - name >)$;
    (DataConstraint $< name >$)*;
    (TimeConstraint $< name >$)*;
$\}$

SafetyProperty $< name > \{$
    (ServiceType $< name >$)*;
    Constraint $< FOPL >;\}$

ContractType $< name > \{$
    (Reactivity $< name >$)+;
    (SafetyProperty $< name >$)*;$\}$

Fig. 3. The TADL syntax of Time and Data Constraint, Reactivity, Safety Property, and Contract

When a request for service is received by a component, it reacts by providing a response. The association between requested services and their provided responses is defined using *reactivity*. Reactivity specification is important for ensuring predictability which is an essential requirement of safety critical systems. Reactivity can be governed by a time constraint. That is, the response should occur within the maximum safe time. In general, a service request may have more than one possible response. Data constraints are used to avoid this nondeterminism. For each possible response, a data constraint is defined such that only one data constraint can be true at an instant. Therefore, only one response will be selected. Figure 3 includes the syntax definition of reactivity.

Safety properties are defined at the interfaces of a component to enforce safe behavior. A safety property is an invariant over the behavior of a component. The behavior can be defined using timed automata. In [2] we have provided an automated approach for generating the behavior of a component by analyzing its architecture. A safety property is regarded as a special type of constraint over the services provided by the component. Figure 3 includes the syntax of safety property definition.

A safety contract type defines a nonempty set of reactivities and safety properties. The rationale behind specifying the contract outside of the component type definition is to allow reuse of a contract for other components that provide similar services, and to enable reconfiguration of its specification. The reconfiguration updates maximum safe time, data constraints, and reactivity for different system configurations and deployment plans. Figure 3 includes the syntax of safety contract type definition.

Component architecture: The structural description of a component includes definitions of *interface types, connector role types, connector types, architecture types,* and *component types*. An interface type enumerates a finite set of services communicated through it. An interface type can have a set of attributes and a protocol specification, stored in an external file.

A connector role type serves as an interface to a connector. It links a connector to a component interface. A connector is a special component that defines the connectivity between components. A connector type definition includes a non-empty finite set of connector role types in addition to attributes and constraints.

A component can be primitive or composite. A composite component is built by assembling existing components and specifying their connectors. An *architecture type* defines the structure of a composite component in which the constituent components and their internal connections are specified. A component type can have multiple possible architecture types. An architecture type comprises connector types, attributes, constraints, and *attachments*. An attachment specifies how components are connected. This is specified by linking the interface type of a connector role type with an interface type of a component at both ends of a connector. Defining the architecture outside of the component type definition increases reuse and allows reconfiguration of architecture without changing the component definition.

A component type definition includes definitions of interface types, architecture types, a contract, attributes, and constraints. If no architecture is specified then the component type denotes a primitive component. In a composite component's type definition, the list of interface types that are not attached to connector role types form the external interface types, whereas the attached ones form the internal interface types. Figure 4 presents the syntax of the structural elements' definitions.

```
InterfaceType < name > {
    String Protocol;
    (Attribute < name >)*;
    (ServiceType < name >)*;}


ConnectorRoleType < name > {
    (Attribute < name >)*;
    (Constraint < FOPL >)*;
    InterfaceType < name >;}


ConnectorType < name > {
    (ConnectorRoleType < name >)+;
    (Attribute < name >)*;
    (Constraint < FOPL >)*;}
```

```
ArchitectureType < name > {
    (ComponentType < name >)+;
    (ConnectorType < name >)+;
    (Attribute < name >)*;
    (Constraint < FOPL >)*;
    (Attachment
    (ConnectorType.RoleType.InterfaceType,
    ComponentType.InterfaceType))*;}


ComponentType < name > {
    (Attribute < name >)*;
    (Constraint < FOPL >)*;
    User u;
    (InterfaceType < name >)+;
    (ArchitectureType < name >)*;
    ContractType < name >;}
```

Fig. 4. The TADL syntax of Interface Type, Connector Role Type, Connector Type, Architecture Type, and Component Type

Security mechanism: The component type definition includes a *user* attribute. This attribute is set at component's instantiation time with a value that denotes the identity of the user on whose behalf the component executes. The value is assigned from a domain of user identities defined at system level and represented by the *user* element.

The security mechanism is based on role-based security access control (RBAC). The mechanism restricts access of services and data parameters to authorized users only. In [1] we have defined the security property in terms of *service security* and *data security*. Service security states that: (1) for every request received at the interfaces of a component, the request should be received from a user who has permission to request the service, and (2) for every response sent by the component, the user who will receive the response should have permission to receive it. Data security states that: (1) for every request received, for every data parameter in the request, the user sending the request should have permission to access the data parameter, and (2) for every response sent, for every data parameter associated with the response, the user receiving the response should have permission to access the data parameter. If a user does not have a permission to send a request then the request will be ignored. Also, if a user does not have a permission to receive a response, the response will not be sent. On the same manner, if a user does not have a permission to access a data parameter, the data parameter value is set to null value. The main concepts in RBAC are user, *group*, *role*, and *privilege*. A group defines a set of related users. A user can be part of many groups. A role defines a security responsibility that a user or a group of users can take in the system. A privilege defines a permission to access a service or a data parameter. A role comprises many privileges. A privilege can be assigned to many roles.

```
User< name > {
    (Attribute < name >)*;
    (Constraint < FOPL >)*;}

Group< name > {
    (Attribute < name >)*;
    (Constraint < FOPL >)*;}

Role< name > {
    (Attribute < name >)*;
    (Constraint < FOPL >)*;}

Privilege< name > {
    (Attribute < name >)*;
    (Constraint < FOPL >)*;}
```

```
RBAC< name > {
    (Users < name >)*;
    (Groups < name >)*;
    (Roles < name >)*;
    (Privilege < name >)*;
    (User-Groups-Assignment(User,Group))*;
    (User-Roles-Assignment(User,Role))*;
    (Group-Roles-Assignment(Group,Role))*;
    (ServiceType < name >)*;
    (ParameterType < name >)*;
    (Privileges-for-services
            (Service,Privilege,Role))*;
    (Privileges-for-data-parameters
            (DataParameter,Privilege,Role))*;}

Configuration< name > {
    (SystemElement < name >)+;
    (Deploy(HardwareComponentType,
    ComponentType))+; }
```

Fig. 5. The TADL syntax of RBAC and Configuration specification

The functions *User-Groups-Assignment*, *User-Roles-Assignment*, and *Group-Roles-Assignment* are used to assign users to groups, roles to users, and roles to groups accordingly.

Service privilege and data parameter privilege are the only types of privileges in the security mechanism. A service privilege defines an access right for a service. Hence, it is associated with services and roles using the function *Privileges-for-services*. A data parameter privilege defines an access right for a data parameter. Therefore, it is associated with data parameters and roles using the function *Privileges-for-data-parameters*. Figure 5 includes the TADL syntax of the RBAC specification.

System definition: A *package* includes definitions of all the preceding meta-architecture elements. It is used to simplify the specification when reusing related elements. The system definition consists of *hardware components* and *configuration*. A hardware component is a special type of component on which the software components will be deployed i.e. a deployment units. Resource capabilities of deployment units are specified as attributes. For example, a hardware component definition can include attributes such as number of CPUs and memory capacity. The system configuration specification includes: (1) instances of the defined software and hardware component types, and (2) deployment specification, assignments of software instances to hardware instances using the *Deploy* function. Figure 5 includes the TADL syntax of system configuration.

4   Conclusion

This paper introduced a new architecture definition language for describing a formal meta-architecture for the development of trustworthy systems. TADL specifications are supported by automatic analysis techniques to verify the trustworthiness properties. A detailed description of the meta-architecture, the rational for designing the new TADL presented in this paper, methods for analysis and reasoning about trustworthiness, and a case study are presented in [4].

References

1. Alagar, V., Mohammad, M.: A component model for trustworthy real-time reactive systems development. In: International Workshop on Formal Aspects of Component Software (FACS 2007), Sophia-Antipolis, France (September 2007)
2. Alagar, V., Mohammad, M.: Specification and verification of trustworthy component-based real-time reactive systems. In: SAVCBS 2007, Specification and Verification of Component-Based Systems, Dubrovnik, Croatia (September 2007)
3. Avizienis, A., Laprie, J.-C., Randell, B.: Fundamental concepts of dependability. Research report N01145, LAAS-CNRS (April 2001)
4. Mohammad, M., Alagar, V.: TADL - An Architecture Description Language for Trustworthy Component-Based Systems. Technical Report ACTS-Trust-08-02, Concordia University (July 2008), http://users.encs.concordia.ca/~ms_moham/tadl.html
5. Schneider, F.B., Bellovin, S.M., Inouye, A.S.: Building trustworthy systems: Lessons from the PTN and internet. IEEE Internet Computing 3(6), 64–72 (1999)

L-DSMS – A Local Data Stream Management System

Christian Hänsel, Hans Jürgen Ohlbach, and Edgar Stoffel

Department of Computer Science, University of Munich
{haensel,ohlbach,stoffel}@ifi.lmu.de

Abstract. L-DSMS is a Local Data Stream Management System. It is a Java Program which can read an XML-file with a description of a network of processing nodes for streaming data. L-DSMS automatically combines all the processing nodes into a single Java program which then processes the data. L-DSMS has a number of predefined nodes, together with an interface for implementing new processing nodes. The generated network can be remotely monitored and reconfigured by a client, Visu-L-DSMS. An example application of L-DSMS is the transformation of RDS-TMC traffic messages into KML, which, in turn, can be visualised by Google Earth.

1   Introduction

Computer programs can operate in quite different modes. The simplest mode is: they get started, read some data, compute something, output some results and terminate. Another mode is the server mode: they wait for some input from a user or a client, do something, and then wait for the next input. A further mode is the *streaming mode*: they get permanently fed with data, process it, and dump the results somewhere, while the next input is already waiting. The data may come from sensors, or, nowadays more typically, from sources on the Internet.

Data Stream Management Systems [1,2] have been developed to connect networks (grids) of computers in such a way that each computer can receive data, process them and forward the results to some other computer. The ideas behind L-DSMS are quite similar to these kind of Data Stream Management Systems. The main difference is that the processing takes place within a single computer, or, more precisely, within a single Java Virtual Machine (JVM). It realises a pipe-and-filter architecture within a JVM. Several instances of L-DSMS can of course run on different computes and be connected in the same way as Data Stream Management Systems.

Programs which process data streams on a single computer can be implemented in different ways. The easiest way is to implement a concrete application as a single monolithic program. A more flexible and comfortable way is to split the program into separate "processing nodes". Processing nodes receive data from some standard input interface, process them in some way, and deliver the results to some standard output interface. A particular application can then be

R. Morrison, D. Balasubramaniam, and K. Falkner (Eds.): ECSA 2008, LNCS 5292, pp. 298–305, 2008.

realised by writing a program that loads the necessary processing nodes, and connect them such that the data can be forwarded from node to node. This seems to be the approach of the MeDICi Integration Framework [3]. Their system allows one to connect processing nodes which are even written in different programming languages.

Alternatively to writing an application specific program that connects the necessary nodes, one can specify the network of processing nodes in an XML-file. A general network configurator can then read such a specification, load the necessary processing nodes, connects them and starts the processing. The network configurator is completely independent of the actual application. Therefore no programming is necessary any more for generating special applications. This is the approach of the L-DSMS system, presented in this paper.

Instead of specifying the network configuration in an XML-file, one can write a user interface that allows one to specify a particular network by arranging icons on the screen. Yahoo pipes (`http://www.jumpcut.com/pipes_team`) is a nice example for this approach. It has a number of predefined nodes which process, for example, news feeds. A user can use it to specify his particular view on Internet messages. The Visu-L-DSMS component of L-DSMS goes halfway this line. Visu-L-DSMS is a client program which can visualise and monitor L-DSMS networks running on some remote servers. It can also be used to change parameters of processing nodes in a running L-DSMS application, but so far it cannot be used to configure a new network.

The prototype application, which has been used to test L-DSMS is a system which receives traffic information via RDS-TMC radio signals and converts them into KML-files, which in turn, can be displayed by Google Earth. This way, Google Earth is able to integrate traffic information into its displayed road maps. The URL is `http://nihiru.pms.ifi.lmu.de/ge-tmc-server/GeoData.php?type=1&format=1`.

This paper describes the general ideas and concepts. The technical details and the code are available from the L-DSMS home page (`http://www.pms.ifi.lmu.de/rewerse-wga1/ldsms/`) and in a deliverable of the EU Network of Excellence REWERSE [4].

2 Node Types

The L-DSMS system distinguishes three different node types: *sources, drains* and *general processing nodes.* Sources push data into the system (usually by reading them from some external source). Drains receive data from the system, and usually forward them to some destination outside the system. Finally, processing nodes receive data, process them and forward them to other nodes.

A *source* is always at the head of a production path and produces the data that needs to be processed. Each source may produce data in a different way. The L-DSMS core package contains sources that read data from files, sockets or external hardware (cf. Sect. 6). In most of the cases, a source receives its data from outside L-DSMS (e.g. from a sensor or from some data source on the web).

To provide additional information about the produced data, a source can create optional meta information for each produced data package. A data packet together with its optional meta data forms the output of a source. A source needs to have at least one connected component that receives the output. There can be an arbitrary number of drains or processing nodes as connected components of a source node. Which drains or nodes are connected to a source, is specified in the configuration file. When connecting a node to a source node, one has to ensure that the data and meta data output types of the source are subtypes to the data and meta data input types of all connected components. The configuration file contains, beside the relation between sources and their connected components, for each source node two general and some further specific attributes. The general ones are a `name` and a `class`, which can be 'source', 'node' or 'drain'. The `ByteArrayFileSource`, for example, has the additional attributes `file`, `delay` and `repeat`.

A *drain* is the final receiver of data, because it can not have any child components inside of the system boundaries of L-DSMS. The data can of course be forwarded to some receivers outside L-DSMS. A `SocketDrain`, for example, forwards the incoming data to every process connected to this drain via a socket connection. The L-DSMS core package contains drains for writing the incoming data into files, sending them over socket connections, or simply printing them to the console screen.

Drains can receive their data and meta data from one ore more sources or processing nodes. The connections between a drain and its parent components are specified in the configuration file. Besides the `class` attribute, each drain has the optional attribute `sourcerefs` which contains the names of the parent components for this drain. A drain can of course have further specific attributes.

Processing nodes are a combination of sources and drains and can be positioned at every possible place within a production line. They receive data and meta data from one ore more components, process them and forward the results to an arbitrary number of consumer nodes. Since processing nodes are sources as well as drains, they inherit the attributes of both of them. Nodes are configured in the same way as sources and drains. Besides node specific attributes, they all have the mandatory `class` attribute and an optional `name` attribute. In addition they have sources (like a drain), which are specified with the `sourcerefs` attribute.

3 How the L-DSMS Network Operates

When it gets started, the L-DSMS system reads a configuration file and arranges the network of processing nodes. The network, hopefully, has some source nodes, possibly some further processing nodes and some drain nodes. Each node, except the drains, have a list of successor nodes, the *consumer nodes*, and each of them has a `consume` method. The source nodes have a `start` method.

After the network is ready for operation, a network broker calls the `start` method of each source node. It is the responsibility of the source node's `start` method to start a thread that does the actual work. If a source node does not start a thread, then the **start** method is just called only once. If this call terminates, it is never called again. This makes sense if there is only one single source node.

After a source node has assembled a packet of data, it calls a **send** method for the data packet together with the meta data. The **send** method in turn calls the **consume** methods for all attached consumers. The **consume** method of a node N can do some processing and then call its **send** method, which in turn calls the **consume** methods of all consumers attached to N. This way, eventually the **consume** methods of the drain nodes get called and dump the data somewhere outside the system.

If there is a single source node and the network has a tree structure then this procedure passes the data through the tree in a depth first left to right order. The **consume** methods could, however, start their own threads when they get called first. Each time they get called next, they just forward the data to the corresponding thread and terminate. The threads can then process the data in parallel. This would result in a more breadth first like traversal through the net.

Another alternative is to implement node classes whose **consume** methods *synchronise* data from different sources. The first time, such a **consume** method is called from one source, it just stores the data locally and terminates. If it is called a second time, maybe from a different source, it can combine the new data with the previously stored data.

With this architecture the network broker need not manage any threads. It depends on the implementation of the **consume** methods to operate with or without threads. Even an agent architecture platform can be implemented this way

This example illustrates a very basic configuration, that prints "Hello World" onto the screen.

Listing 1.1. examples/hello_world/config.xml

```xml
 1  <?xml version="1.0" encoding="ISO-8859-1" ?>
 2
 3  <server>
 4    <logging level="INFO" />
 5    <services>
 6      <network>
 7        <source class="generics.StringFileSource" file="
 8            examples/hello_world/input.txt">
 8          <drain class="generics.ConsoleDrain" />
 9        </source>
10      </network>
11    </services>
12  </server>
```

In line 7 of the configuration file, a **StringFileSource** was specified. This FileSource reads every data from the text file, specified by the *file* attribute of the source element ('examples/hello_world/input.txt' in this case). In line 8, a `ConsoleDrain` was specified. A ConsoleDrain prints every input to the console. Because the `ConsoleDrain` is specified as a child element of `StringFileSource`, every output of the `StringFileSource` (here, the data from the text file) is passed to the input of the `ConsoleDrain`.

4   How to Extend L-DSMS

Although the L-DSMS library contains already a number of predefined node types, every new application will need its own specific processing nodes. L-DSMS supports adding new node types by providing corresponding interfaces and abstract classes. They specify exactly how the new classes have to be implemented.

Every component that should be treated as a source node has to implement, either directly or indirectly, the interface ⟨ldsms core package⟩.network.Source A detailed description of its methods can be found in the JavaDoc documentation at the L-DSMS project page (http://www.pms.ifi.lmu.de/rewerse-wga1/ldsms/). The abstract class `SourceImpl` already implements the interface 'Source'. It can be used as the superclass for new Source classes.

Every new drain class has to implement, either directly or indirectly, the interface ⟨ldsms core package⟩.network.Drain. The abstract class `DrainImpl` already implements this interface and can be used as superclass of a new drain class. Drains that need additional attributes from the configuration file, additionally have to implement the interface **org.apache.avalon.framework.configuration. Configurable**. This ensures, that the configuration information from the configuration file are passed to the Drain. Drains that need to be started or stopped, additionally have to implement the interface **oorg.apache.avalon. framework.activity.Startable**. This ensures, that the server starts the drain after the configuration has been finished and that the server stops the drain if the system is forced to terminate. This is useful, if additionally threads are used or streams have to be opened and closed.

Processing nodes are a combination of a drain and a source. Every node has therefore to implement both interfaces, for drains and for sources. The abstract class `Node` implements both interfaces already. It can therefore be inherited by a new node class. The most important method to implement for processing nodes and drain nodes is `consume(data,metadata)`. It is called by other nodes to pass data and meta data to the current node.

5   Managing L-DSMS with VISU-L-DSMS

VISU-L-DSMS is the graphic user interface for L-DSMS that was developed to ease the management of L-DSMS. It can manage instances of L-DSMS located at the same host as VISU-L-DSMS, as well as instances located on remote hosts.

As shown in Fig. 1, the VISU-L-DSMS main window contains three areas and one menu panel. At the left hand side there is the **Network View**, a graphic representation of all components, together with their relationship to

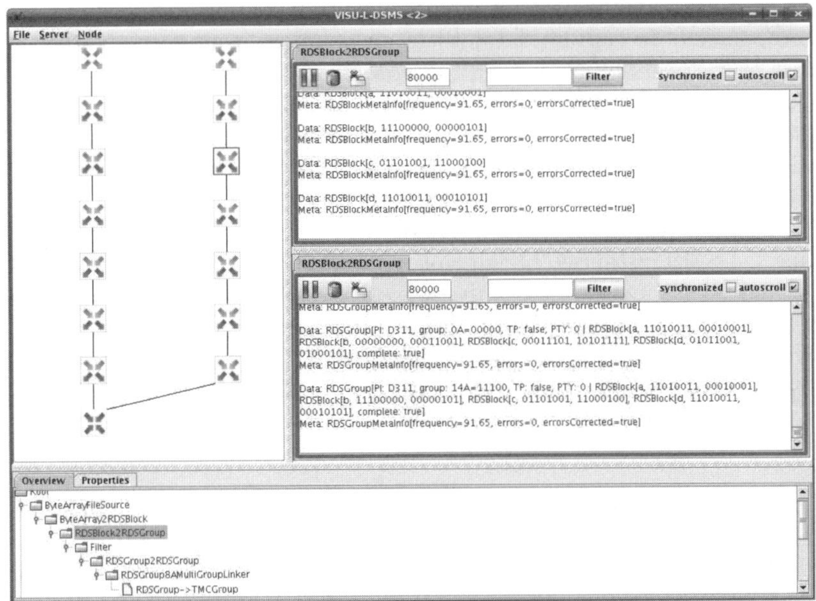

Fig. 1. VISU-L-DSMS Window

each other. Each component is represented as a node (coloured symbol) and their relationships to each other by edges (black lines).

At the right hand side there is the **Capturing View**. This area contains two frames. The upper frame is used to show the incoming data of a component selected in the network area. The lower frame is used to show the outgoing data of a component (the same or another one).

In the bottom area there are two tabs that provide additional information about the selected components of the network window (the **Overview Tab**) and their attributes (the **Properties tab**).

Once VISU-L-DSMS is connected to a running L-DSMS instance, the overview tab shows the names of all components in a tree structure with sources being the parents and their drains being the children (recursively). If a component is selected in the network area, its representation in the overview tab is selected as well, and vice versa. This gives a compact overview about the network structure while the names of the components are listed in the overview tab.

The properties tab is used to *display* and *edit* the attributes for the last component that has been selected. Each property is presented either as a text field, a list or a check box. Not all attributes, however, can be edited. Editing values doesn't affect the L-DSMS instance, until the changes are saved. Saving attributes causes the new values to be sent over the network to the observed L-DSMS instance and to change the corresponding node attributes. This way, a running L-DSMS system can be controlled remotely.

The capturing area is used for monitoring the incoming and outgoing data of the components. To capture data, select one or more components, either in the network or the overview area, open the `node` menu and select `start listening`. This opens a tab for the incoming data in the upper frame and a tab for the outgoing data in the lower frame for each selected component. If only selected data is to be displayed, a regular expression can be defined in the *filter field*. Only the data matching the regular expression is then displayed.

The current version of VISU-L-DSMS can only change node attributes of running L-DSMS instances. In principle it would be possible to extend VISU-L-DSMS and allow it to also change the network configuration. This way, a program for processing data streams could be generated just by arranging some graphic symbols in a suitable graphical editor. The only Java programming which would then still be necessary would be to extend the the L-DSMS library with new types of processing nodes.

6   Predefined Node Types

The L-DSMS core package contains a library of predefined node types. In this paper we list only the general purpose node types. A number of additional node types have been implemented for the test application, a system that feeds traffic information into Google Earth.

`ByteArrayFileSource` produces binary data by reading it from a file stream. `ByteArraySocketSource` reads binary data from a socket connection. `ObjectSocketSource` reads objects from a socket connection. `StringFileSource` reads a file as a list of strings. `StringSocketSource` reads strings from a socket connection and sends them in the same way as StringFileSource.

`ByteArrayFileDrain` writes the incoming data byte arrays and meta data byte arrays into the specified file. `ByteArraySocketDrain` sends the incoming data byte arrays and meta data byte arrays into the specified socket. `ConsoleDrain` prints every incoming data without any formating to the console. `ObjectSocketDrain` writes the incoming data and meta data into the output stream of a socket. `StringFileDrain` writes the incoming data strings with UTF-8 encoding into the specified file. `StringSocketDrain` writes the incoming byte strings to every client, connected at the specified port. `SpexNode` filters data from an XML stream, using the SpexProcessor and a XPath expression. The SpexProcessor extracts from streaming XML data the elements which are described by the given XPath expression [5].

`Buffer` caches information until it can be delivered to attached consumers. `ByteArray2String` transforms incoming byte arrays into strings, using the specified encoding format. `Cast` casts the input to the specified type and filters out any incompatible data or meta data objects. `Filter` tests whether the data and meta data meets a certain condition and passes it to its drains only if the condition is met. There is an elaborated language for specifying filters. `String2ByteArray` takes as input Strings and forwards them as byte arrays. The parameter 'encoding' can be used to specify the encoding format (e.g. US-ASCII, UTF-8, UTF-16BE, UTF-16LE, UTF-16 etc.).

7   Summary

L-DSMS is a local data stream management system. The configuration XML-files specify the structure of a processing network connecting source nodes with drain nodes via intermediate processing nodes. A network broker, implemented in Java, can read a configuration file and turn it into an executable Java program. A running L-DSMS instance can be monitored and, to a certain degree, modified remotely by Visu-L-DSMS. The system and its documentation is open source. It comes with a library of predefined node classes, together with interfaces for adding new node classes.

So far, only the parameters of node instances can be modified remotely by Visu-L-DSMS. A next step could be to specify and modify the whole network remotely, such that no XML editing would be necessary any more to configure a data stream processing system.

Acknowledgements

This research has been funded by the European Commission and by the Swiss Federal Office for Education and Science within the 6th Framework Programme project REWERSE number 506779 (cf. http://rewerse.net).

References

1. Babcock, B., Babu, S., Data, M., Motwani, R., Widom, J.: Models and issues in data stream systems. In: Proceedings of 21st ACM Symposium on Principles of Database Systems (PODS 2002) (2002)
2. Golab, L., Özsu, M.T.: Issues in data stream management. ACM SIGMOD Record (2003)
3. Gorton, I., Wynne, A., Almquist, J., Chatterton, J.: The medici integration framework: A platform for high performance data streaming applications. In: WICSA 2008: Proceedings of the Seventh Working IEEE/IFIP Conference on Software Architecture (WICSA 2008), Washington, DC, USA, pp. 95–104. IEEE Computer Society, Los Alamitos (2008)
4. Hänsel, C.: Implementation: L-DSMS - A Local Data Stream Management System. REWERSE deliverable A1-D10-3, Institute for Informatics, Ludwig-Maximilians-Universität München (2008), `http://idefix.pms.ifi.lmu.de:8080/rewerse/index.html#REWERSE-DEL-2008-A1-D10-3`
5. Olteanu, D.: Evaluation of XPath Queries against XML Streams. Dissertation/Ph.D. thesis, Institute of Computer Science, LMU, Munich, 2005. PhD Thesis, Institute for Informatics, University of Munich (2005)

Towards Independent Software Architecture Review*

Antony Tang, Fei-Ching Kuo, and Man F. Lau

Faculty of Information and Communication Technologies
Swinburne University of Technology, Australia
`{atang,dkuo,elau}@ict.swin.edu.au`

Abstract. Many software architecture evaluation methods, proposed by the research community, have a common problem of engaging the same architects to perform architecture design and evaluation. This violates the independence of quality assurance and hence may lead to biased evaluation, thereby resulting in inferior architectural design. In this paper, we analyze current approaches and issues to software architecture quality assurance. We propose seven conditions for architectural design quality assurance and discuss existing challenges towards independent software architecture design review.

1 Introduction

Software architecture has been studied for over two decades. There are various standards such as IEEE 1471-2000 [1] which define software architecture, and research articles such as [2] and [3] which discuss different aspects of software architecture. In the industry, most sizeable software development organizations have a software architect role, and some of them employ architectural frameworks such as Zachman framework, TOGAF or RM-ODP to represent architectural information.

The IEEE 1471-2000 standards defines architecture as the *fundamental organization of a system* [1] and Perry and Wolf define it as a model of *elements*, *forms* and *rationale* [2]. Such definitions are generic and subject to interpretations. As a result, different architects may have different interpretations of the scope and the level of details of an architectural design. It can logically be assumed that the more details are included in the architectural design, the easier it is to validate the design. Such assumption depends on the level of certainty that an architectural design is viable and of good quality whilst it still depicts an abstract view of the system [4]. In other words, *how can one be assured that the architectural design would lead to a finished system that satisfies all its requirements, both functional and non-functional?*

In practice, many architecture design evaluation methods were proposed to answer this question. However, their scope of work and process vary widely depending on their objectives. For example, some measuring techniques evaluate quality attributes only rather than the entire design as a whole. Moreover, some architectural review methods only aim at evaluating selected aspects of an architecture design. Since software architecture design is influenced by many factors, the challenge is to find a

* This work was supported in part by a grant from the DCRG scheme, Faculty of Information and Communication Technologies, Swinburne University of Technology.

R. Morrison, D. Balasubramaniam, and K. Falkner (Eds.): ECSA 2008, LNCS 5292, pp. 306–313, 2008.

review method(s) that can address the quality of architectural design holistically while keeping unnecessary subjective interpretations to a minimum. In this paper, we propose an independent software architecture review (ISAR) approach.

2 Issues of Existing Techniques

Evaluation techniques [4, 5], such as *questioning techniques* and *measuring techniques*, are used for architectural design quality assurance. Among these evaluation techniques, expert reviewers are often required to assess the architectural design. When an evaluation is depended heavily on human expertise and face-to-face meetings, its soundness relies on the review team, especially when the contents and the details of architectural design description are not sufficiently documented. Under such circumstances, review team and architectural team may have different interpretations on the same design. Such phenomenon has been observed by the authors in real-life projects. Architects who argue most strongly can win a design argument, sometimes undermining objective assessments. This kind of scenarios has an adverse effect on the quality assurance capability of an evaluation technique.

Questioning Techniques assess the quality of architecture via qualitative questions. Architecture reviewers perform these qualitative evaluations via design reviews and inspections. Scenarios-based and attribute-based analysis methods such as SAAM [6], ATAM [7], SBAR [8]; and architectural review methodologies such as AT&T's software architecture review and assessment methods [9, 10] belong to this category. In these methods, reviewers analyze scenarios and quality attributes with the architecture team to determine if an architectural design satisfies the goals of a system.

There are four major issues related to these methods. First, they rely on expert analysis which is quite often a subjective process particularly when the analysis is based on incomplete specification and unavailability of architects' expertise. Second, architecture design reviews rely on reviewers' objectivity and expertise in uncovering issues in the architecture design. The objectivity and independence of the design evaluation may be compromised when the evaluation does not involve independent parties.

Third, some of these methods depend on the selection of relevant scenarios to identify critical assumptions and weakness of the architectural design [5]. What scenarios and architectural significant requirements (ASRs) [6, 7] are included in the evaluation would influence the quality. When the selected scenarios are incomplete or their relative priorities are unclear, there would be a lot of assumptions to be made by the architecture reviewers affecting the quality of the evaluation. Fourth, the architectural scenarios used to test the design can remain at a conceptual level and not all aspects of the architectural designs can be reviewed in details [8]. Thus architectural design flaws can be hidden from the reviewers unless sufficient details become available.

The first two issues relate to the dependency of human interpretation and its objectivity and the latter two issues relate to the quality and sufficiency of documentation.

Measuring Techniques assess the quality of architecture via quantitative measurements. These methods include the use of metrics, simulations and prototyping to collect information for evaluation. For instances, SBAR [9] supports simulation and mathematical models to analyze software qualities such as performance or fault-tolerance;

CBAM [10] and ArchDesigner [11] use utility measures for trade-off analyses; a metrics-based approach [12] evaluates an architecture by using module coupling and cohesion to predict the software quality.

Measuring techniques are useful in dealing with certain aspects of an architectural design but they are not comprehensive enough to assure the overall quality of the architectural design. They have two problems. First, for all measuring models, the input sensitivities for the studied quality attributes are crucial. Sensitivity degrees have an impact on the confidence of predicting design quality with respect to the quality attribute. For example, in Architecture Level Prediction of Software Maintenance (ALPSM) method, the accuracy of the sensitivity of the inputs used in the software modification model would affect the predicted maintenance effort [5]. Second, there is a lack of accurate estimates for quality requirement budgets, and a lack of accurate estimates on how a design model satisfies those quality properties such as performance and reliability [5, 13]. This is true for different levels of the architectural design, especially in the detailed levels.

3   Independent Software Architecture Review (ISAR)

Early detection of problems in architectural design through evaluation techniques reduces development costs and improves the quality of systems [5, 8, 14]. Thus, improving the effectiveness of evaluation techniques (in terms of problem detection) for architectural design is important. There are two approaches. First, one might propose totally new evaluation techniques that outperform existing ones. Second, one might enhance existing evaluation techniques by removing the problematic issues or reducing their negative impacts in order to achieve better evaluation. In this paper, we adopt the latter approach.

As discussed previously, most existing evaluation techniques face the problem of using the same architects to design and review the architectural design. Hence, human factors may lead to biased evaluation. To obtain an objective evaluation outcome, we argue that an Independent Software Architecture Review approach (ISAR) should be adopted as a standard practice of independent validation and verification (IV&V) [15]. In this section, we first analyze the barriers towards ISAR. Then, we propose seven conditions to facilitate better reviews through ISAR, and finally discuss the benefits as well as drawbacks towards applying ISAR.

3.1   Barriers towards an Independent Review

As discussed earlier, one key barrier of attaining independent evaluation is related to the lack of sufficient information provided to review teams for quality evaluation, which hinders the quality of the review process. Currently there are little or no standards on the minimum set of information necessary to support such evaluation. To address this, architecture design evaluation should be based on a well-defined engineering-style architectural design specification. The architectural description contained in such specifications must be structured, precise and detailed to avoid subjective interpretations.

Another key barrier towards an ISAR approach is the subjectivity of architects and evaluators based on their prior experience. There is no doubt that the expertise of architecture design and review teams is important. However, as noted in [4], there is sometimes a skepticism that exists between design and evaluation teams, the mentality of *"Why Should I Believe You?"* It hints strongly about the recognition of experience and the existence of subjective views based on that experience in the evaluation. Such phenomenon has been observed by the authors in real-life projects. Architects who have the experiences and expertise can play a dominating role during design review meetings, making it difficult for evaluators who are less experienced to argue their case.

To alleviate this problem, we suggest that the architecture team capture design rationale to provide further evidences and explanations to justify their decisions. Architectural design rationale helps to explain why a design decision is made and to justify any trade-offs [16]. They can articulate implicit constraints and assumptions in a design [17]. Most evaluation techniques, however, do not mandate the review of design rationale. Therefore, these techniques do not validate whether the design under evaluation was properly made under reasonable assumptions and constraints.

3.2 Supporting Independent Software Architecture Review (ISAR)

Software testing requires that the software to be tested is already programmed. Similarly, to enable an independent review, sufficiently documented information must be available. We argue that current software architecture practice does not provide all necessary documented information for an independent review. Reviews or evaluations are very much people dependent causing the problems discussed earlier. We therefore propose to work towards a design specification format that supports an ISAR approach based on the following conditions.

1. **Requirement completeness** – Based on the agreed ASRs of a system, there are no new requirements and scenarios arising from these ASRs and from the architectural design implementation.
2. **Requirement conflicts detection** – There are no requirements that conflict with each other in terms of achieving the business goals of the system.
3. **Architectural design completeness** – All functional and non-functional ASRs are satisfied by some design components.
4. **Architectural design conflict detection** – No parts of the architectural design will be in conflict with the other parts of the design because they cannot satisfy the constraints set by ASRs or a design.
5. **Quantifiable non-functional requirements fulfillment** – All quantifiable non-functional requirements should be explicitly documented, and the architectural design should describe how the requirements are fulfilled.
6. **Soundness of design decisions** – The design rationale has been sufficiently captured so that the quality assurance team can judge the soundness of key architectural design decisions.
7. **Architectural design sufficiency** – The architectural design description should have sufficient details and there are no design omissions that could cause architectural design changes.

These seven conditions for architectural design are based on the fundamental relationships that exist between the requirements, design outcomes and their design rationale [18]. That is, a requirement causes a design issue, therefore a decision must be made to create or select a design to satisfy or resolve the design issue.

The seven conditions underpin the quality of a review and they are subtly related to each other, further complicating their impacts on the review quality. First, we make a fundamental assumption about the scope of a system as defined by the requirement specification. We assume that the requirement statements are complete (*condition 1*) but this can be proved to be wrong during architectural review if reviewers uncover missing scenarios or find conflicting requirements (*condition 2*). The architectural specification would need to demonstrate that the design can satisfy all the requirements (*condition 3*), and that there are no conflicting design elements (*condition 4*). Often non-functional requirements such as performance and reliability are vaguely specified or not quantified. A verifiable specification would describe explicitly how these requirements can be fulfilled, for instance, a design component can process x transactions per second to fulfill the requirement (*condition 5*). All key design decisions must be justifiable. The justifications can be illustrated by what design options have been considered, as well as documenting the design trade-offs, the pros and cons that have been considered (*condition 6*). Finally, there must be enough details in the design to demonstrate that indeed the design is implementable and further design details would not change the architecture design (*condition 7*).

3.3 The Benefits of ISAR Approach

The seven review conditions discussed in previous section are applicable to both designers who prepare the architectural design specifications as well as to review teams who use an ISAR approach. Besides establishing certain guidelines for the architecture team to follow for supporting better software architecture review, they help to create a software architecture quality assurance baseline. Such baseline can further support quality assurance: (a) it supports independent quality assurance of the work delivered by the software suppliers; (b) it provides a check and balance mechanism to the architecture development team; (c) it assures the quality and the viability of the architectural design before development and implementation thus preventing costly rework; (d) it systematically measures the risks involved in the architectural design through exploring design details.

An ISAR approach alleviates two major existing problems of architecture review, namely, subjective interpretations of and lack of (or imprecise) information in architecture design. This can be achieved by identifying necessary information and conditions that can enable an objective software architecture design evaluation. The ISAR approach differs from existing evaluation techniques in a number of ways:

- **Objective of review.** ISAR approach focuses on verifying the technical feasibility and the requirements fulfillment of an architectural design. It does not review other aspects such as project management issues [13] or skills and responsibilities issues [6].
- **Specification-based assessment.** An engineering-style architectural design description would provide a better structured and more detailed specification than

the existing practice. Instead of questioning and interviewing architects, quality assurance teams can rely on architectural description.

- **Design rationale centric.** ISAR approach requires software architects to justify and document the design. Information such as design rationale, alternative design options and traceability of design to requirements allow the quality assurance team to understand the design's viability and justifications.

- **Sufficiency of details.** ISAR approach requires software architects to document the architectural design to a sufficient level of details to prove the viability of the design. Such details should be sufficient to a point where assumptions and risks would not adversely affect the implementation of such a design.

- **Less reliance on expert reviewers.** Although knowledgeable architects are required to perform the review, the ISAR approach has less reliance on the expertise of reviewers as existing architectural review techniques.

The ISAR approach would provide a more stringent review on the architectural design by strengthening the architectural design based on architectural descriptions. It complements rather than replaces architectural evaluation techniques. Similar to IV&V, ISAR approach has some drawbacks too. For example, the selection of the review team may play a part in achieving objective evaluation because, in some cases, bias may be introduced due to human factors such as past experience and prejudice.

4   The Next Step

In this paper, we suggest that the quality assurance function of existing software architecture evaluation techniques is not independent of the architects who create the design. However, a comprehensive quality assurance technique should be independent of the architects. Thus, it should depend on the information in the design specification as well as the review process. We posit that in order to improve the effectiveness of quality assurance of architecture design, we must first consider a software architecture design specification standard that meets the seven conditions. We suggest a number of further research directions in software architecture specification and architectural review:

- **Meta-model(s) for documenting architecture design.** Such meta-models are used to guide the architects to better prepare architecture design documentation for architecture evaluation. One issue of assessing the quality of architecture specifications is a lack of assessment criteria. Although this is to some extent addressed by having a standard such as IEEE 1471-2000 [1] for architectural description, a more detailed guideline from the perspective of quality assurance of architectural specification would be advantageous. An architectural design meta-model should encompass elements such as ASRs, design decisions, design components and their interrelationships. The interrelationships between model elements ought to provide traceability to allow reviewers to understand and assess the architectural design.

- **Quantifiable quality attributes.** Quality attributes in design, e.g. performance, should be specified in a verifiable way. This means the specification can show how quality requirements can be achieved by each relevant design component.

Often the design for such quality requirements is based on the judgments of architects without objective justifications. Condition 5 suggests that engineering-style specifications should be provided. This implies that standard templates and guidelines need to be created to help architects gather the information for the design specification.

- **Specification of design rationale.** Design rationale as an integral part of an architectural design specification should contain enough details to justify the key decisions of an architectural design. Architecture design is a set of design decisions but often this tacit knowledge is undocumented. It makes independent architectural review very difficult. To fulfill condition 6 and enable independent architecture design review, the documentation of design rationale in architecture specification needs to be improved.

- **Software architectural knowledge and design pattern.** Software architecture design is a function of designers' experience and knowledge that are inherently subjective. So checking the fulfillment of conditions 6 and 7 can be difficult. If architects claim to have fulfilled these conditions, how to verify these claims become the tasks of the review team. The study of architectural knowledge and architectural design patterns may provide support in this area, at least for similar design problems that have been solved previously. Assessment of the soundness of new design and its design reasoning could be based on previous design cases. The similarities and differences when comparing their requirements, design rationale and design outcomes can provide a baseline for reviewers.

In order to overcome subjective interpretation and insufficient or imprecise information in architectural design evaluation, we need to find ways to improve and standardize software architecture description. Such research should attract attention from the research community as well as from the software industry because of the impact to software architecture design in the development life-cycle, especially when an improved quality assurance process could potentially reduce the failures and the rework costs in system and software development. We have received supports from organizations in Australia to carry out case studies into the areas of architectural specification and architectural quality assurance process. We hope that the case studies would help improve their current practices in these two areas.

References

1. IEEE: IEEE Recommended Practice for Architecture Description of Software-Intensive System (IEEE Std 1471-2000). IEEE Computer Society, Los Alamitos (2000)
2. Perry, D.E., Wolf, A.L.: Foundation for the Study of Software Architecture. ACM SIGSOFT Software Engineering Notes 17(4), 40–52 (1992)
3. Bosch, J.: Software Architecture: The Next Step. In: Oquendo, F., Warboys, B.C., Morrison, R. (eds.) EWSA 2004. LNCS, vol. 3047, pp. 194–199. Springer, Heidelberg (2004)
4. Clements, P., Kazman, R., Klein, M.: Evaluating Software Architectures: Methods & Case Studies. Addison-Wesley, Reading (2002)
5. Dobrica, L., Niemela, E.: A survey on software architecture analysis methods. IEEE Transactions on Software Engineering 28(7), 638–653 (2002)

6. Obbink, H., Kruchten, P., Kozaczynski, W., Postema, H., Ran, A., Dominick, L., Kazman, R., Hilliard, R., Tracz, W., Kahane, E.: Software Architecture Review and Assessment (SARA) Report (version 1.0) (2002)
7. Bass, L., Clements, P., Kazman, R.: Software Architecture in Practice. Addison Wesley, Boston (2003)
8. Maranzano, J.F., Rozsypal, S.A., Zimmerman, G.H., Warnken, G.W., Wirth, P.E., Weiss, D.M.: Architecture reviews: practice and experience. IEEE Software 22(2), 34–43 (2005)
9. Bengtsson, P., Bosch, J.: Scenario-based software architecture reengineering. In: Proceedings of Fifth International Conference on Software Reuse, pp. 308–317 (1998)
10. Kazman, R., Asundi, J., Klein, M.: Quantifying the costs and benefits of architectural decisions. In: Proceedings of the 23rd International Conference on Software Engineering (ICSE 2001), pp. 297–306 (2001)
11. Al-Naeem, T., Gorton, I., Babar, M.A., Rabhi, F., Benatallah, B.: A quality-driven systematic approach for architecting distributed software applications. In: Proceedings. 27th International Conference on Software Engineering (ICSE 2005), pp. 244–253 (2005)
12. Briand, L.C., Morasca, S., Basili, V.R.: Measuring and Assessing Maintainability at the End of High Level Design. In: Proceedings of IEEE Conference in Software Maintenance, pp. 88–97 (1993)
13. Avritzer, A., Weyuker, E.J.: Investigating Metrics for Architectural Assessment. In: Proceedings of the Fifth International Software Metrics Symposium, pp. 4–10 (1998)
14. Babar, M.A., Zhu, L., Jeffery, R.: A Framework for Classifying and Comparing Software Architecture Evaluation Methods. In: Proceedings 2004 Australian Software Engineering Conference, pp. 309–318 (2004)
15. IEEE: IEEE Standard for Software Verification and Validation (IEEE Std 1012 - 2004) (2004)
16. Clements, P., Bachmann, F., Bass, L., Garlan, D., Ivers, J., Little, R., Nord, R., Stafford, J.: Documenting Software Architectures: Views and Beyond. Addison-Wesley, Reading (2002)
17. Lee, J.: Design Rationale Systems: Understanding the Issues. IEEE Expert 12(3), 78–85 (1997)
18. Tang, A., Jin, Y., Han, J.: A rationale-based architecture model for design traceability and reasoning. Journal of Systems and Software 80(6), 918–934 (2007)

On the Interplay of Aspects and Dynamic Reconfiguration in a Specification-to-Deployment Environment

Thais Batista[1], Antônio T.A. Gomes[2], Geoff Coulson[3],
Christina Chavez[4], and Alessandro Garcia[3]

[1] Federal University of Rio Grande do Norte (UFRN) – Natal, RN, Brazil
[2] National Laboratory for Scientific Computing (LNCC) – Petrópolis, RJ, Brazil
[3] Lancaster University – Lancaster, UK
[4] Federal University of Bahia (UFBA) – Salvador, BA, Brazil
thais@ufrnet.br, atagomes@lncc.br, geoff@comp.lancs.ac.uk,
flach@dcc.ufba.br, a.garcia@lancaster.ac.uk

Abstract. In this paper, we propose the application of concepts from aspect-oriented software development to facilitate modular treatment of dynamic reconfiguration descriptions in specification-to-deployment environments. Our strategy differs from earlier work in the area by blending aspects and architecture abstractions simply and seamlessly through a special kind of connector — called an *aspectual connector* — that encapsulates reconfiguration interactions. More specifically, we propose an aspect-oriented specification-to-deployment environment, called AO-Plastik, that uses our AspectualAcme ADL to specify dynamic reconfiguration by means of aspectual connectors, and maps these specifications onto a reflective component runtime platform.

Keywords: Dynamic reconfiguration, Aspect-oriented software development, Architecture description language, Component-based software.

1 Introduction

There has recently been significant research [1,3,8] on dynamic reconfiguration in environments that couple Architecture Description Languages (ADLs) with underlying runtime environments in a systematic and integrated way—so-called "specification-to-deployment" environments. Most of this research has proposed annotating conventional ADL abstractions—components, connectors, etc.—with additional reconfiguration statements. Nevertheless, dynamic reconfiguration is a *crosscutting concern*, and as such cannot be effectively modularized at the architecture level using only conventional ADL abstractions. To enable a better modularized specification of crosscutting concerns at the architecture level, Aspect-Oriented Software Development (AOSD) [4] has received increasing attention from the software architecture community. In spite of several Aspect-Oriented ADLs (AO-ADLs) being proposed [3,5], few researchers have considered dynamic reconfiguration as a crosscutting concern at the architecture level. Moreover, the approaches that do so have in common the introduction of whole new sets of ADL abstractions—usually derived

R. Morrison, D. Balasubramaniam, and K. Falkner (Eds.): ECSA 2008, LNCS 5292, pp. 314–317, 2008.

directly from AO implementation techniques—which overburden architects used to the conventional ADL abstractions.

In this paper, we propose an aspect-oriented specification-to-deployment environment called AO-Plastik, which builds on our previous work on the Plastik environment [8] and on the AspectualAcme ADL [5]. The first Plastik release supports dynamic reconfiguration both at the architecture and runtime levels, which were causally connected. At the architecture level Plastik used the original Acme ADL [6] extended with reconfiguration statements such as '*on-do*' clauses. In AO-Plastik, we provide a more modular way of specifying such statements by employing AspectualAcme, a general-purpose ADL that extends the Acme's metamodel with a special kind of connector—an *aspectual connector (AC)*—for representing crosscutting interactions. AC is used in AO-Plastik for encapsulating reconfiguration interactions. At the runtime level Plastik employed the OpenCOM reflective component runtime [2] extended with services such as configuration management, style enforcement, and reconfiguration transactions and notifications. In the AO-Plastik environment, we add to the configuration management service (CMS) a set of facilities for mapping aspectual connector specifications onto OpenCOM reflective primitives.

2 AO-Plastik

2.1 The Architecture Level

AO-Plastik system specifications must follow an *AOPlastikMF* style in order to support the mapping of AO-Plastik architectural elements onto the runtime level. This style packages one port type (*BasePort*) and one component type (*BaseComponent*). An architectural rule is defined on instances of *BaseComponent* so that they are required to have one port of type *BasePort*.

Reconfiguration statements in AO-Plastik are always defined over ports of type *BasePort*. The semantic of this port type is that it exposes the internal structure of its enclosing component; therefore, any component on which architectural reconfigurations may be effected must be an instance of *BaseComponent*. This is particularly useful for representing reconfigurations on composite components. An Acme system in AO-Plastik is regarded as a special case of outermost composite which implicitly offers a port *basePort* (of type *BasePort*). Reconfiguration is always triggered by conditions (specified by the *on-do* clause) occurring within an instance of *BaseComponent* (or the system itself). The aspectual connector encapsulates this reconfiguration protocol by associating the conditions with actions specified in a (aspectual) component to which this connector is attached through its crosscutting role. Such actions—resembling '*advices*' in AOSD parlance—are specified in AspectualAcme through a new clause introduced by AO-Plastik: the '*action*' clause.

Fig.1 illustrates the use of AOPlastik in the specification of a client-server system. In this example, the aspectual connector *ReconfConn* has its base role attached to the system's implicit port *basePort*. The reconfiguration protocol in this connector, as indicated in its *glue* clause, is responsible for triggering an action (*changeServer*) in component *Reconfigurer* after the condition happens. As Fig.1 shows, two new functions are also defined in AO-Plastik for handling architectural elements involved in a reconfiguration protocol. The function *BaseElement()* is usually applied to the 'on' part of the *on-do* clause. It receives as its only argument a base role and returns the architectural element—either an instance of component type *BaseComponent* or a system—to which this role is attached. The function *AttachedPort()* is usually applied to the 'do' part of the *on-do* clause. It receives as its only argument a crosscutting role and returns the port of the aspectual component to which this role is attached. This port will be typically the place where the *action* clause will be defined. In Fig.1 the port returned by *AttachedPort*() is used for triggering the action *changeServer* defined in the *changerPort* port of the *Reconfigurer* component.

```
System ClientServer = new ClientServerFam, AOPlastikMF extended with {
 Component Client = new ClientT;
 Component PrimServer = new ServerT extended with {
  Property failure: boolean = false; }
 Connector Conn = { Role requestor; Role servicer; }
 AspectualConnector ReconfConn = {
  BaseRole triggerRole;
  CrosscuttingRole changerRole;
  Glue after = {
   On (exists cp: Component in BaseElement(triggerRole).Components |
        exists cn: Connector in BaseElement(triggerRole).Connectors |
         attached(cn, cp) and declaresType(cp, "ServerT") and
         cp.failure == true)
   Do { AttachedPort(changerRole).changeServer(cp, cn); }
  }
 }//end of ReconfConn
 Component Reconfigurer = {
  Port changerPort = new ProvidedPort extended with {
   Action changeServer(cp: Component, cn: Connector) = {
    Detach cn.servicer from cp.service;
    Remove cp;
    Component BackupServer = new ServerT extended with {
     Dependencies { Attachments { cn.servicer to BackupServer.service; } } }
   }
  }
 } //end of Reconfigurer
 Attachments { Client.request to Conn.requestor;
               Conn.servicer to PrimServer.service;
               Reconfigurer.changerPort to ReconfConn.changerRole;
               ReconfConn.triggerRole to self.basePort; }
} //end of ClientServer
```

Fig. 1. A dependable client-server description in AO-Plastik

The modularization of reconfiguration statements into aspectual components—and the separation between aspectual components and aspectual connectors that localize the reconfiguration protocols—introduce an additional level of architectural flexibility as they allow the same aspectual component to define reconfiguration statements that may act over different systems, according to different conditions expressed in differ- ent aspectual connectors. Thus, *AO-Plastik promotes better modularized reconfigura- tion specifications, and better reuse.*

2.2 The Runtime Level

OpenCOM is originally a non-AO component runtime. A suite of AO extensions is therefore needed to support the mapping from the AspectualAcme abstractions to this runtime. We propose AO extensions that are compliant to the generic 'AO middleware reference architecture' defined by the AOSD-Europe consortia [7]. In the reference architecture, aspects and advices are roles played in a non-AO middleware by components and interface operations, respectively. This is directly in line with the AO extensions available in AspectualAcme, which implies that the mapping is therefore trivial. The reference architecture also defines a new kind of binding, the *AO binding*, which supports the composition between aspectual components and regular components, similarly to aspectual connectors and attachments of AspectualAcme. In other words, aspectual connectors and attachments are mapped to AO bindings.

The reference architecture also states that aspects in a non-AO middleware should be provided by an *aspect management functionality* built on top of a reflective meta-model layer. We added this functionality to the configuration management service (CMS) in the original Plastik environment. In AO-Plastik, this service is also in charge of parsing action clauses and attachments involving aspectual connectors and inserting interceptors at the interfaces these attachments comprise. This allows CMS to receive notifications from these interfaces, which can trigger reconfiguration actions. Since causality is kept in the mapping, *AO-Plastik provides better alignment between the architecture and runtime levels*, thereby promoting on-line traceability.

3 Final Remarks

So far we have successfully trialed key aspects of AO-Plastik design, including the runtime support and the parsing of AspectualAcme specifications. Some planned future work includes: (i) handling conflicts or accommodating several reconfiguration strategies in AO-Plastik systems by means of *'precedence'* and *'xor'* relationships [5] between aspectual connectors and crosscutting ports, and (ii) packaging family-oriented reconfiguration strategies that can promote an even higher level of reuse.

References

1. Batista, T., Joolia, A., Coulson, G.: Managing Dynamic Reconfiguration in Component-Based Systems. In: Morrison, R., Oquendo, F. (eds.) EWSA 2005. LNCS, vol. 3527, pp. 1–17. Springer, Heidelberg (2005)
2. Coulson, G., Blair, G., Grace, P., Taiani, F., Joolia, A., Lee, K., Ueyama, J., Sivaharan, T.: A Generic Component Model for Building Systems Software. ACM Transactions on Computer Systems 26(1) (February 2008)
3. Costa, C., Ali, N., Pérez, J., Carsí, J.A., Ramos, I.: Dynamic Reconfiguration of Software Architectures Through Aspects. In: Oquendo, F. (ed.) ECSA 2007. LNCS, vol. 4758, pp. 279–283. Springer, Heidelberg (2007)
4. Filman, R., Elrad, T., Clarke, S., Aksit, M.: Aspect-Oriented Software Development. Addison-Wesley, Boston (2005)
5. Garcia, A., Chavez, C., Batista, T., Santanna, C., Kulesza, U., Rashid, A., Lucena, C.: On the Modular Representation of Architectural Aspects. In: Gruhn, V., Oquendo, F. (eds.) EWSA 2006. LNCS, vol. 4344, pp. 82–97. Springer, Heidelberg (2006)
6. Garlan, D., Monroe, R., Wile, D.: Acme: An Architecture Description Interchange Language. In: CASCON 1997, Toronto, Canada, November 1997, pp. 169–183 (1997)
7. Greenwood, P., et al.: Validation of the Reference Architecture. AOSD-Europe Deliverable D-68, Lancaster University, pp. 1–38 (March 2007)
8. Joolia, A., Batista, T., Coulson, G., Gomes, A.T.A.: Mapping ADL Specifications to an Efficient and Reconfigurable Runtime Component Platform. In: WICSA 2005, Pittsburgh, USA (November 2005)

Extending the ANSI/SPARC Architecture Database with Explicit Data Semantics: An Ontology-Based Approach

Chimène Fankam, Stéphane Jean, Ladjel Bellatreche, and Yamine Aït-Ameur

LISI/ENSMA and University of Poitiers - BP 40109, 86961 Futuroscope, France
{fankamc,jean,bellatreche,yamine}@ensma.fr

1   Introduction

The database (DB) design process follows the traditional ANSI/SPARC architecture proposed by Bachman [1]. A conceptual model (CM) is translated into a logical model corresponding to a data specification implemented in a DB system. The physical model defines how data are stored and accessed. External models allow a DB designer to adapting data according to user's requirements. Regarding the semantic exploitation of data models, this architecture has two major drawbacks [2]: (1) a strong dependency of models with designers and specific application requirements; (2) a gap between conceptual and logical models that increases with the discrepancy of the conceptual modelling languages.

The maintenance and/or evolution of the CM, that must be consensual when dealing with semantic integration of data sources (semantics and schema conflicts), are in the kernel of these problems. Recently, some works give more importance to CMs by materializing them in a DB [3]. In these works, the design of a CM is preceded by the design or by pre-existence of ontology. In this case, both ontology and data are represented in the DB. Such a DB is called an *ontology-based database* (OBDB). Hence our proposition is to extend the ANSI/SPARC architecture to support OBDBs.

2   Ontologies and Databases

This paper is based on our analysis of domain ontologies presented in [4]. Ontologies can be combined into a layered model, called the Onion Model and shown on Figure 1. Compared to DB requirements, (1) *Conceptual Canonical Ontologies (CCOs)* can be considered as shared CMs. They may play the role of a global schema in a DB integration architecture. (2) *Non Conceptual Canonical Ontologies (NCCOs)* provide mechanisms similar to views in DBs; non canonical concepts can be seen as virtual concepts defined from canonical concepts. These mechanisms may be used to represent the mapping between different DBs. (3) *Linguistic Ontologies (LOs)* may be used to localize similarities between DB schemas [5], to document existing DBs or to improve the DB-user dialog.

With the increasingly amount of data represented as instances of ontology classes (*ontology-based data*), a novel approach for processing these data in DBs,

R. Morrison, D. Balasubramaniam, and K. Falkner (Eds.): ECSA 2008, LNCS 5292, pp. 318–321, 2008.

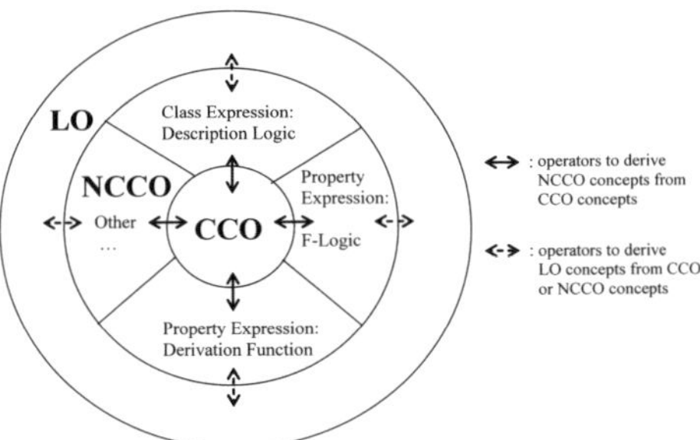

Fig. 1. The Onion Model of domain ontology

called Ontology-Based DataBases, emerges. An OBDB represents explicitly (1) ontologies, (2) data structure or data schema, (3) data, and (4) links between data and their schema and between data and the ontology. The ANSI/SPARC architecture with its three levels (conceptual, logical and external levels) does not support directly OBDB that introduces an additional data access level: the ontological level integrating semantics of data in a DB. As a consequence, we propose an extension of this architecture.

3   New Capabilities of the Proposed Architecture

Figure 2 shows our proposed extended architecture. The CM references the ontology using semantic links. It is defined using a subset of of the ontology that fulfill the application requirements. Compared to the ANSI/SPARC architecture, the proposed database architecture offers new capabilities.

Capabilities resulting from the Onion Model. Our proposed architecture introduces a new level to separate the logical (structure) and the ontological (semantics) representation of data.

Capability 1. *The database management system (DBMS) allows to expressing query at the ontological level independently of the logical representation of data.* Exploiting non canonical concepts of the NCCO layer is a new capability.

Capability 2. *The DBMS supports the definition of non canonical concepts using canonical concepts of an ontology. Queries shall be expressed using canonical and non canonical concepts.*

For the LO layer, users shall be able to use terms in their own language.

Capability 3. *The DBMS supports the definition and exploitation of linguistic definitions of concepts that may be defined in different natural languages.*

Another characteristic of our proposed architecture is to enforce upward compatibility with the ANSI/SPARC architecture which leads to other capabilities.

Capabilities for Preserving Compatibility with the ANSI/SPARC Architecture. The SQL language is the standard defined to manipulate data. As a consequence, compatibility with the SQL language is required.

Capability 4. *The DBMS permits the manipulation of data at the logical level preserving SQL compatibility.*

320   C. Fankam et al.

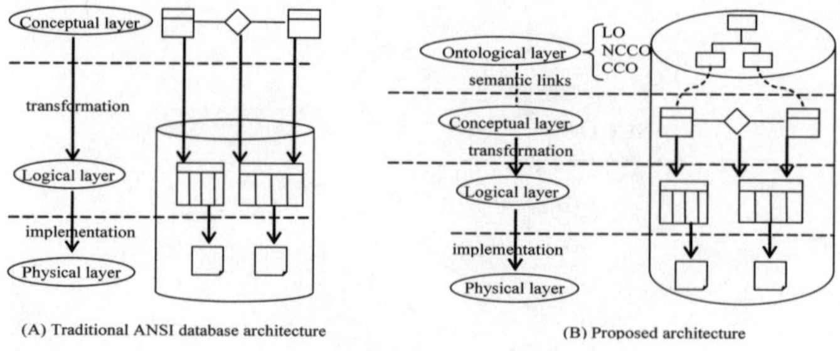

Fig. 2. Proposed extension of ANSI/SPARC architecture

To optimize query processing at the ontological level, the DBMS shall provide an access to the lower level, i.e., the conceptual level.

Capability 5. *The DBMS handles access to data at the conceptual level from the ontological level.*

These capabilities have been implemented in the OBDB OntoDB2 introduced in [6]. In particular, OntoDB2 supports the definition of non canonical concepts (capability 2). To our knowledge, this feature is not available on most existing OBDBs, it is described in next section.

4   Representation of Non Canonical Concepts

The non canonical concepts constructions permit a richer semantic expression and characterization of the data stored in the DB. According to their origin, these constructors can be grouped in three categories (1) constructors of defined classes (Union, Intersection, Restriction) and properties (inverse, symmetric, transitive). They come from Description Logic; (2) logical rules issues from Frame Logic. They require a rule based reasoning engine to deduce new facts from existing ones; (3) Algebraic expressions (e.g, `diameter = 2*radius`). They come from the data processing community. They require an interpreter for algebraic expressions. Thus, a challenge is now to define a flexible OBDB architecture allowing using these various constructors.

From a DB point of view, non canonical ontologies introduce redundancy requiring specific treatments. The difficulty to have a kernel (non-deductive) DB covering the Onion Model is increased. As a consequence, to design such a DBMS, each level of the Onion Model must be managed specifically.

- **Defined Classes.** As stated before, non canonical classes (union, intersection, restriction) instances will be computed using the view mechanism (with triggers) that can be used to compute union, intersection or selection on a set of data.

- **Algebraic Characteristics of Properties**

(a) Symmetry: we propose to automatically materialize a posteriori all data.

(b) Transitivity: to avoid overhead due to transitive closure, we assume at the beginning that all data are materialized. When a new relation concerning a

transitive property is added, the new facts are materialized by a trigger in a non recursive manner. The trigger works as follows. When a new pair P(x,y) is added, for each existing pair P(i,x) in the DB, a new pair P(i,y) is added.
- **Algebraic Expressions.** Like for defined classes, the value of a derived property is computed by evaluating its expression (may be encapsulated by a view).

5   Conclusion and Future Work

In this paper, we have presented a new database architecture extending the traditional ANSI/SPARC architecture with the semantic of data : the ontology layer. Each concept references, by its unique identifier, the semantic definition available in ontologies. The resulting DB is an ontology-based database (OBDB). OBDBs support access to data at the knowledge level. They also provide help to the DB designer by defining the conceptual model as a fragment of ontologies. Notice that proceeding this way preserves an upward compatibility with the traditional ANSI/SPARC architecture. Indeed, when references to the ontology are omitted, we obtain the classical database architecture.

The developed architecture together with the associated exploitation language OntoQL has been implemented in the OntoDB database. Some demos are available on `http://www.plib.ensma.fr/plib/demos/ontodb/index.html`.

As future work, we plan to extend this approach to other software architectures and principally we intend to study how Architecture Description Languages (ADL) can be extended with an ontological layer. We believe that this approach scales up to other software architectures and helps to reduce the heterogeneity of software architectures and software architecture models.

References

1. Bachman, C.W.: Summary of current work - ansi/x3/sparc/study group - database systems, vol. 6, pp. 16–39 (1974)
2. Dehainsala, H., Pierra, G., Bellatreche, L., Aït-Ameur, Y.: Conception de bases de données á partir d'ontologies de domaine: Application aux bases de données du domaine technique. In: Actes des 1ère Journées Francophones sur les Ontologies (JFO 2007), pp. 215–230 (2007)
3. Sugumaran, V., Storey, V.C.: The role of domain ontologies in database design: An ontology management and conceptual modeling environment. ACM Transactions on Database Systems (TODS) 31(3), 1064–1094 (2006)
4. Jean, S., Pierra, G., Aït-Ameur, Y.: Domain Ontologies: a Database-Oriented Analysis. In: Filipe, J., Cordeiro, J., Pedrosa, V. (eds.) WEBIST 2005 and WEBIST 2006. LNBIP, vol. 1, pp. 238–254. Springer, Heidelberg (2007)
5. Beneventano, D., Bergamaschi, S., Castano, S., Corni, A., Guidetti, R., Malvezzi, G., Melchiori, M., Vincini, M.: Information integration: The momis project demonstration. In: Proceedings of 26th International Conference on Very Large Data Bases (VLDB 2000), pp. 611–614. Morgan Kaufmann, San Francisco (2000)
6. Fankam, C.: OntoDB2: Support of Multiple Ontology Models within Ontology. In: Proceedings of the EDBT 2008 PhD Workshop. Co-located with the 11th International Conference on Extending Database Technology (EDBT 2008) (2008)

Search-Based Extraction of Component-Based Architecture from Object-Oriented Systems

Sylvain Chardigny[1], Abdelhak Seriai[1],
Mourad Oussalah[2], and Dalila Tamzalit[2]

[1] Ecole des Mines de Douai, 941 rue Charles Bourseul, 59508 Douai France
[2] LINA, university of Nantes, 2 rue de la Houssinière, 44322 Nantes France

Abstract. Software architecture modeling and representation are a main phase of the development process of complex systems. In fact, software architecture representation provides many advantages during all phases of software life cycle. Nevertheless, for many systems, like legacy or eroded ones, there is no available representation of their architectures. In order to benefit from this representation, we propose an approach called ROMANTIC which focuses on extracting a component-based architecture of an existing object-oriented system. This approach considers this problem as a balancing problem of competing constraints which aims to select the best solution among all the possible architectures. Consequently, we present in this paper the identified constraints of this problem and its formulation as a search-based problem.

1 Introduction and Motivation

A representation of the system software architecture provides many advantages during the software life cycle [1]. Indeed a component-based software architecture is a high level abstraction of a system using the architectural elements: components which describe functional computing, connectors which describe interactions and configuration which represents the topology of connections between components. This distinction makes easier the understanding of a system. This comprehension is crucial during the maintenance and evolution phases, to localize software defects and to reduce the risk of misplacing new system functionality. Moreover a component-based architecture is also useful in order to facilitate the reuse of some system parts represented as components.

However most existing systems do not have a reliable architecture representation. Indeed these systems could have been designed without an architecture design phase, as it is the case for most legacy systems. In other systems, the available representation can diverge from the system implementation. This divergence, between the representation and the reality of the system is the result of the erosion phenomenon. This appears, first, during the implementation phase due to gaps between the expected architecture and the implemented one. These gaps become greater because of lack of synchronization between software documentation and implementation.

R. Morrison, D. Balasubramaniam, and K. Falkner (Eds.): ECSA 2008, LNCS 5292, pp. 322–325, 2008.

Taking into account the previous considerations, several approaches of architecture extraction are proposed and can be classified according to their automation level. Firstly some approaches are quasi manual. For example, Focus [2] proposes a guideline to a hybrid process which regroups system classes and maps the extracted entities to an conceptual architecture obtained from an architectural style according to the human expertise. Secondly most approaches propose semi or quasi-automatic techniques. These approaches automate repetitive aspects of the extraction process [3] or use search-based algorithms to identified modules in the system [4]. These last avoid the need for human expertise which is costly and not always available but they fail to extract some dependencies which can be detected by experts. Finally the output of most of existing architecture extraction approaches is most of time a module view of a system instead of a real component-based software architecture.

Based on these statements, the need for a quasi-automatic extraction approach which avoid the limits of previous ones is clear. Consequently, we propose an approach called ROMANTIC[1] which focuses on extracting a component-based architecture which reflects truly the implementation of the initial object-oriented system. ROMANTIC is a quasi-automatic extraction approach which decreases the need for human expertise and uses all the class dependencies. To achieve this goal, we consider the extraction problem as a balancing problem of competing constraints, as for example the architectural quality or the hardware architecture. To solve this balancing constraint problem, we formulate it as a search-based problem where the problem constraints drive a search in the space of all possible architectures. This choice is motivated by the recent works on the search-based engineering showing that these techniques are very effective to solve this kind of problems [5]. To define the extraction problem as a search-based problem, we present, in this paper the definition of the two required elements: the search space which is the set of all the solutions of the problem; the fitness function which is used to measure the fitness of the explored solutions in the search space and to select the best solution.

The remainder of the paper is structured as follows. Our definition of the search-space of the extraction problem is introduced in the section 2. Section 3 defines the constraints of the extraction problem and presents how they drive the process through the fitness function and a reduction of the search space. Conclusion and future work are given in Section 4.

2   Definition of the Search-Space

Architecture extraction is the reverse process of the design one. Indeed the extraction process uses existing implementation code and the architect's skills to obtain a system abstraction and determine architectural elements : components which describe functional computing, connectors which describe interactions and configuration which represents the topology of connections between components.

---

[1] ROMANTIC: Re-engineering of Object-oriented systeMs by Architecture extractioN and migraTIon to Component based ones.

Consequently, extracting an architecture from an object-oriented system consists of finding a correspondence between object-oriented programming concepts (*i.e.* classes, interfaces, packages, etc.) and architectural ones (*i.e.* components, connectors, interfaces, etc.).

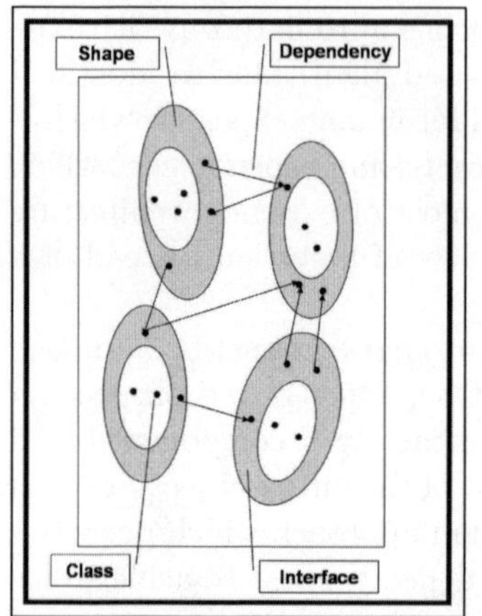

Fig. 1. Object-component correspondence

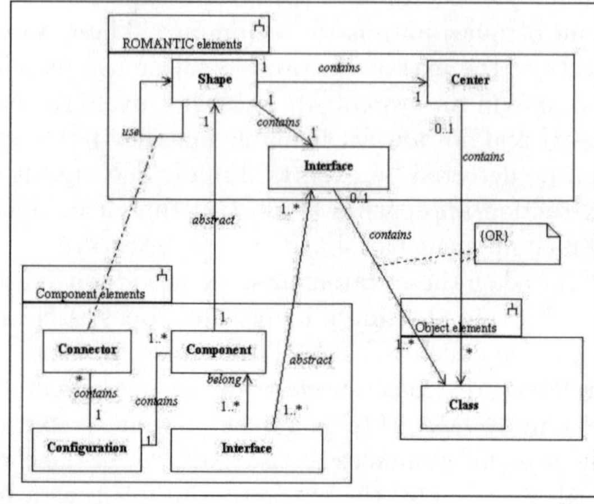

Fig. 2. Our model of object-component correspondence

This correspondence model defines an architecture as a partition of the system classes. Each element of this partition represents a component. These elements are named "shape" and contain classes which can belong to different object-oriented packages (*cf.* Fig.1). Each shape is composed of two sets of classes: the "shape interface" which is the set of classes which have a link with some classes from the outside of the shape, *e.g.* a method call to the outside; and the "center" which is the remainder of shape. As shown in Fig.2, we assimilate component interface set to "shape interface" and component to shape.

Consequently the search-space of our search-based problem is composed of all partitions of the system classes. This means that, in a system which contains n classes, the search-space contains $O(n!)$ possible architectures.

3   Guides of the Architecture Extraction Process

In addition to the search-space we need to define the guides which drive our search in this space. Thus we identify several elements which can be classified into two groups according to the way they can influence the search-based process.

On the one hand, two elements can be used to define the fitness function. The semantic properties define what is an architecture whereas the quality properties define what is a good architecture. Consequently we propose to reify the most commonly admitted semantic and quality properties of an architecture to define the fitness function. Thus our fitness function, defined using these two guides, measures the quality and the semantic correctness of the architecture.

On the other hand, we use other elements as guides to drive our process. In fact available design documents (e.g use-case diagrams) and the recommendations of the architect can be used to guide the extraction process. They allow us to modify the results according to existing functionalities of the system, for example, by rejecting a solution according to the recommended number of components. Finally as deployment constraints can affect the system architecture design, we use hardware architecture properties to guide the extraction process in order to obtain an architecture which is adapted to it.

4   Conclusion

We present, in this paper, a modelization of the architecture extraction problem as a search-based one. Then we propose to define the extraction of a component-based architecture from an object-oriented system as a search in the space of all possible system architectures. This search-space is defined according to our correspondence model as the space of all the partitions of the system classes. We present too the constraints of the extraction problem that we have identified. We use these constraints as guides in order to drive our process as a fitness function or to reduce the search-space.

This use of the extraction problem constraints as guides of our process is our main difference with existing works on architecture extraction. For example our fitness function is defined by a refinement of the commonly used definitions of components into semantic characteristics and measurement models whereas others works use the expertise of the authors in order to define rules driving the process.

We have already defined a fitness function, according the semantic and quality guides, which aims to identify the components. Then we have used the documentation to reduce the search space. Consequently, our future works are the connector identification and the use of the deployment constraints.

References

1. Shaw, M., Garlan, D.: Software architecture: perspectives on an emerging discipline. Prentice-Hall, USA (1996)
2. Medvidovic, N., Jakobac, V.: Using software evolution to focus architectural recovery. Automated Software Engineering 13, 225–256 (2006)
3. Harris, D.R., Reubenstein, H.B., Yeh, A.S.: Reverse engineering to the architectural level. In: Proc. of ICSE, pp. 186–195. ACM, New York (1995)
4. Mancoridis, S., Mitchell, B.S., Chen, Y.-F., Gansner, E.R.: Bunch: A clustering tool for the recovery and maintenance of software system structures. In: ICSM, p. 50 (1999)
5. Harman, M.: The current state and future of search based software engineering. In: Future of Software Engineering, pp. 342–357. IEEE, Los Alamitos (2007)

A Security Model for Internet-Based
Digital Asset Management Systems*

I. Chatzigiannakis, V. Liagkou, D. Salouros, and P. Spirakis

Research and Academic Computer Technology Institute
N. Kazantzaki, University of Patras, 26500, Rio, Patras, Greece
Department of Computer Engineering and Informatics,
University of Patras, 26500, Rio, Patras, Greece
{ichatz,liagkou,salouros,spirakis}@cti.gr

Abstract. Usage and exploitation of the Internet is a critical requirement for managing and distributing valuable digital assets. This requirement introduces a great number of threats for commercial (or not) organizations that may cause huge data and financial losses, harm their reputation as well as people's trust on them. In this paper we present the research challenges for secure digital asset management over the web by proposing a model that provides data safety and secure user interaction on especially demanding on-line collaboration environments.

1   Introduction

Nowadays, rich-media organizations tend to produce, manage, present, exchange, organize, store and distribute their material over the web. However, Internet increases the vulnerability of digital content commercial (or not) exploitation since it is a possibly hostile environment for secure data management. The relation between content (digital files) and the proper *intellectual property rights (IPR)* for use and manage it, results in *digital assets*, as concluded in (1). Copies of digital assets, usually of lower quality, that carry copyright information in order to secure IPR on the originals are referred to as *proxies*. An information system that manages digital assets is called a *Digital Asset Management System (DAMS)*. From a comprehensive summary of (2, 3, 4), a DAMS performs administrative functions on assets such as: ingest, categorize, store and retrieve, workflow control, manage IPR, preview and search, repurpose, encode and transform, preserve and destruct, and, finally, distribute on web portals, broadcasting stations, streaming services and collaborative environments.

2   Research Challenges on DAMS

Till now, a large number of commercial and open-source DAMS platforms, has been developed. (2) gives a classification according to market and commercial

---

* Partially supported by the IST Programme of the European Union under contact number IST-2005-15964 (AEOLUS).

R. Morrison, D. Balasubramaniam, and K. Falkner (Eds.): ECSA 2008, LNCS 5292, pp. 326–329, 2008.

demands (desktop, workgroup/collaborative, mid-range, pay-as-you-go and enterprise systems). (4) present a system for online learning and asset dissemination to researchers, students or even the general public. (5) describes a detailed top-down system architecture based on selected software and hardware technologies. Today, modern rich-media enterprises seek ways to effectively manage their digital material using Internet-based DAMS. Such systems provide advantages such as: (i) data management can be performed in a distributed fashion by utilizing different servers across a network. (ii) users activate system applications even if they are far away from the system infrastructure. (iii) commercial exploitation of digital assets opens to an endless list of possible consumers. (iv) uninterruptible availability on system data and applications can be achieved. (v) system software/hardware can be separated into autonomous modules *(multi-tier scheme)* in order to handle more resource needs and increasing numbers of users.

The vast majority of today's DAMS platforms are not relied upon a unifying model that can sustain a well defined security level. Their development is primarily based on the requirements of specific application domains and they usually need to co-operate with external systems such as Digital Rights Management, watermark platforms, etc. But even then, *there are still open security problems* concerning privilege and IPR assignment, licensing policies and safe access to assets, etc. The demand of expertised staff and the adoption of particular software/hardware solutions are extra disadvantages.

2.1 Security Challenges and Requirements

Despite the advantages, Internet is vulnerable to various threats coming from cyber criminals, hackers, unprincipled authorities, etc. We summarize the most common threats in terms of our application domain:

1. *Unauthorized access*: an Internet user pretends to be a system user and illegally gains access to system data or applications.
2. *Unprivileged activity*: a user of a certain group illegitimately acquires privileges of other groups and proceeds to prohibitive actions.
3. *Repudiation*: a user denies an action that caused a potential damage and the system cannot trace him back.
4. *Illicit interference with transferred data*: packet sniffing, modification or deletion is possible when an unscrupulous entity gains access to a communication channel.
5. *Manipulations on stored content*: an entity tampers with and forges valuable assets and illegally downloads or distributes them on the net.
6. *Virus spreading*: generation and propagation of malicious programs (i.e. viruses, worms, etc.) and other hacking techniques (like denial of service attacks) over the web may infect computers, lower performance, stop system operation, delete and steal confidential data, etc.

Our research direction necessitates a very careful consideration of all possible security challenges. Below, we list our resulted security requirements and give certain design directives in order to eliminate the threats and increase people's trust on the provided system services.

1. *Confidentiality*: leakage of critical information to unauthorized single users or entire user groups is unacceptable. Confidentiality can be achieved through VPN networks, watermarking techniques and effective privileges and IPR management.
2. *Integrity*: no unauthorized changes should be made on stored and transferred data. Data integrity can be achieved through computating hash and MAC functions.
3. *State stamping*: an IPR enforced asset locks into a state and no modifications are possible without detection. State stamping can be achieved by utilizing electronic fingerprints and checking hash values.
4. *Availability*: system data and applications should be available anytime by any authorized user. Availability can be achieved through central failover clusters that perform data path replication and load balancing when needed.
5. *Accountability*: unauthorized access, modification or illegal distribution on media files should be detected and, possibly, traced to specific sources. Accountability can be achieved using electronic signing, commitment and digital watermarking.
6. *Robustness*: the system should be shielded against all possible Internet attacks and threats. Robustness can be achieved through the placement of hardware firewalls, with automatically updated antivirus software, and physical protection to confront natural disasters.

3   Our Proposed DAMS Architecture

We can imagine our Internet-based DAMS as a large data repository that provides specific web applications for handling and distributing digital assets over the web. The system is based on an architectural model that was designed according to the previously discussed requirements. It follows the open-source idea in order to be software/hardware platform independent, lower development and maintenance costs and adapt easier in broader management infrastructures or to future changes.

More specifically, in our model users are separated into distinct groups of specific privileges and discrete roles. A distributed architecture based on median servers connected with a central server farm of failover clusters offers scalability and high-availability. Servers follow a multi-tier scheme to achieve modular organization and flexible adaptation to environmental or future changes. A disciplinary workflow mechanism introduces interdependencies between user tasks and data. Network technologies such as VPN networks, a hierarchical Public Key Infrastructure (PKI) and hardware firewalls guarantee integrity and confidentiality on transferred data. Cryptographic techniques such as bit commitments, electronic fingerprints and signing, computing hash and MAC functions as well as watermarking methods and effective IPR enforcements are utilized in order to prevent potential counterfeiting and unauthorized use of digital files and other administrative information. Especially for IPR enforced assets, the system checks hash values so that no system user or Internet attacker is able to modify them without detection (state stamping).

We are currently developing a prototype for our model that will serve as a reference implementation. In particular, we wish to examine the security levels achieved as well as the scalability of the system to large number of user requests. We also plan to examine alternative techniques and cryptographic tools for achieving a more advanced security level and also investigate the trade-offs between security and overall performance in large scale environments.

References

1. Austerberry, D.: Digital Asset Management - How to realise the value of video and image libraries. Focal Press/Elsevier Ltd (2004)
2. Frey, F., Williams-Allen, S., Vogl, H., Chandra, L.: Digital Asset Management - A Closer Look at the Literature, Printing Industry Center (March 2005) (Technical Report No. PICRM-2004-08),
   http://www.edsf.org/img/picrm200408.pdf
3. Geser, G., et al.: Digital Asset Management Systems for the Cultural and Scientific Heritage Sector. DigiCULT Project (IST-2001-34898), Thematic Issue 2 (December 2002)
4. Walter, M.: Architectural Considerations in Digital Asset Management, The Gilbane Report (October 2004),
   http://www.ancept.com/talks/GilbaneWP_Ancept_IBM_1.0.pdf
5. Digital Asset Management (DAM) Infrastructure Reference Architecture, v. 1.0, Sun Microsystems, Artesia Technologies (February 2003)

A Large Scope Transformational Approach for Distributed Architecture Design

Fabian Gilson, Vincent Englebert, and Raimundas Matulevičius

University of Namur
Faculty of Computer Science
PRECISE Research Center in Information Systems Engineering
{fgi,ven,rma}@info.fundp.ac.be

Abstract. Many Architecture Description Languages (ADLs) appeared in order to model complex software solutions. Unfortunately, current modeling approaches do not take into account infrastructure related constraints and do not add non-functional requirements to architecture constructs. This paper describes a transformation-oriented method to design distributed software architectures. Our method is based on an ADL named IODASS. It uses semantically extensible building blocks with qualitative attributes that specify non-functional or infrastructure related requirements.

1   Introduction

With the growth in size and complexity of distributed information systems, many new architecture description languages (ADLs) are proposed. However, some are error-prone (e.g. Wrigth [1]) and others are difficult to use (e.g. Archware [2]). Elsewhere, we also saw the emergence of domain specific modeling (DSM) that aims building domain specific languages (DSL) in order to create specific solutions [3]. But, DSLs are by definition poorly reusable. Further, some works show the need of using model transformations to refine high-level solutions into more detailed ones [4] [5]. This eases the understanding and the manipulation of the model. In this paper we investigate how *to model distributed information systems with their non-functional requirements (NFRs) and infrastructure constraints*. To this purpose, we define a transformation-oriented design method to create distributed architectures. The method is called *Define-Assemble-Deploy* (DAD) and uses an ADL, named *Infrastructure-Oriented Dynamic Architecture with Subsitutable Semantics* (IODASS). It allows designers to specify component types with the required or provided services and to refine the construct semantics with qualitative attributes. These attributes are used to build and apply transformations on the architecture in order to implement them. Every architecture model is then mapped onto the target infrastructure to identify possible deployment problems.

In Section 2, we present the related work. In Section 3, we introduce IODASS. Next, in Section 4 we describe the DAD method. Finally, in Section 5, we conclude and present the future work.

R. Morrison, D. Balasubramaniam, and K. Falkner (Eds.): ECSA 2008, LNCS 5292, pp. 330–333, 2008.

2   Related Work

As discussed in [6], a set of ADLs does not integrate NFRs to the architecture itself. More recent approaches addressed these requirements, but they focused on particular type of NFRs (e.g. Quality of Services [7]). In our proposal, we intend to cover a wider range of NFRs including infrastructure-related constraints.

In [5], Bosch and Molin describe a method to evaluate architectures against their non-functional requirements. However, this is performed at the end of the development process. In our approach, we want to integrate the NFRs from the first architecture model and validate them at each refinement step.

Recent works focused on running system architectures and their evolution (like, Archware [2] and Plastik [8]). The method presented in this paper focuses on design phase only.

3   IODASS Language

We defined an ADL called *Infrastructure Oriented Dynamic Architecture with Substitutable Semantics* (IODASS) [9]. IODASS models describe architectures of distributed information systems. Quality attributes expressing NFRs are defined inside most of IODASS constructs (see Caption of Fig. 1). A ComponentType classifies SetOfInstances into types and both can be hierarchically organised. They share the same quality attributes and expose the same Facets. A Facet is a set of logically grouped services, called Features. ComponentTypes are connected together via ConnectorTypes and SetsOfInstances via Connectors through a *required-provided* Contract. PhysicalNodes define the infrastructure elements used for the deployment, such as computers, cables, etc.

IODASS semantics is defined with a minimum of hypotheses. It can be seen as a naive semantics. We let the designer refining the construct semantics with the characteristics specific to an environment. For that reason, the language is defined as a framework where the constructs definition can be refined. The quality attributes express non-functional *requirements* or *properties*. A requirement describes a quality that a construct **must have** and a property describes a quality that a construct **has**. These requirements can be used to trigger model transformations and the architecture can be validated against its properties.

4   DAD Method

The *Define-Assemble-Deploy* method uses IODASS to design distributed IS architectures. To illustrate it, we define a simplified client-server system (Fig. 1).

Our model is divided in three parts: *Definition, Assemblance* and *Deployment*. First, designers *define* the **types** of constructs the architecture uses (Fig. 1 a). Our example counts three construct types: a Client, a Server and a Connector. The building blocks are extended with attributes. In the example, the Server type must handle a client request in less than 60 seconds. These component types are connected under a given contract binding a required and a provided

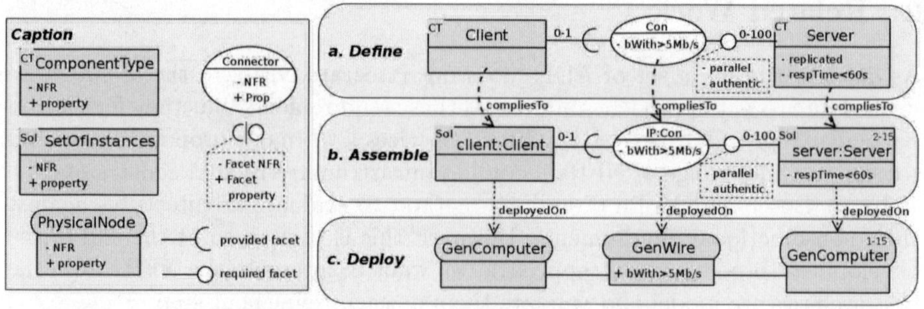

Fig. 1. First architecture of the Client-Server system

facet. The contract also specifies the **Connector** type used by the components and is constrained by a set of NFRs. In Fig. 1 a, the connection bandwith must be at least 5Mb/s. The second step is the *Assemblance* (Fig. 1 b). We instantiate the component types. Here, the **server** instance must be replicated, thus we decide to instantiate it twice and we arbitrary book 13 other available *slots*. The **SetsOfInstances** are then connected using the template given at the *Definition* level. Finally, the logical blocks are mapped to the physical infrastructure in the *Deployment* part (Fig. 1 c). We check the compliance using two techniques: quality attributes and specification of the component types. Quality attributes can express performance properties needed by a component and offered by a concrete node. The component specification is mainly used to validate the compliance between the model connections and the infrastructure links. In the example, the concrete medium used to connect the components must support the given minimum bandwith and the IP communication protocol.

After we have defined our model using IODASS, we can apply transformations to *refine* it or to *resolve* an attribute. A refinement is a transformation that hierarchically decomposes a component (or a component type). An attribute resolution can be more intrusive and modifies the component's inner processes. An example is presented in [10] where a security requirement is implemented into a cypher component. In [11] [12], design decisions constitute an important part of the design process, so we plan to apply a goal-oriented approach like [13] [14], to keep traceability in order to justify the alternative solutions.

5   Conclusion and Future Work

In this paper, we present IODASS, an ADL that uses quality attributes to specify non-functional requirements on architectural constructs. The language is the basis of a transformation-oriented method, called *Define-Assemble-Deploy*. Our approach closely relates the software architecture to its target infrastructure and validates it against the physical constraints during the whole design process. It also uses extensible component semantics in order to refine the construct definition. In the future, we will design a case study to validate our suggestions. We will develop the attributes list and build tools supporting the DAD method.

Acknowledgment. This work is partially funded by the Interuniversity Attraction Poles Programme, Belgian State, Belgian Science Policy.

References

1. Allen, R.: A Formal Approach to Software Architecture. PhD thesis, Carnegie Mellon, School of Computer Science, Issued as CMU Technical Report CMU-CS-97-144 (January 1997)
2. Morrison, R., Kirby, G., Balasubramaniam, D., Mickan, K., Oquendo, F., Cîmpan, S., Warboys, B., Snowdon, B., Greenwood, R.: Constructing Active Architectures in the ArchWare ADL (2003)
3. Kelly, S., Tolvanen, J.P.: Domain-Specific Modeling: Enabling Full Code Generation. Wiley-IEEE Computer Society Press (March 2008)
4. Khriss, I., Keller, R.K., Hamid, I.A.: Supporting Design by Pattern-based Transformations. In: Second International Workshop on Strategic Knowledge and Concept Formation
5. Bosch, J., Molin, P.: Software Architecture Design: Evaluation and Transformation, pp. 4–10. IEEE Computer Society, Los Alamitos (1999)
6. Medvidovic, N., Taylor, R.: A Classification and Comparison Framework for Software Architecture Description Languages. IEEE Trans. Softw. Eng. 26(1), 70–93 (2000)
7. Röttger, S., Zschaler, S.: Model-Driven Development for Non-functional Properties: Refinement Through Model Transformation. In: Baar, T., Strohmeier, A., Moreira, A., Mellor, S.J. (eds.) UML 2004. LNCS, vol. 3273, pp. 275–289. Springer, Heidelberg (2004)
8. Joolia, A., Batista, T.V., Coulson, G., Gomes, A.T.A.: Mapping ADL Specifications to an Efficient and Reconfigurable Runtime Component Platform. In: WICSA, pp. 131–140 (2005)
9. Gilson, F., Englebert, V.: IODASS Overview: Technical Report, University of Namur, Faculty of Computer Science (2008), http://www.info.fundp.ac.be/fgi/pub/iodass/tech-report_iodass-overview_1.0.pdf
10. Englebert, V., Vermaut, F.: Attribute-Based Refinement of Software Architectures. In: Proc. of the 4th Working IEEE/IFIP Conference on Software Architecture (WICSA 2004), p. 301 (2004)
11. Jansen, A., Bosch, J.: Software Architecture as a Set of Architectural Design Decisions. In: Proc. of the 5th Working IEEE/IFIP Conference on Software Architecture (WICSA 2005), Washington, DC, USA, pp. 109–120. IEEE Computer Society, Los Alamitos (2005)
12. Ernst, N.A., Mylopoulos, J.: Tracing Software Evolution History with Design Goals. In: Third International IEEE Workshop on Software Evolvability, 2007, pp. 36–41 (2007)
13. Yu, E.: Towards Modeling and Reasoning Support for Early-Phase Requirements Engineering. In: Proc. of the 3rd IEEE International Symposium on Requirements Engineering (RE 1997), Washington, DC, USA, p. 226. IEEE Computer Society, Los Alamitos (1997)
14. van Lamsweerde, A.: From System Goals to Software Architecture. In: Formal Methods for Software Architectures, pp. 25–43 (2003)

Towards a Software Process for Aspect-Oriented Modeling of Quality Attributes[*]

Mónica Pinto and Lidia Fuentes

Dept. Lenguajes y Ciencias de la Computación, University of Málaga, Spain
{pinto,lff}@lcc.uma.es
http://caosd.lcc.uma.es

Abstract. This paper defines a process for the aspect-oriented modeling of quality attributes, especially those with high functional implications. The goal of this process is to produce "built-in" reusable and parameterizable architectural solutions for each quality attribute. We propose using the AO-ADL Tool Suite to specify and store these solutions.

1 Introduction

Modeling a Quality Attribute (QA) is not a straightforward task (1). They are usually complex enough to be decomposed into a set of concerns, with dependencies and interactions among them. This is especially true for those QAs which have major implications on the core functionality of applications. Thus, there are nowadays several proposals suggesting that QAs with strong implications on the application core should be incorporated into the architecture as functional concerns (2, 3, 4). However, these approaches have two important shortcomings.

The first is that existing solutions do not usually take into account the crosscutting nature of the functional concerns of a QA. Such concerns may be tangled, i.e., several concerns may be encapsulated in the same software artifact, or they may be scattered, i.e., the same concern split across different software artifacts, within the core functionality of the system. In this paper we propose to cope with this shortcoming using Aspect-Oriented Software Development (AOSD), which focuses on identifying, modeling and composing crosscutting concerns throughout the software life cycle. Specifically, we propose the definition of a software process to identify and specify built-in aspect-oriented architectural patterns.

The second shortcoming is that QA patterns are mainly specified by filling in a table with the architectural implications (4), or by means of textual descriptions of intricate scenarios (5). Thus, a ready-to-use solution that the software architect can (re)use in different applications is not provided. In order to cope with this limitation we propose the use of an AO architectural language with support to store the specified models in a repository for later instantiation and reuse. Specifically, we propose the use of AO-ADL (6) and the AO-ADL Tool Suite.

After this introduction, section 2 outlines the motivation for our approach, section 3 describes the software process, section 4 the support provided by the AO-ADL Tool Suite and section 5 our conclusions.

---

[*] Supported by AOSD-Europe project IST-2-004349 and AMPLE Project IST-033710.

R. Morrison, D. Balasubramaniam, and K. Falkner (Eds.): ECSA 2008, LNCS 5292, pp. 334–337, 2008.

2   Motivation and Related Work

We have studied several non-AO and AO taxonomies of QAs with functional implications (2, 5, 7, 8) that are complex enough to be decomposed into a set of related concerns and sub-concerns. For instance, *usability* is decomposed into the *feedback, validation* and *contextual help* concerns among others. These taxonomies suggest that it is not possible to reason about many QAs at the architectural level without adding attribute-specific functionalities to the core application. Moreover, they reveal that it is crucial to start from an accurate and complete taxonomy of concerns modeling a particular QA (2, 7).

Another important issue is that the same concerns are normally shared by several QAs and their modeling is usually repeated for each framework. For instance, fault-tolerance is modeled as a concern of the usability attribute in (2) and of the security attribute in (5). The goal would be to associate a concern to the most suitable QAs and then identify the dependencies created among QA. For instance, there is a dependency between the *usability* and the *security* QAs because a user needs to be *authenticated* in order to provide *contextual help*.

Finally, the format used for presenting architectural solutions does not help to understand the peculiarities of each concern. Details regarding the different alternatives satisfying a particular concern, dependencies with other concerns and about constraints that a QA imposes on the core application and the impossibility of defining completely reusable architectural solutions for some concerns are not well-documented from early stages of the development.

The primary aim of our process is to cope with these shortcomings.

3   A Process for AO Modeling of Quality Attributes

The most important contribution of the process defined in this section is that it makes explicit the multiple considerations that need to be taken into account and highlights important information and decisions that need to be considered and documented for later (re)use of the architectural solutions.

The two first steps of our process (Figure 1) are: (1) selecting an existing taxonomy of concerns or defining a new one (activity 'Reuse/Define Taxonomy of Concerns'), and (2) deciding if the QA is suitable or not to be modeled following our approach, depending on whether or not the attribute has important functional implications, and on the number of concerns with a crosscutting nature.

The third step consists of modeling each concern in the QA (structured activity 'Model the Concern'). The internal workflow of this activity is: (1) Identify existing AO and non-AO solutions to avoid modeling a concern from scratch (activity 'Identify Existing Solutions to Address the Concern'); (2) Identify the architectural implications of the concern in order to identify the main functionalities to be modeled at the architectural level (activity 'Identify Architectural Implications'), (3) Identify the tangled (activity 'Identify Tangled Behavior') and scattered (activity 'Identify Scattered Behavior') behaviors, (4) Identify an architectural solution (notice that more than one is possible), and (5) Model the identified architectural solution

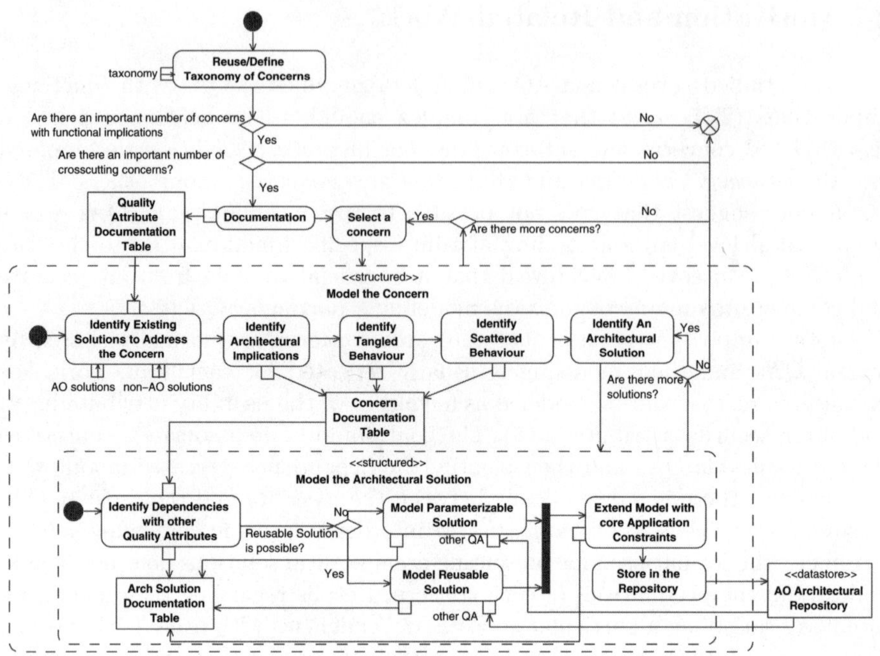

Fig. 1. Activity Diagram of the AO Modeling Process

(structured activity 'Model the Architectural Solution' described below). This information is documented in the ('Concern Documentation Table').

Modeling a particular architectural solution implies that the dependencies with concerns in other QAs need to be identified and conveniently modeled to avoid repeating the same concerns in different quality models (activity 'Identify Dependencies with other quality attributes'). With this information the software architect is ready to decide wether a reusable or a parameterizable solution should be modeled. A Reusable Solution is one in which the concerns can be modeled completely independently of the behaviors of the core functionality. A Parameterizable Solution is one in which the behavior of the concern has to be adapted to each particular application and thus the sub-architecture modeling the concern has to be seen as a template that must be instantiated before it can be used in a particular application architecture. Independently of the kind of solution used, adding one to an existing architecture may require that this architecture satisfies certain constraints (e.g. expose their components' state). These constraints should also be modeled and documented when modeling the QA (activity 'Extend Model with Core Application Constraints'). Finally, the complete QA specification, modeled following an AO approach, is obtained and stored in a repository ('AO Architectural Repository') of reusable architectural solutions. This is an important contribution that considerably increases the possibilities of reusing the QA models in different contexts, since all the dependencies either with the core application or with other QA' concerns are considered. Moreover, models are available to be directly reused.

4   Process Support Using AO-ADL

In order to support the software process described in the previous section, the following requirements must be fulfilled: (1) An AO architectural language able to specify the aspectual bindings between the QA sub-architectures and the core application architecture must be used; (2) Similarly, an architectural modeling language able to define and instantiate architectural templates must be used, and (3) There must be tool Support to store templates and instantiated sub-architectures for later (re)use in different contexts.

These requirements are satisfied by AO-ADL (6), which defines the concepts of components and connector templates and provides a repository of components, connectors and templates that can be imported and reused in the specification of different software architectures. The AO-ADL language is supported by the AO-ADL Tool Suite, implemented as an Eclipse plug-in [1]. This suite can provide a catalogue of architectural templates that are ready to be instantiated.

5   Conclusions

In this paper we have defined a process to guide software architects in the use of AOSD to model those QAs that have a crosscutting nature and important functional implications. This process promotes the understanding of QAs and increases their reusability in different contexts by using a repository of reusable and parameterizable architectural solutions. We propose using the AO-ADL Tool Suite for this purpose, though other AO architectural approaches may be used.

References

1. Bachmann, F., Bass, L., Klein, M., Shelton, C.: Designing software architectures to achieve quality attribute requirements. IEE Proceedings 152(4), 153–165 (2005)
2. Juristo, N., Moreno, A.M., Sanchez, M.I.: Guidelines for eliciting usability functionalities. IEEE Transactions on Software Engineering 33(11), 744–757 (2007)
3. Welie, M.V.: The amsterdam collection of patterns in user interface design (2007)
4. Folmer, E., Bosch, J.: Architecting for usability; a survey. Journal of Systems and Software 70(1), 61–78 (2004)
5. Geebelen, K., et al.: Design of frameworks for aspects addressing 2 additional key concerns. Technical Report AOSD-Europe D117, AOSD-Europe-KUL-14 (2008)
6. Pinto, M., Fuentes, L.: AO-ADL: An ADL for describing aspect-oriented architectures. In: Early Aspect Workshop at AOSD 2007 (2007)
7. Barbacci, M., et al.: Quality attributes. Technical Report CMU/SEI-95-TR-021 (1995)
8. Tanter, E., Gybels, K., Denker, M., Bergel, A.: Context-aware aspects. In: Löwe, W., Südholt, M. (eds.) SC 2006. LNCS, vol. 4089, pp. 227–242. Springer, Heidelberg (2006)

---

[1] Visit our Eclipse Update Site in http://caosd.lcc.uma.es/AO-ADLUpdates

Domain Ontology-Based Generative Component Design Using Feature Diagrams and Meta-programming Techniques

Robertas Damaševičius, Vytautas Štuikys, and Jevgenijus Toldinas

Kaunas University of Technology, Studentų 50, LT-51368, Kaunas, Lithuania
`robertas.damasevicius@ktu.lt, vystu@if.ktu.lt,`
`eugenijus.toldinas@ktu.lt`

Abstract. In domains, where great variability of requirements and products exists such as embedded system design domain, a product line (PL) approach is emerging as the most promising design paradigm. The key for the PL implementation is the use of domain analysis and domain modelling methods. We propose to represent domain variability using feature models enriched with lightweight domain ontology. We transform such models into generative component specifications using meta-programming techniques. We suggest: 1) to use domain analysis methods from two perspectives, software engineering and cognitive science; 2) to enrich domain variability models explicitly by contextualization and repurposing (i.e., by lightweight domain ontology); 3) to represent the model using the enriched feature diagrams (EFDs); 4) to encode EFDs using heterogeneous meta-programming.

1 Introduction

Current approaches for architectural design of systems mostly use the product line (PL) concept. A software PL is a set of software systems that share a common, managed set of features satisfying the specific needs and are developed from a common set of core assets in a prescribed way [1]. The PL concept, if applied systematically, allows increasing of software design quality, productivity, provides a capability for mass customization, and leads to the 'industrial' software design [1].

The key for PL implementation are domain analysis and domain modelling methods. A majority of these methods (e.g., FODA [2], FAST [1]) exploit such domain properties as scope, commonality and variability [3]. These concepts express domain content in systems' features and model a domain through identification of structural, functional and other features and their relationships. However, with further growth of complexity, which is inspired by ever-growing technology capabilities, market demands, and user requirements, it is not enough to rely on content-based and feature-centric analysis in system development.

The extension of the scope of analysis is needed to extract along with the content-oriented features other domain relevant knowledge that may be, e.g., related with the context of use. Context awareness is a very important feature because it hides or

R. Morrison, D. Balasubramaniam, and K. Falkner (Eds.): ECSA 2008, LNCS 5292, pp. 338–341, 2008.
© Springer-Verlag Berlin Heidelberg 2008

brings more complex relationships of features that can be treated as knowledge. Software engineering approaches (such as FODA) do not neglect the importance of a context; however, these approaches deal with a context in a narrow sense (e.g., FODA neglects possible changes in a context).

The problems we discuss are: 1) the representation of system architecture (its components) using Feature Diagrams (FDs) enriched by lightweight domain ontology and 2) the transformation of such feature models into a specification, which describes generative components encoded using meta-programming techniques.

We suggest: 1) to use domain analysis methods from two perspectives, software engineering and cognitive science (at least in a narrow sense with context change and design repurposing); 2) to represent a domain variability model, which is enriched by context changes and repurposing (i.e., by lightweight ontology), explicitly; 3) to represent the model using the Enriched Feature Diagrams (EFDs); 4) to encode EFDs using the heterogeneous meta-programming techniques.

2   Basics of Feature Diagrams and Motivation of Their Extension

Feature Diagrams (FDs) describe the features of a system or a component at a higher abstraction level. Conventional FD [2] is a tree-like directed acyclic graph, in which the root represents the initial concept, intermediate nodes represent compound features, leaves represent non-decomposable atomic features that may have values (aka variants), and branches represent the parent-child relationships among compound features or among compound features and atomic features. Furthermore, additional relationships such as constraints (e.g., <require>, <mutual exclusion>, etc.) between leaves derived from different parents are identified.

There are mandatory, optional and alternative feature types. *Mandatory* feature is always selected (marked by a black circle above its box). *Optional* feature may be selected or not. *Alternative* feature is selected depending on some alternative (condition). Both are marked by a white circle above its box (see Table 1). If an atomic feature has values (variants), it is also treated as a variant point.

We propose to enrich FDs by lightweight domain ontologies and provide extensions to the FD notation. Our aim is similar to Batory [4], who is the proponent of moving FDs closer towards domain ontologies. The structure and meaning of a specific FD is dependable on the context and the goal of a FD. By changing the <goal> and <context> attributes we alter the representation and semantics of the FD (e.g., feature types). In the PL approach, the context is inevitably changing in architectural design. This property further leads to treating the <goal> and <context> attributes as generic categories meaning that each attribute has pre-specified values taken from a defined value space. Generic context is understood as a higher-level feature having at least two different values. When representing the same initial concept, the use of generic context results in the construction of a set of the related FDs. The latter corresponds to the PL approach, in which the related groups of features model product families. Table 1 summarizes the syntax and semantics of conventional attributes as well as innovative attributes of enriched FDs (EFDs).

Table 1. Feature types, ontology and constraints for feature model representation

Feature type	Definition, formalism and semantics of relationships	Graphical notation (syntax)
Concept and its context	Concept is represented by the root with the explicitly stated context on the left at the same level; context is seen as the highest mandatory feature with variants	
Mandatory	Feature B (C, D) is included if its parent A is included: a) *if* A *then* B; b) *if* A *then* C *and* D (Relationship-and: **<R-and>**)	
Optional	Feature B (C, D) may be included if its parent A is included: a) *if* A *then* B *or* **<no feature>** b) *if* A *then* C *or* D *or* **<no feature>**	
Alternative 1 (*R-case*)	Exactly one feature (B or C or D) has to be selected if its parent A is selected: a) *if* A *then* case-of (B, C) b) *if* A *then* case-of (B, C, D) (Relationship-case: **<R-case>**)	
Alternative 2 (*R-or*)	At least one feature has to be selected if its parent A is selected: a) *if* A *then* any-of (B, C) b) *if* A *then* any-of (B, C, D) (Relationship-or: **<R-or>**)	
Alternative 3 (*R-xor*)	*if* A *then* (B *but* ¬C) *or* (C *but* ¬B) (Relationship-xor: **<R-xor>**; differences from **<R–case>**: 1) two sons only; 2) label "**xor**" is written at the parent's node)	
Ontology	A compound of atomic features and their relationships; ontology expresses the domain knowledge in some way	
Constraint *xor*	*if* F *then* ¬K *and if* ¬F *then* K (**<R-xor>** between atomic features F & K derived from different parents: K **xor** F	
Constraint *require*	Feature K requires feature F: K **requires** F	

3   Encoding of EFDs as Ontology-Based Generative Components

A generative component allows generating component instances specified by meta-parameter values on demand. An ontology-based generative component implements the ontology and other features represented in the EFD using heterogeneous meta-programming [5] as a generative technology. We consider encoding as a model transformation, i.e., a process that transforms a source model (EFD) into a target model (meta-program). As meta-program is a compound specification of two languages (meta-language and domain language), we use two-level model transformations. By transformations we mean the rewriting of a graphical notation of the EFD into a textual meta-language notation. At Level 1, the EFD is transformed into a meta-program model. At Level 2, the meta-program model is transformed into a meta-program itself.

Transformation rules at Level 1 are as follows:

A. *Context* as a higher-level feature (variant point) is transformed into the highest-level meta-parameter(s).
B. *Feature constraints* are transformed into constraints that are expressed in terms of meta-parameters and their relationships using meta-constructs.
C. *Variant points* that describe ontology-based features in the EFD are transformed into the ontology related meta-parameters; and the remaining variant points are transformed into other meta-parameters.
D. *Meta-parameter values* are identified.

Transformation rules at Level 2 are as follows.

- Locations that relate to variant points (variants) are identified and variability is described using meta-language constructs (e.g., meta-for, meta-if, etc.).
- Completeness of encoding of the EFD as well as encoding correctness is checked using tools that support meta-programming.

4 Conclusions

In many cases, architecture of an embedded system is not a purely static structure but rather is a dynamic structure. The higher complexity of architecture (in terms of features), the greater need to model domain variability is. Architecture may depend on the context leading to the introduction of new features and specification of more complex relationships among features (i.e., domain ontology). Although Feature Diagrams can model and manage domain complexity and variability, their expressiveness for modelling domain ontologies is not enough.

We consider two challenging tasks: 1) to enrich Feature Diagrams with context information and repurposing (i.e., by domain ontology) and then to represent domain variability in a feature model explicitly; 2) to encode Enriched Feature Diagrams using the heterogeneous meta-programming techniques, thus resulting in the creation of generative components for specifying families of domain systems.

References

1. Weiss, D.M., Lai, C.T.R.: Software Product-Line Engineering: A Family-Based Software Development Approach. Addison-Wesley, Reading (1999)
2. Kang, K.C., Lee, K., Lee, J., Kim, S.: Feature-Oriented Product Line Software Engineering: Principles and Guidelines. In: Itoh, K., Kumagai, S., Hirota, T. (eds.) Domain Oriented Systems Development - Practices and Perspectives. Taylor & Francis, Abington (2003)
3. Coplien, J., Hoffman, D., Weiss, D.: Commonality and Variability in Software Engineering 15(6), 37–45 (1998)
4. Batory, D.S.: Feature Models, Grammars, and Propositional Formulas. In: Obbink, H., Pohl, K. (eds.) SPLC 2005. LNCS, vol. 3714, pp. 7–20. Springer, Heidelberg (2005)
5. Štuikys, V., Damaševičius, R.: Metaprogramming Techniques for Designing Embedded Components for Ambient Intelligence. In: Basten, T., et al. (eds.) Ambient Intelligence: Impact on Embedded System Design, pp. 229–250. Kluwer Academic Publishers, Dordrecht (2003)

Facets of Adaptivity

Claudia Raibulet

Università degli Studi di Milano-Bicocca, DISCo, Viale Sarca 336, U14, 20126, Milan, Italy
`raibulet@disco.unimib.it`

Abstract. Adaptivity is one of the key requirements of today's information systems. It is used in various areas which may range from control and operating systems to networks, from robotics to intelligent systems, from multimedia to information retrieval and Web Services. Essentially, it is related to changes performed in the systems at run-time. These changes may regard various aspects: architectural, structural, behavioral or content. Considering the diversity of its application areas and of ways of achievement, this paper aims to discuss the *facets* of adaptivity by raising the following questions: Why is it needed? Which are its objectives? Which are its main open research issues?

Keywords: definition of adaptivity, facets of adaptivity.

1 Introduction

More and more information systems are *adaptive*. The concept of adaptivity is gaining the attention of the researchers working in various fields. These affirmations are sustained by the growing number of courses, books, journals, conferences focused on adaptivity. Adaptivity may be used to achieve different objectives through different mechanisms. Hence, there are various understandings of adaptivity. It is difficult, if not impossible (yet), to find a precise or complete definition of adaptivity. Each work specifies what it means through adaptivity and how it achieves adaptivity.

This paper aims to discuss several facets of adaptivity by addressing the following questions: why is adaptivity used and which are the areas in which it is successfully exploited. The objective of this discussion is to identify the key points of a possible definition of adaptivity as well as its related open research issues.

2 Why Is Adaptivity Used?

The various different reasons claiming for adaptivity derive mostly from the growing complexity of today's information systems as well as from the need to improve productivity and performance, and automate configuration, re-configuration, control and management tasks. Three of the most important reasons are identified in [9]: (1) systems should run continuously in the presence of components' faults, variability in resources or users' needs, (2) administrative overheads should be reduced allowing smooth operation with minimal human oversight, and (3) systems should provide various levels of services to different users depending on their needs and context.

R. Morrison, D. Balasubramaniam, and K. Falkner (Eds.): ECSA 2008, LNCS 5292, pp. 342–345, 2008.

Ubiquitous and autonomic computing contribute to the growing interest in adaptivity [8]. They have different objectives: ubiquitous computing aims to remove the boundaries on how, when, and where humans and computer interact, while autonomic computing regards self-managing systems which require only high-level human guidance. Although, they share common requirements regarding adaptivity: survival of components failure or security attacks, automation of configuration and management tasks, modification of architectural or behavioral aspects at run-time.

An organizational point of view on adaptivity in an enterprise network infrastructure regards: the fortification of security, increase of productivity, and reduction of the complexity [7].

3 Where Is Adaptivity Used?

Primarily, adaptivity has been used in the context of control engineering to address *unpredicted situations* and to ensure an *optimal working* of a system in the presence of *internal* or *external* changes [1]. Currently, its advantages are exploited in various types of systems and domains: operating systems, networks, robotics, artificial intelligence, e-learning, multimedia, information retrieval and Web Services.

An *extensible* operating system enables applications to adapt the environment to their current needs by managing services through a *late binding* mechanism. This enables the modification of the *architecture* and *behavior* of the system at run-time.

A network is considered adaptive if it is able to obtain the maximum profit from the minimum network resources by *managing* properly the network traffic based on the *user service requests*. Adaptivity comes to complement the QoS or mobility issues. Essentially, it is translated in terms of *flexibility*, *security* and *availability*.

In robotics, adaptivity addresses the *dynamic behaviour*, *situations* and *environmental* modifications. Robot systems *observe* their environment and their current status, *reflect* on them and *make changes* in their *behaviour*. Multi robot systems *reconfigure* themselves by changing their *topology* and *behaviour* to achieve a common goal, Intelligent systems *observe* and *learn* by acquiring information and *reason* about it to recognize new situations and to address them properly in the future. Hence, adaptivity may *improve* or *extend the functionalities* of intelligent systems.

In e-learning, adaptivity aims to improve the *efficiency* of the educational systems in *heterogeneous environments* where students have *different backgrounds* and *abilities* to comprehend knowledge. An adaptive system provides a *personalized* mechanism for students to achieve a similar level of knowledge.

Multimedia and information retrieval systems exploit adaptivity to *manage* properly information according to the *available computational* and *communication resources*. Users work in *different environments*. In this context, adaptivity is based on the *networks, devices, users' environments* and *type of required information*.

Web services can be required in *various contexts* and with *different characteristics*. Adaptivity consists in the ability of the provider to offer a service in the *most appropriate way* for the *current customer* and its *current context*.

4 Definition and Open Issues

In 1963 Zadeh sustained that "it is difficult to find a satisfactory explanation, much less precise definition of this notion in the literature. Much of the vagueness surrounding the notion of adaptivity is attributable to the lack of clear differentiation between the external manifestations of adaptive behavior on the one hand, and the internal mechanism by which it is achieved on the other" [10]. Further, he motivates this affirmation through "the large ways in which adaptive behavior can be realized".

These affirmations are still true today: each work explains what it intends for adaptivity. Examples of possible definitions for adaptivity are listed in the following.

Architectural adaptation focuses on the changes made at run-time in the structure of the components of a system and/or in the interactions among them by using an architectural model of a system [4].

Compositional adaptation regards the modifications of the structure and behavior of a software made at run-time due to the changes occurred in its execution environment [8].

Structural adaptation of a software component consists in updating its structure while preserving its behavior and services [2]. Structural adaptation means changing dynamically the type of application components such as a method signature [5].

Behavioral adaptation focuses on the changes made dynamically in the execution of software components in a non intrusive way (e.g., by changing its configuration or by intercepting its requests and replies) [5].

Content adaptation deals with the transformation and manipulation of contents based on the features of the application or device requiring them [6].

Service adaptation is translated into content as well as behavioral adaptation [3].

These interpretations of adaptivity are characterized by three recurring concepts:

1. *Adaptivity is requested by changes occurred internally inside a system or externally in its execution environment*

An immediate consequence of this affirmation is that an adaptive system should be *introspective* and/or *context-aware*. Open issues are related to the answers to questions such as: Which are those changes claiming for adaptivity? Which are the changes not claiming for adaptivity? How to monitor a system and/or its execution environment to reveal the meaningful changes for adaptivity? Can changes occur simultaneously or independently? Can they be addressed independently from each other? Usually, changes are revealed by capturing information about various internal/external aspects. How to represent and manage this knowledge?

2. *Adaptivity consists in changes performed in a system by the system itself*

An immediate consequence of this affirmation is that an adaptive system should be *autonomous* and *reflective*. Open issues are related to the answers to questions such as: How to identify the changes which should be done? How to define them? How to apply them? Are there changes which cannot be considered part of adaptivity? What should not be changed in an adaptive system? Which are the criteria to define an adaptive change? Are there many levels of adaptivity? Are there any metrics to express the levels of adaptivity of systems? Can a system evolve through adaptivity?

3. Adaptivity is performed at run-time
Open issues are related to the answers to questions such as: Are there any verification/validation mechanisms of the functional and non-functional aspects of an adaptive system after the application of changes at run-time? Is simulation a possible solution to this problem? Are there any simulation models for adaptive systems?

5 Conclusions

Considering the reasons *why adaptivity is used* its possible facets may include: automation of human tasks, performance and productivity improvement, content access and exploitation enhancement, reduction of complexity, fortification of security, management of critical situations. From its *application domains*, the facets may result in: controlling, networking, automation, intelligence, content and service personalization. Is adaptivity a common term for all these different issues? Can it be confounded with scalability, mobility, late-binding or evolution mechanisms? In [9], the authors assert that an adaptive system may be characterized by one or more of the following properties: self-healing, self-configuration, self-management and self-optimization. Can these properties be considered additional facets of adaptvity?

Adaptivity plays an important role in the development of today's information systems. [8] identifies four of its main issues: assurance, security, decision support, and interoperability. This list should be extended with formalisms, models, patterns, tools for design and testing, criteria and metrics, and evaluation mechanisms.

References

1. Astrom, K.J., Wittenmark, B.: Adaptive Control. Addison Wesley, Reading (1995)
2. Bastide, G., Seriai, A., Oussalah, M.: Software Component Re-engineering for their Runtime Structural Adaptation. In: Proceedings of the 31st Annual International Computer Software and Applications Conference, pp. 109–114. IEEE Computer Society Press, Los Alamitos (2007)
3. Choi, O., Yoon, Y.: A Meta Data Model of Context Information for Dynamic Service Adaptation on User Centric Environment. In: Proceedings of the International Conference on Multimedia and Ubiquitous engineering, pp. 108–113. IEEE Computer Society Press, Los Alamitos (2007)
4. Garlan, D., Cheng, S.W., Huang, A.-C., Schmerl, B., Steenkiste, P.: Rainbow: Architecture-based Self-Adaptation with Reusable Infrastructure. IEEE Computer 37(10), 46–54 (2004)
5. Gorton, I., Liu, Y., Trivedi, N.: An extensible and lightweight architecture for adaptive server applications. Software – Practice and Experience Journal (2007)
6. He, J., Gao, T., Hao, W., Yen, I.-L., Bastani, F.: A Flexible Content Adaptation System Using a Rule-Based Approach. IEEE Transactions on Knowledge and Data Engineering 19(1), 127–140 (2007)
7. McHugh, J.: Adaptive Networks Vision. ProCurve Networking, HP Innovation (2007),
   http://www.hp.com/md/pdfs/
   Adaptive_Networks_Vision_White_Paper.pdf
8. McKinley, P.K., Sadjadi, S.M., Kasten, E.P., Cheng, B.H.C.: Composing Adaptive Software. Computer 37(7), 56–64 (2004)
9. Seceleanu, T., Garlan., D.: Synchronized Architectures for Adaptive Systems. In: Proceedings of the 29th Annual International Computer Software and Applications Conference, Edinburgh, UK, pp. 146–151 (2005)
10. Zadeh, L.A.: On the Definition of Adaptivity. Proceedings of the IEEE, 469–470 (1963)

Transition to Service-Oriented Enterprise Architecture

Martin Assmann[1,3] and Gregor Engels[2,3]

[1] International Graduate School of Dynamic Intelligent Systems
[2] Dept. of Computer Science
[3] University of Paderborn
Warburger Straße 100, 33098 Paderborn, Germany
{martin.assmann,engels}@upb.de

Abstract. Enterprise Architecture (EA) has undergone many changes since the IT has found its way into enterprises. At the moment the Service-Oriented Architecture (SOA) is being hyped but has also gained some importance. Implementing SOA can have many implications for an enterprise, depending on how visionary the implemented architecture is. This paper provides the description of an enterprise architecture that is fully-fledged concerning service-orientation and points out the architectural challenges that have to be mastered with future research results.

Keywords: Enterprise Architecture, Service-Oriented Architecture.

1 Introduction

"Change is the only constant" is a citation used often by business analysts. As depicted in [1], over the years the factor change has steadily increased. It is pointed out that several average life cycle times, namely those for products, applications, and processes, have been decreased by magnitudes. During this time enterprise architecture has changed significantly several times. In the seventies computers found their way into enterprises, followed by IT-concepts like Component Based Architecture and Enterprise Application Integration. The implementation of these concepts has often lead to huge projects that heavily influenced the enterprise architecture (a brief definition is given in 1.1).

One of the most recent concepts is Service-Oriented Architecture, whereas it is not really clear what it means as a common definition is not available. Definitions are given in [1], [2], and [3] for example. While [3] merely addresses technical issues, [1] and [2] refer to process and organizational aspects. As no fitting definition is available, this paper presents a description of a fully developed SOA for enterprises. This allows deriving tasks for enterprise architects and formulating research questions. The goal of the research intends helping the architect fulfilling his tasks.

1.1 Enterprise Architecture and Service-Oriented Architecture

Enterprise Architecture addresses nearly the whole enterprise. It comprises business and IT architecture and also addresses their cohesion. The business architecture itself

R. Morrison, D. Balasubramaniam, and K. Falkner (Eds.): ECSA 2008, LNCS 5292, pp. 346–349, 2008.
© Springer-Verlag Berlin Heidelberg 2008

consists of business goals, organization and processes. The IT-architecture consists of software and infrastructure architecture. All these parts define enterprise architecture. In order to develop a complex enterprise architecture its architects have to be aware of all these different sub-architectures and their coherence. A detailed description for EA including a meta-model is given in [4].

The notion Service-Oriented Architecture spans several topics and a comprehensive definition here clearly exceeds the space limit. For extensive descriptions on SOA we refer to [1] and [2]. In the following we focus on the aspects being important for the statements of this paper. We regard SOA as an architectural style for enterprise architecture that aims at an optimal IT realization (automation) of business processes.

1.2   Relation between SOA and EA

As shown in figure 1, one of the main ideas of SOA is to bridge the gap between the business process layer and the application layer. The service layer is introduced for this purpose. Bridging the gap means to ease the implementation of processes with IT while fostering the reuse of services. Therefore SOA influences the business process, the service and the application layer. Hence, the introduction of such a Service-Oriented Architecture affects nearly the complete enterprise architecture.

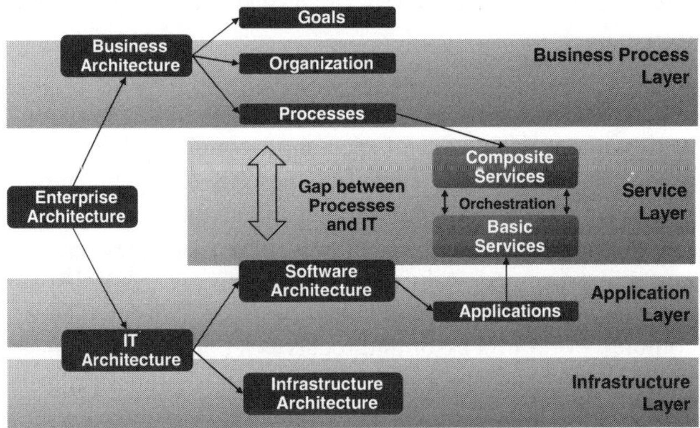

Fig. 1. Relation between SOA and EA

2   Service-Oriented Enterprise Architecture

In figure 2 our conception of a fully developed Service-Oriented Enterprise Architecture (SOEA) is depicted. It describes the most important elements of the three layers and also the problems an enterprise architect is confronted with. An extensive description of the evolution from the beginning to the here depicted enterprise architecture style is given in [5]. We will explain the figure bottom up.

Services abstract from the application layer and are published in the service registry. Furthermore they can be orchestrated in two ways. On the one hand this can be hard-wired, (Incoming order service), so that a service directly uses other services. On the other hand soft-wired by an orchestration engine that allows to model processes

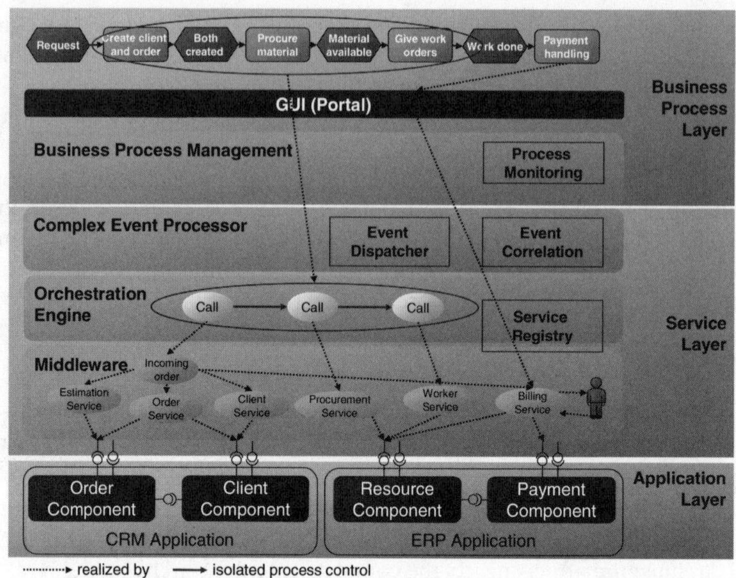

Fig. 2. Fully developed Service-Oriented Enterprise Architecture

with services and that can execute these process plans afterwards. In the latter case the process logic that defines the process control flow exists in a very explicit form. It can be easily changed (without knowledge of special programming languages like Java) and therefore provides a high flexibility regarding process changes. The architect has to decide how services are tailored and orchestrated so that their reuse potential is optimal.

Services should implement event communication so that business events can be immediately sent and processed. All events are sent to the event dispatcher and from there to all subscribers of the event (publish-subscriber pattern). The event correlator is part of the complex event processor and receives a copy of all events. It is watching incoming events over time and checks whether they fit to predefined rules. On the one hand the complex event processor allows describing business logic in the explicit form of rules. A usual case would be that an event triggers the execution of a service orchestration. On the other hand business events can be perfectly used for business process monitoring purposes. Without events it would be hard to gather all the information online. The monitoring information itself could be used for process improvement. The architect has to define event types and the rules for complex event processing, so that the relevant information can be monitored.

With all this the means for Business Process Management (BPM) are given, because the four steps designing, building, operating and monitoring processes are realized. Designing and building is realized by modeling processes with a tool for a service orchestration language like BPEL. Operating is done by the orchestration engine when interpreting the predefined process models. Of course the orchestration engine only triggers the operation of services that do most of the work. The monitoring component delivers information for redesigning the processes. By this the management cycle is closed. A business analyst that controls the BPM will define change requests that have to planned and realized by the enterprise architect.

The GUIs should be as flexible as the processes because often with a change of a process a change in the GUI becomes mandatory. In every case the GUIs functionality has to be decoupled from applications, i.e. they interact with services only. The architect has to consider that the GUIs must be flexible and reusable. Therefore he has to allow reuse in different environments and also tailor the reusable parts in the right granularity.

3 Emerging Research Questions

SOA sure brings up a plethora of research questions, but we will focus on those that concern enterprise architecture and Service-Oriented Architecture.

The evolution from enterprises today to enterprises that implement the presented form of EA is drastic. It is drastic because SOA is the first architectural style for EA, hence it affects large parts of the enterprise. Because of this the evolution demands managing enterprise architecture in whole. Moreover, the new architectural style increases complexity of EA, which makes it hard for the architect to keep the full picture. The first research question derived from these tasks is: „How to model and plan EA-evolution to SOA-style in a holistic way?" A good starting point for this is the EA meta-model model given in [4]. With minor changes regarding to some SOA aspects like service orchestrations and complex event processing, the approach in [4] is suitable to describe a targeted service-oriented enterprise architecture. Such a model supports in planning enterprise evolution, which includes the tailoring of services, orchestrating them and defining events and their corresponding rules.

A step further is not only to plan evolution but also to manage it. Therefore the EA (steadily) has to be evaluated if it conforms to the aimed style (in our case SOA). For this task criteria have to be defined that describe such an SOEA. Of course it would be helpful if the criteria and the model of the enterprise architecture were on a formal basis, so that further research for automation could be done. A question that might be partially answered: "How to automatically decide whether the EA conforms to SOA-style?" and secondly "How to bring up suggestions for changes that evolve the enterprise towards SOA-style?" If other EA styles will emerge, the developed methods could also help for the evaluation of the new styles.

References

1. Krafzig, D., Banke, K., Slama, D.: Enterprise SOA. Service-oriented architecture best practices. The Coad series. Prentice-Hall, Upper Saddle River (2006) (6th print)
2. Erl, T.: Service-oriented architecture. Concepts, technology, and design. Prentice-Hall, Upper Saddle River (2006) (6th print)
3. Dostal, W.: Service-orientierte Architekturen mit Web Services. Konzepte - Standards - Praxis. 1. Elsevier Spektrum Akad. Verl., Aufl. München (2005)
4. Braun, C., Winter, R.: A Comprehensive Enterprise Architecture Metamodel and Its Implementation Using a Metamodeling Platform. In: Desel, J., Frank, U. (eds.) Enterprise Modelling and Information Systems Architectures (EMISA), Proc. of the Workshop in Klagenfurt, October 24-25. LNI, Bd, vol. 75, pp. 64–79. Gesellschaft für Informatik (GI) (2005)
5. Engels, G., Assmann, A.: Service-Oriented Architecture: Evolution of Concepts and Methods. In: Proc. of the Twelfth IEEE International EDOC Conference. IEEE Press, Los Alamitos (2008)

Diagrammatic Modeling of Architectural Decisions

Andrzej Zalewski and Marcin Ludzia

Warsaw University of Technology, Institute of Automatic Control and Computational
Engineering, Warsaw, Poland
`a.zalewski@ia.pw.edu.pl`

Abstract. The paper presents a semi formal model of architectural decisions referred to as Maps of Architectural Decisions (MAD). In a form of a diagram they represent the most important components of architectural decisions (concerns, possible choices, constraints etc.) as well as logic of architectural decision making, i.e. dependencies between architectural decisions. This increases the level of formalism of the architectural decisions documentation, improves its readability and makes architectural knowledge gathered during the decision making process easier to comprehend, share and maintain.

1 Introduction

Modeling of architectural decisions is a focal issue of software architecture researchers. According to the classical paper by [1] they should include the following attributes: addressed issue, considered decision variants (positions), requirements, constraints, decision made, rationale (argument), implications. This provides a structured form of textual documentation of architectural decisions. The drawbacks of textual documentation have already been fully investigated in the software engineering discipline: it is error prone thus often inconsistent and ambiguous, difficult to analyse and verify, inefficient in presenting complex concepts.

In the software engineering discipline, such drawbacks have often been resolved by increasing the level of model's formality according to the scheme: textual (informal) – semi-formal (diagrammatical) – formal (mathematical) model. Increasing the level of formality of the models of architectural decisions seems to be an important research challenge. The most important developments towards further formalization of architectural decision models were so far:

- A tool called 'Archium' supporting architectural decision making has been presented in [3]. It concentrates on documenting the decision making process: the decisions are modeled as text records, however, their dependencies are modeled in the form of dependency graph. The tool supports traceability, basic completeness verification, detection of superfluous decisions;
- Knowledge management techniques based on ontologies have been used for managing architectural decisions in [2], however, these ideas have not been fully prover in practice yet;

R. Morrison, D. Balasubramaniam, and K. Falkner (Eds.): ECSA 2008, LNCS 5292, pp. 350–353, 2008.

– Extension of Tyree's templates to support decision makers collaboration and knowledge reuse – proposed in [4];
– Attribute decision graph presented in [5] in fact models the process of making architectural decisions driven by satisfying predefined attributes.

Maps of Architectural Decisions is another approach to the challenge of formalizing architectural decisions.

2   MAD – Models and Notation

MAD consists of two basic models: Architectural Decision Relationship Diagram (ADRD) and Architectural Decision Problem Map (ADPM), for an example – see fig. 2. The ADRD represents the set of identified architectural problems (concerns) and dependencies between them. The ADPM diagram is used to model all the important details of a given architectural decision problem and consists of the following objects: Architectural Decision Problem (ADP), Decision Variant (DV), Constraint (DC), Requirement (DR), Decision maker/Stakeholder and Connector (Constraint-Variant Connector or Variant-Problem Connector). The summary of MAD notation has been shown in fig. 1.

Each of the objects in ADRD or ADPM is additionally characterized with a set of attributes (they have been omitted due to the limit of space).

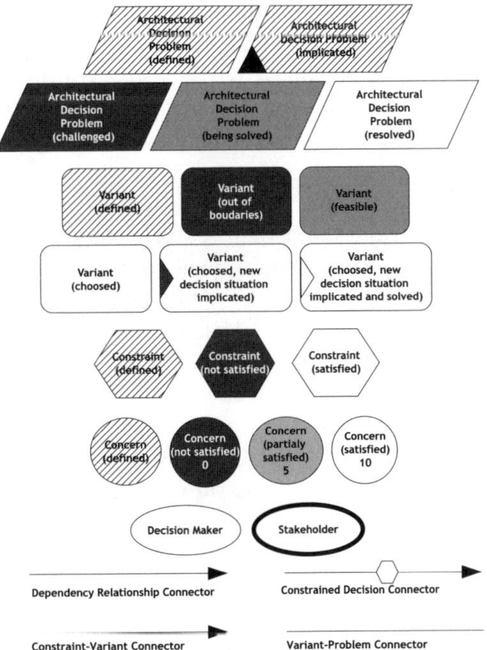

Fig. 1. Maps of Architectural Decisions – notation summary

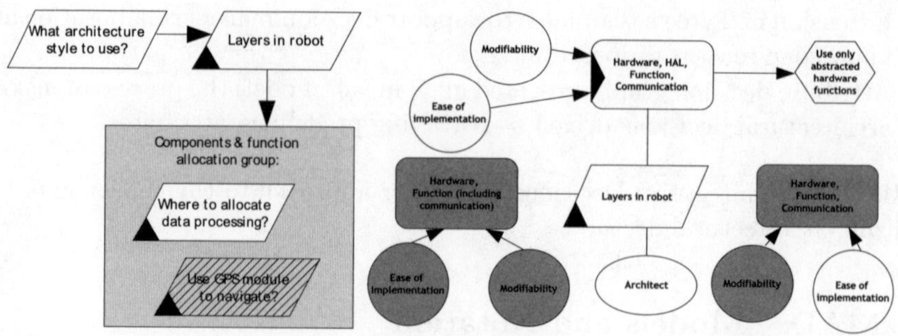

Fig. 2. MAD models for architectural decisions concerning architecting robot control system

The application of MAD has been illustrated on an example of robot control system presented in [6] – see fig. 2. We can comprehend from the ADRD, that there were three decision problems resolved so far and the fourth decision problem was added.

Each of the architectural decision problems can be modelled in detail with ADPM. An example decision problem is shown in fig. 2 (to the right). The central object of this diagram is an ADP object. These objects should first be defined in ADRD. The model of architectural decision problem consists of i) a set of considered solution variants modelled with DV objects attached to the ADP object; ii) Constraints and Requirements – instantiated from the dictionary of constraints and requirements (each Decision Variant should be assigned its own Constraints/Requirement set of instances, the constraints and requirements objects should be linked to Decision Variant by Constraint and Requirement Connector (CRC) with an arrowhead pointing the variant object), iii) Stakeholders involved in decision making process represented by an Decision Maker/Stakeholder object.

Architects evaluate all the Constraints and Requirements for each of the Decision Variants. The constraints and requirements may turn out to be satisfied, not satisfied or partially satisfied (requirements only). The variants, that do not satisfy all the constraints are marked as "Out of boundaries" and excluded as from the set of potential choices in the decision making process.

Variants meeting the requirements and satisfying the constraints should be marked as "Feasible". Architect chooses one of the "Feasible" variants and marks it as "Chosen". If chosen DV necessitates making some other decision, it is reflected as a triangle on the left side of a DV object. Additionally, architect should consider if there are any new constraint introduced by the decision. If so, the constraint should be defined in a diagram and linked with a variant object by CRC with an arrowhead directed to the Constraint object. The constraint will be automatically added to the constraints dictionary.

The entire architecture design is finished and properly documented, when all defined decision problems are described by ADPM models and all the decisions have been made and none of them is in challenged state (does not require reconsidering because of some other decision, which has been made).

3   Conclusion Further Research

The paper has been devoted to the presentation of a novel approach to the modeling of architectural decisions and the process of architectural decision making. The MAD models can be perceived as a tool for "mind-mapping" architectural decisions. Their unique feature is that they document the internal structure of architectural decisions in the form of a diagram. The notation assists both making an individual architectural decision – depicting all the important components on a single diagram – as well as documenting the whole process of architectural decision making – showing the dependencies between architectural decisions in the form of a diagram. As the level of formalism has been increased an automated checking similar to those described in [3] should be possible to implement.

Further research should include:

- interfacing the MAD and traditional modeling approaches (views, ADL's);
- predefining the dictionaries of the attributes of diagram's objects;
- providing formal definitions of diagrammatic models and their semantic;,
- defining the desired properties of the graphical models (consistency, completeness, others) and methods of their analysis;
- developing software tools supporting architecting with MAD.

References

1. Tyree, J., Akerman, A.: Architecture Decisions: Demystifying Architecture. IEEE Software (March/April 2005)
2. Kruchten, P.: An Ontology of Architectural Design Decisions in Software-Intensive Systems. In: Proc. of 2nd Groningen Workshop on Software Variability, Rijksuniversiteit Groningen, pp. 54–61 (2004)
3. Jansen, A., et al.: Tool Support for Architectural Decisions. In: Proceedings of the Working IEEE/IFIP Conference on Software Architecture (WICSA 2007). IEEE, Los Alamitos (2007)
4. Zimmermann, O., et al.: Reusable architectural decision models for enterprise application development. In: Overhage, S., Szyperski, C.A., Reussner, R., Stafford, J.A. (eds.) QoSA 2007. LNCS, vol. 4880, pp. 15–32. Springer, Heidelberg (2008)
5. Schwanke, R.W.: Layers, Decisions, Patterns, Styles, and Architectures. In: Proceedings of the Working IEEE/IFIP Conference on Software Architecture (WICSA 2001), pp. 137–147. IEEE, Los Alamitos (2001)
6. Gueorguiev, A., et al.: Design, Architecture and Control of a Mobile Site-Modeling Robot. In: Proceedings of the IEEE 2000 International Conference of Robotic and Automation, San Francisco. IEEE, Los Alamitos (2000)

Web Services Domain Analysis Based on Quality Standards[*]

F. Losavio[**], A. Matteo, and R. Rahamut

Centro ISYS, Escuela de Computación, Facultad de Ciencias
Universidad Central de Venezuela
Apdo. 47567, Los Chaguaramos 1041-A, Caracas, Venezuela
{flosav,almatteo,rrahamut}@cantv.net

Abstract. Web Services (WS) are an alternative to the lack of interoperability of applications, to facilitate integration via Service Oriented Architecture (SOA). The main goal of this paper is to establish a correspondence between three WS-related standards, WSA (Web Services Architecture) representing industrial and marketing requirements, ISO/IEC 9126-1 quality model to specify standard quality requirements, and ISO/IEC 13236 to specify the measurement model for WS-based applications. A domain analysis process is defined to provide guidelines to integrate the information of the three standards, facilitating the automatic generation of standardized quality of service contracts between clients and providers.

Keywords: web-services architecture; domain analysis; quality requirements; ISO/IEC 9126-1; ISO/IEC 13236.

1 Introduction

A *Web Services* (WS) is considered a software component offering a service. WS can be grouped on the basis of the functionality or service they provide. The WSA requirements document of the W3C describes seven critical top-level quality goals that are the minimal set of requirements for a common architecture that a WS-based application should comply: Interoperability, Reliability, WWW Integration, Security, Scalability and Extensibility, Team Goals, Management and Provisioning [1]. A broad initial analysis of the *domain of WS-based applications* is given by identifying the quality goals for the base-line or generic architecture, shared by a family of applications within the domain [2]. This paper aims to define a process, which on one hand establishes a correspondence between the WSA top-level critical goals and the ISO/IEC 9126-1 standard for software product quality, to facilitate at a high abstraction level, common understanding of the WS domain architectural properties [3, 4]. Moreover, the quality requirements associated with the functionality of each

[*] This work is partially supported by the Consejo de Desarrollo Científico y Humanístico de la Universidad Central de Venezuela, MODABAC* Project No. 03-005821-2008 and GEMOCLASS Project No. 03-006051-2005.
[**] Corresponding author.

R. Morrison, D. Balasubramaniam, and K. Falkner (Eds.): ECSA 2008, LNCS 5292, pp. 354–358, 2008.

WS type, defining sub-families of applications, are also specified using the ISO/IEC 9126-1 quality model. On the other hand, the ISO/IEC 13236 standard [5] which specifies the quality of services (QoS), is used to define a measurement model by specifying the measurable attributes, according to general quality of service metrics. In consequence, a standard quality model and measurement model for the WS application domain are defined.

This paper is structured as follows, besides this introduction: a central section describing the process to characterize the WS application domain and a final section presenting the conclusion and future work. The case study for Transactional WS is not presented in this paper for lack of space; it can be seen in [8].

2   Analysis of the WS Domain

Step 1. Define functionality. Classification of WS

This classification of WS is based on functional requirements (see Table 1) [6, 7].

Table 1. Functionality based WS classification

WS family	Functional requirements	Examples
Information and collaborative environments	Data Base operations	Distributed authoring systems
Transactional	E-commerce operations, encrypting	On-line banking
Workflow	Process monitoring operations	Planning/Scheduling systems
Web Portal	E-search and e-communication	Search engines, On-line news
Security	Access control, encrypting	Authentication and authorization

Step 2. Define Quality Model

The ISO/IEC 9126-1 standard defines a hierarchical model based on six main high level quality characteristics, also called quality requirements: Functionality, Reliability, Usability, Efficiency, Maintainability and Portability; these are the minimal set of non functional properties characterizing applications within a domain. A correspondence with the WSA critical goals is established to specify standard architectural quality (see Table 2).

The quality model shows the minimal characteristics that providers must comply to guarantee *user satisfaction*. In consequence, a WS must satisfy some of the quality properties indicated in Table 2. According also to this table, a WSA compliant service is now also compliant with the ISO/IEC 9126-1 standard characteristics for internal/external software product quality, to which a high, medium or low goal ranking has been assigned by consensus by an expert group. Usability and efficiency are ranked low because they are not present as WSA critical goals [1]; they are not shown in the table. In consequence, *the quality model for WS domain considering relevant architectural properties* is conformed only by characteristics ranked high or medium, which are the following: *functionality (interoperability, security, suitability), reliability (availability), maintainability (Changeability (extensibility, management and provision)) and portability (adaptability (scalability))*.

Table 2. Quality Model for WS-based application domain, showing traceability among ISO/IEC 9126-1 and WSA. The codes of the WSA goals are taken from [1].

ISO/IEC9126-1 characteristics	Correspondence between ISO/IEC9126-1 sub-characteristics and WSA critical goals		
Functionality	**Interoperability**		Semantics is similar. The capability to interoperate within different environment **Goal: high**
	ISO/IEC	Interoperability	
	WSA	Interoperability (AG001)	
	Security		Semantics is similar. It means access control. **Goal: high**
	ISO/IEC	Security	
	WSA	Security (AG004)	
	Suitability		Semantics is similar. It means to satisfy the user specific tasks. **Goal: medium**
	ISO/IEC	Suitability	
	WSA	Team Goals (AG006)	
Reliability	**Availability**		Semantics is similar. It means a combination of maturity, fault tolerance and recovery from failures **Goal: high**
	ISO/IEC	Availability	
	WSA	Reliability (AG006)	
Maintainability	**Extensibility**		The WSA *extensibility* goal is considered as sub-sub-characteristic of changeability. ***Goal: high.***
	ISO/IEC	Changeability	
	WSA	Scalability and Extensibility (AG006)	
	Management and provisioning		The WSA management and provisioning goal is considered a sub-sub-characteristic of changeability **Goal: high.**
	ISO/IEC	Changeability	
	WSA	Management and Provisioning (AG007)	
	Integration		The WSA integration goal is considered a sub-sub-characteristic of changeability. **Goal: medium**
	ISO/IEC	Changeability	
	WSA	Integration (AG003)	
Portability	**Scalability**		The WSA scalability goal will be considered a sub-sub-characteristic of adaptability. **Goal: medium**
	ISO/IEC	Adaptability	
	WSA	Scalability and extensibility (AG006)	

Notice that the WSA critical goals *extensibility* and *management and provision* are shown as sub-sub-characteristics of maintainability. Now, for each type of WS, quality properties are assigned to the functional requirements to express quality goals they should fulfill. New sub-characteristics or sub-sub-characteristics can be added accordingly, if needed. Table 3 shows that **efficiency** for Transactional and Web portals and **accuracy** for Transactional and Collaborative environments were not considered as WSA requirements [1], since they are concerned on how the functionality must be accomplished. Observe that the fulfillment of some of the quality requirements imply a commitment or trade-off with other requirements.

Table 3. Quality requirements for each WS type

WS Type	Quality requirements for sub-families of WS-based applications - characteristics and sub-characteristics according to ISO/IEC 9126-1				
	Functionality	Reliability	Maintainability	Portability	**Efficiency**
Information and collaborative environments	**-accuracy**	-availability	-changeability		
Transactional	**-security** (integrity) **-accuracy**	-availability			**-time behavior -resource utilization**
Workflow	-suitability				
Web Portals				-adaptability: scalability	**-time behavior -resource utilization**
Security	-security				

The WSA quality model, enriched with the qualities related to WS functionality, constitutes the *standard quality model for the WS-based application domain*. It expresses the overall *architectural quality* for WS-based applications. The enrichment is obtained considering all the quality characteristics shown before for WSA and adding the quality characteristics (shown in boldface), derived from the functionality quality goal for each WS, shown in Table 3: **efficiency** (*time behavior, resource utilization*) is required for some of the WS and the sub-characteristic **compliance to standards and regulations** is required to achieve interoperability, in order that the service conforms to standards like SOAP, UDI, WSDL in their respective versions. We assume that this characteristic is present for all WS types and so it is not specified in Table 3. The sub-characteristic **accuracy** has been included for data transactions indicating the precision of an event, set of events, condition or data [5]. Notice that often the term *integrity* is used in WS transactions to denote the fact of maintaining the correction of the transaction with respect to the source, which we are considering in the model as *security*.

Step 3. Define Measurement Model

The QoS, which are quantifiable aspects or parameters, are considered here as *attributes of the sub-characteristics* of the WS domain quality model. Observe that traceability between ISO/IEC 13236 [5] and ISO/IEC 9126-1 [4] is not explicitly provided by the standards, making difficult their practical usage. This work is a contribution towards the fulfillment of this gap. It is clear that the metrics presented are quite general and should be customized to establish the contractual part when using the service in a particular application. In what follows, the quality model is further refined for each WS type of Table 3. The refinement consists in finding the attributes or measurable elements and their metrics, for each WS quality property. These attributes and metrics correspond to the QoS characteristics considered in the ISO/IEC 13236 standard [5]. Table 4 shows the refinement only for the transactional WS category, since this is a complex WS type. The other refinements can be obtained

Table 4. Measurement Model: QoS metrics for Transactional WS

WS	Quality characteristics and sub-characteristics, ISO/IEC 9126-1		Attributes (QoS characteristics, ISO/IEC 13236)	Metrics, ISO/IEC 13236
Transactional WS	Functionality	Security	protection	Probability
			access control	Value or level derived from an access control policy.
			data protection	Value or level derived from the data integrity policy.
			confidentiality	Value or level derived from the data confidentiality policy.
			authenticity	Value or level derived from the data authentication policy.
		Accuracy	{addressing, delivery, transfer, transfer integrity, allowable, release establishment} error	Probability
	Reliability	Availability	fault-tolerance	$MTBF^a = MTTF^b + MTTR^c$
			fault-containment	Probability
			resilience, recovery error	Probability
			Agreed service time (channel, connection, processing)	A=MTBF/(MTBF+MTTR) when maintainability is involved, $0 \leq A \leq 1$
	Efficiency	Time behavior	date/time	Any unit of time
			time delay: transit, request/reply, request/confirm	TD=T2- T1
			lifetime	Any unit of time
			remaining lifetime	Any unit of time
			freshness (or age of data)	Any unit of time
			capacity	Any unit of time
		Resource utilization	throughput (communication capacity)	Units depend on the resource type
			processing capacity	Rate (bits/seconds, bytes/seconds)
			operation loading	Instructions/seconds.

Table notes: [a] MTBF: mean time between failures, [b] MTTR: mean time to replace, [c] MTTF: Mean Time to Failure.

in a similar way and they will not be shown here to ease the presentation; they are detailed in [8]. Notice also that Table 4 only shows some of the attributes, to facilitate legibility. They must be used depending on the application requiring the WS and on what is to be measured. For more detailed information on attributes and metrics, see the ISO/IEC13236 [5] standard document.

3 Conclusion and Future Work

The standard specification of the quality properties for a WS has been emphasized and a process has been proposed for domain analysis, integrating three separate standards: the WSA critical goals that a family of WS applications must hold [1]; a quality model for this domain, according to ISO/IEC 9126-1 [4], enriched to characterize the family of WS, by the quality properties inherent to each functionality. Finally, this quality model is instantiated for families of WS, considering the attributes or QoS metrics, according to ISO/IEC 13236 [5]. In this way, three standards have been related and put into a practical use for domain analysis. Common understanding among stakeholders has been set by this correspondence. Notice also that from the standard measurement model, the Service Level Agreement (SLA) contract can be automatically generated. Ongoing research works are: the generalization of the quality-based WS domain analysis process to any domain, and its usage as an initial step of architecture design methods.

References

[1] World Wide Web Consortium. Web Services Architecture Requirements. W3C Working Group Note (February 11, 2004) Copyright © W3C ® (MIT, ERCIM, Keio) (2004), http://www.w3.org/TR/wsa-reqs

[2] Berard, E.: Essays in Object-Oriented Software Engineering. Prentice-Hall, Englewood Cliffs (1992)

[3] Losavio, F., Chirinos, L., Matteo, A., Lévy, N., Ramdane-Cherif, A.: ISO quality standards to measure architectures. Journal of Systems and Software 72, 209–223 (2004)

[4] ISO/IEC 9126-1, 2, Quality characteristics and guidelines for their use (1, 2), International Organisation for Standardisation / International Electrotechnical Commission (1999)

[5] ISO/IEC 13236. Quality of Service: Framework. Version 1. International Organisation for Standardisation / International Electrotechnical Commission (1999)

[6] Menascé, D., Almeida, V.: Cappacity Planning and Performance Modeling. Prentice-Hall, Englewood Cliffs (2000)

[7] World Wide Web Consortium. Web Service Modeling Ontology. W3C Member (submission June 3, 2005) W3C Working Draft (October 28, 2002). Copyright © 2005 W3C ®, http://www.w3.org/Submission/WSMO/

[8] Rahamut, R.: Patrón de especificación de contratos de calidad con servicios Web, MSc. dissertation, Universidad Central de Venezuela (2008)

Visualizing Software Architectural Design Decisions

Larix Lee and Philippe Kruchten

University of British Columbia
`{llee,pbk}@ece.ubc.ca`

Abstract. Software architecture can be represented as a set of design decisions. Exploring and analyzing architectural design decisions are difficult due to how the decisions are represented and displayed. We describe four visualization aspects that apply to architectural design decision exploration and analysis: 1) tabular listing; 2) decision structure visualization; 3) decision chronology visualization; and 4) decision impact visualization. These aspects address some situations where visualization helps people understand and utilize decisions.

1 Introduction

Designing software is the process of making many design decisions that defines and guides the development of a software system. Some of these decisions are architectural design decisions, as they govern the overarching goals and characteristics of the system being developed. For example, the decision to support which target platforms or the decision to use a particular communication topology are architectural design decisions. These decisions intertwine with many other decisions such that changing one of these decisions may significantly affect other aspects of the design [3], leading to the view that these decisions are a fundamental part of software architecture [1, 2].

Keeping track of architectural design decisions is important in the later stages of software development and maintenance, when the original software architects are no longer available to answer various questions on the design intents and what decisions they made or had previously rejected. We addressed the issues of decision capture in a previous work [6]; however, it can be difficult to explore and analyze the captured decisions effectively. We propose that visualizing the decisions with different aspects may help with architectural design decision exploration and analysis by highlighting certain decision information that will assist the software architect, designer, or developer in performing their tasks. We describe these aspects and how they could contribute to architectural design decision exploration and analysis. We also present conceptual examples using screenshots of a decision visualization tool [7] that we developed.

2 Architectural Decision Exploration and Visualization

Exploration and analysis of architectural design decisions depend on how we structure and represent the information of each decision. Various design decision representation models have been proposed and these models focus on different aspects or attributes.

R. Morrison, D. Balasubramaniam, and K. Falkner (Eds.): ECSA 2008, LNCS 5292, pp. 359–362, 2008.

The argumentative design rationale approaches like the Issue-Based Information Systems [5] focus on the background information, context, and available options at the time the decision was made, while other models focus more on the decisions' attributes and interconnectivities by representing them as first-class entities, such as the architecture decision description template [8] and our decision ontology model [4]. We chose our decision model as it includes aspects of development processes like decision states (e.g., "idea", "tentative", "decided" or "approved") and it makes decision relationships explicit. Relationships include how decisions constrain, forbid, enable, subsume, override, comprise, bind, conflict with, or are alternatives to other decisions.

Exploring and analyzing design decisions also depend on the way the structured decision information is conveyed. Visualization is often used to explore large networks or to understand complex systems like in program comprehension. Visualization is also an identified requirement for the decision view of software architecture [2]. Decision visualization helps people build mental models of the decision space when the decision set gets large (several hundred architectural design decisions) and reveals information hidden in a set of design decisions by supporting associations, groupings, and layout (where we can identify patterns). Since different tasks and situations focus on different decision attributes, different visualization views into the decision model can help prioritize or filter out information that is not directly relevant to a particular exploratory or analytical task. We propose four visualization aspects to visualize software architectural design decisions: tabular listing, decision structure visualization, decision chronology visualization, and decision impact visualization.

Tabular Listing. The purpose of this visualization aspect is to provide a quick and effective way to browse and retrieve information from design decisions. The textual tabular representation facilitates decision querying and simple decision entry because the data representation can be easily parsed on a computer screen or on a paper printout. Although tables provide efficient textual display of decision information, it is difficult to quickly trace and assess decision structures, relationships, and properties when the decision sets get large or change relationships frequently. Fig. 1a shows a list of design decisions for a project. Relationship lists are not shown in this figure.

Decision Structure Visualization. The goal of this aspect is to increase understanding of the architecture's decision structure. The decision structure guides the capture, perusal, and manipulation of decisions and their relationships without sacrificing comprehension of the architecture the decision represents and the decision interconnectivities. An effective way to sort and analyze decision information is to represent the decisions visually using graphs. Decisions are represented as nodes and the relationships are directed edges, as shown in Fig. 1b. Viewing design as the result of applying a set of design decisions, the visualization may display decisions, their attributes, and their relationships separate from the architectural components, that is, a "decision-only" view of the software architecture.

A significant benefit for graphical structure visualization is its cognitive assistance, in the context of helping people create a mental map of the decisions. Other benefits include the ability to detect missing or orphaned decisions that may denote design incompleteness and the preservation of decision contexts in relation to one another.

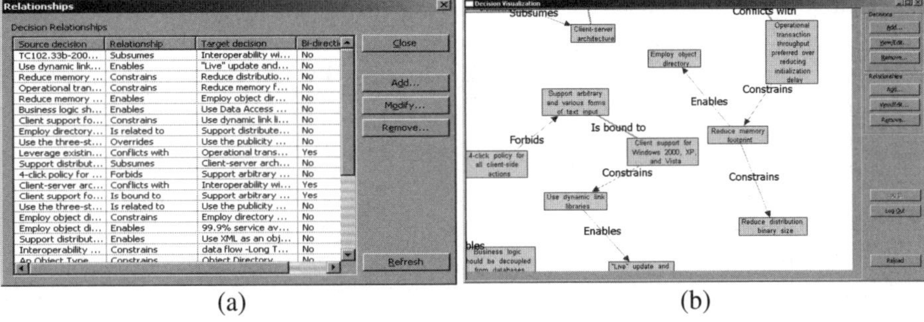

(a)   (b)

Fig. 1. Screenshots of our visualization tool implementing the tabular listing and graphical structure visualization: (a) Decision list showing the current set of design decisions, (b) structure visualization of a set of design decisions and their relationships as a directed graph

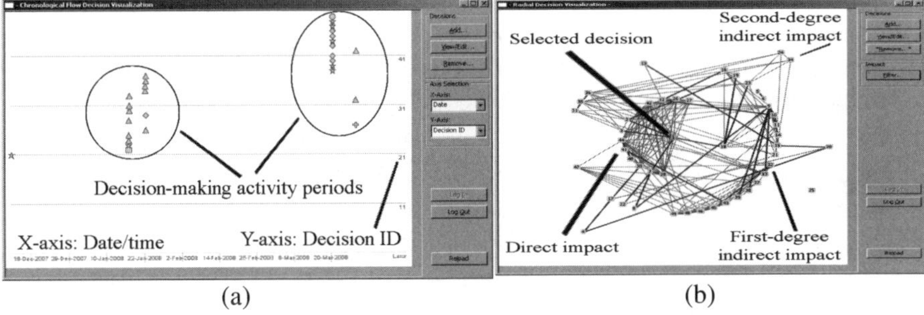

(a)   (b)

Fig. 2. Screenshots of our visualization tool implementing the chronological and decision impact visualization aspects: (a) Chronological view showing two decision activity periods within a five-month interval, (b) decision impact view of a design decision (center node of the concentric node circles). Nodes represent decisions and edges represent decision impact-relationships.

Decision Chronology Visualization. The goal of this aspect is to increase understanding of the architecture's dynamic nature. Software design changes over time, so the design decisions made will also change. The visualization should handle the evolution of the design decisions by supporting versioning and decision states. Links to previous decision versions show design progression and traceability.

Keeping track of the history of the changes would better explain the architectural story and reasons behind the design. Moreover, a timeline view would display decisions that were created or modified during a specified time interval. This would be beneficial in periodic design reviews by determining what has changed since the last review or by identifying which areas are still being actively designed. Fig. 2a shows how the visualization highlights decision-making sessions via decision clusters.

Decision Impact Visualization. The goal of this aspect is to increase the understanding of the architecture's dependencies on its set of design decisions. This visualization helps to visually identify the impact decisions have on each other using decision relationships and properties. More concisely, the impact visualization aspect utilizes the traceability provided by the decision attributes represented in the structural aspect to create a potential impact matrix upon which software architects, designers, and developers draw conclusions. Fig 2b visualizes this matrix by showing how one decision (in the center) can directly impact (innermost concentric node circle) or indirectly impact decisions to the nth-degree (outer concentric circles).

3 Conclusions

The four proposed aspects to visualize software architectural design decisions provide a means to explore and analyze large sets of decisions. Visualization helps people create mental maps of the decisions and it highlights information that is not directly visible. Moreover, each visualization aspect can highlight or reveal different decision attributes to support specific tasks, such as risk analysis, system cleanup, or other uses of architectural decisions [9]. Although we identified four aspects, these aspects do not cover all situations and there may be other aspects that could reveal more information provided by a set of decisions or reveal them more effectively. Using various decision representation models or discovering other visualization aspects should be investigated to enhance support for architectural decision exploration and analysis.

References

1. Bosch, J.: Software Architecture: The Next Step. In: Oquendo, F., Warboys, B.C., Morrison, R. (eds.) EWSA 2004. LNCS, vol. 3047, pp. 194–199. Springer, Heidelberg (2004)
2. Duenas, J.C., Capilla, R.: The Decision View of Software Architecture. In: Morrison, R., Oquendo, F. (eds.) EWSA 2005. LNCS, vol. 3527, pp. 222–230. Springer, Heidelberg (2005)
3. Jansen, A., Bosch, J.: Software Architecture as a Set of Architectural Design Decisions. In: Proc. 5th Working IEEE/IFIP Conference on Software Architecture (WICSA 2005), pp. 109–120. IEEE Computer Society, Pittsburgh (2005)
4. Kruchten, P.: An Ontology of Architectural Design Decisions. In: Bosch, J. (ed.) Proc. 2nd Groningen Workshop on Software Variability Management, pp. 55–62. Rijksuniversiteit Groningen, Groningen (2004)
5. Kunz, W., Rittel, H.W.J.: Issues as Elements of Information Systems, Working Paper 131. Institute of Urban and Regional Development. The University of California at Berkeley, Berkeley (1970)
6. Lee, L., Kruchten, P.: Customizing the Capture of Software Architectural Design Decisions. In: Proc. 21st Canadian Conference on Electrical and Computer Engineering, pp. 693–698. IEEE, Niagara Falls (2008)
7. Lee, L., Kruchten, P.: A Tool to Visualize Architectural Design Decisions. In: Becker, S., Plasil, F. (eds.) QoSA 2008. LNCS, vol. 5281, pp. 43–54. Springer, Heidelberg (2008)
8. Tyree, J., Ackerman, A.: Architecture Decisions: Demystifying Architecture. IEEE Software 22(2), 19–27 (2005)
9. van der Ven, J.S., Jansen, A.G.J., Avgeriou, P., Hammer, D.K.: Using Architectural Decisions. In: Hofmeister, C., Crnković, I., Reussner, R. (eds.) QoSA 2006. LNCS, vol. 4214, pp. 1–10. Springer, Heidelberg (2006)

Author Index